REVOLUTIONS AND MILITARY RULE IN THE MIDDLE EAST: THE ARAB STATES
PT. II: EGYPT, THE SUDAN, YEMEN AND LIBYA

REVOLUTIONS AND MILITARY RULE IN THE MIDDLE EAST: THE ARAB STATES
PT. II: EGYPT, THE SUDAN, YEMEN AND LIBYA

GEORGE M. HADDAD

University of California, Santa Barbara

Volume 3

ROBERT SPELLER & SONS, PUBLISHERS, INC.
10 EAST 23RD STREET
NEW YORK, NEW YORK 10010

©1973 by GEORGE M. HADDAD

Library of Congress Catalog Card No. 65-20537   ISBN 0-8315-0061-1

Printed in the United States of America

**DEDICATED TO
FRESIA
My wife**

TABLE OF CONTENTS

		Page
Preface		IX
Chapter I.	Revolution and Socialism in Egypt	1
I.	The Old Regime: Egypt on the Eve of Revolution	1
II.	The Free Officers and the Coup d'Etat of July 23, 1952	11
III.	The Coup Turns into a Military Dictatorship: End of the Old Political Order	26
IV.	Nasser Versus Naguib: Coups and Counter-Coups February-March 1954	33
V.	Military Adventures in Democracy	43
VI.	Military Experiments in Socialism	54
Chapter II.	Nasser and Nasserism: The Methods and the Results	78
I.	Nasserism in Egypt	78
II.	Nasserism Outside Egypt: Initial Successes 1954-1958	82
III.	Nasser and the Arabs	88
IV.	Nasserism, Palestine and the Great Powers	96
V.	Nasserism and the War Ordeal	114
A.	Nasserist Motives	114
B.	The Egyptian Defeat and its Explanation	118
C.	The Consequences of Defeat in Egypt	122
VI.	The Two Sides of the Coin	142
VII.	Egypt After Nasser: Problems of Succession and Continuity	154
Chapter III.	The Sudan: Military Rule and Popular Revolution	174
I.	Background and Problems	174
II.	The Four Military Coups 1958-1959 and the Military Regime	183
III.	The Popular Revolution of October 1964 and the Restoration of Democratic Rule	194
IV.	The Leftist Coup d'Etat of May 1969	209
Chapter IV.	Revolution and Civil War in Yemen	220
I.	The Coup Against Imam Yahya 1948	221
II.	Abortive Attempts Against Imam Ahmad	239
III.	The Coup d'Etat of September 1962 and the Yemeni Arab Republic	244

	IV.	Characteristics of the New Revolutionary Regime	254
		A. The Civil War and the Egyptian Involvement	254
		B. Problems of Recognition of the Republic.	262
		C. Experiments in Government and Republican Dissensions	266
	V.	Inter-Arab Tensions and Attitude of the Great Powers	274
	VI.	The Coup Against Sallal and Other Results of Egyptian Withdrawal	284
Chapter V.		The Junior Officers' Coup d'Etat and the New Republic in Libya	308
	I.	State and Society Under the Sanusi Monarchy and the Oil Producing Revolution	308
	II.	Tensions and Pressures and the Army Officers	318
	III.	The Coup d'Etat of September 1, 1969	325
	IV.	Characteristics and First Results of the New Military Regime	331
	V.	The Meaning of the Libyan Coup	345
Chapter VI.		Conclusion: Motives, Characteristics and Results of Arab Revolutions and Military Rule	352
	I.	General Remarks on Arab Revolutions and Coups d'Etat	352
	II.	Motives of Military Coups d'Etat	357
	III.	Patterns of Military Coups d'Etat	369
	IV.	Characteristics of Military Rule	379
		A. The Nature of Political Change	379
		B. Reform and the Socialist System	384
		C. Arab Nationalism and Arab Division	386
		D. Instability and Military Anarchy	387
	V.	Results of Revolutions and Military Rule	393
		A. Those Who Ruled by the Sword	393
		B. Where is the Dignity? Democracy, the Socialist Revolution and Palestine	400
	VI.	Back to the Barracks	412
	VII.	After the End of Military Rule	419
Appendix			429
Select Bibliography			431
Index			445

ILLUSTRATIONS

1. King Farouk (1920-1965) and Winston Churchill in 1942 (From Barrie St. Clair McBride, "Farouk of Egypt", Robert Hale, London 1968).

2. Mustafa al-Nahas Pasha (1879-1965), leader of the Egyptian Wafd party until its dissolution in January 1953 (From "The New York Times", August 24, 1965 — AP photo 1950).

3. King Farouk and Mustafa al-Nahas Pasha, Egyptian prime minister and leader of the Wafd party, May 1951 (Keystone Press Agency, from Harry Hopkins, "Egypt the Crucible", Secker and Warburg, London 1969).

4. General Muhammad Naguib (born 1901) and Lt. Col. Gamal Abdul Nasser (born 1918).

5. Lt. Col. Abdul Nasser, Secretary of State John Foster Dulles, and Gen. Muhammad Naguib in Cairo, May 1953 (Keystone, from Harry Hopkins "Egypt the Crucible").

6. Field Marshal Abdul Hakim Amer (born 1919) in Moscow, early December 1960 (From "The Scribe", January 1961).

7. Advertisement in "al-Ahram", July 23, 1964 conveying the congratulations of a state-owned corporation to President Nasser on the 12th Anniversary of the revolution and mentioning twelve achievements under Nasser's leadership.

8. The Nile diversion ceremony at the Aswan High Dam in mid May 1964 showing from the left: President Nasser, Nikita Khruschev, Abdul Salam Aref of Iraq, and Abdallah al-Sallal of Yemen (Keystone, from Harry Hopkins, "Egypt the Crucible").

9. President Nasser in Moscow with Soviet leaders, Alexei Kosygin, Leonid Brezhnev, and Anastas Mikoyan, late August 1965 (from "The New York Times", August 29, 1965).

10. Ismail al-Azhari (1900-1970) leader of the National Unionist party greeting al-Sayyid Abdul Rahman al-Mahdi (1885-1959), son of the Mahdi, head of the Ansar religious brotherhood, and patron of the Umma party (From P.M. Holt, "A Modern History of the Sudan", Grove Press, New York 1961).

11. General Ibrahim Abboud (born 1900), head of the Sudanese State after the coup d'etat of November 17, 1958 (From P.M. Holt, "A Modern History of the Sudan.")

12. Colonel Jaafar al-Numairi, leader of the coup d'etat of May 25, 1969 in the Sudan (From "al Anwar" — Beirut — May 28, 1969).

13. Imam Yahya Hamiduddin of Yemen, ruled 1904-1948 (sketch made by Ameen Rihani was only known portrait of the Imam; from Harold Ingrams, "The Yemen: Imams, Rulers and Revolutions", John Murray, London 1963).

14. Imam Ahmad 1891-1962 (Photo Planet News Ltd., from Harold Ingrams, "The Yemen, Imams, Rulers and Revolutions").

15. Imam Muhammad al-Badr, born 1926 (The Central Press Photos Ltd., from Harold Ingrams "The Yemen: Imams, Rulers and Revolutions").

16. General (later Marshal) Abdallah al-Sallal (born 1917?) chief of State in Yemen after the coup d'etat of September 26, 1962 (from "Time", September 13, 1963).

17. Imam Muhammad al-Badr (center seated) and his royalist warriors in the Yemen civil war.

18. Sayyid Muhammad Idris al-Sanusi (born 1890), King of Libya 1951-1969 (From Henry Serrano Villard "Libya, The New Arab Kingdom of North Africa," Ithaca: Cornell University Press, 1956).

19. First Lieutenant (later Colonel) Mu'ammar al-Qadhafi (born 1942?) leader of the junior officers' coup of September, 1969 in Libya (From "The Economist", December 20, 1969).

PREFACE

The present volume continues the study of revolutions and military rule in the Middle East that began in the first volume on the non-Arab countries of the northern tier, and in the second volume on the four Arab states of the Fertile Crescent. This third and last volume in the series deals with twenty revolutions and coups d'etat between 1948 and 1969 in four other Arab states - five in Egypt, seven in each of the Sudan and Yemen, and one in Libya.

The author's purpose in writing the last two volumes was, first, to contribute to the understanding of the contemporary Arab world and its turmoil by making a comprehensive study of its revolutionary movements and their background; second, to explain the consequences of the intrusion of the military into radical politics and the results of the controversial innovations and policies they imposed at a critical period in the history of the Arab nation.

As in the other volumes, the coups d'etat and revolutions of each country have been studied here in separate chapters. Comparisons have been made between the coups of each individual country and also between those of several countries in order to emphasize the similarities and contrasts in their motives, patterns and results. In the study of each coup the background and causes were explained, the role of the officers and their civilian partners in planning and carrying out the coup was outlined, the new institutions and changes that followed the coup were critically described, and the account was ended with an analysis of how and why the regime established by the coup was destroyed. In each case the personality and character of the leaders involved in the coup as well as their methods, achievements and failures have been assessed. Controversial issues related to certain coups and regimes have been discussed and the reactions and opinions of native and foreign observers and scholars have been recorded.

On the basis of evidence provided in this and the preceding volume, the author has had to refute the assumption that the military were the only force for reform and stability in the Arab world and that their socialist revolutionary regimes gave the Arabs more dignity, unity and strength. The assumptions were made for obvious reasons by the leaders of the new regimes and their partisans, and by enthusiastic foreign authors who wrote at the height of Nasser's popularity in the late 1950's and early 1960's before the full unfolding of the record of military rule or the establishment of the socialist system, and before the disaster of June 1967.

The first five chapters in this volume study in detail the revolutions and military regimes in each of the four Arab states, with two chapters on Egypt. The sixth or last chapter is a general conclusion that sums up and compares the motives and patterns of the fifty-nine coups and revolutions in the eight Arab states (described in this and the preceding volume) and the features and results of their military rule. It ends with a detailed statement on the return of the officers to their barracks and the developments that might follow the restoration of the liberal democratic system. The last chapter is followed, as in the second volume, by a chronological table of the coups and revolutions discussed in this volume and by a select bibliography.

The author wants to register his gratitude to the authorities of the University of California and their General Research and Humanities Institute grants, and to the Ford Foundation and its Non-Western Studies grants for their unfailing support of his research. He is indebted to many scholars and writers, within and outside the Arab countries, whose researches and insights on the subject have been of invaluable help. Their names and publications are mentioned in the notes and in the select bibliography. The author lived at one time through some of the events described in the last two volumes and he later returned to the area for observation and study in 1966-1967. He gratefully remembers the helpful kindness of the many persons who answered his questions on various developments in which they were personally involved or on which they were well informed. The author has based his description of the revolutionary movements and his analysis and conclusions on primary source material, mostly in Arabic, and on direct observation and reports both oral and written. He has also profited from the many monographs and articles in various periodicals on the varied aspects of the developments and their interpretation.

For the patient and competent work of typing the manuscript I am pleased to thank Mrs. Melva McClatchey and her unfailing kindness and diligence. For providing the needed publications and illustrations, I am indebted to the cooperation of the acquisitions and inter-library loan departments of the university library at Santa Barbara and the university photographic service. In concluding this series I want to thank, last but not least, my wife and children for their gracious cooperation and understanding during the long process of preparing and writing the three volumes.

I have generally followed the standard system of transliteration of Arabic names, but without the use of diacritical signs. For certain familiar names I have adopted the most commonly used and accepted spelling.

George M. Haddad

Santa Barbara, California
May 1970

CHAPTER I

REVOLUTION AND SOCIALISM IN EGYPT

Among the military coups d'état in the Arab world, the Egyptian officers' coup of July 23, 1952 was the first to develop into a revolution and to be known as such. It started as a modest local army movement against arbitrary royal rule and corruption in the military establishment, but it soon assumed the character of a revolution against the established political and social order in Egypt and set out to provoke revolutionary changes in the other Arab countries. Although Egyptian conditions under the old regime do not necessarily explain the radical transformations, they can at least help an understanding of the developments of the revolution in its early stages, the motives of its leaders, and the special characteristics which it was soon to acquire.

I The Old Regime: Egypt on the Eve of the Revolution

Egyptian state and society in the nineteenth and the first half of the twentieth centuries presented a number of contrasts with the other Arab countries of the Middle East. Under the rule of Muhammad Ali and his dynasty, Egypt began to develop into an almost independent nation-state while most of the other Arab countries remained divided into provinces under the direct rule of the Ottoman Empire. Egyptian territory remained, as it always has been, united and fairly well defined, and when its rulers dreamed of empire building, their expansion carried them either southward to the Sudan and western Arabia, or eastward in the direction of Syria. Egyptian administration remained centralized and the rulers of Egypt were, in the tradition of the old divine pharaohs, a combination of graciousness and terror.[1]

The population of Egypt, in contrast with that of the neighboring Fertile Crescent, presented an aspect of unity and homogeneity and was not plagued by the same religious schisms and ethnic diversity. It had also developed an awareness of its Egyptian identity as a result of its close connection with the valuable fertile soil and its identification with the native land and its old civilization. It was also a self-confident population, for it was assured that the Nile in its regular annual rise would enrich the land and help produce its crops. This self confidence and feeling of security and "unimpaired destiny" gave the ancient as well as the modern Egyptian a sense of superiority and self conceit[2] enhanced by the pride in the old pharaonic heritage and in the fact that Egypt became the first modern nation-state as well as the most important cultural center in the Arab world and had the largest population. Because of this security and self assurance, however, the Egyptian soldier lacked aggressive spirit, and the Egyptian generally was superficial, frivolous and disinclined to exert himself.[3] He was dependent on a strong central authority to control the distribution of the Nile waters and regulate various aspects of his life. He was consequently more disciplined, docile and submissive to that authority and less individualistic than the Arabs of Western Asia. The Egyptian rulers of the Muhammad Ali dynasty were able to command and obtain almost without question the loyalty and obedience of their subjects until the last years of King Farouk's reign in spite of their autocracy and extravagance, for which the Egyptians sometimes tried to find excuses. There seems to be no foundation for the notion, created after the revolution and the fall of the monarchy in 1952, that the people of Egypt were resentful of the foreign origin of their dynasty.

In 1882 Egypt became the first Arab country in the Middle East to be occupied and ruled by a European power. The occupation was preceded by the revolt of Arabi Pasha and his group of native "peasant officers" against the domination of the officers of Turco-Circassian origin, and against European influence and intervention in the internal affairs of Egypt. Before and after the British occupation, the Egyptian ruling dynasty, following the tradition of the Ottoman sultans, allowed thousands of Europeans - Greeks, Italians, French, British, Syro-Lebanese Arabs and others - to settle in Egypt and enjoy the privileges of the capitulations and the millet system. Yet, in no other country in the Ottoman Empire and the Middle East were Christian foreign communities as numerous as in Egypt, or as influential in the economic, social, and cultural life of the country. The foreign population of Egypt, however, made valuable contributions to the economy and cultural life of their adopted country. After the Conference of Montreux in May 1937, that followed the treaty of independence of 1936, their privileges were gradually lost and during the decade before the revolution the greatest number of foreign residents had become Egyptian citizens. At the same time there appeared among the native Egyptians, who had been unused to responsibility after long years of foreign rule, an Egyptian middle class of businessmen, industrialists, financiers and professional people, and this class was growing in size, wealth, and prestige.

The distinctive feature of Egyptian society under the monarchy was the extremely uneven distribution of land and wealth among its members, the relatively small size of its middle class, and the abject poverty and degradation of its masses, mostly peasant farmers and agricultural laborers. The limited size of the cultivable land, estimated at about six million feddans (approximately acres) in 1952 had only increased by some twenty per cent since 1882, whereas the population of Egypt had tripled. The great majority of land owning families could hardly subsist on their income, and their holdings were being constantly divided by inheritance. In 1952, in an agricultural population numbering 14 1/2 million people or 68 per cent of the total population, less than one fifth owned land. Of these landowners, two million (or 72 per cent) held only 13 per cent of the cultivable land at the rate of one acre or a fraction of it for each landowner while 2,100 landlords forming 0.1 per cent of the landowners owned 19.8 per cent of the land or more than one million acres with over 200 acres each.[4] The landed aristocracy consisted either of the members of the ruling dynasty, or of the descendants of officers and dignitaries to whom Muhammad Ali and his successors had granted tenure or full ownership of the land. Among the big landlords were also some successful Egyptian and foreign businessmen who invested their earnings in profitable landed estates.

The political leadership belonged largely to the landed aristocracy and the professional and business group. The higher levels of the civil and military service belonged at one time to the landed aristocracy or the wealthy middle class, but Egyptians of the lower and the lower middle classes were increasingly drawn to the bureaucracy and particularly to service in the army. It must be said also that Egyptian society under the old regime, and even before the treaty of 1936, gave full opportunity to men of modest means and recognized talent to study at government expense and rise to the highest national and international positions, as the two cases of Taha Hussein, the well-known dean of Arabic letters, and Abdul Hamid Badawi, the famous jurist, illustrate.[5] Moreover, legislation to prevent the abuse of authority and economic pressure on the peasant and improve his condition had been introduced and carried out during the British occupation.

The struggle against the British occupation was long and often violent, as in the revolution of 1919. All classes contributed to it except the army officers. Independence was won gradually after the declaration of February 1922 and the treaty of August 1936 by the activities of the organized political parties, the Wafd party in particular. Independence, however, was still incomplete as long as the British were allowed to maintain troops in the Suez Canal zone. The question of their evacuation and the abolition of the treaty with Britain became vital issues after the Second World War and contributed to the tensions that were exploited by the leaders of the military coup.

In its nationalist struggle with the British, Egypt did not emphasize its Arab identity, of which it was probably not aware. It fought its battle separately under the banner of Egyptian nationalism. Egyptian political and intellectual leaders like Zaghlul and Taha Hussein and others proclaimed that they were Egyptians first and refused to consider the idea of an Arab union. In the 1940's Egyptian politicians such as Nahas, and King Farouk himself began to show interest in Arabism primarily to promote their own position in Egypt as well as Egyptian influence and leadership in the Arab countries whose importance for the security and vital economic interest of Egypt came to be recognized. Egypt opposed the Greater Syria project of Emir Abdallah of Transjordan, and the Fertile Crescent unity proposed by Nuri al-Said of Iraq.[6] In the talks and conferences that led to the formation of the Arab League in March 1945, Nahas Pasha took the initiative from Nuri al-Said, and Britain did her share in including Egypt and giving her the leadership in the League in the hope of controlling the whole Arab area.[7] Among the Arab states that fought in Palestine in 1948, Egypt was the only Arab belligerent whose leaders hesitated to join in the struggle and were later blamed by the military revolutionaries because they did join.[8]

In the decade that preceded the revolution, the three forces - the Palace, the Wafd, and the British - that usually held the balance of power in Egypt became increasingly unpopular. Marked expressions of discontent and turbulence, however, did not appear until after the Palestine war. Small ideological groups such as the several small Communist factions, and the Young Egypt fascists, who later turned socialists, incited trouble but were silenced. The Muslim Brotherhood, on the other hand, was most difficult to deal with as it became an entrenched militant nationalist and religious force and turned to terrorism. It was outlawed by the government in

December 1948 after its involvement in the assassination of the Cairo chief of police. It retaliated by assassinating the prime minister, Nuqrashi Pasha, on December 28, but its Chief Guide, Hasan al-Banna, was liquidated shortly after on February 12, 1949.

King Farouk was seventeen years old when he was proclaimed king after his father's death on April 28, 1936. The regency council that exercised authority during his minority was dissolved on July 29, 1937 when Farouk attained the age of eighteen - in lunar years. The people were very fond of their young and handsome king and showed him every sign of love and affection. His popularity was enhanced by his marriage in January 1938 to Farida Dhul-Fiqar, an upper middle class young lady of great personal charm and noble character. Two dangerous signs of deviation, however, soon were revealed by Farouk's behavior and gradually exhausted the reserve of love and goodwill of his subjects because they showed his indifference to the dignity and interests of the state and its people. They were his reckless exercise of arbitrary power, and his openly scandalous and dissolute private life.

Farouk began his quarrels with the Wafd soon after his accession and dismissed the Nahas Pasha cabinet in December 1937 although it was supported by Parliament. Nahas Pasha was later imposed on him as prime minister in the famous incident of February 4, 1942 when the British ambassador, Sir Miles Lampson, surrounded the royal palace with armored cars and presented an ultimatum which the king accepted. Civilians and military officers were then shocked by this insult to their king, but they and the king had to swallow the insult at the time. One officer only, Lieutenant-Colonel (later General) Muhammad Naguib, one of the future leaders of the coup, presented his resignation in protest, but it was refused.[9] Farouk is said to have lost since then his faith in the people and decided to rule as he pleased.

The Palestine war of 1948 exposed the weaknesses of the Egyptian army and discredited Farouk's administration. Egypt was more humiliated than the other Arab participants, and was the first to sign the armistice with Israel in February 1949. Among the armies of the new emerging Arab states, the Egyptian army was the oldest and the most numerous, and was expected to demonstrate competence and win victories, but it did not. The frustrated younger officers attributed Egypt's poor performance to the defective and antiquated arms and to the high ranking officers who fought the war from their offices in Cairo. General Naguib has explained that several supply officers were in league with the king and his cronies, and they bought substandard munitions and pocketed the difference between what they charged the government and what they paid. The defective arms scandal was exposed in the press, and the government ordered an investigation in the summer of 1950, but the prosecutor-general was ordered to quash the investigation when some members of the king's circle were involved and their arrest was decided by the prosecution.[10]

Farouk contributed to the degradation of his own image within and outside Egypt by his addiction to gambling and his lust for women. Before the end of the war with Israel he divorced Queen Farida, who was the victim of flagrant infidelities and bad treatment. In the summer of 1950 foreign newspapers scornfully related sensational reports about Farouk's trip to France, the fabulous amounts of money he lost in the casinos, and the dancers and women of doubtful reputation who flocked to Deauville to meet him. The story of how he met his second wife, Nariman Sadeq, in the fall of 1950 through the cooperation of his jeweler, and how he ordered her and her parents to annul her engagement to a government official, added another scandal to his record.

Farouk depended increasingly in his last years on servants and palace employees for communication with the government. Some of them were his agents and partners in his embezzlements, and his companions in his pleasure adventures. The most hated among his personal advisers and companions was his press secretary, Karim Tabet, a journalist of Christian Lebanese descent who became, with Farouk's insistence, a cabinet minister in early July 1952, a few weeks before the revolution. According to General Naguib, he was guilty of cynically encouraging Farouk to declare himself a Sayyid - descendant of the Prophet - in spite of the king's well-known foreign origin.[11] When Tabet was brought to trial before the Tribunal of the Revolution on October 12, 1953 to answer for the fortune he acquired since he became Farouk's press secretary, he tried to explain, among other things, Farouk's misconduct. He believed that the two factors that had their destructive influence on the king were: first, his addiction to gambling, and second, his physical constitution. Tabet suggested that Farouk's glands affected his body and mind and made him stubborn, suspicious, and incapable of any sustained effort. The causes of Farouk's deviations, said Tabet, were his physical abnormalities, and these increased as he grew older; Farouk therefore was believed to be a sick man.[12]

Farouk's attitudes suggested to certain observers that he expected the eventual loss of his throne and the end of the monarchy. Whenever he was advised to be moderate or was warned about the results of his behavior, he allegedly answered, "In a few years there will be only five kings, the king of England and the four kings in a pack of cards." This is why, one observer believed, he frantically set out after 1946 to amass an exportable fortune and deposit his millions in Italian, Swiss and other banks.[13] His lust for money and possessions was even more than his lust for pleasure and women, and invariably at the expense of the state, in spite of his vast personal wealth, mostly in landed estate, and his budgetary allowances of L.E. 100,000 (about $280,000 at the time). When the head of the Audit Bureau objected to certain expenses and deals, he was removed on May 19, 1950. The senator-lawyer, Mustafa Meri, raised the question of the forced resignation of the Audit Bureau chief in the Senate and asked for an investigation. Farouk answered on June 17 by dismissing several leading senators of the opposition and replaced them by members favorable to the Palace.

In his scandals and deviations in private and public life,

Farouk had no parallel among the constitutional monarchs of the Arab world. His vices were aggravated by the fact that they were practiced more or less openly in a traditionalist Muslim country with an overwhelmingly poor population. The Egyptian masses in spite of this paid little attention to his deviations on account of the great distance that separates the ruler and the ruled in Egypt. The political leaders themselves were careful not to offend him and in their rivalries, many strove to win his favor. The one notable protest against the king's behavior was voiced on October 18, 1950 in a petition signed by leading members of the oppostion, and it was partly directed against the ruling Wafd party. The signatories of the petition wanted the king to help stop corruption, purge his entourage, and respect constitutional principles; they ended their petition by telling him that "the people's endurance, no matter how long it might last, would inevitably end."[14]

In the press and among the intellectuals, the criticisms of Farouk and his regime were voiced particularly after the Palestine war, notably in the weekly **Rose al-Yusif** whose editor, Ihsan Abdul-Quddus, raised the question of the defective arms, and in the daily *al-Misri*. But it was Khalid Muhammad Khalid who raised the cry for far reaching changes in order to insure economic and social justice in his book "From Here We Start," published in February 1950. The book was banned on charges of anti-religious agitation and propagating a doctrine that aims at changing the fundamental principles of society, and of inciting hatred against the capitalists. Yet, it is remarkable that on May 27, 1950 the president of the tribunal in Cairo to whom the case was assigned had enough courage and independent judgment to annul the prosecutor's order that had banned the book.[15] Critical writers and advocates of reform, however, wanted the changes to be achieved gradually and following real democratic parliamentary procedures.

Generally, it can be said that Farouk's rule was arbitrary in certain aspects but it was not oppressive. In the speeches and proclamations of the revolution of July 1952 he was denounced as the "corrupt king" rather than as "the tyrannical king." Intellectuals, political leaders, and journalists were largely able to manifest their opposition and criticism in what was still a free constitutional monarchy. Farouk was thus able to rule comfortably for sixteen years and would have probably ruled longer if revolutionary action had depended on the people's initiative. His increasing unpopularity, however, made it easier for the military revolutionaries to strike their blow. The officers who overthrew him were led to revolt by those aspects of his arbitrary and corrupt rule that affected their military institution and contributed to their humiliation in Palestine.

Among the political parties, the Wafd that had prestigiuosly led the nationalist movement since 1919 began to be discredited when the British imposed its leaders on the king in February 1942. In the election of January 1950, the Wafd was still popular enough to gain a majority of 228 out of 319 seats in the Chamber of Deputies, and Nahas Pasha, who was then seventy- one years old, was asked to form the cabinet. The Wafd government was expected to take advantage of its party victory to start a battle against the king's arbitrary power. The king himself, as it seemed, was apprehensive of what might happen. But the government of the Wafd evidently preferred to enjoy peacefully the benefits of rule with the king's favor, and thus when Nahas met the king for the first time after his appointment as prime minister he expressed one desire and that was "to be allowed to kiss the king's hand."[16]

The Wafd government was unable to reach an agreement with the British on the problems of evacuation and the Sudan. In a move motivated partly by the desire to regain popularity and hide corruption, it abrogated unilaterally the treaty of 1936 and proclaimed Farouk king of the Sudan in October 1951. This was followed by ineffective guerrilla warfare with the British in the Canal Zone in which volunteers were organized into "liberation units" supported by the police to fight the British forces. The Egyptian army did not participate in the struggle. In the most eventful of the episodes of the guerrilla warfare, some fifty policemen were killed at Ismailiya on

January 25, 1952 in the defense of their barracks and of the governorate against the British as a result of the Egyptian Interior minister's order to the police force to fight to the last bullet. On the following day, known as Black Saturday, the embittered police failed to prevent a damaging and violent riot that has been referred to since then as "the burning of Cairo." King Farouk was then giving a banquet for the birth of his first male child, Crown Prince Ahmad Fuad. The participants in the riots and burning included Muslim Brethren, socialists, communists and other discontented elements. The rumors attributed the seemingly prearranged and well organized action to various sources including the communist embassies, the socialist party of Ahmad Hussein, the Palace, the Wafd, and even to Gamal Abdul Nasser, who was then the chairman of the Free Officers Committee. The significant results of Black Saturday were the imposition of martial law by the government and the call addressed to the army to restore order and end the riot, as well as the dismissal of the Wafd cabinet on the following day. The officers saw in the chaos that discredited both the Palace and the Wafd their chance to advance the date of their movement against the regime of King Farouk.

II. The Free Officers and the Coup d'Etat of July 23, 1952

A. The Free Officers and Their Motives and Role

The coup d'état of July 23, 1952 was known in Egypt at the time it occurred as "the Army movement" *(Harakat al-Jaysh)* and was never referred to as a coup*(Inqilab)*.[17] Shortly after the consolidation of military rule it was called "the Revolution of 23 July." Its first distinctive character, in contrast with the previous Arab coups in Iraq and Syria, was that it followed a relatively long period of secret preparation, and it was exclusively organized and led by a group of military men known as "the Free Officers." The name "free officers" was adopted after the success of the Egyptian coup by various conspirators who plotted to overthrow the ruling regimes in the other Arab countries.

The free officers' movement was formally organized for the first time in late 1949 with the formation of an executive committee of nine members. The officers in the committee were: Lt. Cols. Gamal Abdul Nasser and Anwar al-Sadat, Wing Commanders Abdul Latif Baghdadi and Gamal Salem, Majors Abdul Hakim Amer, Kemal al-Din Hussein, Salah Salem and Khalid Muhieddin, and Squadron Leader Hasan Ibrahim. The committee had to be enlarged shortly before and after the coup and to seek the cooperation of other officers because its members were mostly staff officers and had no fighting troops. Among those who became members were Lt. Cols. Zakaria Muhieddin, Abdul Munem Amin, Yusif Saddiq, and Hussein al-Shafii who commanded a cavalry (armored) unit. Major-General Muhammad Naguib, who became the front leader of the movement, has claimed that he became a member of the committee in 1949 and its chairman after the burning of Cairo in January 1952. Other sources, however, agree that he first began to attend the committee meetings after the coup and even without voting, and that he only became chairman in mid-August 1952.[18] The original committee of nine had elected Abdul Nasser chairman in January 1950 and re-elected him twice in the following two years. With the admission of Naguib and four others, the free officers' executive committee came to include fourteen members.

The nine officers of the first executive committee were all young; their average age was thirty-three years. They mostly came from lower middle class families of small government employees and farmers with class interests different from those of the superior officers or the ruling elite. Yet, among the officers who cooperated with the committee were a few members who belonged to families of higher standing, like Ahmad Shawqi, Sarwat Okasha, and the two Sabri brothers. They all went to secondary schools in the big cities in the early and mid 1930's in a period of student demonstrations encouraged by the Wafd party after the suspension of the constitution. They all graduated from the Military Academy between 1938 and 1940, and most of them met at the Staff College between 1945 and 1948, and later on participated in the Palestine War of 1948. In their first informal contacts since the early 1940's, they expressed their disappointment with the ruling institution and their resentment of the British authority that was able to impose a new cabinet on the king in the incident of February 4, 1942. Some of them, such as Sadat and Baghdadi, showed their hostility to the British by taking part in the sabotage of British military installations in Egypt during the Second World War. The humiliation of the officers in Palestine and the defective arms scandal weakened their loyalty to the throne. The officers also resented the aspects of social and economic inequality, and one of them wrote with bitterness on the ostentation of the ruling pashas, the summers spent in Europe, the clothes brought from Paris, the luxurious villas, and even the cigars of Fuad Serageddin, the Wafdist Interior minister.[19]

The number of free officers steadily increased, and some of them were recruited during the war in Palestine. Abdul Nasser admitted later that the war gave them "the opportunity to study and investigate and meet in the trenches and command posts," and that "we were fighting in Palestine but our dreams were centered in Egypt."[20] Although they had no common ideology, the free officers generally cooperated with extreme organizations. Some of them like Sadat, Kemal Hussein, and Abdul Munem Abdul Rauf had strong connections with the Muslim Brotherhood. Others were communists like Yusif Saddiq and Khalid Muhieddin, or belonged to the socialist party. Abdul Nasser himself had contacts with all extreme nationalist and left wing organizations, and at one time was claimed as a sympathizer by a communist group called Hadeto that represented the initials of the Arabic equivalent of "the Democratic movement of National Liberation." His friendship with Ahmad Abul-Fath, a left wing Wafdist and editor of *al-Misri,* was particularly useful and lasted until early 1954.[21]

In the early informal meetings of the free officers, Nasser seemed to have been the recognized leader and organizer, but nothing proves Sadat's claim that the organization existed formally in 1943 and that Nasser was its director.[22] Nasser was born in 1918 in Alexandria where his father was a post office clerk. His family came originally from Beni Merr in the province of Assiut. In 1936 he graduated from the Nahda Secondary School in Cairo where he often participated in the students' anti-British demonstrations. He then entered the law school of Cairo University in the fall of 1936 because he was denied admission to the Military Academy. In February 1937 he was accepted at the Military Academy with the help of a former minister called Abdul Mejid Salih Pasha. He graduated as second lieutenant in 1938, and five years later he attained the rank of captain and taught at the Military Academy. In 1945 he attended the Staff College, and like many of his colleagues who were by then in staff jobs, he had more time and energy to spend on fostering friendships and infiltrating the junior army officers. In 1948 he had his first combat experience in Palestine and felt the humiliation of being trapped for several months in Faluja in the Negeb. "Here we are," he said, "in these foxholes surrounded and thrust treacherously into a battle for which we were not ready. Over there is our country, another Faluja on a larger scale."[23] After the Palestine war and during the period of formal orga**nization of the Free Officers Executive Committee he was** instructor in the Army Administration School and later in the Staff College.

Nasser was a revolutionary and the seeds of revolution, as he said, were present within him long before the episode of February 4, 1942, but the episode had an electrifying effect on his spirit.[24] He was nevertheless known to be cautious and calculating. Nasser was also described by one of his closest friends as a man of many complexes that resulted from his unhappy boyhood, the poverty of his family and the comfortable condition of some of his well-to-do classmates, and his inability to enter the Military Academy except with the help of a pasha.[25]

The free officers felt the need to organize themselves formally in 1949 under an executive committee in order to expand their activity and to insure more protection for themselves at a time when the king and his ministers were extending their control to the military hierarchy.[26] The officers, moreover, were encouraged by the example of the Syrian officers and the political role they assumed in the coup d'état of March and August 1949. Nasser and several of his colleagues believed that the ruling regime should be destroyed in order to achieve the liberation of Egypt, and that the army should direct the operation. The revolution, Nasser said later, did not stem from what happened in the Palestinian war or from the defective weapons scandal. These were incidental causes that added impetus for going ahead with the revolution. Its real cause was "to decide our future," to free the nation, and to build a free and strong Egypt.[27] "The situation," Nasser said, "singled out the Army as the force to do the job," because it had more cohesion, its men trusted each other, it was drawn from the heart of the people, it was far removed from the conflict between individuals and classes, and it had "enough material strength at its disposal to guarantee a swift and decisive action."[28]

In his book *Egypt's Destiny,* General Muhammad Naguib also presented his argument in favor of military intervention. The purpose of the military, he said, was not to govern but to defend those who govern from their enemies. To serve its purpose, the military must be given a worthy government to defend. But "if the government it is asked to defend is manifestly indefensible, as it was in Egypt, the military must either resign itself to the prevailing corruption, or intervene in civil affairs long enough to establish a government that will respond to the legitimate needs and desires of the nation." According to Naguib, the Army seized power because "we could no longer endure the humiliation to which we, along with the rest of the Egyptian people, were subjected." [29]

The members of the Society of Free Officers were organized into cells of five to ten members each. Their number was placed at about three hundred officers.[30] Their activities consisted of recruiting more members and of writing and distributing leaflets calling attention to the abuses in the administration and attacking imperialism. In early 1950, they issued a leaflet entitled "An Appeal and a Warning." The leaflets or circulars expressed particular interest in the Army and attacked all those who undermined its strength. The circular of March 22, 1952 criticized the senior officers and declared that "the traitors in command of the Army are also in league with imperialism." In a singular circular on July 14, 1952 they accused the commander of the armed forces, Muhammad Haidar Pasha, of being the servant of imperialism because he sent the army to fight a losing battle in Palestine in order to divert Egypt from its struggle against imperialism and to support British allegations that the Egyptian army cannot defend Egypt.[31] The organization had to take tight security measures and maintained an effective intelligence network that had access through its members to information from the Army Headquarters, the Palace, and the government departments. The Wafd apparently knew about the free officers but did not consider them dangerous, and so did the king as long as he controlled the top army command.

In order to test their own strength, the officers decided to present a full slate of candidates for the elections of the Officers' Club which were scheduled for December 27, 1951. In doing so they effectively challenged the king whose candidates usually won the elections. Farouk supported General Hussein Sirri Amer, who had been commander of the Frontier Corps, for the presidency of the club, but the free officers presented General Naguib. On January 6 the elections took place after they had been adjourned, and the free officers' ticket won. The new board of fifteen members included besides General Naguib, such well known free officers as Zakaria Muhieddin and Hasan Ibrahim, as well as Rashad Muhanna, who apparently was not a free officer but was inclined to be on the free officers' side.[32] General Naguib was elected president by 276 out of 334 votes.[33] The majority of the board were for the first time in club elections majors and lieutenant colonels, and the election was equivalent to a rebellion against the king and a challenge to the senior army officers who were regarded by their junior colleagues as corrupt and obedient servants of the king.

The free officers' executive committee had thought that the revolt could not be staged successfully before 1954 or 1955, but after the burning of Cairo and the fall of the Wafd cabinet in late January 1952, they decided to be ready within a few months.[34] Police activity, on the one hand, had increased and they were in danger of being identified and arrested. On the other hand, the arbitrary change of cabinets by King Farouk, and the unpopularity and weakness of political parties played into the free officers' hands.

The free officers took notice of the king's hostility and determination to act against them when the officers' club board was dissolved on July 15, 1952. The order of dissolution was issued by Muhammad Haidar Pasha, commander of the armed forces and uncle of Abdul Hakim Amer. In the summer capital at Alexandria, a ministerial crisis led to the resignation of Hussein Sirri - who had formed the third cabinet after the burning of Cairo - on July 20 because he wanted General Naguib for the war ministry, which was still vacant and occupied temporarily by the prime minister, while the king wanted General Sirri Amer, the foe of the free officers and of Naguib. The Wafdist editor of *al-Misri*, Ahmad Abul Fath, who was in Alexandria, immediately called his wife's brother, Sarwat Okasha, by telephone and explained the cause of the crisis in order to alert the free officers.[35] They were alarmed by the news and their fears increased when they learned about the appointment of Ismail Shirine, the king's brother-in-law, as minister of war in the new Hilali cabinet which was formed officially on July 22. The king, moreover, gave his brother-in-law the rank of colonel, although he had no formal military training, and this was viewed as a sign of contempt for the dignity of the army.

The free officers had decided in early July to start action on August 5 after having collected their pay. But in their meetings after the dissolution of the officers' club board, the date was advanced to July 21 and then to the night of July 22-23. It is probable that the telephone call of Abul Fath from Alexandria on July 20 about the ministerial crisis and the impending appointment of a war minister hostile to the free officers decided them to act in forty-eight hours. Sadat has mentioned a meeting of the executive committee on July 16 in which two alternate plans of action was discussed: First, to overthrow the ruling regime by a coup d'état; second, to start a wave of assassinations if the first scheme failed.[36] Nasser was reported to have been in favor of the second solution because he thought that the free officers' forces were scattered and a revolt was impossible.[37] Two days later, in the meeting of July 18, Nasser changed his mind and argued for making a coup d'état because the assassinations were risky and would not produce a change in the ruling institution. The timing of the coup was thus an immediate outgrowth of the spreading rumors about the impending arrest of the free officers following the dissolution of the officers' club board and the ministerial crisis of July 20, 1952.

The free officers' executive committee had agreed that a well-known higher officer should assume the leadership of the movement. According to Sadat, they thought of the old veteran military and political leader, General Aziz al-Misri, but he declined the offer and preferred to remain as the spiritual father of the free officers.[38] They then thought of General Fuad Sadeq, who had commanded the Egyptian army in Palestine and was known for his honesty, but he was appointed chief of staff and could not accept the officers' proposal. The appointment turned out to be of short duration and he was succeeded by General Hussein Farid. The committee then asked General Muhammad Naguib to be front leader, but it is not known precisely when Naguib was approached or when he accepted the offer. The evidence on this point and on Naguib's role before and during the coup is colored by the prejudice of most writers in view of Naguib's subsequent quarrel with the revolutionaries and his ultimate dismissal. Naguib has maintained that on July 19 a meeting of the free officers was held in his house and they agreed that Egypt was ripe for revolution. He spoke of the need to act before the king's spies could discover them and before the formation of a new cabinet. The account by Sadat implies that Naguib was not even a free officer and that he did not know about the planned coup except after it had taken place. Abul Fath partly agrees with him when he says that some officers were sent by Nasser at 2 A.M. (July 23) to tell Naguib about the beginning of the movement and to invite him to lead it. [39] But he also mentions that weeks before the coup, Nasser had told him about the work of the free officers and their plans to purge the government, raise the standard of the army, and establish sound constitutional rule. From these and other writings it would seem that Naguib was not a member of the free officers' executive committee, but he might have been regarded as a free officer, for he was in contact with Nasser's group since the end of the Palestine War through Amer who was one of his staff officers; the contact, we are told, became closer when Amer became his aide de camp.[40] Naguib, moreover, was apparently informed about the coup before it occurred. It was eventually carried out without his participation, but Naguib has claimed that it was agreed that he should stay at home until the first phase of the coup had been completed.

Muhammad Naguib was born in 1901 (or 1899) in Khartoum. His father was an Egyptian army captain employed in the Sudan civil service, and his mother was the daughter of an Egyptian officer in the Sudan who was killed two hours before General Gordon. Naguib was already a brigadier general at the time of the war in Palestine, and in December 1950 he became major general. He was known for his courage, honesty, humble manner and hearty laughter. In the Palestine war he fought in more than twenty engagements and was wounded four times, one of them very seriously to the point of being pronounced dead.[41] Since then he occasionally wrote articles criticizing the army administration and the conduct of the war in the weekly *Rose al-Yusif* under the pseudonym "The Unknown Soldier."[42] In 1949 he was appointed commander of the Egyptian Frontier Corps, but was later replaced by General Sirri Amer who was hated by the junior officers and was believed to be a corrupt stooge of the Palace, and this earned Naguib popular sympathy. When he considered resigning from his new job as Director of Infantry, Nasser is said to have told him that the officers wanted him to stay.[43] His candidacy for the presidency of the Officers' Club brought him an indirect warning from the king to withdraw but he refused.

Certain writers on the officers' coup d'état have alluded briefly to the role played by the United States and its Central Intelligence Agency in the coup. One of them has categorically asserted that "the CIA maneuvered an Egyptian revolt that kicked Farouk out and substituted the Naguib-Nasser rule."[44] Another writer has mentioned that after the burning of Cairo in January 1952, the United States and Britain decided that Farouk would have to go. The CIA turned to the Egyptian Army and sent skilled agents to Cairo to keep a close watch on the weakening Farouk regime, and late in July it gave the word. The CIA was supposedly aware of Nasser's behind-the-scenes maneuverings, but it chose Naguib as its man of destiny.[45] Nasser's decision to abandon the scheme of political assassinations, to which he refers in his *Philosophy of the Revolution,* was allegedly taken when a CIA agent was sent to tell him that if he wanted to change the system of rule, he had to seize power, because assassinations would not change the system.[46]

B. The Coup d'Etat and the Fall of King Farouk

The coup d'état of July 23, 1952 was the first military challenge against established legal authority in Egypt since the

Arabi revolt seventy years earlier. Egypt had been independent following the treaty of 1936, but its Suez Canal zone was still occupied by a British force. The free officers, consequently, had to proceed with caution and moderation, for they feared the intervention of the British forces. The preparations were made in secret and Nasser in person had to contact the leading participants and give them instructions about their duties on the eventful night of 22-23 July. Some confusion and mishaps resulted from the fact that the officers did not know who their other participating colleagues were due to the secrecy that surrounded the movement. [47]

Like most other coups, the Egyptian army movement was carried out in the first hours of the day between midnight and 3 A.M. (July 23). Its immediate aim was to seize control of the army, occupy its general headquarters, arrest its higher commanding officers and secure control of the important centers of communication in Cairo including the broadcasting station. In contrast to most other coups, no plans were made in the first stage of the operation to arrest the king and cabinet, who were in Alexandria, and occupy the royal palace. The action was scheduled to start at 1 A.M., [48] but two hours earlier a free officer of the Army Intelligence, Saad Tewfik, told Nasser that the king had been informed about the coup and the chief of staff, General Hussein Farid, had given orders to all commanders to meet at the General Headquarters at Kubri al-Qubba, near Abbasiya, in order to deal with the plot. The free officers had consequently to march one hour earlier with forces estimated at some 3,000 soldiers. Nasser thought it was an excellent opportunity to arrest the commanding generals together in the building, but he had also to move fast to tell the officers about the change in schedule. The entire military area between Abbasiya and Heliopolis was blocked by the armored cars of Khalid Muhieddin. The General Headquarters building was surrounded and taken by force at 1:45 A.M. after a brief resistance in which two guards were killed and two were wounded. Twenty generals and high ranking officers including the chief of staff and Ali Naguib, General Naguib's brother, were arrested and sent to the Military Academy. The accounts differ on who led the attack against the General Headquarters. According to Sadat, it was Amer who entered the building armed with a pistol and followed by soldiers, for Amer "has always been courageous and decisive," says Sadat, "he leads in battle with unshakable faith and with nerves of steel."[49] According to others it was Yusif Saddiq and Ahmad Shawqi, or the latter alone, who occupied the building.[50] At about the same time, Hussein al-Shafii with his tanks occupied the strategic points in Cairo: the broadcasting building, the telephone exchange, the railway station, and the airports. The planes of the air force at the same time flew over the main cities of Egypt to discourage resistance to the movement. The takeover was complete when the important garrison at Arish rallied and its headquarters was taken over by Salah and Gamal Salem at 4:30 A.M.

General Naguib was brought to the General Headquarters by two officers at about 3 A.M., and was appointed commander-in-chief of the armed forces to lead the successful movement. The first communique about the coup, apparently written by Amer, was broadcast at 7 A.M. (July 23) by Anwar Sadat in the name of General Naguib. Its text had been communicated earlier to the press. It neither proclaimed a revolution, nor did it say that a coup d'état had just been carried out against the old regime of King Farouk, whose name it did not even mention. The statement was an apology for the military takeover and showed primarily the military motives behind the officers' action and their concern about the army's reputation. It spoke of the bribery, corruption, and government instability that had a great influence on the army and contributed to defeat in the Palestine War. The statement reassured the people that "the entire army is today working for the interests of the fatherland within the constitution and without any designs of its own," and gave assurances to the foreign residents, "our brothers," about the safety of their lives and property.⁵¹ The declaration, according to Sadat, was part of a maneuver intended, first, to avert foreign intervention before the king was expelled, and second, to make the king believe for a while that the only goal of the coup was the determination of the army to purge its ranks.⁵²

The successful first stage of the officers' coup had to be followed by the nomination of a new government that was imposed on the king. Nasser and his colleagues decided to stay in the background and appoint a civilian cabinet headed by Ali Maher Pasha, a former prime minister and head of the royal cabinet, and an independent in politics. Ali Maher accepted the offer presented by Sadat, but it is not known under what conditions and whether Ali Maher was expected to help persuade the king to abdicate. Maher left for Alexandria on July 24, and the king immediately accepted the resignation of Hilali and appointed Maher officially and wished him "success in what is beneficial for the country." The exchange of letters between the king and Hilali and Maher with all the customary formulas relating to the formation of a new cabinet created the impression that the king was to stay.⁵³ This impression was strengthened by the fact that the officers addressed certain demands to the king through Maher, and he accepted them. They involved the dismissal of six objectionable persons of the king's entourage. Sadat has stated that this also was a part of the maneuver to deceive the king and gain time, and the king and even Maher thought that this was the end of the crisis.

The fate of Farouk was probably decided before the coup, but the officers took three days to force his abdication. The immediate pretext for their action was the rumor that spread in the first two days on Farouk's attempt to prepare a counter-coup and his radio messages to the British in the Canal Zone asking for military assistance.⁵⁴ On July 24, Zakaria Muhieddin was sent to Alexandria with a batallion of motorized infantry supported by tanks, artillery, and armored cars to besiege and, if necessary, attack the two royal palaces on the evening of the following day. Naguib and Sadat left separately for Alexandria on July 25. Sadat has related that

Nasser told him before leaving, "Today, or at the utmost tomorrow we should get rid of Farouk for the situation does not allow us any other course." Sadat has also claimed that Ali Maher was surprised when he was told that the Command decided to depose Farouk and that in the evening General Naguib would bring the ultimatum to be presented to the king.[55] On the evening of July 25, Muhieddin asked to postpone action against the king to the following day because his forces had to rest. In the meantime, Farouk, alarmed by the arrival of the armed forces, left al-Muntazah Palace at the eastern end of the beach for Ras al-Tin Palace hoping perhaps to escape more easily.

In the night of July 25, those of the free officers who had come to Alexandria engaged in a hot argument about what to do with Farouk after his abdication. Gamal Salem argued for his trial and execution, but some others disagreed, and they finally decided to send Salem to Cairo to consult Nasser and the other members of the executive committee. Salem brought back the decision of the majority on the morning of July 26 and it was in favor of exiling Farouk without trial. The discussion and vote of the committee on that night of July 25 amounted to an informal trial of Farouk, and the verdict was to allow him to live. In the morning of July 26, the troops surrounded the two royal palaces and the guards of al-Muntazah Palace surrendered without incident. At Ras al-Tin Palace, where Farouk lived, the soldiers of the guard surrendered after a lively exchange of fire caused by the mistake of a junior officer. Six soldiers of the palace guard were wounded. On the same morning, Ali Maher carried the ultimatum to King Farouk. It was addressed by Naguib on behalf of the officers and men in the army and contained a series of charges against the king and his regime. The ultimatum ended by saying that the Army, representing the power of the people, demanded that "Your Majesty abdicate the throne in favor of your crown prince, His Highness Prince Ahmad Fuad... at the latest at noon today, Saturday, July 26, 1952... and that you leave the country before 6 P.M. of the same day." [56] Farouk accepted the ultimatum and expressed the desire to carry with him his coin and stamp collections and to be accompanied by Antonio Pulli and Muhammad Hasan of his royal household, and to leave on the yacht *al-Mahrusa*. This last request was granted and the others were denied.

The language of the act of abdication, in contrast with that of the ultimatum, was very moderate and respectful of the king, because it was written in his name. It began with the phrase, "We, Farouk the First, King of Egypt and the Sudan." It gave as causes for his abdication, his concern over the welfare of "our nation," and his wish "to save the country from the difficulties it is facing." The statement that represented him abdicating "in conformity with the will of the people" was reportedly added by Gamal Salem.[57] Farouk left Alexandria dressed in an admiral's uniform at 6 P.M., July 26, 1952 with full military honors. He was accompanied by his three daughters, his wife Nariman, and the six-month-old crown prince who was proclaimed "King Ahmad Fuad II" immediately after Farouk had left. According to a journalist's report, Farouk took with him 204 pieces of baggage. The king's departure was attended by Ali Maher, General Naguib, Gamal Salem, Hussein Shafii and the American Ambassador, James Caffery. The Palace band played national anthems as he stepped aboard the cutter that took him to *al-Mahrusa,* and the cruiser *Farouk* gave him the twenty-one-gun salute. Naguib has related that on the bridge of the yacht he told Farouk, "Effendim [Sir], you remember that I was the only Egyptian officer who submitted his resignation in 1942," and the king said he remembered. Then Naguib added, "We were loyal to the throne in 1942 but many things have changed since then," and Farouk answered, "Yes I know," and then said, "I hope you will take good care of the Army. My grandfather, you know, created it," and Naguib answered, "The Egyptian army is in good hands."[58]

III. The Coup Turns into a Military Dictatorship: End of the Old Political Order

The first apparent feature of the military coup of July 23 in its early stages were its deceptive moderation, and its apparent legalism and expression of respect for democracy and the constitution. At the end of the first week following the coup, the well known jurist and president of the Council of State, Dr. Sanhouri, spoke with optimism of the Egyptian Army movement as "the first military movement in the world to stop at the limit where it should, for the military coups that took place before have given various results."[59] The first restrained statements of the coup by General Naguib, followed by the establishment of a civilian cabinet, the peaceful departure of King Farouk and the preservation of the monarchy led other observers and writers to believe that the officers had no intention to seize power or turn their coup into a political and social revolution, and that when they did effectively seize power and make changes later, they did so because their hand was forced by the circumstances.

The officers in reality did not all hold the same views on the question of their political role or on changing the political and social order. It was the hard core revolutionaries who wanted revolutionary changes and consequently strove to seize power in order to carry out the revolution - and later strove to expand the revolution in order to maintain power. These differences of opinion ultimately led to the forced withdrawal of those free officers who disagreed with the radical group. The eventual takeover of the government by the free officers should therefore need no apology as long as there is evidence to prove that what their influential leaders wanted from the very beginning was not a mere coup but a revolutionary change in the system of government, as Sadat admitted, and also in the social and economic domain. The Charter presented by Nasser in 1962 to the Congress of Popular Forces is very clear in this connection. It mentioned that the vanguard after the coup had no guide for action except the six principles which had been published in the secret circulars before the coup and later became a part of the preamble to the constitution of 1956.⁶⁰ The six principles contained clearly the seeds and directives of a revolution and included: The destruction of imperialism and its treacherous Egyptian agents; the abolition of feudalism: the ending of monopolies and of the domination of the government by capital; the establishment of social justice; the building of a powerful national army; and the establishment of a sound democratic system.[61] In this light one should therefore regard the statements in the *Philosophy of the Revolution* about Nasser's disappointment with the masses and with the leaders of opinion after the coup as mere apologies for taking over the government and for justifying his conclusion: "I realized that the task of the vanguard, far from being completed, had only begun."[62] At the same time one can dismiss as completely unwarranted by the facts those statements of contemporary writers who asserted that the free officers never expected to govern and that they were disillusioned by the end of the first week because they thought that the new regime could function with the old politicians.[63]

Two other features of the military coup can be deduced in addition to its deceptive moderation. One of them is the much repeated claim of the officers that all their actions and changes were carried out in the name of the people and expressed their will, even though the people were apathetic and had really no voice in the officers' decisions. Another feature is that the officers overthrew the old political order and established their own dictatorship gradually, not overnight as in the case of the Iraqi and Yemeni revolutions. The Egyptian free officers displayed patience and tactical skill in removing their opponents and operating their changes. The reforms and the innovations which they introduced as they were acquiring total power were generally calculated to help in the weakening or elimination of their opponents. For one month and a half, the rule of the officers' junta or the Revolution Command Council was indirect and limited under the Ali Maher cabinet (July 23 - September 7, 1952). A three-member council of regency for the infant king was established under Prince Abdul Munem, son of Khedive Abbas II, with Colonel Rashad Muhanna as a member representing the Army.[64] In the first week after the coup, two important measures were taken, marking a breach with the old regime and its practices. On July 28, it was decided that the seat of government, which was normally in Alexandria during the summer months, was to be in Cairo throughout the whole year. Two days later (July 30), all honorary titles of Pasha and Bey were abolished, but the medals that accompanied the titles could be retained.

The outstanding development during this first period of rule under Ali Maher was the beginning of the open struggle between the powerful Wafd party led by Nahas and the military. The Wafd party supported the new cabinet and accepted the Army movement on the basis of Naguib's promise of respecting the constitution and conducting elections in October. The military junta, however, was not prepared to return to the old parliamentary system or cooperate with the old parties and their leaders. During the second half of August, Nahas challenged the military leaders and insisted on the return to parliamentary rule. At the same time, Maher showed reluctance to pass the agrarian reform law prepared by the officers, and was consequently dismissed on September 7. The military junta thus moved one step farther toward dictatorial rule as it ordered on the same day the arrest of forty-three political leaders of the old regime, and appointed General Naguib prime minister of a new civilian cabinet with Sulaiman Hafez, the opponent of the Wafd, as deputy premier and interior minister. The Wafdist spokesman and writer, Ahmad Abul Fath, was unable to dissuade his old friend Nasser, who at this time dominated the decisions of the Revolution Command Council, from arresting the politicians. He consequently wrote an editorial in his newspaper, *al- Misri,* entitled "Whereto Are We Going: To Democracy or to Dictatorship?"

On September 9, 1952, the new cabinet enacted the agrarian reform law. It provided for the expropriation of landed estates that exceeded 200-300 feddans (approximately acres) and for their redistribution among peasants, reduced rents for the benefit of tenant farmers, and increased the wages of agricultural laborers. The RCC and the cabinet expected, among other things, to gain popularity among the masses and to break the political power of the land-owning class.[65] The new government was not as yet ready to dissolve political parties, but as a step in that direction it ordered them on September 10 to reorganize within a month and list their objectives, the sources of their funds, and the names of their officers. The parties complied. Nahas withdrew from the active leadership of the Wafd after some resistance and was elected honorary president, but the party reorganization was judged unacceptable. The officers basically wanted no parties and their excuse was that the parties were against the concept of the revolution.[66] All the maneuverings and orders to purge and reorganize were therefore intended to gain time and prepare public opinion for the inevitable result. When the Wafd sought to challenge the decision of the RCC through the courts, the cabinet gave Naguib supreme power for six months without being subject to judicial review. This action was accompanied by more arrests of politicians and by retiring some 450 army officers. In another step towards direct military rule, the RCC decided at the end of September to assign officers, known as "Delegates of the Command," to several departments of government in order to insure the coordination of army policy and administrative action. The constitution of 1923 had been standing for more than four months after the coup, but on December 10, 1952, Naguib abrogated it "in the name of the people," and direct rule thus passed to the military junta.

The abrogation of the constitution was followed by the dissolution of all political parties on January 16, 1953 with the exception of the Muslim Brotherhood which the military could not afford to alienate while they were concentrating on the destruction of the Wafd. In the proclamation of January 16 that dissolved the parties and confiscated their funds, the military rulers began to use the theme of "foreign conspiracy" and "reactionary mentality" to justify their action. A three-year transitional period was established "in order that the country may enjoy stability and productivity," and "to enable us to set up a sound democratic and constitutional government." The system of government during the transitional period was defined in the eleven-article constitutional proclamation of February 10, 1953 which declared the nation to be the source of all powers and granted various personal freedoms "within the limits of the law." The council of ministers was given legislative and executive power (articles 9 and 10), and a congress of both the RCC and the cabinet was established to define the general policy of the State and discuss the conduct of every minister in his ministry (article 11).[67] Supreme sovereign powers were entrusted to the commander of the revolution in the Revolution Command Council (article 8), and Naguib candidly admitted, "I thus became a reluctant dictator." He explained the new development by the fact that the revolution was actively supported by only a small minority of the people and its enemies were strong.[68] The ultimate authority during the transitional period was the RCC whose chairman was General Naguib since Nasser resigned in his favor on August 17, 1952. Decisions in the RCC, however, were taken by majority vote, and Nasser and his old supporters continued to play the decisive role.

The establishment of the military dictatorship meant the abandonment of the principles and ideas for which the military leaders had fought against the old regime. They had attacked martial law under Farouk, the censorship of the press, the political arrest of persons, and the dissolution of parliament. But in less than six months after their coup, they had by far exceeded the aspects of Farouk's arbitrary rule. As they apparently fell in love with the power that came so easily to them, they found it difficult to disengage themselves and return to their barracks. They sought to justify their dictatorship by assuming that they were the custodians of national interest and had to take all necessary measures to implement the needed reforms. As in most dictatorships that follow a military coup, they had to lead a continuous struggle for eliminating all opposition, including that of their former partners in the coup.

Among the officers who opposed the military regime, the first to be dealt with was Rashad Muhanna, the imposing artillery colonel who had become a member of the regency council. On October 14, 1952, he was dismissed from his post and placed under house arrest because he allegedly scoffed at agrarian reform and considered it a communist measure; he was also too much involved with the Muslim Brotherhood, and, according to Nasser, wanted to wreck the foundations of the military revolution.[69] On January 16, 1953, Muhanna was arrested with twenty-four other officers and fifteen civilians for preparing a counter-revolution. He was tried by a military tribunal under Nasser, who was then acting chief-of-staff, with the members of the RCC as judges, and at the end of March was sentenced to life in jail while thirteen fellow conspirators were given prison terms of one to fifteen years. The timing of the dissolution of political parties with Muhanna's arrest on January 16 was intended to justify the Junta's action because, as Sadat said later, there was a danger of collusion between Muhanna and the parties, and the revolution therefore had to crush them before they could stab it in the back.[70] With the dismissal of Muhanna, the council of regency was dissolved and one sole regent was left, Prince Abdul Munem.

Arrested at the same time as Muhanna, was the governor of the Western Desert, Lt. Col. Muhammad al-Damanhuri, for plotting a counter-coup of his own. On January 20, he received a death sentence which was commuted to life in jail. Another independent and immature attempt to seize power was made by a military police officer called Ra'fat Chelebi. It has been related that this was one of the first occasions in which tape recording machines were used by the military to incriminate their opponents, and Nasser himself is said to have boasted of how the officers entered Chelebi's house with their machines and pretended they were ready to support him. Since then the most modern and varied recording instruments were utilized in the army, the government offices, the universities, the hotels and the factories by spies, intelligence agents, and informers of the regime who included, among others, chauffeurs, shoe shiners, waiters, and house servants.[71]

On June 18, 1953, the Revolution Command Council proclaimed by decree and "in the name of the people" the end of the monarchy and of the dynasty of Muhammad Ali, and the establishment of a republic. The infant king, Ahmad Faud II was deposed, and General Naguib was proclaimed president. The officers believed that the regency gave no guarantee of stability and encouraged the enemies of the regime to plot. According to Naguib, his junior colleagues would have proclaimed the republic earlier, but he preferred to wait until the people could vote on a constitution.[72] It is also claimed that Naguib opposed the overthrow of the monarchy and thereby provoked the fierce criticism of Nasser who angrily told him, "We made you and appointed you our president and you still speak of our commitment to the people."[73] The RCC evidently had thought of giving Naguib the presidency only and reserving the premiership to Nasser, but Naguib's hesitation to accept the proclamation of a republic decided his colleagues to give him both, and he thus combined in his person the posts of president, prime minister, and chairman of the RCC. Nasser became deputy prime minister and minister of the interior, and for the first time since the coup he became openly known to the public. The number of civilians in the cabinet was reduced and all the key posts were given to officers. General Naguib believed that this "militarization of the cabinet" was of doubtful wisdom.[74]

Three months after the proclamation of the republic, the officers announced in September the formation of a tribunal of the revolution in order to try those who endangered the security of the state and its new regime and supported colonialism and corrupt rule in the past. Prominent politicians under the monarchy were arrested on September 20, 1953 and after, and included Ibrahim Abdul Hadi, former prime minister and leader of the Saadist party, as well as Fuad Serageddin, the prominent Wafdist leader. The RCC was evidently worried by mounting criticism and hostile rumors about the regime and by the open demand for a constitution. The trials were intended to silence the critics and discredit and destroy the influential political leaders by using the same theme of conspiracy with foreign powers that it was to utilize throughout the entire period of military and Nasserist rule. The tribunal was presided by Badgdadi and the two members were two other officers of the RCC, Anwar Sadat and Hasan Ibrahim. Under the pretext that the tribunal was revolutionary, the RCC defined the judicial procedure, appointed the prosecutor and the judges from among its own members, and ratified the sentences of the tribunal. Former Prime Minister Abdul Hadi was sentenced to death for alleged treason and corruption, while Serageddin received fifteen years in jail for various offenses including responsibility in the burning of Cairo. Nahas was condemned, but not sentenced, for condoning the misbehavior of his Wafdist associates. General Naguib confided later that Serageddin's sentence was "a blunder and an injustice." He also declared that no one liked the tribunal "and we abolished it as soon as we safely could." From September 26, 1953, when it held its first trial, to June 30, 1954, when it ended, thirty-one cases were tried.[75] One of the results of the end of the monarchy and of the revolutionary trials was the confiscation of 180,000 acres of land that belonged to the royal family.

IV. *Nasser Versus Naguib: Coups and Counter-Coups February - March 1954*

The struggle between General Naguib and his younger colleagues led by Colonel Gamal Abdul Nasser began with a series of differences and disagreements on matters of policy and procedure and entered its decisive phase on February 25,

1954. It ended on March 29 with Naguib's defeat and the emergence of Nasser as Egypt's strongman after thirty-four days of coups and counter-coups attended by demonstrations and disorder. The basic underlying factors of the conflict were, first, the misunderstanding between the two parties on the role and the powers of General Naguib; second, the disagreement on the disengagement of the military from politics and the restoration of constitutional rule; third, the different outlook and views on the extent and speed of the revolutionary changes to be made. Along with these factors, one can mention the personal jealousies, suspicions, and intrigues characteristic of military rule.

The free officers had asked General Naguib to be the front leader of their movement in order to give it an appearance of respectability in view of the General's age, integrity and popularity. They thought he would be satisfied with the titles and honors of the various positions and would not claim more power than that which his vote in the RCC gave him. Naguib thought that as president, prime minister, and leader of the revolution, he should exercise some control, but real control was exercised by the majority in the RCC, and effectively by Nasser who dominated that majority. Naguib was expected, in view of his position, to be responsible for every action taken by the government, but he could not, as he said, assume responsibility for actions of which he did not approve or regarding which he was not consulted. He could no longer go on pretending to run things that were run by others.[76]

Naguib's moderation and popularity were largely responsible for the first successes of the army movement. The people viewed his presence as a guarantee for the fulfillment of the promises made by the army to restore constitutional rule and to eradicate corruption. In the showdown with the political parties, Naguib supported his junior colleagues and helped insure stability for the regime. But Naguib was a devout Muslim and hated injustice and arbitrary rule. He heard the people complain about the arbitrary behavior of the young officers in the administration, and he made no secret of his disappointment with his colleagues when he said, "These young men are imprudent . . . .they no longer listen to me. They are piling up stupid mistakes and heading for disaster."[77] Naguib believed that the army should return to the barracks because, for one thing, it was weakened by engaging in state administration and politics. Yet, Naguib has claimed that he did not intend to dissolve the RCC or restore the old parties or call a halt to the revolution, but he wanted to gain popular support for the movement by gradually demilitarizing the government, creating a constituent assembly, and preparing the people for free elections.[78]

According to Sadat, Naguib feared the word "revolution" and tried to stop it with the fallacy of the constitution, elections and parties. But Sadat wondered through whom Naguib was to realize democracy and achieve the aims of the revolution. The younger group of officers which included Sadat and Nasser feared that constitutional rule and democracy would mean the return of the old parties and their leaders. They were apparently obsessed by the frightening thought of what would happen to them if democracy and with it the old politicians returned, and by the no less disturbing idea that the revolution would not continue its march, or would not be able to stand on its feet, without them. The revolution, said Sadat, should be directed by those who participated in it, otherwise "what would be the role of those who made the revolution? Would they join the Dervish orders and grow beards, or what would they do?"[79] The fear of the old democracy and the sincere or pretended concern about the fate of the revolution were valid reasons, in their view, to retain power and prevent Naguib or anyone else from taking it away from them.

Naguib's position from the very beginning was precarious, and under the special conditions of military rule, his kind of leadership would not have lasted as long as it did. His colleagues believed that they built up his stature and that he owed them everything. They, moreover, dominated the various commands in the army. Yet, it is to Naguib's credit that through his simple honesty and moderation, he was able to command respect and become immensely popular in the army and among the masses. He never understood his position to be that of a figurehead. Nasser took the freedom of issuing policy statements in cooperation with Salah Salem without consulting Naguib in an attempt to isolate him. He also called cabinet ministers to his office and made decisions and imposed them on Naguib in the cabinet meetings or in the joint meetings of the cabinet and the RCC.

The open crisis between Naguib and Nasser was brought about by the outlawing of the Muslim Brotherhood on January 13, 1954 without consulting Naguib. On the preceding day, students belonging to the Brotherhood cursed Nasser as a dictator and an Anglo-American pawn in a demonstration at Cairo University. The police tried to intervene and one of their jeeps was set on fire. Several students were injured in the fighting between the Muslim Brethren and members of the Liberation Rally. As a result, Nasser banned the Muslim Brotherhood, closed its premises, and arrested its supreme guide, Hasan al-Hodeiby, along with hundreds of its members. Naguib criticised the arrests and the repressive measures and asked for the right of veto on the decisions of the RCC. The officers told him that this would mean dictatorship and refused his demand. Some believed that he was trying to carry off a "genuine coup d'état ." Naguib, however, claimed that he was asking for a limited veto that could be overridden if the Council did so openly.[80]

On February 23, 1954, Naguib presented his resignation to the RCC saying, " . . . . I can no longer carry out my duties in the manner I consider best calculated to serve the national interests."[81] The time was well chosen because he was scheduled to leave for the Sudan with Salah Salem on February 28 to attend the inauguration of a newly elected parliament. The RCC immediately sent Shafii and Gamal Salem to Naguib's house and an agreement was reached, according to Naguib, to keep the resignation a secret until after his return from the Sudan and then the council would decide on his powers. The RCC apparently changed its mind shortly after. It held a long meeting on the evening of February 25 at the Gezira Palace where unusually loud voices were heard and Sadat reportedly placed his pistol on the table. At the end of the lively discussion, Salah Salem announced that Naguib's resignation was accepted and Nasser was appointed in his place as prime minister and chairman of the Council, while the presidency of the republic remained vacant.[82] In the press and radio, the younger Salem attacked Naguib, but this only made the people more irritated against the RCC. Naguib was placed under house arrest, his telephones were cut off, republican guards were replaced by military police and infantry troops, and movement in and out of Naguib's house was prohibited.[83]

The bloodless coup of February 25 that removed Naguib was followed after less than twenty-four hours by a counter-coup that forced his return. The people were worried and grieved on hearing the news of Naguib's removal, and the government of the Sudan which had great respect for Naguib expressed its disapproval and later sent a delegation that asked to take Naguib to the Sudan or obtain a promise to set him free. The decisive action in Naguib's favor, however, came from the liberal elements in the army and particularly Khalid Muhieddin and the cavalry officers who were close to Naguib. On the evening of February 26 they met with Nasser and protested vehemently against what he did to Naguib. They told him that authority had gone to his head, that he preferred power to the army, and that instead of liberation, he replaced Farouk's autocracy by his own. Their armored forces with guns directed towards the building at Abbasiya helped force Nasser's hands. He tried in vain to appeal to their self interest as officers and he warned them against the return of parliamentary rule which would bring with it Fuad Serageddin and other old politicians. He finally gave up and agreed to call back Naguib on condition that Khalid Muhieddin would become prime minister. Khalid went to Naguib's house and persuaded him to accept this condition. Naguib gave his approval but expected the other members of the RCC to continue their cooperation.[84]

On the early morning of February 27, shortly after he had accepted Khalid's proposal, General Naguib was abducted from his home by two military police officers and taken to the artillery headquarters at Almaza. He was then removed through a backdoor and driven to the desert, and he thought he would be murdered. Nasser, however, ordered his release and kept his promise to return him to the presidency. One of the explanations given for Naguib's abduction after the cavalry officers' counter-coup suggested that the pro-Nasser army units thought that Nasser had been apprehended by the rebels and they consequently made a counter strike against Naguib. Another explanation, by Naguib himself, said that the RCC was trying to avoid an unequal battle between its sympathizers and those who outnumbered them on Naguib's side.[85]

On February 27, the radio announced Naguib's return to the presidency but Nasser — not Khalid Muhieddin — remained prime minister. The RCC appealed to the people to close their ranks and forget what happened. Photographs appeared very soon in the press showing Nasser and Naguib smiling and arm in arm. On the following day, February 28, Naguib was driven to the Republican Palace (Abdin Palace), and from the balcony he told the enormous crowd who came to cheer him that the crisis was "a summer cloud that had quickly passed away." Naguib at the same time announced, without being authorized by the RCC, that the people would soon be invited to elect a parliament. The crowds responded with delirious applause as they hoped to win back their constitutional liberites. The old political parties and the forces opposing the military regime in general attempted to take advantage of Naguib's position in the crisis, while foreign circles counted on his success because they were disturbed by the horrible growth of leftism under Nasser's rule. The United

States alone reportedly supported and encouraged Nasser during the crisis and was not favorable to restoration of parliamentary democracy.[86]

The first phase of the crucial struggle thus ended on February 28 with Nasser's defeat, but the defeat was temporary. Although the majority of the country and most of the army were against him, he still had the support of his colleagues in the RCC and it proved to be very valuable. The tactics he adopted consisted of making concessions to Naguib and the people on the issue of constitutional rule, but at the same time he strove to win back the army with General Amer's help, and paralyze Naguib's power and exploit his mistakes. On February 29 Naguib left for the Sudan with S. Salem, but he returned hastily on account of the bloody riots in Khartum that were organized by anti-Egyptian elements and resulted in the death of more than twenty persons.

On March 5, 1954, shortly after Naguib's return to Cairo, the RCC announced that censorship was abolished and martial law would be lifted, and that a constituent assembly would meet on July 23 to adopt a draft constitution after discussion, and to act as a provisional parliament until a new parliament is elected. This concession could have been a manifestation of what has been called Nasser's "tactical genius," but one should not discount popular pressure on Nasser and the RCC, and the backing given to Naguib by such eminent personalities as Ali Maher and Dr. Sanhouri. Four days later, March 9, Naguib regained his post of prime minister and was thus theoretically in full possesssion of the powers he had held before the crisis of February 25. While Nasser remained in the background with his old position of vice-prime minister, General Amer helped consolidate his friend's control over the officers by intriguing against Nasser's opponents and transferring or dismissing them, and rewarding his supporters with promotions. Nasser himself again appealed to the officers' self interest and reminded them how they had been nothing before the military regime and had become everything. He told them that they would again be badly paid, badly armed and despised if the army lost power.[87] With similar warnings he also tried to incite the labor unions against the restoration of constitutional government.

On March 20, 1954, King Saud of Saudi Arabia began a long state visit to Egypt. Nasser saw no more appropriate time than this to launch his second, but decisive, coup against Naguib. On March 25, the RCC issued a communiqué drafted by Nasser in which it pretended that it would transfer sovereignty to a constituent assembly on July 24, and that the revolution would end there. The announcements in the communiqué were a tactical maneuver calculated to set the stage for the disturbances which Nasser and his junior colleagues had prepared. Naguib felt out-maneuvered because the text of the communiqué went beyond what he wanted.

The well-calculated maneuver of March 25 was accompanied by the release of Hodeiby and other leaders and members of the Muslim Brotherhood. At the same time the forces prepared by Nasser and his RCC colleagues began their violent protest against the return of civilian rule. On the morning of March 26, the officers of the National Guard which had been organized by the Liberation Rally to serve as Nasser's militia, started various demonstrations in Cairo and exploded bombs to disturb public security. Army buses and trains were used to transport national guardsmen from the provinces, while the commander of the National Guard, Kemal Hussein, and prominent members of the Liberation Movement like Tuaima and Tahawi directed the protest movement.

On the morning of March 27, the Federation of Transport Workers in Cairo, whose president Sawi Ahmad al-Sawi had been won over by Nasser, declared a general strike that paralyzed Cairo. It is claimed that the strike had been already scheduled on that day because of the disagreement between the workers and the transport companies, but Nasser exploited it and distributed leaflets saying that the transport workers were protesting against elections and parties and were asking the RCC to continue its rule. Demonstrations, it is claimed, moved in Cairo in army cars while hired speakers and demonstrators under the supervision of the national guardsmen chanted, "Down with freedom .... Down with democracy .... Down with parliament." Students, however, were able to reach the university to denounce the plot against the restoration of civilian rule and issue resolutions supporting the decisions of March 5 and 25, but they were soon dispersed. On the other hand, the mob which had been gathered by the military for participation in the disturbances surrounded the ministerial and other government offices on March 28 and shouted slogans in support of the RCC and the revolution. On the following day the demonstrators headed for the State Council to humiliate its president, Dr. Sanhouri, for his cooperation with Naguib in favor of constitutional rule. He was attacked and beaten and was carried to his home with a head wound.

When King Saud left Cairo on March 29, Naguib and the RCC members accompanied him to the Almaza Airport. At one moment before Saud's departure, some officers reportedly thought that Naguib tried to escape with the King and they prevented him by tearing him from the King's embrace. It is even said that Sadat slapped him on the face.[88] Naguib, who had already shown signs of exhaustion collapsed in the airport and was carried to his home. The duel between him and his younger colleagues ended in his defeat. In the evening of March 29, Nasser and the RCC reaped the fruits of their efforts over the last four days. They issued a statement announcing that the RCC would assume again full responsibility, and postpone the decisions that had been taken on March 5 and 25 until the end of the transitional period. The statement was followed by student strikes and demonstrations against military dictatorship but the demonstrations were ended by troops and the universities were closed during the first week of April. Naguib retained his title of president until he was deposed on November 14, but he lost his post of prime minister to Nasser on April 18. The RCC was purged of three of its members for their support of Naguib. They were Khalid

Muhieddin, Yusif Saddiq, and Abdul Munem Amin. Khalid was sent to Europe on April 6 and his expenses were paid by the government. Strict censorship of the press was restored and the press syndicate council was dissolved. Parties were again abolished with the exception of the Muslim Brotherhhod. The universities were reorganized and purged.

When Nasser became prime minister on April 18 - for the second time in two months - he appointed Hasan Ibrahim minister of state for presidential affairs and Hussein Shafii minister of war. On September 1, the cabinet was re-shuffled and it prepared for more purges and challenges. Amer was appointed minister of war, and Sadat became minister of state. All ten members of the RCC were now included in the cabinet. In its first month in office, the cabinet pensioned forty university professors and more than one hundred high ranking police officers. The only opposition group left and with whom the new regime had compromised after March 1954 was the Muslim Brotherhood, but it soon resumed opposition and clashed with the government. The Brethren distributed pamphlets praising Naguib as "the savior and leader of the country." They criticized the initial agreement with Britain on the Suez Canal zone in July. On October 26, 1954, one week after the signature of the formal agreement for the evacuation of the Suez Canal zone with Britain, a Cairo plumber called Mahmud Abdul Latif, who belonged to the "secret order" in the Muslim Brotherhood, fired eight shots at Nasser in the course of a mass rally in Alexandria. The unsuccessful attempt on Nasser's life gave him the opportunity to break the power of the Muslim Brotherhood. About one thousand leaders and members including Hodeiby, the supreme guide, were arrested and a "Special People's Tribunal" under three RCC members - Gamal Salem as president and Sadat and Shafii as members - began the trial of the Brethren on November 9. Testimony at the trial tended to involve President Naguib in the conspiracy, and Nasser immediately deposed him. On November 14, 1954, Hasan Ibrahim and Amer called on Naguib in Abdin Palace and escorted him to a villa in a suburb of Cairo where he was placed under house arrest. A brief statement on the radio said, "General Naguib was relieved today of his position as president." The people of Cairo did not react as they had done when his resignation was announced for the first time in February 1954 because times had changed. The political students, the Muslim Brotherhood, the communists, the Wafdist leaders, and the army officers who would have reacted had been all dispersed or rounded up and the dictatorship was firmly entrenched. The trials ended with the condemnation of seven leading defendants to death, and the conviction of hundreds of others. Six of the condemned were executed while the supreme guide's sentence was commuted to life in jail.

The success of the second coup against Naguib at the end of March 1954 is a most significant event in the modern history of Egypt and the Arab world. It meant the end of that spirit of moderation and compromise that had hitherto characterized all Arab military regimes. It also meant the decisive defeat of the attempts to restore freedom and parliamentary government in Egypt. The military dictatorship under Nasser, in the absence of any successful opposition, felt free to carry Egypt and with it other Arab states on a revolutionary course whose benefits and achievements have remained doubtful.

V. Military Adventures in Democracy

Under Nasser's rule and leadership, the radical changes in the political and social system were officially explained as prerequisites for national liberation and strength, and for the achievement of social justice. The changes which are usually referred to as the political and social revolution, were decreed by a succession of more or less dictatorial governments that imposed their own version of democracy and socialism, emphasized class conflict, and nationalized private enterprise.

Nasser and the ruling military junta found it relatively easy after the fall of Farouk to destroy the old political regime in Egypt by dissolving parties, eliminating the military and civilian opposition, and degrading the leaders of the country by arrests and trials and confiscating their property. The military rulers were able to go through this negative phase of the revolution by their control of the means of violence, and were also aided by the submissiveness of the Egyptian people. They were unable, however, to substitute a new stable democratic political order for the one they destroyed. The transitional period under the RCC (1953-1956), in contrast to that of certain military regimes in other countries, was not a period of training and preparation for democracy. On the contrary, Nasser and his military and civilian supporters concentrated a good part of their efforts on denouncing the entire Western system of democracy to the point of evolving a doctrine against it, and ended by adopting a system of popular or totalitarian democracy that knows neither parties nor free elections but is based on the following: a single mass organization created and controlled by the government, a national assembly that exercises no real power and whose candidates are screened and almost chosen before the elections, and on the use of plebiscites for obtaining the people's consent to certain measures already decided by the government such as the adoption of a constitution and the election of the president.[89]

On January 23, 1953, six months after the revolution, the ruling junta or the RCC created a mass organization known as the Liberation Rally to provide popular support for the military regime. Nasser became the head of the organization that depended for its membership mainly on the laborers and the youth. The masses remained largely indifferent to it but the Muslim Brethren and the communists tried to infiltrate the organization. The Liberation Rally was used for organizing demonstrations against the enemies of the ruling RCC. The role it played in the disturbances of March 1954 against Naguib discredited it, and it was finally abolished. The RCC announced the "immediate" formation of a national consultative assembly in the declaration of March 29, 1954 after Naguib's defeat, but this assembly was not established. Nasser disliked to share authority with an elected assembly and therefore tried to avoid elections, but at the same time he had to provide a foundation for his government, and the three-year transitional period of direct military rule was coming to an end.

On January 16, 1956, a draft constitution prepared by a small committee dominated by the RCC was presented to the Egyptians.[90] It was the third constitutional proclamation since the revolution, after those of February 10 and June 18, 1953. The constitution provided for a presidential republic with a strong president who was his own prime minister and was elected by popular vote, and a national assembly which was to be elected later according to an electoral law enacted in March 1957. The constitution mentioned for the first time in any Arab document of this kind the formation of a mass organization called the National Union, whose first duty according to Article 192 was "to present the candidates for the elections to the national assembly." It thus became a characteristic of the new Egyptian democracy to create a mass organization every time a national assembly was contemplated, and to make the national assembly an emanation of the mass organization that was virtually created and controlled by the government. The same action was repeated in 1962 when the Arab Socialist Union became the new mass organization and preceded the drafting of a new constitution and the elections for a national assembly. Another characteristic of this new democracy was the slow pace of the military regime in creating the democratic machinery, as illustrated by the long period of time that was calculated to pass between the drafting of a constitution, its approval by plebiscite, and the elections for the national assembly.

The constitution of January 1956 was ratified in a double referendum on June 23, 1956 in which Nasser was elected president of the republic. The referendum took place five days after the complete evacuation of British forces from Egypt. Nasser, as an unopposed candidate, was elected by a fabulous majority of 99.9 per cent, and the constitution was ratified by

99.8 per cent of the votes. On June 24, the Revolution Command Council was dissolved and its members changed into civilian clothes. Out of the fourteen original members, only six remained active in the government.

On July 3, 1957, one year after the constitution had been accepted by plebiscite, the national assembly was elected. The executive committee of the National Union had excluded all candidates it did not consider fit, because they were "imperialist agents, reactionaries, and opportunists." The national assembly met on July 22, but it lasted about six months and was dissolved after the proclamation of unity with Syria in February 1958. It played no role in policy making. The assembly members, however, were bold enough to question and challenge the actions and declarations of ministers and highly placed officials. The debate on the corrupt administration of the Liberation Province by Magdi Hassanein, for example, was sensational and led to the dismissal of the administrator who was an officer and a friend of Nasser.

A double referendum was held soon after the proclamation of the United Arab Republic to approve the unity of Syria and Egypt and elect the president. Nasser was the only candidate. On February 21, the people of Egypt and Syria elected him president by 99.99 per cent of the votes. He then promulgated a provisional constitution of the presidential type for the UAR on March 5, 1958. It was the fourth constitution since the revolution. It gave the president the power to appoint and dismiss the vice presidents and ministers. The constitution provided for a national assembly, half of whose members were to be drawn from the dissolved Egyptian national assembly and the Syrian chamber of deputies. Three cabinets were appointed by Nasser on March 6: a central cabinet for the UAR, and an executive council or local cabinet for Syria and another for Egypt.

The new national assembly was not a representative assembly; its members were for the first time in the parliamentary history of the Arab world appointed by the president instead of being elected by the people. It met on July 21,

1960, more than two years after the promulgation of the provisional constitution, and only after elections had been terminated for the various committees of the National Union that had been reorganized as a mass organization to include both Egypt and Syria. Nasser's government claimed that the National Union was not a party but the representative of all the classes and groups in the nation. Others saw in it simply the basis of one party rule dominated by Nasser, for he was its chairman and his ministers were appointed to serve as its supreme executive committee. It was this supreme executive committee that helped him select the six hundred members of the national assembly that met on July 21, 1960 and chose Anwar Sadat as its president. Nasser made sure that all the social and professional categories of people, including even singers like the famous Umm Kulthum, were represented in his selection in order to enhance the picture of democracy.

When the union between Syria and Egypt came to an end in September 1961, Nasser dissolved both the national assembly and the National Union. In his speech of October 16, 1961, he declared that he made the mistake of allowing the forces of reaction to infiltrate the National Union and succeed in paralyzing it. He decided that his regime needed more powerful popular support and that the people should be organized in a union that would be an instrument for the national masses alone. He therefore designated 250 persons to act as a preparatory committee for the meeting of a "national congress of popular forces" in order to create another mass organization. The congress was to consist of the 250 appointed members of the preparatory committee and 1500 elected members who represented the various classes and groups in the following proportions: 379 peasants, 300 laborers, 150 representing "national capital,"461 representing government officials, professional unions, and women, and 210 professors and students.

In the opening session of this congress on May 21, 1962, President Nasser took five hours to read the ten chapters of his draft of the "National Charter"and had it approved. The

Charter embodied and explained in detail the three national aims of freedom, socialism, and unity. It described the ideology of the new popular democracy and the "scientific socialism" of the Egyptian state. The fifth chapter entitled "sound democracy" started with an attack on the old parliamentary democracy and called it "the democracy of reaction" because it was based on the alliance of capitalism and feudalism. Democracy in the Charter is based on the alliance of the working forces of the people that consist of the peasant farmers, the laborers, the soldiers, the intelligentsia, *(al-muthaqqafun),* and national capital. The future constitution, according to the Charter, should include the following characteristics: The supremacy of the elected bodies over the executive power, collective leadership, and the award of half of the seats in all elective bodies, including the national assembly, to the peasant farmers and laborers "who have a vested interest in the revolution and have been deprived of their rights for a long time."[91]

In the spirit of the reform announced by the Charter, a constitutional proclamation was promulgated on September 27, 1962 establishing a collective leadership in the form of a presidency council of twelve members - ten of whom were former military officers - under President Nasser, to share some of his powers. The proclamation also provided for an executive council, equivalent to a cabinet, and Ali Sabri was appointed its chairman. Nasser, however, retained extensive powers. This was the fifth constitutional document since the revolution. Plans were made for the formation of the Arab Socialist Union that was intended to play the role of a one party organization under the new socialist regime defined by the Charter. It was the third mass organization since the revolution. Its structure was similar to that of the National Union. Its various committees were selected over a long period of time "so as not to allow reaction to sneak in."

The regime of collective leadership which began on September 27, 1962 was ended when a new provisional constitution, the sixth since the revolution, was announced by President Nasser on March 23, 1964 and became effective two days later. At the same time a new national assembly of 350 members was elected on March 10 and met on March 26. The voters naturally had one list of candidates to choose from and they were all members of the same one-party organization.

The new constitution of March 23, 1964 declared in its first article that the Egyptian people are part of the Arab nation, as in the constitution of 1956, and similarly Islam was mentioned as the religion of the state.[92] But in 1964, the constitution described Egypt, not merely as a democratic republic but as a "democratic, socialist state based on the alliance of the working forces of the people" (Article 1). In Article 3 it mentioned the Arab Socialist Union which is formed by "the alliance of the people's forces representing the working people who include the farmers, the laborers, the soldiers, the intelligentsia, and national capital." The economic foundation of the state is the socialist system, and the two foundations of the socialist society are "sufficiency and justice" (Article 9). The function of the armed forces is "the protection of the social gains of the popular struggle," in addition to "the safeguarding of the country and the security and integrity of its territory" (Article 23).

The new provisional constitution of March 1964 with its 169 articles was made to fit the political, social, and economic system created by Nasser. It was a picture of the new "democratic, socialist state" and contained guarantees to preserve it. On the day it became effective, March 25, 1964, and one day before the meeting of the national assembly a new cabinet was sworn in with Ali Sabri as prime minister, ten deputy prime ministers, and twenty-two ministers. The newly created deputy premierships were like a super cabinet, but none of the deputy premiers was a former RCC member or an intimate friend of Nasser. In January 1965, a campaign, promoted by the regime, began in Cairo for nominating Nasser for a third term. Television sets were placed in the streets and public squares to let the crowds watch the nominating speeches made by the delegations who came from various parts of the country, while demonstrators called for Nasser's nomination.[93] On March 16, 1965, Nasser was elected by referendum, after his nomination by the assembly, by the classical 99.99 per cent of the votes.

In the new democratic socialist state described by the charter of 1962, the role of the Socialist Union was not clearly defined. The constitution of March 1964, Article 3, spoke of it as "the power representative of the people, driver of the revolution's potentialities, and protector of sound democratic values." The Socialist Union, in reality, was dominated by the government which uses it as an instrument of political and administrative pressure. Its General Secretariat, which on October 9, 1965 consisted of thirteen members, was headed by Ali Sabri, who had just lost his post of prime minister. The Higher Executive Committee of the Socialist Union, which was reduced from twenty-five members in October 1965 to seven members in November 1966, consisted of President Nasser, the three vice presidents, the secretary general, the president of the national assembly, and the prime minister.

Following the war with Israel in early June 1967, a new development in government occurred. President Nasser took over on June 19 the functions of prime minister as well as those of secretary general of the Socialist Union. The purpose, as it was explained, was to insure full unity between the State and the people's forces represented by the Socialist Union. The three former prime ministers, Ali Sabri, Z. Muhieddin, and S. Sulaiman, in addition to Shafii, became vice-prime ministers.[94]

The military adventures in democracy with their successive constitutional proclamations, mass organizations, and national assemblies had one basic and persistent objective, namely, the search for total political power and the monopoly of political activity by those who made the coup of 1952 and then became the self-appointed trustees of the revolution.

While government machinery was represented as the instrument of the popular will, the rulers refused to share power with the people under the pretext, expressed by Sadat, that "the leadership of the revolution defines what it thinks the interests and needs of the people are."[95] Certain similarities have been found between the one party organization in the Egyptian system and the Communist Party in the Soviet Union. In both, the one party organization is an officially recognized entity and its leaders are high state officials. But, whereas in Russia the Soviet State was a creature of the Communist Party and served as its instrument, in Egypt the one party organization - The Socialist Union - is the creature of the State and is subservient to it.[96]

The officers in civilian clothes became under the revolutionary regime a new ruling class and a political interest group that replaced the old bourgeois elite and were no longer inclined to lose their acquired privileges.[97] In their opportunism and techniques for manipulating the masses, and in certain aspects of corruption, abuse of power, and disregard of the rule of law, they sometimes surpassed the rulers of the old regime, but their weaknesses and scandals were often ignored and could not be publicized. Nasser consistently refused to take stern measures against those of his colleagues who were flagrantly responsible for mismanagement or embezzlement as in the cases of Magdi Hassanein of the Liberation Province in 1957, the smuggling ring that operated from Marshal Amer's office, or the officers who helped themselves to some of the indemnities for the families of soldiers who died in Yemen in 1966. Bureaucratic routine and red tape remained an object of bitter, but silent, general complaint. Civil service officials were still criticized for their arrogance, negligence, and abuse of privilege,[98] while officers without experience and qualifications were appointed to supervise the work of indignant professionals.

Under the new democratic socialist society, educational facilities were expanded especially at the elementary level, and education in its various stages became free, but educational standards were degraded, and the universities in particular suffered from lack of qualified professors and from confusion in the new regulations and programs and in the preparation of needed text books that sometimes were made available only in the middle of the academic year.[99] Professors were dismissed for not following the government official line in their teaching. Private and foreign schools were placed under strict supervision "to protect the students against religious, national, and political deviations." Programs and books were revised to include propaganda material for the revolutionary regime and to indoctrinate the students in its goals, policies, and institutions.[100] Academic organizations such as the Higher Council of Sciences, Arts and Letters, founded in 1958, were established to encourage research that would benefit the government system and also to regiment the intellectuals and keep them obligated to the state for the various indemnities they received as members of the many committees and conferences.

Under the pretext that they were in a state of revolution and that they were attempting to establish social justice for the oppressed against their oppressors, the military have deprived both the old elite and the rest of the people of the most precious gains realized during the long struggle for independence, namely, freedom and civil liberties without which no real democracy can exist. The people have felt insecure in their person and property after the successive waves of nationalization, confiscation, and trials. As in the days of the Mameluks and Ottomans, they had to avoid conspicuous consumption for fear of attracting attention and inviting trouble.

Freedom of expression, oral or written, became restricted and rigidly regulated. Any comments on government policies had to be accompanied by caution and glancing over the shoulders due to the presence of spies and informers. Correspondence by mail was opened and letters were not always sure of reaching their destination. Topics for the Friday sermon in the mosques were sometimes specified, and one minister of Waqfs (Religious Endowments), Sheikh Hasan al-Baquri, who held the post between 1952 and 1958, was accused even of dictating the complete text of the Friday sermon.[101] In the press, newspaper editors received official directions on the handling of the news, especially editorials, and reaction to major developments had to wait until the editor received the official line from the government. Local news was sometimes blacked out completely by direct order as though it never happened, whereas distorted and fabricated news was often published. Dispatches of foreign correspondents sometimes were withheld.[102] In May 1960 the Egyptian press was nationalized and placed under the direction of the National Union. The nationalized newspapers and publishing companies were later grouped in semi-autonomous organizations under state control. Nationalization and state control of the press was justified, according to the Charter of 1962, by the claim that the press had lost its freedom under the old regime and was supported and dominated by the interests of feudalism and capitalism through advertising.

Among the contradictions in the Nasserist version of the democratic socialist society, one of the most obvious was religious and ethnic discrimination in spite of the constitutional provision that declared, "Egyptians are equal before the law and they have equal public rights and duties without discrimination between them due to race, origin, language, religion, or creed."[103] Nasser's regime apparently believed that the only Egyptians worthy of civil rights were those of nattive Egyptian ancestry while other Egyptian citizens of Syro-Lebanese, Greek, Italian or other ancestral origins, who were usually non-Muslim, were not real Egyptians. Pressures amounting to depriving them of the means of livelihood or degrading them morally led to their wholesale departure from the country. Moreover, the Christian Coptic minority, the most Egyptian among the native Egyptians by its origins, began to cite cases of discrimination under the revolutionary regime since the mid-1950's and for the first time in its long history some of its members began to emigrate. An estimated 10,000 Copts were said to have been converted to Islam after 1956.[104] Others have continued the practice, which had started before the revolution, of adopting Muslim names to hide their identity or make themselves more acceptable to Muslim society.

VI. Military Experiments in Socialism

The military dictatorship and its adventures in totalitarian democracy were accompanied from the very beginning of the revolution by parallel adventures in socialistic experimentation until July 1961 when Egypt became the first Arab socialist state and enunciated a socialist doctrine in a charter of Marxist inspiration on May 21, 1962. Socialism in fact was the pretext and the justification for building up the dictatorship and the instrument for destroying its opponents. This is one of the reasons why the political and social revolution had to go side by side.

In the first years of the revolution, the military leaders used the slogan of "unity, discipline, and work," and emphasized the idea of "liberation" and the need for "social justice." They avoided socialist slogans and the mention of "socialism" and class struggle. Yet, certain revolutionary socialist elements and aspects of class struggle were inherent from the beginning in their egalitarian ideas and in the six principles of the revolution, particularly those that dealt with the destruction of landlordism, monopolies, and capitalist influence on government.

In the first months of the revolution the military government issued various laws for achieving social justice and preventing the exploitation of the peasant and worker, and also for destroying the political power of the ruling elite and giving the new rulers the satisfaction of exulting at the political and material downfall of the mighty and the wealthy. The earliest and most significant of these laws was the Agrarian

Reform Law no. 178 of September 9, 1952 that set a limit for what a landlord could own and allowed the state to expropriate and distribute the lands that exceeded that limit. The first objective that was easily realized by the military rulers was to destroy political feudalism or the political influence of the landlord over the peasant voter who worked on his estate. The other objectives that took longer time to realize were to allow more peasants to become landowners, to establish state control and modernize agriculture in the newly distributed lands through the creation of cooperatives among new peasant landowners, and to force the landlords to divert their capital to industry. It is alleged that the United States embassy played a role in preparing the law and encouraging the officers in ideas which seemed to be good for the struggle against communism.[105] The law amounted virtually to confiscation, and not merely forced sale of the land, since the landlord received no immediate compensation. The land that was distributed was less than ten per cent of the cultivatible land, and about 200,000 peasant families or one million peasants became landowners while there were still more than five million landless peasants. The tenants were given substantial reductions amounting to about fifty per cent of their rents, but agricultural laborers who were one third of the agricultural population did not profit from the law. The reform was followed by the creation of the appropriate organs for its implementation and by various land reclamation projects, the best known of which was the Tahrir (Liberation) Province that was started in March 1954. The social welfare centers that existed before the revolution were reorganized into combined rural centers that provided agricultural as well as health, social, and educational services and were placed under the Permanent Council for Public Welfare Services organized on March 16, 1954. Cooperative societies of producers and consumers, as well as agricultural cooperatives, multiplied between 1952 and 1955, and the cooperative movement was later reorganized by Law 317 of 1956 and was mentioned and encouraged in the constitution of 1956.

The military rulers issued other decrees to bring the classes and their living standards nearer to each other and to gain popularity among the masses. They lowered rents, raised the taxes on higher incomes, forbade the dismissal of laborers, introduced social insurance, labor arbitration and individual labor contracts. They also sought to increase production and encourage domestic and foreign capital investment in industry, and in 1953 they founded the Permanent Council for Production. Various categories of people, however, were discontented, especially the merchants, because of the decree on maximum profits and fixed prices accompanied by harsh treatment and severe sanctions for violation of the decree, the government officials because their salaries were decreased, and even the workmen sometimes struck because the indemnity of high living was abolished. Certain measures, like forbidding the dismissal of workmen, led to unemployment and thus contradicted their intended goal because industrial enterprises regulated their employment according to their minimum production.[106] The measures, moreover, did not encourage the investment of foreign capital.

In 1956 the military government, evidently frustrated by the flight of capital and the drop in confidence on the part of local and foreign capitalists, began to change its course decisively towards a system of state capitalism and introduce a new slogan, "the establishment of a socialist, democratic, cooperative society free from political, economic, and social exploitation." External and internal developments in 1955-1956 encouraged the rulers to follow this course. Egyptian hostility to the Baghdad Pact of February 1955, the establishment of closer relations with the Communist Bloc after the arms deal of September 1955, and the new policy of positive neutralism and non-alignment after the Bandung Conference of April 1955 possibly led the rulers to believe that Egypt should follow a pattern in its economy which is neither capitalist nor communist. The neutralist policy also, in bringing Egypt closer to Yugoslavia in particular, caused her to be attracted by the Yugoslav emphasis on central planning, state capitalism, and cooperatives. The arms deal, moreover, and the subsequent economic involvements with the communist countries and their centrally planned economies could have imposed the need for parallel Egyptian controls in order to implement these deals and transactions.[107] The Suez War at the end of October 1956 that followed by three months the nationalization of the Suez Canal Company led to the sequestration, Egyptianization, and subsequent nationalization of British, French, and Jewish property along with a large number of foreign banks and insurance companies. The officers who were placed in charge of these companies apparently availed themselves of the opportunity to become wealthy by various illicit means and Nasser knew it and called them "profiteers" but did not punish them.[108]

State ownership since then expanded to include the entire Misr Bank complex of banks and companies in February 1960, Belgian property in December 1960 with the Congo crisis as a pretext, and in May 1960 the Egyptian press was nationalized. In January 1957 the Economic Organization was established as a state holding institution for administering the requisitioned and nationalized properties, and it became the nucleus of the growing public sector of the economy. Two other giant state organizations were formed for the same purpose in February 1961; they were the Misr and the Nasr organizations.

The ruling regime tried to justify the nationalizations and the expansion of state ownership by arguing that state enterprise and central government planning, and not free capitalism and private enterprise, were alone capable of promoting economic development and national strength, and achieving the goals of public welfare. State ownership also had its national and sectarian aspects, for many industries and businesses were in the hands of foreigners and the majority of their employees belonged to the non-Muslim minorities. With the liquidation of foreign capitalism accompanied by Egyptianization and nationalization, the Muslims obtained ninety per cent of the jobs, which corresponds to the proportion of the Muslim population in Egypt. At the same time, Egypt could boast of eliminating the role that foreign capital played in its economy.[109]

Socialism after 1960 began to borrow Marxist arguments and slogans especially in emphasizing the exploitive character of capital and in explaining the connection between socialism, democracy, and social welfare. Nationalization was no longer based only on economic urgency, but also on ideological considerations that called for the creation of a classless society and for equal opportunity, and opposed private enterprise because it allowed the emergence of a wealthy and socially prominent business community. This is one of the main reasons why the economically successful Misr bank and its companies, that were entirely owned by Egyptians, were nationalized. At the end of 1960, Nasser gave himself the right and the responsibility to carry his program to all the Arab world when he said, "We are responsible for the attainment of social justice not only here, but in every part of the Arab nation."[110]

It was in July 1961, shortly before and after the celebrations of the ninth anniversary of the revolution, that socialism emerged as the official social and economic system of Egypt, and a decisive blow was dealt to private enterprise and large incomes. The national assembly was not in session, and Nasser's government issued the socialist laws without an assembly vote on the new radical changes. Syria was then a part of the United Arab Republic, and the July decree-laws applied to both Egypt and Syria and were among the causes of Syrian withdrawal from the UAR. The decree-law no. 117 of July 1961 transferred to complete state ownership 149 companies (75 in Egypt and 74 in Syria) including 17 banks and 17 insurance companies, and decree-law no. 118 nationalized partially 91 other companies (79 in Egypt and 12 in Syria) with the state taking a share of not less than fifty per cent.[111] Decree-law no. 119 made it illegal for any individual to own shares worth more than L.E. 10,000 (or 100,000 Syrian pounds, equivalent to about $24,000). Anything owned over this amount was transferred to the state. Companies and individuals were compensated for what they lost to the state by fifteen-year bonds bearing four per cent interest. A subsequent declaration promised cash payment of L.E. 1,000 on the shares of those who owned only L.E. 5,000 worth of stock. Another decree reduced land holdings to a maximum of 100 feddans, instead of the 200 feddans of 1952, and forbade individuals from renting more than 50 feddans or acres. Decree-law no, 135 forbade any individual from holding more than one position. The boards of directors of all companies, according to decree-law no. 137, were to consist of seven members, two of whom should represent the workers and staff employees, and no individual was allowed to be a member of more than one board of directors. The salary of any board member or official or consultant in a company or institution was limited to a maximum of L.E. 5,000. The staff employees and workers in the various companies were awarded 25 per cent of the profits, but only ten per cent were to be given in cash payments and the rest in social and other services. The income tax law of 1949 was replaced by a new law that raised the rate in the upper brackets to as much as 90 per cent for those whose income exceeded L.E. 10,000. The Charter of May 1962 later gave details and explanations on these nationalizations and added that foreign trade in imports should be entirely nationalized, and exports should be 75 per cent in state hands, while the public sector would have only 25 per cent of internal trade, but the state imposed the notion of reasonable profit.[112]

The new socialist laws of July 1961 were preceded and accompanied by various propaganda articles in the press, and by official explanatory and apologetic statements and declarations. The statement of the minister of state for information, Dr. Abdul Qader Hatem, on July 19, 1961 declared that the revolution was not merely a change in the form of government, for in that case it would have been a mere *inqilab* (coup); it was basically a real change in society to realize the hopes of the people and build their life on solid foundations of freedom. To insure this freedom, two foundations were essential, namely, sufficiency and justice, the first requiring the mobilization of the resources of the nation for higher production and enlarging the basis of national wealth, and the second requiring the award of equal opportunity for every citizen to obtain an equitable share of that wealth.[113] The charter of May 21, 1962 later spoke of sufficiency and justice as "the two foundations of socialism which is the road to social freedom."[114]

The laws of July 1961 and the nationalizations that preceded them in 1960 meant the end of large scale private enterprise and the liquidation of the bourgeoisie as an active enterprising class. The revolutionary change was done without the violence of a proletarian revolution, and the government underlined this aspect as well as the fact that it promised compensation for the nationalized property. Yet, it must be said that no Egyptian to whom this writer has spoken believes that compensation was paid; the nationalizations effectively amounted to outright confiscation. Nasser's government, on this basis, was compared to that of the predatory Ali Bey and the other Mameluks with this difference, that Nasser's action was based theoretically on the ultimate good of the people and on the hope of establishing social justice. Another important difference, on the other hand, is that the Mameluks extorted money from the wealthy but left them the initiative and the freedom to restore their wealth and make up their losses.

The coup d'état of September 28, 1961 in Syria against unity with Egypt was followed by a violent government reaction in Egypt against the remains of the wealthy upper class, and by the dissolution of the national assembly as well as the National Union because it was said to have been infiltrated by reactionaries. On October 16, 1961, Nasser attacked reactionaries who relied on imperialism and said that reaction hides in the palaces and safes of the millionaires. He therefore announced that the hour of revolutionary action has come for isolating the people's enemies. In order to prevent the wealthy, whom he equated with reactionaries, from serving the interests of exploitation and monopoly and attempting a coup as the

Syrians did, his government arrested a group of rich Egyptians and sequestrated the property of some 850 persons, one-fourth of whom were Muslim Egyptians and the others were Syro-Lebanese, Jews, Armenians, and Greeks and various other Europeans. The attitude towards the upper classes became more belligerent as they were called "the enemies of the people." New socialist slogans of class warfare were used and the regime sought the support of the masses. The charter of May 21, 1962 was prepared during this period and contained the doctrinal basis for the Egyptian socialist system. A new political organization or one-party movement called the Arab Socialist Union was created to form the popular base of the new socialist regime.

The Charter and the writings of responsible Egyptians since 1962 abound in slogans and statements borrowed from the Marxist system. In the Charter, the struggle between classes is referred to as "inevitable and natural and cannot be ignored or denied." The fierceness and bloodiness of class struggle and its dangers are attributed to reaction because it does not want to abandon its monopolies and privileged positions through which it exploits the masses. Experience has proved, according to the Charter, that it is inevitable that the revolution should liquidate reaction and disarm it completely.[115] The alliance of reaction and exploitive capital, said the Charter, should end, and interaction should become possible between the active popular forces which are: the peasants, the workers, the soldiers, the intelligentsia, and national capitalism. The complete domination of the people over the means of production is emphasized. The socialist solution in Egypt is described as a "historical inevitability." "Scientific socialism" is mentioned as "the convenient formula for finding the sound program for progress."[116] The Charter also declared that "the unity of purpose" (or objective) - which means the adoption of revolutionism and socialism - "should be the motto of Arab unity in moving from the stage of the political to that of the social revolution." Egypt, moreover, assumed the responsibility of communicating its appeal and its principles to the other Arab countries.[117] In other writings, a distinction was made between the two levels on which Egypt operates, namely, as a "state," and as a "revolution." Nasser, moreover, mentioned in his speech in the national assembly in March 1964, that the revolution was not for the Egyptian people alone but for the Arabs in general.[118]

The Egyptian government could not ignore the importance of religion as a spiritual and social force and its opposition to Marxism or communism. The rulers tried, therefore, to remove the suspicions of the masses about the new socialist order by claiming that Arab socialism was different from Marxism and that it agreed with Islam which is itself a socialist religion. In addition, the socialist regime used religion and the religious institution for supporting and spreading socialism. Nasser himself gave the reassurance about socialism in a speech of March 12, 1965. "Is socialism," he asked, "opposed in its principles to religion? Some pretend it is; but this would mean that religion could justify exploitation, and religion never said that." Then he asserted that "the Muslim religion is a socialist religion one hundred per cent." Various writers in religious, literary, and other magazines, as well as authors were mobilized to prove that Islam is a socialist religion, that socialism "springs from the depths of our faith," that "the Koran is the work of a socialist society," and that the Charter drew its genuineness from the Koran, the sayings of the Prophet, and from the conditions of Egypt.[119] The identification of early Islam and certain early Muslims, even Muhammad himself, with socialism sometimes reached ridiculous proportions. Khadija, the first wife of the Prophet was, according to one author, the mother of socialism because she employed young men - including Muhammad her future husband - in her trade and paid them wages or a share of the profit. The Prophet Muhammad was called "the leader of the left" in one of a series of articles in which Islamic history was rewritten according to Marxist interpretation, and Islam was called a leftist revolution.[120] The Caliph Umar was mentioned by Nasser in his speech of July 22, 1961 as the first to nationalize land and distribute it to the peasants. Actually Umar distributed lands that did not belong to Muslims but were spoils of conquest, and Islam strictly prohibited taking people's property without agreement, attested by a contract, with the owner.

Arab socialism has thus resorted to the practice of "revising religion," or "bolshevizing" it to make it compatible with socialism and enlist its support.[121] Among the aspects of this bolshevization of Islam were the attempts to persuade the masses that Islam is a revolution and that it is the first religion to proclaim socialism, and at the same time to subject the Ulama (religious scholars) to the revolutionary plan and make them cooperate in spreading socialism. Plans were made to retrain the Imams (mosque officials) so that they could teach socialism to the masses. The venerable old religious university of al-Azhar was told, after its reorganization in 1961 and the loss of its autonomy, that its task in its new era was "to inculcate the new revolutionary thoughts and understanding in the people's minds.[122] The Ulama, who were basically opposed to the innovations of the revolution, had to accept them with reserve in order to save their position. Periodic meetings were held for the Ulama and Imams in the Bureau of Religious Affairs of the Socialist Union in order to enable them to deliver their "religious" message.

Communist writers outside Egypt noted with approval Egypt's advance towards scientific socialism. The *Pravda* writer, E. Primakof, reported with evident satisfaction that in early 1964 all "communists and democrats" were released from Egyptian jails and that they occupy important positions in the press, state organizations, and the Arab Socialist Union.[123] Communists were actually released shortly before Khruschev's visit to Egypt in May 1964. They later announced the dissolution of their party in February 1965 and joined the socialist union. They were given certain key posts in the press and in the various organs of indoctrination and propaganda. One of them, Ibrahim Saadeddin, became the director of the

Higher Socialist Institute, and another, Lutfi al-Khawly, was editor of *al-Talia* magazine which was established by the state for socialist propaganda.

The Egyptian government created various institutes and centers for teaching socialism. One of them was the above mentioned Higher Socialist Institute. Another was the Institute of Socialist Youth, and both prepared socialist workers to fill the positions in the smaller institutes of political training in the provinces. The government had also to supervise and control the formation of executive committees of the socialist union in the country and the behavior of their members. In November 1965 the supreme executive committee of the socialist union dismissed 2500 members, charged them with being "reactionary, deviationist, and negative," and promised that others who infiltrated the ranks would be dismissed.[124] Among the many functions of the late Field Marshal Amer was the chairmanship of "the committee for the liquidation of feudalism." The committee was expected to investigate all aspects of non-compliance with the socialist and agrarian laws, and to denounce and fight "reactionaries."

The achievements of the socialist revolution benefited the people only to a small extent because the revolution did not bring with it the expected degree of sufficiency and justice, and it gave Egypt only an illusory feeling of power and prestige. In the new totalitarian socialist state, the real beneficiaries were the new class of military and civilian bureaucrats, mostly of lower middle-class origin, in whose hands political and economic power was concentrated. The old inequalities of wealth and income were drastically reduced, but enormous inequalities, material and moral, remained between various categories of salaried people or workers for the socialist state. In economic growth and per capita income, Egypt stood behind such Arab countries as Saudi Arabia, Jordan, Iraq, and Lebanon in the period 1957 to 1965 in spite of the fact that the rate of increase in population was not more than that of Jordan and Saudi Arabia.[125] The income of the small landowning fellah and the laborers' wages increased slightly, and the tenant's rent was reduced, but more restrictions on their freedom were imposed by the state. The peasant farmer had to sell his crops at a price imposed by the government, pay higher taxes and various dues, and buy his consumer articles and fertilizer and seeds at prices imposed by the government. Salaries of government officials were generally reduced and no extra hours or indemnities for various kinds of work were permitted. The socialist state tried to provide work and jobs for the Egyptians, but in so doing it appointed persons to jobs and positions in which they were not needed and for which they were not trained.[126] The salaries of a large category of these - many of whom had poured in from the rural areas to the big cities - were extremely low and varied between ten and twenty Egyptian pounds (about twenty four to forty eight dollars) a month.

The Egyptians under the socialist regime have experienced, for the first time in the contemporary history of Egypt, shortages in basic food supplies, and in various consumer goods and medical products due to the inefficiency in production or the exportation of certain needed products in order to obtain foreign exchange. Egypt had to import most of its needs in wheat, and between 1963 and 1965, the United States government provided it with close to 450 million dollars worth of surplus food. Housewives sometimes could not find on the market, even at relatively high prices, such common food articles as lentils and potatoes, while the consumption of meat was restricted in 1966-1967 to four days a week. Shortages of soap, oil and halva were discussed on November 17, 1966 by the executive committee of the socialist union and by the administration in Cairo. The most critical shortage was in pharmaceutical products which doctors sometimes prescribed even though they could not be found, while certain equivalent products produced locally were ineffective.[127] One month after he became prime minister, Zakaria Muhieddin painted a gloomy picture of the economic situation in a statement to the national assembly on December 4, 1965, and asked the people for more sacrifice as he decreed higher taxes and increases in the price of articles. An indication of labor unrest over certain measures tending to cut down wages or lengthen the working day was the protest strike of 3000 dockers at Port Said on October 9, 1966 in spite of the fact that they belonged to closely controlled trade unions. The strike leaders were arrested and the vessels had to be unloaded by soldiers and sailors.[128]

The socialist state succeeded since it began its nationalizations in 1956 in concentrating enormous financial resources in its hands. The nationalized properties of the king and the royal family, the income from the nationalized Suez Canal, the nationalized foreign properties since 1956, the assets of the Misr Bank and its affiliates and of the nationalized companies after the socialist laws of July 1961, in addition to the sequestrated properties of the "reactionaries" in October 1961 - all these gave the Egyptian government and its public sector billions of pounds to spend on the various development projects. Other billions came from foreign loans and aid from the Soviet Union, the United States, Western Germany, Kuwait, and others. With all these financial resources the socialist state was unable to carry out its development plans as expected, and instead of creating "a society in which well-being prevails," as the official slogan said, it created shortages and hardships. In December, 1964, it began to sell discreetly a part of the gold cover for its currency in order to pay its bills. In 1966, in eight weeks, Egypt was forced to sell $50 million, or a third of its gold reserves. Short term debts at the end of that year amounted to $200 million, and the foreign debt was estimated at nearly three billion dollars, while the trade deficit was $250 million in the preceding year.[129] Creditors became so concerned about Egyptian finances that they were reluctant to advance loans. Italy, among others, refused in the spring of 1966 to deliver any more automobile parts for the Fiat factory in Egypt until it could get overdue back payments. The Egyptian pound had been devaluated several times and in 1967 the black market price of the pound was about half that of the official price. Nationalizations and confiscations not only prevented the flow of foreign capital to Egypt, but also resulted in the continuous flight of capital from Egypt by various devices and tricks. The feeling of insecurity and lack of confidence discouraged depositing savings in nationalized banks and the government ordered compulsory savings of half a day's pay to be deducted from the employee's salary.

The socialist state has spent a good part of its enormous resources on weapons and military equipment from the Soviet Bloc, industrial and agricultural projects like the Helwan iron and steel factory south of Cairo, and the High Dam at Aswan. But it has also spent an average of $150 million a year on its troops in Yemen until mid-1967, and extravagant amounts on pro-Egyptian revolutionary and socialist propaganda and on conspiracies in the Arab countries. One of the most serious mistakes of the revolutionary regime is that it has sought to maintain revolutionary fervor through an artificial class warfare that has prevented economic progress. It has entrusted the nationalized companies and enterprises to an inefficient and corrupt bureaucracy in which political reliability rather than professional competence is the main consideration for awarding key jobs. Waste and innumerable scandals were the result.

The state-owned press can be given some credit in exposing and commenting on some of that waste and on certain scandals. Dismissals of officials and executives have been often reported in the press for "deviation" which, under the socialist regime, is a mitigated equivalent of embezzlement and robbery. In February 1967, the Higher Committee of the Public Sector under Marshal Amer ended the services of 140 officials in the general consumer organization and the organization of flour mills and rice processing, and in the bakeries sector. The property of eighteen of them was sequestrated because of "deviation."[130] In 1965 a committee of the national assembly conducted an investigation in the Nasr car factory. It found that there was extravagance in appointments caused by the vanity of the executives, each of whom believed that his prestige was measured by the number of his employees. It found the stores inadequate for all the equipment and that some spare parts in their boxes were placed behind the warehouse in the sand. It realized that often production stopped because some small machine was missing, and that the factory worked regularly only when a distinguished visitor came.[131] Another report was made about thefts from the government warehouses and the absence of statistics on the losses incurred every year. In the medical services, reports in *al-Ahram* were made on the Qasr al-Ayni hospital and they showed that the patients complained of lack of care, inhumane treatment, bad food, lack of medicines, and low standards of cleanliness. The reports said that there were many physicians and nurses in the hospital but most of them were not doing their professional duties; they were rather in the administrative services. Assistants in the laboratories had no qualifications, and many workers without any training served in the operation rooms, while surgical instruments and the medical equipment in general were not properly kept. The reports mentioned that the average monthly salary of the nurse was fourteen pounds (35 dollars).[132]

Negligence and indifference, and general inadequacy of public services can be seen and felt everywhere in the cities of Egypt. Public buildings are very poorly kept with no paint and no repairs. Most of them have been inherited from the old regime and are deteriorating fast. The public parks, and almost anything that is public, is in an abject state of negligence and deterioration, and compares poorly with what it used to be before the revolution. The shortages and interruptions of electrical power, the inadequacy and poor quality of the city transportation system are among the visible aspects that underline the mediocrity and ineptitude of the socialist administration. The socialist revolution certainly produced no miracles in the Egyptian economy, in the public services, and in the social and economic standards of living; in many ways it has moved the country backward.

CHAPTER I
NOTES

1. John A. Wilson in *Before Philosophy,* ed. Henry Frankfort (Baltimore: Penguin Books, 1954), 80.

2. For these elements of Egyptian psychology in ancient times, see John A. Wilson, *The Culture of Ancient Egypt* (Chicago: University of Chicago Press, 1951), 145; Jon Manchip White, *Everyday Life in Ancient Egypt* (New York: G.P. Putnam's Sons, 1963).

3. See for this opinion of Taha Hussein on the Egyptians, *al-Makshuf* (Beirut), November 21, 1938, quoted in *al-Nasr,* November 24, 1961.

4. *Statistical Pocket Yearbook,* 1953; see also Eva Garzouzi, *Old Ills and New Remedies in Egypt* (Cairo, 1958), 77.

5. Abdul Hamid Badawi 1887-1965 was the first Egyptian, and Arab, to be named a member of the International Court of Justice in 1946. He served as foreign minister in Egypt and headed the Egyptian delegation to the San Francisco conference in 1945. He was one of eleven sons born in humble conditions on a small family farm. Nine of the children rose to distinguished positions.

6. On the attitude of Egypt towards Arabism, see Anwar Chejne, "Egyptian Attitudes Towards Pan-Arabism," *The Middle East Journal,* XI (1957), 253-268; Sati al-Husri, *al-Uruba Awalan* (Arabism First), 4th ed. (Beirut, 1961), 115, 129, 145, 163; see also Patrick Seale *The Struggle for Syria* (London: Oxford University Press, 1965), 19-22.

7. On this point, see Patrick Seale, 21-23.

8. On the attitude of Premier Nuqrashi at the time of the Palestine War, see Muhammad Hussein Haikal, *Mudhakkarat fil Siyasa al-Misriya* (Memoirs on Egyptian Politics), II (Cairo, 1953), 331; on General Naguib's opinion, see Muhammad Naguib, *Egypt's Destiny* (New York: Doubleday, 1955), 17.

9. Naguib, 16.

10. See Naguib, 18; on the declaration of the prosecutor general to Ali Maher after the revolution, see *al-Ahram,* July 30, 1952.

11. Abdul Rahman Rafii, *Muqaddimat Thawrat 23 Yulio* (Preliminaries of the Revolution of 23 July (Cairo, 1957), 134 does not mention Tabet, but he says that on May 5, 1952 the Naqib al-Ashraf (the representative of the Muslims claiming descent from the Prophet) presented a report to King Farouk on his descent from the Prophet through his mother.
12. *Muhakamat al-Thawrah* (The Trials Under the Revolution), ed. Kemal Kire (Cairo: Ministry of National Guidance, n.d.), 689.
13. Haikal, II, 329, 381.
14. The text can be seen in Rafii, 208; Haikal, II, 355-357.
15. Khalid Muhammad Khalid, *Min Huna Nabda'* (Cairo, 1950). The book was in its tenth edition in 1963. The text of the decision of the court is on pages 12-32. There is an English translation of the book by I. R. Faruqi, Washington, D.C., 1953.
16. See Rafii, 189; Anwar al-Sadat, *Qissat al-Thawrah Kamilah* (The Complete Story of the Revolution), (Cairo: Dar al-Hilal, n.d. 1956?), 145.
17. See for example the issues of *al-Ahram* after July 24, 1952.
18. See Naguib, 30-32, Sadat, 137; Ahmad Abul Fath, *Gamal Adbul Nasser* (n. p.n.d., 1961?), 41.
19. Sadat, 35-44.
20. Gamal Abdul Nasser, *Egypt's Liberation: The Philosophy of the Revolution* (Washington, D.C.: Public Affairs Press, 1955), 21.
21. See the account of their relationship in Abul Fath, 9 ff.
22. Sadat, 60.
23. Abdul Nasser, *Philosophy of the Revolution*, 23.
24. *Ibid.* 24.
25. Abul Fath quoted by *al-Nasr,* March 28, 1962.
26. P. J. Vatikiotis, *The Egyptian Army in Politics* (Bloomington: Indiana University Press, 1961), 59.
27. Abdul Nasser, 19, 30-31, 43, 49. For a detailed account of the political, military, and social causes of the revolution, see Rafii, 153-173.
28. Abdul Nasser, 42.
29. Naguib, 15.

30. Robert St. John, *The Boss* (New York: McGraw-Hill Co., 1960), 115; Naguib, 101 says they were several hundred; Andrew Tully, *CIA, The Inside Story* (New York; William Morrow & Co., 1962), speaks of 700 free officers in 1952.

31. For these circulars and their contents, see Rashed al-Barawy, *The Military Coup in Egypt* (Cairo: Renaissance Bookshop, 1952), 200-204.

32. Naguib, 90 and Sadat, 63 claim that he was not a free officer, but Abul Fath believes he was one of the founders.

33. Naguib, 89.

34. Naguib, 89; Sadat, 62 said "After the burning of Cairo we decided to be ready within a month."

35. Abul Fath, 35-36 says that Nasser later told him, "If it were not for your telephone call to Okasha, the army movement would have taken place on the third Saturday in November, the date at which the parliamentary sessions used to begin."

36. Sadat, 68.

37. Robert St. John, 111.

38. Sadat, 54-57.

39. Abul Fath, 39.

40. See Jean and Simonne Lacouture, *Egypt in Transition* (Translation from the French "L'Egypte en Mouvement" by Francis Scarfe), (New York: Criterion Books, 1958), 139, 144.

41. Naguib, 21.

42. Lacouture, 142.

43. Sadat, 57.

44. Drew Pearson Column, January 22, 1962.

45. Andrew Tully, 101-105.

46. Abdul Nasser, 52; Tully, 105.

47. Robert St. John, 115 speaks of 90 out of 300 free officers who participated; *al-Ahram,* July 24, 1952 mentions 300 participants.

48. Naguib, 103; St. John 115; *al-Ahram,* July 24, 1952 said the action was to begin at 2 A.M. but was advanced thirty minutes; Abul Fath, 36 mentions midnight and so does Lacouture, 147. Lacouture says that the meeting with the chief-of-staff was called for 10 P.M. and that Saad Tewfik came to tell Nasser at 7 P.M.

49. Sadat, 81; St. John, 120 mentions that a company in the battalion commanded by Yusif Saddiq began moving towards the Headquarters and Amer took charge of the operation.

50. Abul Fath, 37 says that Saddiq sent Shawqi to occupy the building; S.E. Finer, 158 says that Shawqi's 13th Infantry and Saddiq's tanks occupied the building.

51. See the text in Muhammad Khalil, *The Arab States and the Arab League,* I (Beirut: Khayat, 1962), 492.

52. Sadat, 94-97.

53. The text of the letters can be seen in Barawy, 216-217, and in *al-Ahram* July 25, 1952.

54. Naguib, 115-116 relates that the king asked the U.S. ambassador, Jefferson Caffery to inform the British that he deserved their help. Caffery refused and promised to protect the king's life.

55. Sadat, 104, 107.

56. Text of the ultimatum and of the act of abdication in Muhammad Khalil, I, 493-494.

57. Sadat, 116.

58. Naguib, 126-127.

59. His declaration in *al-Ahram,* July 31, 1952.

60. Sadat, 164; *The Charter* (1962), 5.

61. *The Charter,* 5-6.

62. Nasser, 33 said that the vanguard performed its task and for a long time it waited; the masses that came were disunited, divided groups of stragglers. Then after consulting the university professors and experienced leaders, he concluded that the task of the vanguard had only begun.

63. See for example Keith Wheelock, *Nasser's Modern Egypt*, (New York: F. A. Praeger, 1960), 12-13; Georgiana Stevens, *Egypt, Yesterday and Today* (New York: Holt, Rinehart and Winston, 1963), 107 ff; Charles Cremeans, *The Arabs and the World* (New ;York:: Praeger, 1963), 28; John Badeau, "A Role in Search of a Hero," *MEJ* IX, 4 (1955), who almost makes an apology for dictatorship.

64. Constitutional practice required the swearing in of the regents by Parliament, but the Council of State under Sanhouri decided it was unnecessary to reconvene the dissolved Parliament; see Abul Fath, 49.

65. Sadat, 169 admits that land reform was not a mere economic question but it was in the very heart of politics.

66. On Sadat's ideas on parties and the revolution, see *Ibid.*, 178-180.

67. See the text in Khalil, I, pp. 496-497.

68. Naguib, 167.

69. Abul Fath, 56 quoted Nasser's statement about Muhanna's conduct and danger; see also Naguib, 133, 157.

70. Sadat, 185.

71. Abul Fath, 60-61.

72. Naguib, 133, 177.

73. Abul Fath, 142; the author also claims that Naguib asked him to persuade Nasser to avoid the republican issue. *Ibid.*, 111.

74. Naguib, 177.

75. Lacouture, 181; Naguib, 184.

76. See chapter in Naguib, under the title "Why I Resigned," 189 ff.

77. Quoted by Lacouture, 179.

78. Naguib, 206.

79. Sadat, 186.

80. See Naguib, 191; Lacouture, 182.

81. Naguib, 189.

82. From Naguib's account, pp. 193-197, and that of Abul Fath, p. 156 it seems that Naguib did not attend the meeting of the RCC, whereas Lacouture, p. 179, says that Naguib was present and left at midnight.

83. Naguib, 193-197.

84. Abul Fath, 158 claims that Nasser's choice of Khalid Muhieddin as a prime minister was to excite the anger of other army units against Muhieddin and the cavalry officers. Naguib, 202, says it was either a trick on Nasser's part or an act of desperation.
85. See Lacouture, 184; Naguib, 200.
86. Lacouture, p. 186 says that with the exception of U.S. Intelligence services, the foreign powers wanted Naguib's success; Abul Fath, 315 speaks of contacts between the U.S. Embassy and Nasser during the crisis through an Embassy official called Lakeland.
87. Lacouture, 188.
88. Lacouture, 190; Abul Fath, 177 says that Naguib asked King Saud to take him with him, and that Saud asked Nasser but he refused fearing that the people would think that Naguib was exiled. Naguib then went to the plane and stayed long and as he was leaving it, he fainted.
89. See Sadat, 23 on why the revolutionary regime should not grant freedoms, democracy and various rights; Nasser's justification for not having political parties in his speech of July 9, 1960 at the general congress of the National Union, and in *al-Ahram*, January 27, 1960. For details and explanations on Nasserist popular or totalitarian democracy, see Malcolm Kerr, "Arab Radical Notions of Democracy," *St. Antony's Papers*, no. 16, ed. Albert Hourani (Carbondale: Southern Illinois University Press, 1963?), 10; see also for an explanation on what is called populist democracy, Morroe Berger, *The Arab World Today*, (Garden City, N.Y.: Doubleday & CO., 1964), 393 ff.
90. See the text of the constitution in Khalil, I, 499 ff.; see also Don Peretz, "Democracy and the Revolution in Egypt," *MEJ*, XIII, (1959), 26-40.
91. *The Charter*, 39 ff.
92. *The United Arab Republic, The Constitution* (Cairo: Information Department, March 25, 1964).
93. *The New York Times*, January 21, 1965.
94. *The Herald Tribune*, June 20, 1967.
95. Sadat, 29-35 quotes from Mao tse-Tung to justify the dictatorship of one category of people over another.
96. Malcolm Kerr, *Egypt Under Nasser* (New York: Headline Series, Foreign Policy Association, September-October, 1963), 13.

97. See Vatikiotis, 256 ff; Lacouture, 292 ff.

98. For the complaints of Nasser against the bureaucracy, and the campaign of Z. Muhieddin against red tape, see *The New York Times* September 25, 1967, and November 14, 1965; see also *Rose al-Yusif,* January 9, 1967.

99. See *al-Musawwar,* January 22, 1960; *al-Ahram,* November 7, 1966.

100. As an example, one can mention a school book entitled *al-Mujtama al-Arabi* (Arab Society) by Hamid Ammar et. al. (Cairo, 1964) for the second year of high school.

101. *The Egyptian Gazette,* October 6, 1954; see also Daniel Crecelius, "Religion in the Service of the State," (mimeographed English text kindly communicated by its author), note 14. This article appeared in German translation in *Bustan,* VIII, 3 (1967), 13-20.

102. See Frank Kearns, *Near East Report* (Washington, D.C.), February 2, 1959.

103. Article 24 of the Constitution of March 23, 1964; the provision exists in previous constitutions.

104. Reported in Bernard Vernier, "L'évolution du régime militaire en Egypte," *Revue Francaise de Science Politique,* XIII, no. 3 (September 1963), 601, n. 1; see also Wheelock, 49, 62 where he cites sources according to which certain firms told Christian applicants that they had instructions to hire Muslims only.

105. Doreen Warriner, *Land Reform and Development in the Middle East,* 2nd ed. (London: Oxford University Press, 1962), 13. F. Bertier, "L'idéologie sociale de la revolution egyptienne," *Orient,* no. 6 (1958, 2), 58.

106. Bertier, 60.

107. See Salah Serafy, "Economic Development by Revolution: The Case of the UAR," *MEJ* XVIII, (1963), 222-224; Charles Issawi, *Egypt in Revolution: An Economic Analysis* (London: Oxford University Press, 1963), 49.

108. Abul Fath, 333 said that the methods of plunder used by the officers after 1956 "exceeded the stories of Ali Baba and the forty thieves."

109. See Bertier, 64-68 who puts it bluntly, "for the Muslims of Egypt, socialism meant jobs and money."

110. For this speech, see *The Scribe,* January 1961, p.9.

111. For these and other socialist laws of 1961 and 1962 see *al-Qawanin al-Ishtirakiyah* (Cairo: UAR Information Service, 1962?); for a good resumé and comments, see M. Kerr, "The Emergence of a Socialist Ideology in Egypt," *MEJ*, XVI (1962), 127-144.

112. *The Charter*, 64.

113. See this declaration by Hatem in *al-Qawanin al-Ishtirakiyah*, pp. 5-6.

114. *The Charter*, 57.

115. *Ibid.*, 51.

116. *Ibid.*, 57-61; for Marxism in the Charter and non-Marxian interpretations of Arab socialism see Fauzi M. Najjar, "Islam and Socialism in the United Arab Republic" *Journal of Contemporary History*, III, 3 (July 1968), 184 ff.

117. *The Charter*, 109, 111.

118. See Haikal in *al-Ahram*, April 19, 1964; Nasser's speech of March 26 in *The New York Times*, March 27, 1964; see also Malcolm Kerr, *The Arab Cold War 1957-1964: A Study of Ideology in Politics* (London: Oxford University Press, 1965), 40-41; see also Salaheddin Munajjed, *al-Tadlil al-Ishtiraki* (Socialist Deception), 3rd ed. (Beirut: Dar al-Kitab al-Jadid, 1966), pp. 35 ff. on the similarities and parallels between Arab socialism and Marxism.

119. Articles in *Minbar al-Islam*, June 1965, and other magazines mentioned in Munajjed, *al-Tadlil al-Ishtiraki*, 54-64, and references to a book entitled *al-Mithaq fi Daou' al-Quran* (The Charter in the Light of the Koran) in Munajjed, 77.

120. Munajjed, 66, 89, quoting from a book entitled *Umm al-Ishtirakiyah Khadija Bint Khuwailid* (The Mother of Socialism, Khadija Bint Khuwailid) by Ibrahim al-Sibai, and quoting also from a series of articles on the struggle between the right and the left in Islam, in *Majallat al-Katib*.

121. See Munajjed, *Balshafat al-Islam Ind al-Marxiyin wal Ishtirakiyin al-Arab* (The Bolshevization of Islam by Arab Marxists and Socialists) (Beirut: Dar al-Kitab al-Jadid, 1966), 45 ff for the various aspects of Bolshevization.

122. Daniel Crecelius, "al-Azhar in the Revolution," *MEJ* XX (1966), 43 quoting *Rose al-Yusif*, November 5, 1962, and *Majallat al-Azhar* (English supplement) March 1962.

123. See *Mizan,* a review of Soviet writing on the Middle East and Africa, vol. VII, no. 8 (September 1965), 1, 11 quoting Aziz al-Hajj, an Iraqi communist writer, and Primakov in *Pravda,* July 23, 1965.

124. *Akhbar al-Yawm,* November 20, 1965; *Mideast Mirror,* November 27, 1965.

125. See article in *The Economist,* April 1, 1967, pp. 15-16.

126. In his speech on February 22, 1967, President Nasser admitted employing people who were not needed and said humorously, "We want the young men to be outside the home working and able to marry and the girls to find husbands."

127. *al-Ahram,* November 18, 1966; Muhammad al-Tabii in *Akhbar al-Yawm* May 8, 1965, quoted in *al-Mu'jizah al-Ishtirakiyah* (The Socialist Miracle, evidently a sarcastic title), ed. George Yaqub Mansur (Beirut, 1965?), 150; many reports heard by travelers in Egypt about the gravity of the shortages in pharmaceuticals.

128. Hedrick Smith in *The New York Times,* October 27, 1966.

129. See the article in *Business Week,* May 21, 1966, pp. 87 ff.; *The New York Times,* October 28 and November 28, 1966.

130. *al-Akhbar,* February 16, 1967.

131. *Akhbar al-Yawm,* May 8, 1965, quoted in George Mansur, pp. 11-28.

132. See the reports in *al-Ahram* April 30 and June 2, 1965, quoted in Mansur,131ff

CHAPTER II

NASSER AND NASSERISM: THE METHODS AND THE RESULTS

Among the many Arab organizers of military revolutions since the days of Bakr Sidqi of Iraq in 1936, Nasser has established an unsurpassed record, first, in his long period of leadership in Egypt and the Arab world, and second, in the extent of his revolutionary experiments and risky policies and challenges that took the name of "Nasserism" and made Nasser himself a controversial world figure.

Internally, Nasserism meant revolutionary changes in government and society that imposed a system of totalitarian democracy and introduced a brand of scientific socialism known as Arab socialism. Externally, Nasserism meant positive neutrality that sought and received economic aid from the western democracies and the communist bloc, but persistently attacked imperialism, defied the western powers and sided with the Soviet Union and depended militarily and diplomatically on it. It also meant the attainment of the goals of Arab nationalism in unity and the restoration of Arab rights in Palestine, along with militant action to spread revolution and socialism in the Arab countries. The ultimate goal of Nasserism was to make Egypt strong and to secure for it a respectable world position and a leading role in what Nasser defined as the Arab, the Islamic, and the African circles.[1]

I. Nasserism in Egypt

In carrying out the political and social revolution and

maintaining himself in power, Nasser depended on the security services — including the *mabahith* or intelligence and secret police services — the army, and the support of the masses. He took no chances in matters touching freedom, and made no concessions for the restoration of political parties, free elections, and a free press. His *mabahith* copied from communism its tactics and organization to protect his person as well as his regime and eliminate all opposition.

The army officers received ample rewards for supporting the regime. Their salaries were raised and they had priorities and exemptions in obtaining low rent housing and purchasing cars and appliances which they sometimes sold in the black market. Purges and transfers of officers were made on the basis of political considerations, and Nasser's concern about maintaining himself in power had evidently a higher priority than the efficiency and strength of the military establishment.

The officers, in spite of the many privileges and benefits, were not always passive and subservient to Nasser. They sometimes challenged his policy, but the challenge invariably marked the end of their political and military career. After the Syrian military coup of September 1961 against unity with Egypt, the daily *al-Nasr* in Damascus gave several reports about military unrest in Egypt where certain officers, encouraged by the Syrian action, voiced their criticism of Nasser's rule. Some officers close to Amer, including his secretary Daoud Uways, were arrested.[2] Disagreements about the war in Yemen similarly led to conspiracies and attempts against the regime. One of them led to the arrest in early April 1966 of twenty officers who advocated rapid withdrawal of Egyptian forces. This was described as the most serious move by the military, and the officers were to be tried secretly on charges of treason in wartime because the regime could not admit publicly that there was opposition in the army.[3]

The six out of the original fourteen members of the Revolution Command Council who remained active in the government after June 1956 often quarreled with Nasser on matters of basic policy or government appointments. In 1964, Kemal

Hussein and Baghdadi disappeared from the public scene after twelve years of cooperation with Nasser, marked by occasional disagreements, quarrels and reconciliations. Their loss of power was probably a result of their opposition to the Yemeni war and the socialist regime. After losing his last public function of vice president in March 1964, Kemal Hussein was constantly watched, and in October 1965, he was arrested supposedly for attempting to make contacts in military circles.[4]

The war with Israel showed the tragic results of Nasser's preoccupation with revolution, socialism, and political power to the detriment of his country's unity and strength. The disastrous war in early June 1967 ended with the forced resignation of Marshal Amer and the dismissal of the incompetent commanders, but the man who had been the closest associate of Nasser for fifteen years after the revolution and many years before refused to bear alone the responsibility for defeat without being heard publicly. He tried with his supporters to mount a coup and regain his post in the command of the armed forces, but his attempt led to his arrest on August 26, 1967 and soon after to his suicide under suspicious conditions on September 14.

While Nasser depended for survival on the secret police and the army, he drew the legality of his authority and of his political and social revolution from the support of the masses. In order to insure the support of the people and keep them impressed with the results and successes of the revolution and with Nasser's paternalistic concern for their welfare and his wise leadership at home and abroad, the Nasserist regime developed a highly sophisticated propaganda machine. Its most potent instruments were the communication media, including the press, radio, and television, as well as the holding of mass rallies and of public trials of the enemies of the regime. Extensive propaganda inevitably led to the development of a cult of Nasser which spread in certain other Arab countries even more than in Egypt.

In Egypt, the visits of Nasser to the national assembly, his presence at the mass rallies, and his movements with foreign visitors were all accompanied by organized cheering, the mobilization of the army and police who lined the streets through which he passed even in the late night hours, and the transportation of thousands of persons from other sections of Cairo or its suburbs by buses to applaud him at the rallies. Nasser's official visits abroad and his attendance at conferences outside Egypt were accompanied by a costly display of splendor and munificence along with security precautions that contrasted with his supposed austerity and simplicity, and by far surpassed the extravagance of similar displays under the old regime. When Nasser, for example, visited Algeria in 1963, he left Alexandria on April 20 in a white luxury yacht with a large entourage and was accompanied by two warships, while hundreds of secret service men converged on Algiers. A ship loaded with Egyptian arms was also brought as Nasser's gift to Algeria.[5] In Egypt, whenever a Diesel motor was installed to electrify fifty houses in a village, or whenever some other small project was inaugurated, a celebration was organized in the presence of the minister of municipal and rural affairs or his delegate, pavilions were erected with costly decorations, and sometimes a banquet was given that cost as much as the project itself.[6]

In the daily press as well as in magazines and books, the "nationalized" writers and authors flattered Nasser sometimes to the extent of idolization and represented him as a miraculous and providential being. A good example is a book by Taha Abdul Baqi Srur, member of the Journalists' Syndicate, on "Gamal Abdul Nasser, the Man Who Changed the Face of History."[7] The author, instead of writing a biography, made a panegyric that exalted the revolution and tried to show how Allah entrusted Nasser with a mission of salvation and restoration for His Islamic and Arab people. More than a political leader, a statesman, and a national hero, Nasser was viewed as the providential being predestined by God to be a second Saladin to remove the humiliation endured by the Arab and Muslim world.

The extensive propaganda, with all its efforts to create an

impressive image of Nasser and Nasserism and to perpetuate the people's admiration and support of Nasser's regime, did not eliminate all civilian opposition or dissatisfaction, nor did it destroy the people's loyalty to some of their old leaders. The death of the former Wafd leader Mustafa al-Nahas on August 23, 1965 gave some dissenters in Egypt a chance to manifest their dissatisfaction with the Nasserist era. The funeral of Nahas turned into a demonstration which had to be dispersed by riot police.[8] The widespread conspiracy of the Muslim Brotherhood, discovered on July 2, 1965 led to clashes with government forces in Damietta and the Cairo suburb of Kerdasa, and to the trial of forty-three ring leaders of whom seven were sentenced to death on August 21, 1966 for conspiring to kill Nasser and overthrow the regime.

II. Nasserism Outside Egypt: Initial Successes 1954-58

Nasser's legend and the spectacular, but short-lived, rise in his prestige were not so much the product of his revolutionary changes within Egypt as of his challenges and initial successes as an Arab national leader whom the Arabs viewed for some time as a symbol of their hopes and aspirations.

For two years after the revolution (1952-54), Nasser's action had to be centered within Egypt in order to consolidate his power, destroy the powerful opponents of the military dictatorship, and secure the end of the British occupation of the Suez Canal zone. On October 19, 1954, Nasser's transitional military government signed an agreement with Britain for ending the treaty of 1936 and with it the British military presence in the Canal Zone. Twenty months earlier, on February 12, 1953, the problem of the Sudan between Britain and Egypt was solved on the basis of allowing the Sudanese to decide whether they wanted to be independent or united with Egypt after a three years' transition.

Between the agreement of October 1954 and the end of

1956, Nasser's relations with the West increasingly deteriorated as his interests shifted from internal problems to international and inter-Arab issues. One reason for this shift was to divert the attention of the Egyptians from his failure to achieve the desired degree of internal progress, and to counteract the wave of criticism resulting from the agreement with the British and from the severe suppression of the Muslim Brotherhood.[9] The conclusion of the pact of mutual cooperation, known as the Baghdad pact, between Iraq and Turkey on February 24, 1955 and joined later by Britain, Iran, and Pakistan, was the beginning of a violently worded campaign against the Western powers, and especially against their Arab allies and friends, who were now viewed as the tools of the imperialists. Nasser's reasons for fighting the Baghdad Pact were related primarily to Egypt's national fears, hopes, and ambitions. Nasser was afraid that other Arab states in the Middle East, such as Syria and Jordan, might join the Pact, and that the Fertile Crescent concept, which Egypt as well as Saudi Arabia opposed, might be achieved by a backdoor method that would lead to Egypt's isolation.[10] His main concern was that the Western powers might strengthen Iraq and deprive Egypt of her leadership in the Eastern Arab world at a time when he envisaged the creation around Egypt of a group of states that would be free from foreign control with a unified military and foreign policy under Egyptian leadership.[11] This is why he indulged in the attack against Iraq and accused its government of breaking Arab solidarity and linking the fate of the country with that of Turkey and the West. His radio described Nuri al-Said and the Iraqi crown prince, Abdul Ilah, as enemies of Arab unity and friends of Israel.

The important development in Nasser's new interventionist policy was his utilization of the concept of Arab unity and solidarity to fight Iraq and any other Arab state that refused to follow his direction. Nasser's sudden interest in Arabism and Arab solidarity was obviously the result of the Baghdad Pact and its threat to Egypt's leadership, because it was only by making Arabism the basis of his attack and by portraying the Pact as a western conspiracy intended to undermine Arab nationalism that he could inflame the feelings of the Iraqis and other Arabs against the Pact and those who signed it or were likely to sign it.

Nasser's propaganda campaign against Iraq, the Baghdad Pact, and the Western powers started him on his career as an Arab nationalist leader and inaugurated his Arab offensive which continued, with evolving motives and goals, and with peaceful interludes, until the spring of 1967. Leadership, however, required sensational positive action that would go beyond the negative and hostile attitude towards the Iraqi government and its new pact. The arms deal that was concluded in September 1955 with the communist bloc was Nasser's first positive act that impressed the Arab masses and made the leadership of Egypt acceptable to most Arabs. The arms deal was made under the combined influence of the Israeli attack of February 28, 1955 on Gaza, the difficulty of purchasing arms from the West, and the new neutralism to which Nasser was converted at the Bandung Conference in April. The Soviet Union under the leadership of Khruschev also wanted to gain the good will of Nasser and the Arabs at a time when it was looking for Arab leadership to counteract the Western system of anti-communist pacts.

As a result of the arms deal, Nasser gained support in Egypt which he did not have. In the Arab world, the reaction was hysterical. It was not only that the arms that were needed for defense, or attack, against Israel were now available, but that Nasser was able to defy the West openly and prove his independence from it, and no leader before Nasser had done it. This is why Nasser began to look like a "new Saladin" and to be called savior of the Arabs, even before the arms were in the hands of the Egyptian officers and soldiers, and before it could be proved that the arms would be properly used. Nasser's speeches about the arms and his boasting about refusing to submit to Western conditions gave rise to propaganda slogans that filled the Arabic press and radio broadcasts. "I want arms to buy, not arms by which I could be bought," one slogan said. Another slogan answered the charge about the Russian influence that could come with the arms, and it said, "The Soviet arms in the hands of the Arabs become Arab arms."

Through the prestige gained by the arms deal, the neutralist policy and the campaign against the Baghdad Pact, Nasser was able to appropriate and control the two movements that aroused the greatest emotional interest in the Arab countries: Arab nationalism and unity, and restoration of Palestine to the Arabs. For Nasser, however, the interest of Egypt and the popularity of his regime were foremost in his plans and calculations. He soon began to indulge in two dangerous practices, first, taking momentous decisions that could affect or involve other Arab countries without consulting them, and second, exploiting the conditions of the cold war by making the United States and the Soviet Union compete in offering him aid and blackmailing the United States and the West when they stopped that aid. The two lines of policy succeeded for some time but eventually led to disastrous results for Egypt and for the other Arab states.

The nationalization of the Suez Canal Company on July 26, 1956 was Nasser's second sensational act, and it came nine months after the Czech arms deal. The motives for the nationalization were purely Egyptian motives and involved Egyptian interests, and the circumstances that led to the nationalization were the outcome of Nasser's independent policies and maneuvers. The nationalization was a quick and angry response to the withdrawal of the American offer to make loans, in cooperation with Britain and the World Bank, to help finance the construction of the High Dam at Aswan. Nasser felt that the explanation given by Dulles on the causes for withdrawing the offer on July 19 was insulting to Egypt, because it cast doubt on Egypt's ability to devote sufficient funds to the project after the arms agreement had been made with the Communist Bloc. The explanation given by Dulles was also a rebuke to Nasser for his attacks against the West, his close cooperation with the Soviet Union and the invitation of its foreign minister, Shepilov, to attend the evacuation ceremony in June 1956, his recognition of Communist China on May 16, 1956, and his attempt to spread rumors about a better offer of support by the Soviet Union that did not come immediately. Nasser's quick response to the affront by Dulles, his defiance of the Western powers, and his assertion of the unshaken independent will of Egypt to finance the Aswan Dam with the revenues of the Suez Canal won him the admiration of the Arab people within and outside Egypt. Many Arab governments, in spite of this admiration, were apprehensive of the nationalization and its implications.

The nationalization of the Suez Canal Company eventually led to war. Israel attacked in the Gaza Strip and the Sinai Desert on October 29 after reaching an understanding with France and Britain that they would fight on her side. Israel was not involved directly in the nationalization, but it was concerned about the steady increase of the Egyptian armaments and about the raids of Egyptian Fedayeen (commandos) in its territory. Nasser's forces made proof of complete incompetence and lack of dedication and discipline, and lost some six thousand prisoners and valuable Russian equipment to Israel. The Egyptian air force did not participate in the battle and no Arab states came to Egypt's support. The British and French occupied Port Said on November 5 after some resistance by the inhabitants, not by the army, and the death of some six hundred Egyptians. The United Nations saved the day for Nasser with the cooperation of both the United States and the Soviet Union, and issued resolutions for a cease fire and for the evacuation of foreign forces from Egypt. Britain and France complied on November 7, and by December 22 the canal area was evacuated. Israel withdrew from the Gaza Strip only on March 9, 1957 after heavy pressure from President Eisenhower and a guarantee of free navigation in the Gulf of Aqaba and the Strait of Tiran. Egypt did not have to sign a peace treaty with Israel, but it accepted the presence of a U. N. Emergency Force on its border with

Israel and along the Gulf of Aqaba and thus assured the security of Israel's southern borders and Israeli free navigation in the Red Sea. The Suez Canal was opened to navigation after it had been blocked and was operated efficiently by the Egyptians. In Syria, the Iraq Petroleum Company pipelines that were destroyed during the attack were repaired after the evacuation of foreign troops from Egyptian soil.

The humiliating military defeat suffered by Nasser's forces in Sinai and Port Said was turned into a political victory that consolidated Nasser's position in Egypt after it had been in danger of total collapse. The evacuation of French and British forces in the midst of their success and the subsequent fall of the British prime minister, Anthony Eden, made it possible for Nasser to tell the people of Egypt, "You have sent Anthony Eden to his doom . . . . Once Anthony Eden could remove any prime minister in Egypt in twenty-four hours."[12] Several factors helped Nasser in this crisis: world opinion was on Nasser's side and the triple attack was considered an act of aggression; the Arab countries reacted strongly and expressed their support by violent demonstrations, destruction of the oil pipelines in Syria, and readiness to enter the battle on Nasser's side; the conditions of the cold war and the secret nature of the Anglo-French collusion with Israel placed the United States on the side of Egypt; British opinion was divided, the British government was violently attacked and one of its members, Anthony Nutting, resigned and later viewed the operation as the most disastrous of all British blunders in the Middle East.[13]

The Suez crisis that came two years after Nasser had become the ruler of Egypt, contributed perhaps more than anything else in his career to making him a world figure. At the same time it can be credited with consolidating his prestige and leadership among the Arabs, who since then regarded him as the defender of their dignity and the man whose policy of independence "raised the Arabs several levels upwards among the other nations."[14] Nasser became the symbol of freedom from Western influence and of the ability to enhance the Arab self image and satisfy Arab need for outside admiration. As a Western writer put it in describing the attitude of the Egyptians and of many Arabs, "To a people long used to leaders taking their orders from foreign embassies, it is a pleasure in itself to have a leader on whose word foreign embassies now hang."[15]

Nasser's third prestigious achievement was the unity of Egypt and Syria on Nasser's terms and the formation of the United Arab Republic in February 1958 as a first step in an expected larger Arab unity.[16] The unity with Syria raised Nasser's prestige among the Arab people and in the world to its climax, but it also marked the end of his sensational successes. In fact the unity with Syria in 1958, and the break up of that unity in 1961 showed clearly the precarious character of Nasser's successes and the basically weak and artificial foundations on which Nasser's prestige rested.

III. Nasser and the Arabs

Nasser's pan-Arab leadership before and after the adoption of the socialist system depended on the application of pressures on various Arab countries to bring them closer to him and his system and to destroy his rivals and those who opposed his policies. The means of pressure were varied, but the most frequently used was to draw a distinction between the Arab people of each country and their rulers, to appeal to the people above the heads of their rulers and to portray the rulers or the leaders who do not fall in line as traitors and agents of imperialism, and to flatter the people and describe them as the arbiters in deciding the destiny of the Arabs. "The destiny of the Arab people," he said in December 1960, "is no longer decided at foreign embassies nor by foreign powers in conjunction with imperialist stooges; it is decided by the ordinary people."[17] The campaign against imperialism remained a constant theme in Nasser's speeches even though British and French influence had been removed. Its purpose was to divert the people's attention to imaginary enemies and accuse the rival Arab leaders of complicity with "the imperialists." The campaign, as it has been said, was a fight against a paper tiger in which the regime created the imperialist adversaries and then proceeded to destroy them.[18]

Nasser's appeal to the people against their rulers was accompanied by conspiracies and acts of violence and bloodshed. Nasserist propaganda aroused in the people the most violent and primitive passions of hatred and jealousy and resorted to exaggerations, misrepresentations, and pure fabrications of charges against the persons to be destroyed. The abusive accusations had to be repeated often and with great emotional extremism under the assumption that the people will believe anything if they hear it often enough. The pressures were often exercised through Egyptian agents, especially the military attachés, many of whom were caught smuggling arms and had to be expelled from various Arab capitals. Nasser also employed fifth columnists in the countries he intended to subvert. Some of them acted by conviction as a result of Nasserist propaganda but they needed arms, money, and technical advice. Others had to be bribed, and every cooperating officer or politician had a price depending on his weight and rank. Many fifth columnists were mediocre but ambitious and impatient climbers and opportunists who belonged to such small and radical parties as the Baath in Syria and Iraq and could not hope to reach power legally. They therefore depended on Nasser's maneuvers and the support of some officers' group to stage a military coup. Nasser also unscrupulously employed the communists outside Egypt, although in Egypt he limited their activity, and encouraged them to cooperate with other radical parties whenever he intended to undermine government authority, as he did in Syria and Iraq, but he had to contend later with them when they claimed their share of authority under a new regime. Nasser's methods thus seemed to be more imperialistic and directed to divide and dominate the Arabs rather than unify them and raise their dignity. His policy indeed has generally caused serious setbacks to the unity and dignity of the Arabs.

The United Arab Republic was supposed to be a first step in pan-Arab unity, but no Arab state joined except the Kingdom of Yemen that entered into a loose federation with the UAR in March 1958. The revolution of July 1958 in Iraq and the fall of the monarchy and of Nuri al-Said against whom Nasser had campaigned since 1955 was another climax in Nasser's career. For a while, Nasser seemed to be moving towards absolute domination of the Arab world and to making Iraq the eastern province of the United Arab Republic just as Egypt and Syria had been made its southern and northern provinces respectively. But the new republican Iraq did not join the UAR and six months after the fall of the monarchy, Nasser engaged in a violent campaign against the new republican regime under General Kassem that continued until Kassem's fall in February 1963. Jordan had its bitter experiences with Nasser's intervention and subversion between 1957 and 1967 with periods of truce and reconciliation, but Nasser was not successful in changing Jordan's pro-Western trend, or overthrowing its monarch and turning Jordan into a socialist republic. Lebanon's civil war in the summer of 1958 was the product of Nasser's miscalculation, as was the civil war in Yemen four years later, and both showed the degree of opposition to Nasser's search for domination.[19]

The Syrian coup of September 28, 1961 against unity with Egypt was a humiliating blow to Nasser's prestige and pride. For about one year after the coup, he concentrated on transforming Egypt into a socialist state, creating the socialist foundations, and issuing the socialist charter. Nasser realized that his impatience for achieving Arab unity under his leadership, and his violent Arab offensive with all the revolts and civil wars it created did not give the quick results he expected. Nasserism therefore decided to follow a new policy, that of emphasizing the inevitability of the socialist revolution as a prerequisite for Arab unity, and imposing Egypt's leadership of that revolution which should be the main Arab objective.

Egypt consequently declared in early 1962 that it would not continue its solidarity with the Arab states which she thought were not revolutionary, and these were not only Saudi Arabia, Imamic Yemen, and Jordan, but also Iraq under Kassem and Syria under Dr. Qudsi. Egypt then adopted a new slogan, "the unity of objective," instead of the old formula, "unity of ranks." The Nasserist spokesman, Haikal, expounded the new policy in an article in *al-Ahram* of March 9, 1962 entitled "We Do Not Want Solidarity", to explain that the lack of solidarity between Arab states — that is between the progressive revolutionary states and the so-called reactionary or non-revolutionary ones — should be sharpened, and the differences and clashes between them should occur because otherwise the Arab revolution would be frozen, and bargaining and compromises would be accepted and would become an obstacle to the expected great changes. Later in January 1963, Haikal made it clear that the completion of the political and social revolution in any Arab country should precede any thinking about unity in any way.[20]

The new policy did not mean the end of Nasserist interventionism. In fact, the Charter of May 1962 openly placed the principles of its socialist revolutionary appeal at the disposal of every Arab citizen, and declared that Egypt would not be stopped by the old argument that might consider this action as intervention in the affairs of others.[21]

Egypt again seemed to score new negative successes when the Yemeni revolt occurred on September 28, 1962 and declared the end of the Imamate, and when a few months later Kassem's regime was ended in Iraq on February 8, 1963, and the moderate regime of Dr. Qudsi was swept away in Syria on March 8 by military coups. Nasserist vocabulary now introduced a new term, "the liberated Arab states," to identify those states that were under revolutionary military rule and were socialist or on their way to become socialist. The group included Egypt, Syria, Iraq, Yemen, and Algeria. The dream of Arab unity was immediately revived, and on February 22, 1963, on the anniversary of the defunct unity of Egypt and

Syria, Nasser launched the movement for "unity, freedom, and socialism." Shortly after the end of the "secessionist" regime in Syria on March 8, discussions began for a federation between Egypt, Iraq, and Syria in March and April 1963. Nasser was cautious and suspicious of the Baathists who then ruled in both Syria and Iraq. The Baathist regimes insisted on a collective leadership for the federation and on maintaining the preeminence of their party in Iraq and Syria. The charter of the federation was finally signed after much bargaining on April 17, 1963, but it was never implemented because Nasser and the Baathists did not trust each other, and the Baathists were particularly afraid about losing their leadership in their own countries. Nasser's supporters in Syria tried to seize power from the Baathists in July 1963 and failed, while in Iraq the Baathists lost power in November. Attacks and counter-attacks between the two revolutionary socialist regimes of Nasser in Egypt and the Baath in Syria continued until the summer of 1966.

The Arab unity of ranks was thus shattered between 1962 and 1964, and the unity of objective was not reached. Nasser, however, still believed that "the Egyptian revolution is for all the Arabs, not for Egypt alone," and his spokesman, the editor of *al-Ahram,* made it clear in an article of April 19, 1964 that Egypt acted in two capacities, "as a state and as a revolution," and that as a revolution, it has the right to be in contact with the various popular forces and movements in the Arab countries.[22] In mid-1964, Nasser concluded agreements with the governments of Iraq (May 26, 1964) and Yemen (July 13, 1964) for coordinating their political and other policies as a step towards complete unity. A coordinating council was formed after each agreement, and a few meetings of these councils were held, but unity did not materialize. The agreements were intended to maintain an image of Egyptian leadership and to prove to the Saudi and Jordanian monarchies as well as to Syria that Nasser still had Arab allies.

Nasser continued in the midst of his successes and failures to have the initiative in Arab affairs. He could increase the intensity of the cold war between the Arabs, then call for a truce, and then resume the cold war depending on his interests and calculations and those of his Russian friends, and on the attitudes of Arab public opinion. In early 1964 and until the end of 1965, Arab politics were dominated by what is known as the "summit spirit." Under the pressure of Arab public opinion that was concerned about Israeli diversion of the Jordan waters to the Negev, and also because of the problem of the war in Yemen, Nasser called for a summit conference of Arab heads of state, and the conference met in Cairo on January 13, 1964. A second summit conference later met in Alexandria on September 5, and one year later, in September 1965, a third summit conference was held in Casablanca. Nasser used his influence in the first two conferences to prevent the use of force against Israel, and Arab action was restricted to the diversion of the head waters of the Jordan in the territory of Syria, Lebanon, and Jordan. Before the meeting of the third summit conference, Nasser concluded the Jidda agreement with King Faisal in August 1965 for peace in Yemen, but the agreement was fruitless. In the conference at Casablanca, "a solidarity charter" was signed by the Arab delegates to "clarify the atmosphere" between the Arab states and to stop radio and press attacks by one country against another.

In early 1966 Nasser abandoned his policy of coexistence with the non-revolutionary Arab countries, discarded the summit spirit, and resumed his attacks against Faisal of Saudi Arabia and Hussein of Jordan. The Jidda agreement of August 1965 for peace in Yemen failed to bring peace between the royalists and the republicans. Nasser again voiced his threats against the "bases of aggression" in Saudi Arabia, and made fun of King Faisal's attempts to strengthen his air defenses against possible Egyptian attack. Nasser was infuriated by King Faisal's efforts to strengthen Muslim solidarity in a series of visits to various Muslim countries in late 1965 and early 1966. The movements of King Faisal were clearly intended to rally Muslim opposition to the revolutionary socialist system, but Nasser who had formerly claimed that only socialists were good Arab nationalists, now began to imply that those who were not socialists were not good Muslims, and that non-socialist Muslim states were reactionary and servants of imperialism. A full scale campaign consequently began in Egypt and the other "progressive" Arab countries against what they called the Muslim alliance or pact. On the anniversary of the revolution, July 23, 1966, Nasser moved another step and announced that he would not attend the fourth summit conference that had been scheduled to meet in Algiers in September 1966. Nasser thus inaugurated the summit policy in early 1964 when it suited him, and he ended it in the summer of 1966 when he had no more need for it, and returned to the slogan of "the unity of objective."

During his visit to Cairo in May 1966, Premier Kosygin apparently encouraged a rapprochement between the "progressive" Arab states, and especially between Egypt and Syria. Informal talks about holding a conference of the five revolutionary states in what was called a "revolutionary summit" gave no result. Nasser's attacks, however, against the radical Baath regime in Syria and what he used to call their "opportunist policies" stopped after Kosygin's visit. The two sides, Nasser and the Baath, had to swallow their pride and forget their violent quarrels, and on November 4, 1966 they concluded a mutual defense pact. For the first time since the break-up of unity in 1961, Egypt agreed to exchange ambassadors with Syria. The defense pact was meant to be against Israel, but it was also a symbol of cooperation against the "reactionary" Arab regimes. It was undoubtedly encouraged, and perhaps urged upon the two sides, by the Soviet Union because of the state of isolation in which the rulers of Syria stood.

Following the pact with Syria and until the end of May 1967, Nasserism continued its pressures on the Arab countries by sponsoring and boasting of sabotage activity, as it did in Saudi Arabia in 1966, provoking riots and demonstrations, as it did in Jordan following the Israeli attack on Sammu on

November 13, 1966, and encouraging attacks and threats against King Hussein by Ahmad Shuqairi, the protégé of Cairo and the head of the Palestine Liberation Organization. Nasser himself carried on his invectives against his Arab opponents and made fun of them, sometimes in vulgar terms, as when he spoke of King Faisal in a broadcast speech of February 1967 as *Abul Daqn* (the man with the beard), and of Bourguiba as *Khawaja* Bourguiba.[23]

In its relations with the Arab countries, Nasserism was thus generally aggressive and domineering. From its attack against the Baghdad pact and the Iraqi government in 1955 to its attack against the so-called Muslim pact and the Saudi government in 1967, it had tried to spread and impose its revolutionary policies, domestic as well as foreign, on the Arab states. While Nasserism registered certain successes, mostly negative, it failed to achieve what it always told the Arab people it would give them, namely, Arab unity, and restoration of Arab rights in Palestine. Instead of Arab unity and strength, Nasserism created division, first between what it called the liberated states, and the reactionary — and even democratic — Arab states, and second within each state between the radical socialist supporters who were viewed as the real patriots, and the liberal democrats and various elites who were described as traitors and imperialist agents. While it claimed to defend, or restore, Arab dignity Nasserism deprived the Arab individual of two basic elements of human dignity, freedom and justice, the most precious fruits of the long Arab struggle for independence. Nasserism ended by bringing suffering and humiliation to Egypt and to the Arabs in general in the Israeli war of June 1967 because of its immature diplomatic and military initiatives and its continued military ineptitude that contrasted with Nasser's vociferous threats and claims of military superiority. Nasserism sowed so much division and hatred among the Arabs, created so much instability as a result of the successive military coups that it provoked, and caused such large scale purges of officers in the armed forces that it weakened the Arabs and their armies materially and morally. The Arabs were also distracted from the Israeli challenge by the constant internal quarrels, conspiracies, and class warfare that Nasserism incited.

IV. Nasserism, Palestine, and the Great Powers

The Palestine war of 1948 provided Nasser and the free officers with one of the pretexts for the revolution of July 1952, because the Egyptian army was humiliated by defeat and the officers held the old regime under King Farouk responsible for forcing them into a war for which they were not prepared. Egypt continued to be involved in the Palestine question after 1948 for several reasons: It had common borders with southern Israel along the Gaza Strip and Sinai, it was still technically at war with Israel after the armistice of February 1949 and, as an Arab state, it had to cooperate with other Arab states in their nationalist drive to reduce Israeli power and restore Arab rights in Palestine. In the relations of the Nasserist regime with Israel and the question of Palestine, three characteristics can be noted: First and foremost, the Palestine problem has never been a question of first priority or vital concern in the plans and programs of the Egyptian government. Nasserist policies and actions were dictated primarily by considerations of enhancing Nasser's personal prestige, stabilizing his regime, and advancing Egyptian national interests. Second, Nasser's regime never initiated direct military action against Israel. The two wars that he involuntarily fought in 1956 and 1967 were the outcome of Nasserist policies that sometimes had little or no relation to the Palestine problem. Third, while exploiting Egypt's belligerency with Israel, Nasser involved Egypt and the Arabs in the general cold war to obtain benefits for his own regime, but with no real advantages for the Arabs. Moreover, Nasser's advocacy of neutralism, revolution, and socialism provoked an Arab cold war within each state and between the states that weakened the Arabs and their armies and diverted their attention from the Palestine affair.

Nasser began to exploit the Palestine problem and to play with Arab emotions and inflame Arab feelings when he concluded the arms deal of September 1955 and told the Arabs that the arms would serve for the liberation of Palestine. The arms purchased by Nasser, however, did not liberate Palestine. Instead, they have given false expectations to the Palestinians and brought more suffering to the Arabs of Palestine.

The arms deal and the neutralist policy of Nasser's Egypt "opened the door of the Arab East to the Soviet Union after it had been prevented from setting one foot or even one finger in it from 1917 to 1954." Thus wrote the Egyptian journalist Fikri Abaza in an open letter to Khruschev in March 1959 to remind him of what the Soviet Union owed to Egypt.[24] The door of the Arab East was indeed opened for the Soviet Union, and with every Israeli attack and destruction of Egyptian and Arab military equipment the door opened still more widely. In the emotional and highly explosive Palestine problem, the Soviet Union sought in particular to impress Egypt and the Arabs with its defense of Arab rights, and thus led them to believe that it would support their efforts for the liberation of Palestine. At the same time, the Soviet Union persistently sought to intensify Arab hostility against the West, and the United States in particular, for their pro-Israeli policy and to emphasize the idea that Israel was a creation and a tool of western imperialism.

The Soviet Union in reality was not interested in the solution of the Palestine problem or in the liberation of Palestine and the liquidation of Israel. On the contrary, the Soviet Union had a long range interest in maintaining the confusion and exacerbating the tensions resulting from the Palestine problem in order to exploit them to her advantage. The Russian Ambassador in Cairo, Daniel Solod, knew very well that the Nasserist revolution would serve the interests of Russian power and Russian socialism, because the sole food of this revolution was anti-imperialism and anti-capitalism. Nasser was the strongest among the military revolutionary rulers and he had the greatest potential of supporting socialism and making Egypt a socialist state. This is why the Soviet government gave him its powerful backing and worked to enhance his prestige and raise him to the position of supreme leadership of the Arabs, especially after he began his attacks against the Baghdad Pact.

Nasser exploited his new friendship with the Russians to the fullest extent exactly as they exploited their friendship with him. In fact an identity of interests made each of the two sides use and serve the other at the same time. The Soviet Union used Nasser to oust the Western powers and their interests from the Arab countries, and to spread socialism and revolution and fight the Arab rulers who had any ties with the West. Nasser similarly used the Soviet Union to promote his position in the Arab world, and with its moral support to defy and attack the Western powers and their Arab friends. Nasser soon found out that non-alignment was profitable and he later gave his friend, President Tito of Yugoslavia, the credit of showing him how to get help from both East and West without joining either.[25]

The nationalization of the Suez Canal and the political victory that Nasser achieved after the Suez war gave him such uncontested leadership and popularity that Nasserist subversion and intervention threatened almost every Arab country after the removal of British and French influence. This is why President Eisenhower asked Congress in January 1957 to give him power to help the countries of the Middle East maintain their independence in the face of direct or indirect communist attack. Nasser rejected what came to be known as the Eisenhower Doctrine because it could stand in the way of his ambitious projects and it was considered intervention in the affairs of the various countries, although it was expected to function only if the threatened government applied for help. The result was that the Nasserist anti-Western campaign was directed more against the United States than against Britain and France, and the credit for saving Nasser from the results of his defeat was given almost entirely to the Soviet Union.

While Nasser's friendship with the Soviet Union helped him achieve his initial successes against the Western powers and their Arab friends and raise his international prestige, it contributed nothing positive for the question of Arab rights in Palestine. It only weakened those Arab countries — Syria, Iraq, and Jordan — which could be expected to do anything for Palestine, and for many years to come aggravated their divisions and caused their officers to engage in fruitless internal disputes. The Soviet friendship and armaments, at the same time, gave Egypt neither the genuine strength and military leadership to deal effectively with the Palestine problem, nor the determination to engage in any serious action for the sake of Palestine. Nasserist Egypt was satisfied with the wave of popular support that followed the Suez "victory", and continued to issue declarations and threats against Israel and to speak of the "holy march" for the liberation of Palestine in order to win over the Arab masses and conceal the real aspects and tenets of its policy and the gravity of the concessions she made after the Suez War. Egypt indeed in spite of its inflammatory declarations and slogans had evidently decided to live in peace with Israel by accepting the stationing of a United Nations emergency force on its side of the border in Sinai, the Gaza Strip, and the Gulf of Aqaba. This meant the end of the Egyptian-Palestinian Fedayeen raids which were active shortly before the Israeli attack, and also the freedom of Israeli navigation through the Strait of Tiran and the Gulf of Aqaba. This was actually the price which Egypt had to pay for the evacuation of its territory after negotiations and agreements had been worked out with the UN Secretary General Hammarskjold, and with the knowledge and blessing of the United States. These concessions explain why the nationalization of the Suez Canal and the so-called Nasserist victory in the Suez War were consequently viewed by Arab nationalists as a setback and even as a disaster for the Palestinian question.[26]

During the period of unity with Syria after 1958, Nasser's passive attitude toward the Palestine problem irritated the Arab nationalists in the Syrian region and provoked serious arguments between them and their Egyptian president, especially after Israel announced its intention to begin work for the diversion of the Jordan river waters. In a meeting on November 29, 1959 at Qasr al-Qubba in Cairo, the Syrian vice president of the United Arab Republic, Akram Hourani, raised the question and tried to persuade Nasser to use force for preventing the diversion and explained to him the danger of the Israeli operation that could lead to doubling the population of Israel. Nasser expressed the fear of provoking a general war with Israel for which the UAR was not prepared. He wanted more time to industrialize and to strengthen his forces, and constantly brought up the argument of "what would happen if Israel sent her planes to bombard Damascus?" Hourani, supported by two Syrian ministers from among the military — Ahmad Abdul Karim and Amin Nufuri — answered Nasser that the use of force would not lead to a general war because the international organizations and the powers would immediately intervene, as they did in 1953 when Syria alone was able to prevent diversion works in the demilitarized zone.[27] Nasser eventually allowed the Israeli operation to proceed until it reached its final stage in 1963, but this time Arab official declarations, including those of the Arab League, and Arab pressures were such that Nasser had to call for a summit conference of Arab heads of state in early 1964 to deal with the problem.

Before the meeting of the first summit conference, Nasser had made it clear on more than one occasion to private groups and even to mass rallies that he had no intention of taking immediate action to regain Palestine for the Arabs. When a delegation of Palestinian Arabs from Gaza arrived in Cairo in September 1962 to greet him and renew their loyalty to him, and to ask him to save Palestine, he told them with frankness that shocked and disappointed them that neither he nor any other Arab country had a plan to fight Israel and liberate

Palestine, and that the removal of Israel needed great preparations and a very long time. In mass rallies, his reasons for taking no action in Palestine were different and centered on the priority of accomplishing his revolutionary task against Arab reactionaries.

The first Arab summit conference that met in Cairo in January 1964 to discuss Israel's diversion of the Jordan waters was a disappointment to most Arab nationalists. The Arab heads of state at the conference included the military rulers of five Arab countries who had reached their position of power and were acclaimed as leaders by the masses because of the hope they raised and the claims they made of saving Palestine, and yet they were using the same arguments and pretexts for avoiding a confrontation with Israel that the discredited and assassinated politicians and leaders of the old regime occasionally used. Their pretext was that the powers might intervene against them in case of war, and that in any way they needed time to arm themselves, obtain the necessary funds, and win over world opinion. They had been arming themselves for ten years, and they had attacked the Baghdad Pact precisely because it would have prevented them, as allies of the West, from engaging in a war against Israel. Egypt now imposed on the conference, as a substitute for using force to prevent the diversion of the Jordan, the idea of diverting the tributaries or headwaters of the Jordan in the territories of Lebanon, Syria, and Jordan. The conference also created a Unified Arab Command with an Egyptian general at its head, and a Palestine Liberation Organization that would represent the Palestine entity. Egypt, at any rate, succeeded in diverting Arab efforts to the tributaries and in protecting herself from any Israeli danger caused by the diversion of the tributaries because it was to be in the territories of other Arab states. It thus retained the initiative in the Palestinian question, as well as its position of leadership without sharing responsibility and without being asked about the presence of the UN emergency force on its borders.

At the second summit conference in Alexandria in early

September 1964, it was admitted that the decision to divert the tributaries was not being implemented as it should. Israel in fact had announced its opposition to that diversion, and towards the end of 1964 it began to use force against the zone of the diversion in Syria. Israeli attacks occurred in November and December 1964, and in March and May 1965 but the Unified Command did not react. When Israeli artillery destroyed some Syrian bulldozers and stopped work on the project in March 1965, Nasser answered those who expected that this was a test for the effectiveness of the Unified Military Command that he would not risk war for a few bulldozers. At the end of May 1965, Nasser told a meeting of the second national congress of the Palestine Liberation Organization in Cairo that the Arab governments were unable to regain Palestine by force, and that they were equally unable to protect the diversion of the tributaries and added that the diversion would have to be suspended until the three countries are better prepared to defend themselves.[28] The Baath party regime in Damascus commented on Nasser's speech and declaration by saying, "Because of Palestine, Abdul Nasser came, and because of it he assumed Arab leadership and Syria was offered to him on a silver platter!"[29]

After the second summit conference, Nasser's spokesman, M. H. Haikal, editor of *al-Ahram,* developed a rationale for Nasser's decision not to fight Israel. He compared the Egyptian policy of not fighting Israel to that of the United States in not fighting Russia or Cuba.[30] The weekly *Rose al-Yusif* had already stated on the eve of the meeting of the first summit conference that Egypt could not move her forces against Israel because the anti-Cairo Arab regimes would stab her in the back.[31]

The third summit conference of September 1965 in Casablanca practically killed the idea of diverting the tributaries and Ahmad Shuqairi commented, "The diversion project has been diverted!" When the conference, instead of providing protection for the diversion, issued the Solidarity Charter that required the Arab states to stop their press and radio attacks against each other, the editorialist of *al-Safa* in Beirut wrote with sarcasm, "The world which held its breath through the conference expecting some earth shaking decisions, has been informed that the Arabs have agreed not to curse each other!"³²

Nasser's constant maneuvers to prevent Arab action against Israel, as illustrated by the affair of the diversion of the Jordan waters, and his moderation in dealing with the Palestine question naturally won the approval of the United States government and brought considerable benefits in surplus foods and technical aid to the Nasserist regime. Nasser's relations with the United States had effectively begun to improve in late 1958 after the well-known series of clashes and crises caused by the Czech arms deal and the Baghdad Pact crisis in 1955, the American opposition to the leftist regime of Syria and to the Nasserist subversion in Syria and Iraq in 1955-1958, and the landing of the marines in Lebanon in July 1958. Two developments were responsible for the improved relations. First, the United States softened its attitude towards Nasser's neutralism and was reconciled to it. The State Department specialists evidently believed, in spite of the many crises and revolts that Nasser provoked in the Arab countries, that he was a force for stability in the area, and they were obsessed by the fear of what would happen to Egypt in case of his fall. They were satisfied with his behavior towards Israel and with the absence of tension on the Syrian border during the period of unity with Egypt.

The second development that helped improve American relations with Egypt was Nasser's open denunciation of Arab communists in the United Arab Republic in his strong speech of December 23, 1958 and his quarrel with Kassem's regime in Iraq ostensibly for its close cooperation with the communists, but in reality for Kassem's opposition to the unity of Iraq with the UAR and the role of the communists in influencing Kassem's attitude. The quarrel culminated in the abortive anti-Kassem coup in Mosul in March 1959 which Nasser instigated and financed through the minister of interior in the

Syrian region, Abdul Hamid Sarraj. Nasser's anti-communist campaign in late 1958 and early 1959 provoked an angry Soviet reaction and a brief crisis with the Soviet Union during which Khruschev described Nasser as rash and immature and Egypt's undemocratic regime was denounced, while Egypt was reminded of Soviet support especially in the Suez crisis. The Egyptian-Russian crisis soon ended, but it helped create a more favorable American attitude towards Nasser who, moreover, continued his campaign against the communist-supported Kassem regime in Iraq until its fall in February 1963. Nasser's little skirmish with Russia was almost the only instance in which the two sides angrily criticized each other. The crisis could not be serious because neither side could afford to lose the other. Russia proved to be ready, in this case as in many others, to sacrifice the local communists in Egypt and Syria in order to maintain her prestige and influence in the Arab world.

In early 1964, about 800 communists were released from Egyptian jails in preparation for Khruschev's visit in May, and the Red Major, Kh. Muhieddin, was recalled and appointed editor in chief of the daily *al-Akhbar*. When Khruschev arrived for celebrating the end of the first stage of the Aswan Dam, the editorialist of *al-Ahram* welcomed him with these words of recognition, "It must be said in all fairness that one-half of the success achieved by the Egyptian revolutionary movement depended on Nikita Khruschev."[33] The Soviet Prime Minister promised Egypt a new loan of $220 million for heavy industry, and bestowed on Nasser and Amer the title of "Hero of the Soviet Union," and on Nasser the honors of the "Order of Lenin" and the "Gold Star."[34] Khruschev, however, besides criticizing the quality and the high cost of housing and of wheat production during his visit to Liberation Province, expressed his dissatisfaction with the goal of Arab unity on the basis of nationality and suggested that it should be on the basis of work. He proposed that the motto, "O Arabs, unite," be replaced by, "O Arab peasants, laborers, intellectuals unite against exploitation and exploiters." In this way, he said, "The peoples of the Soviet Union would find a place among the Arabs."³⁵

The United States government was no longer concerned as it had been about Nasser's internal political and economic system and ideology or his close ties with the Soviet Union and his role in the neutralist or "third" world, but it strove to maintain a measure of influence for moderation and restraint in Egypt.³⁶ Nasser, at the same time, was in favor of keeping relations with the West as a counterpoise to his intimate ties with Russia. American loans for economic development and grants-in-aid multiplied under the Kennedy administration especially in 1962 and 1963. The food for peace agreement that ended in June 1965 brought to Egypt for three years an average of 150 million dollars' worth of surplus foods every year that were paid in local Egyptian currency and given back to Egypt in the form of long term loans. American officials were satisfied with what they reportedly considered as "the quiet benefits we get on the side, such as a moderate policy towards Israel."³⁷

The Arab free press, mainly in Lebanon, and the Arab critics of Nasser naturally saw the relation between American assistance and Nasser's "moderate policy toward Israel," and were ready to taunt Nasser for the price he was paying in accepting the massive American aid.³⁸ In the congressional debates about foreign assistance, certain congressmen sometimes criticized the United States government for offering assistance to Egypt claiming that it was preparing for war against Israel, but the State Department spokesmen invariably reassured them that Egypt had no such intention. This is how Deputy Assistant Secretary of State Grant put it in the meeting of April 30, 1963, "In the case of Egypt, I think, one of the accomplishments of the last several years has been that her actions have increasingly become a matter of words against Israel, and not so much of action. In a very real sense, in terms of real actions, the United Arab Republic I think can be said to have put its relationship with Israel in the icebox."³⁹

While Nasser's actions against Israel had indeed become

"a matter of words," his actions in support of leftist revolutionary activities in the Arab countries and in Africa were more than a matter of words. Nasser's relentless action in the Yemeni civil war from October 1962 until May 1967 with its ruthless use of napalm bombs and indiscriminate bombardment of towns puzzled Arab nationalists and moved Imam al-Badr to remind Nasser that "the road to Israel was Sinai, not Yemen!" The fact that the Egyptian role in Yemen was approved, if not ordained, by the Soviet Union and partly financed by it did not improve Nasser's reputation among Arab nationalists and demonstrated his indifference to the Palestine question. Nasser's incitements against Jordan were often made in conditions in which Jordan needed most his moral and material help. When the Jordanian village of Sammu, in the Hebron district, was raided and destroyed by Israeli forces on November 13, 1966 in massive retaliation for commando raids that came from both Syria and Jordan, Nasser and the Baath regime in Syria exploited the occasion to arouse Jordanian public opinion, not against Israel, but against the Jordanian rulers.

It is ironic that in Nasser's relations with the Western powers, disagreements about Israel and Palestine provoked no such anti-Western violence or drastic action as was provoked by his concern over African issues that had no relation to the genuine interests of Egypt and of the Arabs. Because of the Congo, not of Palestine, the American Embassy in Cairo was attacked twice, first on February 14, 1961 as a result of the death of Patrice Lumumba, and second, on November 25, 1964 after the American rescue operation in the Congo. The Belgian Embassy was also attacked in 1961, and Nasser found a good pretext, after rejecting the Belgian protest, for expelling the Belgians, sequestrating their property, and breaking relations with Belgium. In November 1964, Nasser was evidently irritated because the United States helped rescue the white hostages held by the Congo rebels whom he was supporting with arms shipments against the legal Congolese government.[40] The attack on the American Embassy resulted in the burning of the U.S. Information Library and produced a bitter reaction that was reflected partly in delaying the grant of another 35 million dollars' worth of surplus foods requested by Nasser. One month earlier, in October 1964, the second conference of non-aligned nations opened in Cairo. It was the second of its kind after that of Belgrade in September 1961, and the number of nations represented in it was much larger and included some communist and pro-communist delegations. The issues discussed in the conference, moreover, were viewed mostly through communist eyes, and the resolutions touching Vietnam, Cuba, Communist China, Puerto Rican independence and others were largely anti-American in spirit.

The attack on the American Embassy in November 1964 was followed on December 23, by Nasser's famous "drink-the-sea-water" speech at Port Said which cast a heavy shadow on his relations with the United States and was a turning point in the American attitude towards him and his regime. Nasser's angry anti-American tirade was evidently caused by the criticism of his policy in the Congo and his deep involvement in Yemen, and also by delaying the grant of more surplus food. Nasser rejected the American appeal to stop arming the Congo rebels and told the American government to "drink the sea water" if it is not satisfied, "and if the Mediterranean is not big enough we will give them the Red Sea to drink too."[41]

In early 1965, the House of Representatives reacted against Nasser's acts by voting to stop the execution of the 1962 agreement for food deliveries. The American gift, it was said, was freeing money that Nasser spent on arms shipments to the Congo and other countries to oppose the United States and its allies. Before the end of June 1965, however, the suspension of aid to Egypt was lifted and it was decided to send the $37 million in surplus food that was still undelivered. President Johnson explained that the decision was in the American national interest, and a State Department spokesman referred to the improvement in relations caused, among other things, by the discontinued shipments of arms to the Congo rebels, and by "indications in recent statements and actions by Nasser's government which have avoided adding to tensions with Israel." The spokesman mentioned specifically Nasser's speech of May 31, 1965 before the Palestine Liberation Organization Congress in which he warned the Arab states against provocative military action against Israel.[42] It has been even related that in early 1965, the Government of Israel itself intervened to advise the American government that it was unwise to stop the aid to Egypt, and that Vice President Humphrey told the members of Congress secretly that Israel opposed the suspension of food shipments,[43] Palestine thus continued to be an important instrument that Nasser used to win American friendship and assistance when he wanted, or to satisfy the Soviet Union when necessary, regardless of whether the basic Arab interests in the Palestine problem were served or not.

Nasser's bid for African leadership, in addition to Arab leadership, and his involvement in Afro-Asian revolutionary politics absorbed much of his activity and his funds without giving him and Egypt the expected results. His involvements, moreover, were of no benefit for the Arab cause and particularly that of Palestine. Egypt assumed the leadership of the anti-Western movement in Africa since 1958, and tried to act as the defender of the black people and to impose Cairo as the intellectual capital of Africa. The Azhar University began to prepare African religious teachers and send them back to their countries to organize Islamic centers attached to Cairo. It also sent from Egypt cult counselors and religious teachers, whose number reached 782 in 1963, to preach Islam and make propaganda for Egypt. The political-religious propaganda was expected to combat Israel's political and economic action, and expel the West from Africa in order to improve Nasser's position and develop Egyptian influence. Nasser apparently turned to Africa also because he was disappointed by the breakup of the United Arab Republic and by the opposition to his policy of Arab unification under Egyptian hegemony.

Nasser realized by 1963 that his propaganda in Africa bore no fruits. The heads of state were suspicious of his activity and the African states were jealous of their independence. Nasser had no adequate financial facilities or technical possibilities to interest the African countries. Moreover, in emphasizing the anti-imperialist and revolutionary theme, "he played the card of the extremists which was not the good one."[44] Nasser succeeded in inscribing the Palestine question on the agenda of the various conferences, and the resolutions usually contained a polite statement on "supporting the rights of the Arabs in Palestine," in addition to the mention of Israel as a base of imperialism. Yet, many African countries that subscribed to these resolutions continued to carry on their friendly economic and cultural relations with Israel.

Nasser's revolutionary Afro-Asian and anti-Western activities often led him to adopt policies of doubtful benefits against certain states. Along with the other Arab revolutionaries, Nasser, for example, was hostile to Pakistan and friendly to India although Pakistan regularly took the same strong position as the Arabs on the Palestinian question. The criterion for Nasser's friendship in this case, as in several others, was not Palestine but neutralism and the attitude towards the West. The fact that Pakistan joined the Baghdad Pact and therefore was aligned with the West was in the eyes of the Arab revolutionaries a guilt which no Pakistani support for the cause of Palestine could make them forget. In the Rhodesian crisis, Nasser considered Egypt to be at war with Rhodesia on November 18, 1965 because of its internal policies. On December 17 he actually broke diplomatic relations with Britain and even wanted the Arab states to follow his example, but none of them did. Many Arabs have commented that Nasser never broke relations with Britain because of Palestine.

Nasser sometimes dragged the Arab states to disputes in

which they took no initiative and had no interest, as in the dispute with West Germany in 1965. The Arabs had generally maintained friendly relations with Germany and they were satisfied that West Germany had no diplomatic relations with Israel. Germans were active in many economic development projects in the Arab countries. Egypt, in particular, employed scores of Germans in its propaganda services, industrial and technical development projects, and the expansion of its armaments, including rocketry. The crisis between Egypt and West Germany began when Cairo announced on January 14, 1965 that Walter Ulbricht, president of Communist East Germany would visit Egypt in late February. The invitation to Ulbricht had been decided in December 1964 during Soviet Deputy Premier Shelepin's visit because the Soviet Union wanted to assert the existence of the East German entity and to draw attention to the ties of the Soviet Bloc with the Arab world. The visit was apparently imposed on Egypt by Soviet pressure accompanied by a loan of 287 million dollars.[45] Nasser cleverly exploited the question of German arms shipment to Israel about which he had been informed several months before, but which he raised precisely at this time in order to put West Germany on the defensive and to make his invitation to Ulbricht look like a calculated retaliatory act against the West German government for providing Israel with arms. On February 12, West Germany made public its decision to stop the arms shipment to Israel, but already 80 per cent of the 80 million dollars' worth of arms had been delivered, and Nasser in any way was not ready to cancel his invitation to Ulbricht.

Ulbricht arrived in Cairo on February 24, 1965 and was very well received. He was awarded the highest Egyptian decoration, "the collar of the Nile," but East Germany was not officially recognized. On March 7, Erhard's government in West Germany decided to stop economic aid to Egypt, and offered to establish diplomatic relations with Israel. Nine days later, on March 16, the Israeli Knesset accepted the offer. The conferences of Arab heads of state and of Arab foreign ministers in Cairo, on March 9 and 15 respectively, showed the extent of Arab division in the crisis which Nasser provoked by inviting Ulbricht. The Arab leaders disagreed about the boycott of West Germany, but accepted in principle to break diplomatic, not economic relations. They also decided not to give diplomatic recognition to East Germany. Ten Arab states out of thirteen in the Arab League broke diplomatic relations.

The Nasserist crisis with West Germany to which the Arabs were dragged was neither in Nasser's interest nor in that of the Arabs and Palestine. Nasser played the game of the Soviet Union and the Eastern Bloc and was used as a pawn in the cold war. He contributed to the loss of German economic aid and dealt a heavy blow to German friendship with the Arabs and pushed Germany to open diplomatic relations with Israel. He also illogically broke relations only with Germany, which was the instrument for sending the arms to Israel, but could not break relations with the United States, which furnished the arms and told Germany to ship them.

The Nasserist regime in Egypt concentrated its propaganda in 1966 and the first four months of 1967 on the favorite theme of the cooperation between the Arab reactionary governments and imperialism and Zionism. Nasserism, at the same time, began to assert the demagogic claim that the revolutionary regimes alone were responsible for the liberation of Palestine, and it mobilized its protégé, Ahmad Shuqairi, chairman of the executive committee of the Palestine Liberation Organization, against the rulers of Jordan.[46] The conservative weekly, *al-Zaman* in Beirut, predicted with good cause that it was "as if this revolutionism in the Arab world were executing a plan aiming at creating a Palestine disaster in every Arab land in the name of liberating Palestine."[47] The Israeli raid on the Jordanian little town of Sammu on November 13, 1966 brought no response from the Unified Arab Command or from Egypt and Syria. It showed that Cairo and Damascus were more interested in overthrowing King Hussein than in saving Palestine. The Baathist head of the Syrian state, Nureddin Atassi, was quoted saying that the end of the Jordanian regime should come before the end of Israel.[48]

In the meeting of the Arab Higher Defense Council in Cairo on December 7, 1966, Jordan made it clear that it would welcome Arab troops on its territory and other arrangements required by the Unified Arab Command only when the plan of mobilization and air cover is defined, and when all other plans of Arab defense decided in the summit meetings are executed. The Jordanian representatives mentioned that there should be concentration of troops in Sinai as well as on the other borders of Israel, and that the UN emergency forces should be removed and the 50,000 Egyptian troops in Yemen should be withdrawn. When the Jordanian foreign minister, Akram Zuaiter, asked Egypt to withdraw the UN forces in order to be able to implement the Arab defense plan on all borders, the Egyptian foreign minister, Mahmud Riad, answered that they did not form an obstacle to military operations.[49] The Higher Defense Council met again in March 1967, but the relations by then had worsened between Egypt, Syria and the PLO on the one hand, and Saudi Arabia and Jordan on the other. Jordan decided to boycott the meetings of the Arab League as long as they were attended by Shuqairi. The Jordanian government had also decided to resume relations with Western Germany on February 27, 1967. In the stormy meeting of the Arab League Council in Cairo on March 14, 1967, the Jordanian delegate made an opening speech attacking Shuqairi and withdrew, but Shuqairi's right to sit in the Council was defended by the Egyptian delegate and approved by others. The Council then voted a motion censoring Jordan for re-establishing diplomatic relations with West Germany, and Shuqairi proposed expelling Jordan from the Arab League and gave thirty-seven reasons for his proposal.[50] The text of Shuqairi's memoir was given to the Jordanian government in order to defend itself in the following meeting of the Council in September, but the war with Israel occurred in the meantime and put a temporary end to Arab quarrels.

The tensions between Syria and Israel in the demilitarized zone and over commando infiltration from Syrian territory culminated in a violent Israeli air raid that lasted seven hours inside Syria on April 7, 1967. The neighboring Arab countries issued the regular declarations of support for Syria, but Egypt and the Unified Arab Command did not respond to the Israeli attack in which six Syrian planes were destroyed and Israeli planes flew over Damascus. The independent press in Beirut wondered what happened to the mutual defense agreement of November 4, 1966 between Egypt and Syria. A few days after the air raid, the commander of the Egyptian Air Force, Muhammad Sidqy Mahmud, paid a visit to Syria and was followed by an eight-man Egyptian delegation under Prime Minister Muhammad Sidqy Sulaiman. During the visit, the Syrian chief of staff, Major General Ahmad Sweidani, denied the rumors about the establishment of an Egyptian air base in Syria. He accused Israel of massing large concentrations of troops near the Syrian border and added, "but the Syrian army is fully prepared and will this time reply with surprises which will stun Zionism, imperialism and reaction."[51]

Frictions between the Arab states surrounding Israel continued even until after the beginning of the crisis that led to the war with Israel. Syrian officers who had taken asylum in Jordan in the fall of 1966 were encouraged to move to Egypt where they were officially received and employed to spread rumors about Jordanian sabotage in Syria and plots to stir a revolt against the Syrian regime.[52] Later on, when parliamentary elections occurred in Jordan in mid-April, 1967, the Syrian radio broadcasts appealed to the Jordanians to boycott the elections. At the height of the Middle East crisis, when the Arabs were mobilizing their armies for a confrontation with Israel, the explosion of a time bomb on May 21, 1967 at the Jordanian frontier post south of the Syrian border killed fourteen Jordanians and injured twenty-eight others. The bomb was evidently placed in a car by orders of Syrian intelligence officials. Jordan immediatley broke relations with Syria and closed the border.[53] King Hussein, while condemning Syrian action, called on the Arabs to cooperate and forget their differences in view of the impending war with Israel.

V. Nasserism and the War Ordeal
A. Nasserist Motives

Nasser's attitude towards the Palestine problem remained equivocal and cautious, but he could no longer accept to be taunted constantly by the Arab critics for hiding behind the UN emergency forces, and the Soviet Union disliked to see his prestige undermined and the Baath Socialist regime in Syria humiliated. Suddenly in mid-May 1967, Nasser set out to regain his position of leadership in the defense of the Arabs. The moment of truth approached when he declared the Gulf of Aqaba closed to Israeli shipping on May 22. As a result of Israel's strong reaction, he had either to modify his decision or face the possibility of an armed conflict. The choice was imposed on him by Israel on the morning of June 5 because Israel evidently decided that war was inevitable and it could not afford to wait until Nasser attacked, and also because it was probably tempted by the opportunity to destroy Nasser's war machine and gain more territory at a time when world opinion was mostly on its side.

The succession of events that led to the closing of the Gulf of Aqaba on May 22, 1967 began with a sudden declaration of a state of emergency alert in the Egyptian armed forces on May 15, followed by troop movements in the Cairo area and in the military air fields, and a vast troop build up along the Sinai border with Israel. On May 17-18, Egypt asked the Indian commander of the UN forces, General Rikhye, as well as Secretary General U Thant to withdraw the 3,500 UN troops, and U Thant found that he had no other choice but to comply with the request. On May 19 Egypt's request was granted, and the Egyptian forces moved in to take the positions overlooking the Straits of Tiran at the mouth of the Gulf of Aqaba. The closing of the Straits of Tiran was consequently the direct result of the withdrawal of UN troops. On May 24 the Israeli government made it known that the blockade of the Gulf of Aqaba was an act of war, but neither Nasser was ready to withdraw his declaration, nor Israel was prepared to accept the new situation.

The official Egyptian reason for the build up in Sinai was, as General Muhammad Fawzi wrote to the UN commander on May 17, "to be ready for action against Israel immediately after she launches any act of aggression against any Arab state."[54] Egypt evidently believed that Israel was massing troops to invade Syria. The threat made by the Israeli premier, Levi Eshkol, on May 11 "to adopt measures no less drastic than those of April 7," because of what he called continued Syrian provocation, confirmed this belief.[55] Moreover, Nasser wanted to remove the stigma of his passive attitude during the Israeli air attack of April 7, 1967 when six Syrian planes were destroyed and Israeli planes flew over Damascus with no Egyptian response.

On the basis of the well known moderate policy of Nasser towards Israel and various revelations of responsible Egyptians echoed in the world press, it would seem that Nasser's basic motives for the military build up in Sinai were political and that he did not intend to engage in military action against Israel. The Egyptian commanders evidently had warned him against the danger of concentrating troops near the Israeli border and recommended that Egypt should strike first if military action was contemplated, but they were told that the whole affair was a political maneuver.[56] The object of Nasser's noisy brinkmanship and of his dramatic defiance of Israel was probably to regain his Arab leadership and prestige which had been impaired by his unhappy experience in Yemen, the counter attacks of the "reactionary" states, and the taunts for keeping the UN forces on his border in addition to his failure to help Syria on April 7, 1967. He expected that Israel would be prevailed upon to accept his blockade of the Gulf of Aqaba, and that the Arab world, as a result, would acclaim him as the hero who ordered the removal of the UN forces, humbled Israel by the blockade, and deterred her from attacking Syria, exactly as he had been acclaimed in 1956 as the hero who nationalized the Suez Canal, caused the fall of Anthony Eden, and confounded the plans of two great powers allied with Israel.[57]

It must be said that for two weeks after his troop movements began, and particularly after his blockade of the Gulf of Aqaba, Nasser's prestige did rise and the Arab masses thought that the long expected movement of liberating Palestine had come. Nasser scored an easy victory when the UN forces withdrew on May 19 and when Secretary General U Thant came hurriedly to Cairo on May 24 to plead the cause of peace. The tragic aspect of this victory, however, was that it was responsible for Nasser's ultimate defeat. The speedy compliance of U Thant surprised Nasser and confused him because it brought him face to face with the problem of Israeli shipping in the Gulf of Aqaba without giving him time to study the issue. Had Nasser allowed Israel free access to the Gulf while his forces occupied the area overlooking the Straits of Tiran he would have certainly been taunted by the Arabs, even more than when he accepted the presence of the UN emergency forces, and he would have consequently defeated the entire purpose of his military build up. This is why he announced the blockade of the Gulf after the withdrawal of the UN forces. He scored still another victory when his Arab rivals rallied to his cause, and most particularly when King Hussein arrived in Cairo on May 30 and concluded a mutual defense pact with Egypt. This victory also had its tragic aspect, because it produced in Israel the feeling that it was encircled and precipitated the formation of the war cabinet in which Moshe Dayan became minister of defense on June 1, 1967.

It has been said that Nasser acted as if he received the signal from Russia telling him that the conditions were favorable.[58] Certain observers have found a connection between the mysterious three-day visit of the Soviet foreign minister, Andrei Gromyko, to Cairo on March 29, 1967 and Nasser's military movements in May. In the opinion of the American ambassador, Richard Nolte, who was in Cairo during the critical two weeks preceding the war, "the Soviet Union did have a hand in triggering this confrontation with Israel."[59] It was the Soviet government that told Nasser about the massing of Israeli forces near the Syrian border, and it probably agreed with him that Israel should not be allowed to attack Syria again. The Russians stirred the fire in the hope of arousing more anti-Western and pro-Soviet feeling. They wanted in particular to set a trap for the United States so that the more it intervenes or threatens to intervene in favor of Israel, the more its relations with the Arab countries would deteriorate and its interests would be swept away.[60]

Nasser acted in this crisis in his own interest and that of the Soviet Union, but not in that of Palestine and the Arabs. It was as if the Russians prepared the crisis and he executed it without consulting the Arab states who became automatically involved in it. The Soviet Union evidently approved both the withdrawal of UN forces and the blockade of the Gulf of Aqaba, which it considered as a mere return to the position prior to 1956. The Soviet Union and Nasser apparently expected that the United States government would prevail upon Israel to accept the blockade, and that it would restrain Israel more than it ultimately did. The United States viewed the blockade as illegal, and possibly could not, or perhaps did not try hard enough to make Israel accept it.[61] Moreover, the United States evidently had no interest in giving Nasser a triumph that would be eventually accredited to Russian support and that could be used by Nasser against the Arab friends of the United States, especially Saudi Arabia, and ultimately against American interests in the Arabian Peninsula.

Nasser's position hardened and his declarations became more extravagant because of apparent Soviet encouragement. On May 29, after the return of Shamseddin Badran, Egypt's defense minister, from a three-day visit to Moscow, Nasser announced to the national assembly that Prime Minister Kosygin had pledged to stand by Egypt in the battle.[62] Two days before, Nasser was advised by a note from the Soviet ambassador in Cairo not to start the fighting. Nasser was perhaps inclined, in spite of this Soviet double talk that encouraged him and at the same time tried to restrain him, to be optimistic and expect the Soviet Union to lend military support in case of an overwhelming Israeli attack.[63] The movement of Soviet ships into the Mediterranean during the crisis might have had also its share in deceiving Nasser and the Arabs and leading them to think that Russia was going to help them.

B. The Egyptian Defeat and Its Explanation

Nasser can be held responsible for at least five blunders and miscalculations in the crisis that led to the war and to Arab defeat. First, he frivolously allowed himself to be manipulated by the Russians for starting the dangerous crisis without intending to fight. Second, he allowed the crisis to develop by blocking the Gulf of Aqaba without knowing exactly the extent of Russian support in case of war. Third, he thought that the United States would restrain Israel or would persuade her to accept the blockade without realizing that the conditions in 1967 were different from those of 1956. Fourth, he thought that Israel would not fight alone without American military aid and that American participation would automatically lead to Soviet participation and perhaps to a world conflict. He thereby underestimated both the preparedness of Israel and the determination of the United States not to become involved. Fifth, he either ignored the relative weakness and unpreparedness of his own armed forces — which is improbable in view of his many former declarations about the need for more preparation — or, worse, he allowed himself to take an extremely belligerent attitude in spite of what he knew about the condition of his army.

As a result of his blunders, Nasser led the Arabs to the most humiliating defeat — and not mere "setback" — in their modern history. The Six Day War in June 1967 has disproved all Nasser's propaganda and demonstrated the vanity of his and Amer's claim about possessing "the greatest striking force in the Middle East," and about having an air force that "dominates the skies of all the Arab region."[64] The Unified Arab Command established by the summit conferences, the Palestine Liberation Organization, and the mutual defense pacts with Syria and Jordan also proved to be ineffective. The missiles and the rockets developed by the German scientists were not even used, and the billions of dollars' worth of arms including jet fighters and bombers were mostly destroyed before they could be effectively utilized. An estimated 5,000 Egyptians were killed, 4,600 were held as prisoners, and about ten thousand Egyptian soldiers were forced to roam in the Sinai desert for several days before they could reach the Suez Canal. For the first time in the course of the Arab-Israeli conflict, the lands of the belligerent Arab states surrounding Israel were occupied by the Israelis and the Suez Canal remained closed for navigation not because Egypt wanted to keep it closed, but because Israel continued to occupy its eastern bank. A new exodus of over 200,000 Palestinians from the Israeli-occupied western bank aggravated the problem of the refugees and added to their suffering and to the burdens of the Jordanian government. For the first time since the creation of Israel thousands of Egyptians and Syrians also became refugees because their territory was occupied, and some 300,000 Egyptians had to leave their cities in the Egyptian Canal Zone for the Cairo region because of continued hostile attacks after the ceasefire of June 8, 1967.

In the first two days of the war, Egyptian communiqué s were careful not to mention anything about the retreat of the Egyptian forces from Sinai. Nasser sought to give his people an explanation for the disastrous withdrawal and on the second day of the war, June 6, he told the Egyptians and the Arabs that Britain and the United States were providing an air cover for Israel and supporting her militarily. Nasser expected that his charge against the Anglo-Americans would internationalize the conflict and force Russia to enter the war on his side, but Russia disliked what she probably believed to be a bluff and refused to be maneuvered into participation in the war. The charge against the Western powers was believed in Egypt and the other Arab countries and helped maintain Nasser in power. Since then he has acknowledged publicly that the United States and Britain did not send planes against Egypt, but in the meantime certain Arab countries broke their relations with the two powers. Besides Egypt, they were Algeria, Sudan, Iraq, Syria and Yemen, while Lebanon withdrew her ambassador for a short time from Washington and asked the American ambassador to leave Beirut.[65] Nasser's call to cut off the oil and sabotage Anglo-American oil interests was partly obeyed, but only for a brief period.

Several months after the war, responsible Egyptians, including Nasser and his spokesman, Haikal, tried to explain what they called the "June setback." In a series of articles in October 1967, Haikal attributed the land defeat to the fact that the "field officers were too slow to grasp the Israeli offensive tactics and then panicked." For the quasi-complete destruction of the Egyptian air force that left Egypt at the mercy of the enemy, he said that American space satellites and intelligence support helped the Israeli pilots pinpoint the targets in the Egyptian airfields and destroy the planes. The Egyptian military aircraft was harbored in three-sided brick structures and the Israelis knew which was the open vulnerable side for striking from the air. Israeli success, he said, was due to superior planning and intelligence services and communications, and to the fact that Israel jammed the Egyptian radio frequencies and issued false orders so that contacts broke down between the high command and the Egyptian army. The Israeli planes did not come from the Western Desert or from the sea as the Egyptians first thought, but from the direction of Port Said across Lake Burlos through a weak point in the Egyptian air defense.[66] Haikal attributed the lack of coordination in the army and the presence of several centers of power to the circumstances of the formation of the Free Officers' movement and to the precautions that had to be taken to prevent the occurrence of military coups that could threaten the revolution.[67] The Iraqi politician Muhammad Saddiq Shanshal has perhaps explained the defeat more clearly, and also more bluntly and without being apologetic when he described the situation among the Egyptian officers. He mentioned that the reforming regime after the revolution was dependent on the army, and the officers knew it. They felt that they were the protectors of the regime and they consequently asked Field Marshal Amer to grant them various favors, and he did. The officers were busy enjoying what they obtained, and corruption in the army became widespread. The officers as a result did not give sufficient attention to training and military affairs.[68]

In his talk to his troops on the Suez fire line in March 1968, Nasser said that he told the Soviet experts after the war in June to come and "teach us the secrets and methods of employing the arms they gave us."[69] Observers, as a result, have wondered whether the Soviet experts had failed to teach the Egyptian military how to use the arms before the war in June and in the course of the twelve years since the first arms shipments arrived in 1955, or whether the Egyptian military did not learn the secrets of employing the arms between 1955 and 1967 fast enough. One thing seems to be certain. The SAM ground to air anti-aircraft missiles sent by Russia were apparently fired in large number but with little effect; they did not hit their targets. As for the rockets and long-range missiles that were given the impressive names of "the Conqueror" and "the Liberator", it seems that Nasser was fed with fabricated reports on their production and performance, and he became the victim of an elaborate fraud devised by many of his leading officers. Millions of pounds destined for the rocket program were reportedly misappropriated and went to the pockets of Egyptian, German, and Russian officials. When the Egyptian army was moved to Sinai in May, Marshal Amer declared that the Egyptian rockets could destroy any part of Israel. In the first day of the war, when Amer became panicky and ordered the rockets to be used, rockets were not available, and as a result none of the missiles got off the ground.[70]

C. The Consequences of Defeat in Egypt

The defeat in June 1967 was by far the most serious humiliation in Nasser's career. In the past Nasser was always fortunate in gaining victories without fighting, and sometimes even in the midst of defeat as in the Suez war in 1956. The great powers and the Arab states often intervened to save him from his own mistakes. He was also able to find excuses for his setbacks, and these were mostly in his relations with the Arabs. In 1967 he again expected to score a victory without fighting and through a mere display of force, but Israel refused to be intimidated and exploited his miscalculations to the farthest extent, while the United States, the Soviet Union and world opinion did not come to his help. He was consequently obliged to assume responsibility for the defeat for lack of any excuse except that of the alleged British and American collusion with Israel which he later admitted was not true.

The first result of defeat was, therefore, Nasser's resignation on Friday evening June 9, 1968 in a radio-television speech, one day after the ceasefire with Israel had been accepted. In the same speech he again repeated the charge against the Anglo-Americans and their air support for Israel during the war. At the same time, Marshal Amer and the minister of war, Badran, resigned. Nasser's resignation, however, was followed immediately by demonstrations in which thousands of Egyptians went towards his home chanting his name and asking him to stay. The national assembly also held an extraordinary meeting that same night and took a resolution that said "No . . . . no" to Nasser "in the name of the alliance of the working popular forces who have elected us and chose us only because you are their guide and ours." On the following day, June 10, Nasser sent a letter to the national assembly withdrawing his resignation because "the voice of our people," as he said "cannot be rejected."[71]

The resignation, according to certain observers, was a well produced scenario to enable Nasser to regain his popularity. It was also thought to be the result of a struggle for power, or of a plot against Nasser which made him appeal to the people in order to obtain their support. Others have maintained that Nasser's emotional statements along with his dramatic face and sober dignity while making the speech, turned the situation in his favor. There was, moreover, a danger of anarchy and perhaps civil war in a country in full dissolution, and therefore the people wanted him to stay.[72]

Nasser has since then given much importance to the reaction of the people after his resignation and took it for a plebiscite in his favor, or a new *bay'a*. It has been argued, on the other hand, that even if that popular reaction had not been arranged by Nasser and his supporters, it should not be given more importance than it deserves, because, first, it did not represent the general will of the people; second, it was only a spontaneous emotional reaction that occurred before the dimensions of the military disaster were known; third, it occurred under the influence of the belief that there was collusion between the Anglo-Americans and Israel, and Nasser emphasized it in his speech. In a way, Nasser's "bogus resignation" on June 9, 1967 was similar to his offer of March 25, 1954 to dissolve the RCC and end the revolution. In both cases he did not mean what he proposed to do, and the tactical maneuver was expected to elicit a popular reaction that would constitute a vote of confidence for retaining power. The favorable popular reaction was particularly needed after the defeat, because in the following few days certain heads were expected to roll and Nasser wanted to make sure that his head was not among them. He needed sufficient backing and strength to protect himself and to make some difficult decisions.

The second result of the war in June 1967 for Nasser and Nasserism was the dismissal of Marshal Amer and other high ranking commanding officers, and the struggle for power that led to Amer's attempted coup d'état in August 1967 as well as various attempts on Nasser's life. On Sunday June 11, 1967, one day after Nasser withdrew his resignation, Marshal Amer, who had resigned on June 9, was replaced by Lt. Gen. Muhammad Fawzi as deputy commander in chief, and there was speculation that Nasser was under pressure to dismiss his closest friend and designated successor.[73] Amer and Badran, the minister of war, evidently insisted after the debacle on an investigation, whose results would be made public, into the developments and the decisions that led to the war, and a struggle ensued between them and Salah Nasr, the head of military intelligence who was responsible for believing the misleading communications through the secret KGB channel to Moscow, while Amer and Badran mistrusted them. Salah Nasr was evidently able to gather more political power and both Amer and Badran were dismissed.[74] It was only on September 7 that Salah Nasr's turn came. He was dismissed because "his office deviated from its duties."

The three commanders of the land, air, and sea forces were dismissed at the same time as Amer, and by June 23, some 800 officers were said to have been relieved of their duties and some of them were expected to be tried, especially the higher officers of the air force.[75] Among the causes of dismissal were those of alleged treason, sabotage, and collusion of the higher officers with Israel in a deliberate attempt to remove Nasser. As an illustration of the sabotage and treason, it was reported that when the pilots were asked why they did not take off the first day of the war, they answered that they never received orders. A further cause for the purging of the officers was the alleged Soviet intervention to remove the "military bourgeoisie" and the anti-socialist commanders against whom criticism was voiced by the Russians.[76] The dismissals were often sudden and brutal, and they were resented especially when they were ordered by the Russian experts.

At the end of August 1967, while Nasser was attending the Arab summit conference at Khartoum, it was disclosed that he had foiled an attempted coup to overthrow him before leaving Cairo in the weekend of 25-27 August. Fifty officers and four members of the national assembly were arrested in connection with the plot, while Amer was placed under house arrest. Amer and the top officers had evidently planned the coup because they felt that they were made the scapegoats for the defeat, and they wanted to return to their positions and to halt the investigation of the conduct of the war.[77] The charges against the men involved in the plot were made by the public prosecutor on January 22, 1968 in a show trial reported on television. Twelve of the principal defendants were in the dock, and Hussein Shafii presided over the court. The prosecutor mentioned that the conspiracy of Amer and the other defendants began right after the defeat in June and amounted to treason. The coup was scheduled for August 27, 1967, but the arrests were made two days before. The conspirators had set up a stronghold near the Pyramids and prepared to capture some government leaders like Z. Muhieddin and Ali Sabri, and to seize control of four key military headquarters. Among the ring leaders were Badran, Abbas Radwan, former interior minister, Jalal Hreidi, commander of storm troops, and Salah Nasr, chief of military intelligence. The prosecutor represented Amer as a real conspirator in the plot, not an unwilling supporter. He offered sanctuary to the officers in his villa in Giza which was converted into an arsenal of weapons, and his men fired at the security officials who approached the villa. Amer also allegedly engaged several clerks to prepare leaflets and tracts in support of the coup.[78]

Marshal Amer committed suicide on September 14, 1967 shortly after the discovery of the plot and long before the beginning of the trial. The National Guidance ministry broadcast the news of his death on September 15 and described it as "a regrettable and painful incident." It mentioned that he had taken large quantities of toxic products. Amer had been under house arrest since August 26. On September 13, two generals went to question him about the plot and about the causes of defeat and they were told that he took poison. He was then taken to a rest house and the poison was pumped out, but on September 14 he took another dose that was hidden under a piece of plaster on his body. He was buried in his village, Astal, in the province of Minya south of Cairo.

According to a document that is said to be his last testament, Amer had explained to Nasser before his arrest that he had no intention to make a coup, that the visits of officers to his home had nothing to do with politics, and that if he had wanted to seize power he would not have resigned.[79] Amer explained that it was not enough for Nasser to stand up and take full responsibility for the defeat; he "should have explained to the people how the decisions that led to the destruction of our army were taken." This is why Amer resigned. He told Nasser he was prepared to prove his innocence in any military court, but Nasser refused and sent him investigators to his villa. He wanted him to be silent about the events leading to the war. Amer, according to this document, did not think of suicide and claimed that he received threats to silence him forever if he ventured to talk. Amer ended his testament by blaming Nasser for neglecting Egypt altogether, and this was, according to Amer, "the cause of our failure." Amer's suicide has been doubted even before the appearance of this document which, if genuine, offers a strong indication that he was murdered.

Amer's death led to more arrests of officers and civilians and was followed by the trial of the prominent former commanders of the air force who were: the air commander Muhammad Sidqy Mahmud, the air force chief of staff Jamal Afifi, the vice air marshals Ismail Labib and Hamid Dogheishy. On February 20, 1968 the sentences were given. Muhammad Sidqy Mahmud received fifteen years in jail for negligence in the performance of duty, but the exact charges were not known, Ismail Labib received ten years, while the two others were acquitted.

Discontent among the officers, many of whom were loyal

to Amer, was widespread because of the disgrace that fell on them. They resented the diminished respect and prerogatives accorded to the military to the point that some of them did not wear their uniforms in the streets. They were irritated by the large scale dismissals and transfers and by the authority given to the more than one thousand military Soviet advisers in the armed forces. Two conspiracies to kill Nasser were said to have been organized by officers, with civilian help, and they were both discovered between the beginning of May and the end of June 1968. The first conspiracy was organized by eight officers, who were arrested, and a high judge who escaped to Libya. It was scheduled for May 2, when Nasser was expected to cast his vote near Alexandria in a plebiscite on the government's policies. It was not reported in the Egyptian press. The second conspiracy was reportedly thwarted in June and involved thirty-five army and police officers and civilians who were all arrested. The conspirators planned to kidnap Nasser from his rest house at Maamura on the eastern outskirts of Alexandria, where he had been spending his weekends since the beginning of May, and to shoot him after a summary trial, and then overthrow his regime.[80]

The third important result of the defeat for Nasser and Nasserism was the change in the Egyptian attitude towards Nasser, and the growth of dissidence expressed in mass demonstrations and in the demand for change in the system of government. Nasser lost his charisma with the army and with the citizens. He was no longer infallible in the eyes of the masses as a military strategist and a national hero. On February 24, 1968 the most serious mass demonstrations against Nasser's regime since 1952 began at the military factory complex at Helwan, south of Cairo, where many persons were killed. The bloody clash at Helwan led to demonstrations of thousands of students in Cairo and Alexandria where the slogans called for democracy with a multi-party system, a civilian cabinet, freedom of the press, and the abolition of the national assembly and of the socialist union. The demonstrators also denounced the lenient sentences of February 20 against the air commanders. The demonstrations developed into a violent anti-government performance where chants against Nasser and anti-Soviet slogans were heard and stones were thrown at the besieged *al-Ahram* offices in protest against the tight press censorship and against Muhammad Hassanein Haikal, Nasser's spokesman and complacent servant. The government tried to portray the demonstrations as a patriotic reaction against the sentences, but they were more than that. They meant resentment against the military caste that had been ruling Egypt since 1952, and a vote of non-confidence in the Egyptian government. They also represented a delayed manifestation of frustration and indignation of the students and workers for the defeat, and they meant to undermine the government.[81] The government closed the universities on February 25, but it attempted to placate the students by releasing the arrested demonstrators, ordering a retrial of the air commanders - which meant casting doubt on the process of justice in Nasser's regime - and emphasizing in the press that fifty policemen and only twenty demonstrators were injured in the riots.

The appointment of a new cabinet on March 20, 1968 was an indirect result of the demonstrations. Nasser remained prime minister and named fourteen new civilian ministers, many of whom were western-educated and seven of them were university officials, but the important portfolios of foreign affairs and interior were still in the hands of Nasser's former military officers. Shafii remained vice premier, and Ali Sabri was still secretary general of the socialist union, but Zakaria Muhieddin was no longer in the cabinet. The students were dissatisfied because no essential changes were made in the formation of the cabinet or in the political system. Ten days later, on March 30, 1968, Nasser announced a program of political reconstruction and national liberation in a televised speech from the Qubba Palace and called on the Egyptians to vote on it in a referendum on May 2, 1968. The program was assigned attractive and impressive goals: to mobilize the military and economic forces in order to liberate the land, and to mobilize the masses and all their possibilities for liberation. The program generally showed that Nasserist institutions and Nasser's methods and maneuvers remained the same. The socialist union was described in the program as the most appropriate instrument for mobilizing popular forces on a democratic basis. The program expected to elect a congress of delegates of the socialist union by popular vote, and to draft a constitution later by that congress, but it would go into effect only after the withdrawal of Israel from Egyptian territory. Half of the seats in the congress were to be given to farmers and laborers. The new program promised to give greater incentives in industry, and a greater measure of freedom of the press and of personal freedom.

The general impression among intellectuals was that this program of action did not go far enough. It maintained the one party system and did not want to open a debate on whether the socialist union should continue as the only political base. The government, however, was confident, in spite of its awareness of criticism, that it could appease its critics because it was convinced that it still enjoyed the loyalty of the masses. Nasser continued to have a certain mass appeal and was believed to be the only leader capable of binding the elements of Egyptian society together.

In the referendum held on May 2, 1968 for voting on Nasser's program for "the liberation of the land," official results showed that 98.2 percent of the registered voters participated, and that the program was approved by 99.989% of those who voted. The minister of interior, Sharawi Gum'a, a former intelligence officer, commented that the vote was "an affirmation of the revolution and a massive response to counter-revolutionary forces." The critics naturally viewed the whole referendum and the program of action itself as another Nasserist tactical maneuver to obtain a new mandate from the people and to demonstrate their confidence in his own person.[82]

One month after the referendum, Nasser and Ali Sabri proceeded to settle accounts with some critics of the regime.

On June 2, 1968 it was reported from Beirut that twenty-six members of the socialist union, some of whom were members of the national assembly, were purged because they "deviated from the principles of the national charter" and failed to carry out party decisions. One of those purged was Ahmad Said, the well known speaker from the Voice of the Arabs radio, because he apparently criticized the regime in private. It might be thus concluded that the demonstrations, the criticism, the growth of dissidence, and the changed attitude of students and intellectuals have succeeded neither in changing Nasser's basic ideas and institutions, nor in weakening his authority and his determination to claim fabulous majorities in the game of popular referendums.

The elections for the national congress of the socialist union took place on July 14, 1968 directly after Nasser's return from a visit to Moscow (July 4-12), and 1648 members were elected. The new congress of the one party organization held its first session on September 14 and elected the 150-member central committee of the socialist union of whom twenty-five were appointed by Nasser. Two months later, Nasser decided to dissolve the national assembly of 360 members whose five-year term would have ended in March 1969. It was said at the time that the national assembly had lost its prestige after the defeat and that many of its members were not even elected for the membership of the national congress of the socialist union. On January 10, 1969 a new national assembly was elected and a majority of the new members were supporters of Nasser.

Nasser's program of action of March 30, 1968 did not remove the causes of student unrest and in November 1968 rioting broke out again among high school and university students, particularly in the cities of Mansoura and Alexandria. After the riots of February 1968 the students resented the ban on public demonstrations and the authoritarian way by which the government regulated their conduct. They expressed their contempt for what they called "the society of coined slogans" produced by the state-directed press, and they were unhappy with the system of job placements that often assigned the university graduates to fields for which they were unprepared. Their demands for a liberal change in government institutions remained unanswered, while the election of a new congress of the socialist union and of a new central committee were not what they had asked for. Moreover, the forces opposed to socialism and to Soviet influence played their role in student ranks, and similarly those who were expelled from the socialist union tried to provoke student unrest.

The immediate cause of the riots was the new law that tried to raise educational standards by tightening the conditions of promotion from one class to another and restricting the students' right to take the examinations if they failed twice in passing them. On November 21, 1968, about 5000 students of secondary and religious schools demonstrated in Mansoura and were joined by non-students with the possible encouragement of the Muslim Brotherhood. The police opened fire on them as they marched on police headquarters and four youths were killed. The movement soon became one of political protest and on November 23 it spread to Alexandria where the students took over the engineering school. The demands for political parties and a free press were voiced by the demonstrators who also protested against the harsh treatment of students in Mansoura. The riots in Alexandria, according to observers, were the most violent in recent memory and were reminiscent of Black Saturday (the "burning of Cairo") on January 26, 1952. The demonstrators burned or destroyed buses and street cars, and damaged stores and police stations. On November 24 the six universities in Egypt and fourteen other higher schools were closed, but on the following day a battle between the police and several thousand school boys in Alexandria ended with the death of sixteen youths.

The riots of November were ruthlessly put down and resulted in twenty persons killed and some 400 wounded. Nasser did not show in this case the sympathy and patience that he had shown towards the demonstrators in February. The riots were directed against everything that characterized his regime and this is why his government tried to put the blame on "mysterious hands" and external forces. In the emergency session of the congress of the socialist union in December 1968, the interior minister gave a report on the extent of the damage done, and the congress passed a resolution saying that the "shameful events" of Mansoura and Alexandria were the result of a "Zionist-colonialist-reactionary plot." The riots were particularly painful to the leaders of the Egyptian revolution because they were made by the generation that was brought up under the revolution. Many members of this generation, however, in their gloom and uncertainty about their future, expressed their dissatisfaction with the regime as they exclaimed, "We lost the war and we still have Nasser and the police state!"

A fourth result of the defeat in June 1967 has been the change in Nasser's position in the Arab world, and in Nasser's policies and attitudes towards the other Arab states. In the Arab world and among the Arab people, the position and prestige of Nasser and the Nasserist system were seriously weakened. The Arabs were generally dismayed by the incompetence, blunders, and corruption of the Nasserist regime and had no more illusions about the myth of Nasser's striking force or about Nasser's infinite and infallible wisdom. Certain manifestations of pro-Nasserist feeling could still be seen at times, and in some Arab circles Nasser was still at least a respected symbol of the revolution, but the fanatic admiration and confidence in Nasser were past memories, while intensified criticism of his system was more widely heard.

Nasserist policies towards the Arab states underwent a serious change. Egypt could no longer afford to denounce the conservative rulers as reactionary and portray them as the agents of imperialism. It was no longer able to spread the gospel of revolution in their countries and appeal to the masses to destroy them. Nasser needed the friendship and the moral and financial support of the Arab states. He had to agree to a summit meeting of the Arab heads of state suggested by King Hussein. In the summit conference that met at Khartoum on August 29-31, 1967 to discuss the means for "erasing the consequences of aggression," Nasser, who used to be the most influential among the revolutionary leaders, showed more moderation than Iraq, and certainly more than Syria who refused to participate in the conference, and Algeria whose president refused to attend. In a concession to the Arab oil-producing conservative regimes, Nasser accepted to lift the oil embargo against the United States and Britain, and thereby opposed the radical economic sanctions against the supporters of Israel which Iraq had recommended at the Arab economic conference in Baghdad on August 15-20, 1967. In a bilateral agreement with King Faisal of Saudi Arabia, which did not appear in the resolutions of the conference, Nasser accepted to evacuate Yemen before December 15, 1967 and to recognize tacitly that the Arabian Peninsula would not be viewed as Egypt's sphere of influence.[83] The conference gave Egypt $266 million in financial aid supplied by Saudi Arabia, Libya, and Kuwait. This was officially intended to compensate Egypt for her loss of Suez Canal revenues and other war ravages, but it was also meant to be a reward to Nasser for accepting the compromise on lifting the oil embargo and on the withdrawal from Yemen. The conference was rather humiliating to Nasser as well as to Russia, because it was an admission of failure in Yemen, and King Faisal emerged in it as the real victor.

The Arab world has remained divided into conservative and revolutionary camps, and Nasser's Egypt has remained naturally in the latter. Nasser, however, unlike the radical Baath in Syria, was not only ready to cooperate with all the Arab regimes, including the conservative ones, but he also called at times for that cooperation. Shortly after the war in June, Egyptian diplomatic relations were re-established with Tunisia after they had been broken in October 1966. Nasser also agreed that Shuqairi should leave the PLO after a conference of heads of Arab commando groups in Cairo in December 1967.[84] Nasser was more conciliatory with his former Arab rivals and, in trying to find a solution for Israel's occupation of

Arab lands, he seemed to cooperate more with Hussein of Jordan than with the Baath of Syria. In early May 1968, he refused to be persuaded by the president of the radical regime in Syria to leave out Jordan in the Arab plans of military cooperation.[85] He saw the need to reenforce the eastern front and to assure the cooperation between Iraq, Jordan, Syria and Lebanon. Nasser began to act as a mediator and moderator in situations in which he would have acted as an instigator before June 1967. He tried, for example, to reconcile General Asad with his Baath colleagues in Syria in March 1969, and helped freeze Asad's coup. He sent his personal representative, Hasan Sabri al-Khawli, to help solve the crisis between the government of Lebanon and the Palestinian commando organizations after the demonstrations of April 23 and 25, 1969 in the cities of Lebanon and the ministerial crisis that followed.

One of the important developments after June 1967 was the rise in the importance of the Palestinian commandos because of their militant drive against Israel. Until the first months of 1968, Egypt viewed guerilla activity as of little importance but later reversed its attitude and on April 10, 1968 Nasser declared that his country was prepared to support and arm the Palestine resistance movement in guerilla operations. After more than a year of inactivity on the Suez ceasefire line, Egypt began in early September and especially in late October 1968 to challenge the Israeli forces on the eastern side of the canal. The artillery duels and commando raids across the canal escalated after March 1969. It was said that Nasser reacted to criticism about the lack of Egyptian activity and that the accumulation of internal pressures prompted him to provide a military outlet. Nasser also reacted to the rising popularity of Yasser Arafat, leader of al-Fateh commandos and of the PLO, and wanted to tell the Egyptians that Egypt did not leave the fighting entirely to the Palestinian commandos. Other factors that contributed to the continued exchanges across the canal were, first, to prevent Israeli construction work on the eastern side of the canal and the bringing of more material, and second, to impress the four great powers that began consultations for finding an agreeable peace formula in early April 1969 with the urgency of imposing a settlement based on the UN Security Council resolution of November 22, 1967.

The Egyptian commando raids across the canal and the escalation of artillery attacks brought Israeli retaliation that showed the inadequacy of the Egyptian defense system and the lack of sufficient discipline and vigilance. The Israeli commando raid on October 30, 1968 into the region of Qena in Upper Egypt was followed by the raids of April 29 and June 29, 1969 into the Upper Nile valley and by attacks on coastguard posts on the Gulf of Suez. On June 17, 1969 Israeli jet fighters flew over Cairo for photographic reconnaissance without being challenged and the Egyptian air force commander, Mustafa al-Hinnawi, was dismissed for inattention to duty. The Soviet Union had to make it clear in the stern language of the *Pravda* on December 3, 1968 that the Israeli raid of October 30, 1968 to the north of Aswan was a risky step and that it reserved the right to prevent another war in the Middle Eastern area that adjoins its southern borders. The Soviet Union had also to send a note to Cairo on May 8, 1969, as a result of the exchange of commando and artillery attacks in April, recommending that the ceasefire agreement should be carried out. The visits of the Soviet foreign minister, Andrei Gromyko, to Cairo in December 1968 and June 1969 indicated that the Soviet Union did not want the "controlled chaos" to degenerate into another war. Its consultations with Nasser and its answer to the American peace plan in June after Gromyko's visit to Cairo also indicated that it was seeking to obtain for Nasser a peace settlement that he could accept and that would preserve for him his dignity and self respect and for the Soviet Union its special position in Egypt and the Arab countries. Nasser also had to talk occasionally of war and of action against Israel, and while he privately indicated that he favored a peaceful settlement, he sometimes made belligerent speeches in order to retain the confidence of his country and of the militant Arabs. His failure to achieve progress towards Israeli withdrawal from the occupied territories, or towards a sensational display of military strength, as well as the daring raids of Israeli commandos and the downing of Egyptian planes have contributed to a further decline in his prestige.

The fifth result of the war in June 1967 involves the change in relations between the Nasserist regime and the great powers and a modification of the Nasserist attitude towards Israel. The military and diplomatic defeat suffered by Nasserist Egypt has marked the failure of Nasser's non-alignment policy which he had been proclaiming since 1955, and resulted in a shift from that pretended non-alignment to open dependence on the Soviet Union, and even to the acceptance of a measure of Soviet influence in his military establishment. This shift was naturally accompanied by more marked hostility to the United States, and by the expansion of Soviet influence in the Arab socialist states, with more frequent demonstrations of Soviet support expressed by the visits of the Soviet fleet to the ports of Egypt and Syria and even the Persian Gulf. This shift in policy has strengthened the view that Israel's security is a part of American national security, that the Arab menace to Israel meant the furthering of communist penetration, and that Israel was playing the role of defender of threatened American and Western interests against Russian expansion in the area.[86] The Middle Eastern confrontation between Israel and the Arabs, according to this view, has assumed the aspect of an American-Russian confrontation of national interests, and the crisis that preceded the war in June was a Russian challenge to the West and its interests. Israel, in accepting the challenge, has prevented the Middle East from becoming a second Vietnam and caused the Western position to improve, while it enabled the United States "to afford the luxury of doing nothing."[87] Israel's victory in this view, averted the danger to the United States position and was also "a victory for the West."[88]

Whether the Soviet Union intentionally lured the Arabs to a humiliating defeat or not,[89] its opportunistic attitude created bitterness and disillusionment in the Arab countries. In allowing the crisis to develop, with the consent of the Russians, Nasser evidently thought only of the expected easy victory but not of Israel's dangerous reaction. When the reaction took place and Israel fought and won in the first two days, Nasser thought that the Russians would still do something because they could not possibly allow him and the Arabs to be defeated by Israel. It is related that when Russia accepted the proposed cease fire on Wednesday June 7, Nasser was unable to control his rage and, in a stormy meeting with the Soviet ambassador, he threatened to let the United States hold the Middle East "as long as you abandoned us," as he said, adding that the Russians have proved that there were not two great powers but one super power only, the United States, "and you come far behind."[90] The Arabs were not alone in their disillusionment and surprise. Observers everywhere commented on the Soviet Union's bad intelligence estimates and calculations, and even raised questions on the competence of the Russian training missions in Egypt and Syria and on the value of Russian equipment.

The Russians were aware of the Arab reaction and could not afford to lose their preeminent position in Egypt, Syria, and Iraq. They immediately set out to repair their injured prestige and to impress the Arabs with their moral and material support. Between June 10 and 23, 1967 the Russians made four friendly gestures that they thought would regain for them the good will of the Arabs. On June 10 the Soviet Union and the communist nations of eastern Europe, except Rumania, broke diplomatic relations with Israel. In Cairo, the editorialist of *al-Akhbar,* Muhammad al-Tabii, commented, "Israel couldn't care less!" In another move, Prime Minister Kosygin asked for an emergency meeting of the UN General Assembly, and on June 19 presented a draft resolution asking for Israeli withdrawal from all occupied territories and the payment of damages. On June 21, the central committee of the communist party under Brezhnev issued a statement in

Moscow supporting the Arabs, and on the same day the president of the presidium of the USSR, Podgorny, visited Egypt.

Nasser's Egypt similarly could not afford to leave the people with the conviction that the leader of world socialism, the Soviet Union, has failed socialist Egypt. This is why efforts were made before Podgorny's visit, in the socialist union and in the press, to make the people believe that Russia could not have supported Egypt more than it did without starting a nuclear war.[91] Soviet propaganda also asserted that it was the Soviet warning that forced a halt to Israeli aggression and saved the regimes in Cairo and Damascus from being overthrown. Russia was very soon able to re-establish its position in Egypt and the Arab Middle East by airlifting and shipping sorely needed arms to replace the military equipment that was lost in the short war. A succession of Arab heads of state and ministers of defense visited Moscow between June and August 1967 to discuss their needs and press for Soviet help. Even King Hussein, described as the first pro-Western King to visit Moscow, was promised arms and aid during his visit on October 4, 1967, but he decided later not to get involved. Soviet warships visited Alexandria and Port Said on July 10 and October 27, 1967 in a demonstration of friendship and support and as a deterrent to the threat of Israeli attacks across the Canal. Arab bitterness against the Soviet government soon gave place to praise when twelve Arab ambassadors in Moscow declared at the end of June their "heart felt gratitude" to the Soviet Union that "furnished fresh evidence of material, moral, and political support and friendship."[92]

Two developments have shown how the Soviet Union has taken advantage of the new situation created by the war in June and sought to extend the political drive that began in 1955 in Egypt and Western Asia. The first was the expansion of Soviet naval power and the increase of the units of the Soviet fleet in the Mediterranean. The movements of the Soviet fleet in the Eastern Mediterranean and its frequent visits to Egyptian and other Arab ports have led to speculation about the establishment of Soviet bases in Alexandria and

Port Said, or at least the utilization of various facilities in the Egyptian ports. Moreover, the British evacuation of Aden in November 1967 and the continued Soviet support of republican Yemen along with the Russian desire to build up its influence in the Indian Ocean have made it necessary for the Soviet Union to speed the opening of the Suez Canal in order to make it easier for Soviet ships to sail down the Red Sea and the southern shores of Arabia to the Persian Gulf where Soviet ships were seen in May 1968. It is ironic that whereas the closing of the Suez Canal in the past caused serious concern for the Western powers, and Egypt used it as a means of pressure on those powers in order to stop aggression or to obtain a favorable settlement, as in 1956, the same action by Nasser at the beginning of the war in June 1967 left the West largely indifferent and obliged the Nasserist regime and the Soviet Union to seek a way for its opening because of Egyptian financial pressures and Soviet strategic considerations. It is now Israel and not Egypt who can use the opening of the Canal as a means of bargaining, knowing that it is a major necessity for Cairo and Moscow. It is also significant that the expansion of Russian forces in the Mediterranean following the recent crisis has led some Western strategists to worry about turning the southern flank of the North Atlantic Organization by the Soviet Union, exactly as it turned the southern flank of the Baghdad Pact countries after the first arms deal with Egypt in 1955.

The second development was the increase in the number and caliber of Soviet military advisers and experts in influential positions in the Egyptian army and air force. This was the result of the accelerated arms deliveries that had replaced about 80 per cent of the Egyptian war material by January 1968. From about 500 Soviet advisers and officers before the war in June, the number is said to have reached 1500, and some say 3,000, in early 1968. Some of them were taken from key positions in Russia.[93] The Soviet advisory officers are said to have assumed increasing control of the selection of officers for promotion with the resulting ability to mold the armed forces. Moreover, Russian circles have blamed the defeat of Egypt on what they called the "military bourgeoisie" and on the "defeatism" of military commanders and politicians hostile to Nasser's socialist program. They have argued for the reorganization of Egypt along more proletarian and pro-Soviet socialist lines, and the removal of what they called opportunistic nationalist elements and the appointment of elements loyal to Russia.[94]

The almost unsolvable problem of the United States with Nasserism and the Arabs in general has continued to be its close association with, and support of Israel. American effective action against the expansion of Soviet influence in the Arab states has thus been rendered impotent.[95] The resumption of arms deliveries to Israel in addition to the exaggerated Israeli reports on Soviet inroads into the Arab world in order to obtain more American arms, have effectively contributed to make these inroads deeper and to render American counter-action still more difficult. Yet, in spite of the Soviet penetration that every Israeli success tends to strengthen, no communist satellite regime has been established in any Arab country. Several Arab states, on the other hand, have maintained strong ties with the Western powers because of the Arab cautious attitude towards the Soviet Union and Nasserism. The fear of socialism and the loss of economic and personal freedom have been determining factors in obliging many Arab states and Arab groups and personalities to overcome their hostility to the American association with Israel and maintain good relations with the United States. Even in Egypt itself, an article by Nasser's unofficial spokesman, Haikal, has stated only two months after the war in June that it was essential to have diplomatic relations with the United States to balance Cairo's international policy. Haikal added that Egypt cannot afford a head-on crash with the United States, for even the Soviet Union has avoided it.[96] Nasser might have wanted to restore full diplomatic relations with the United States, but according to a report, the Soviet ambassador, Sergei Vinogradov, disapproved and even rejected the attempt in early 1968.⁹⁷ Relations with Britain were restored on October 22, 1967.

The United States has also continued to support its old Arab friends but with more caution. It ended the arms embargo only to the Arab states that were not neighbors of Israel soon after the war ended, and it was only in early June 1968 that it agreed to resume the shipments of arms to Jordan. The new development in some Arab countries such as Morroco, Tunisia and Kuwait is that the Soviet Union has extended its economic diplomacy to them, while in the Sudan, the Russians have been equipping and training the army.

A significant change in the Arab attitude towards Israel, as well as a kind of Arab self-examination have resulted from the war in June 1967. It was no longer Bourguiba of Tunisia alone who could criticize the Arab talk on wiping out Israel and the Arab policies "that have deprived them of all sympathy to the extent that no nation wanted to consider Israel an aggressor."⁹⁸ The Egyptian editorial writer, Ahmad Bahauddin, in his critical analysis of the Egyptian "setback" in *al-Musawar,* two weeks after the end of the war, stated that the Arab slogan on destroying Israel made it easy for Israel to win the propaganda war. In their conferences, declarations, and resolutions since June 1967, the Arabs have defined their goal as "erasing the consequences of aggression," which meant the withdrawal of Israel from the newly occupied Arab lands, but the slogan on the destruction of Israel was no longer mentioned. Arab leaders, moreover, have indicated in their peace proposals in November 1967, and February and April 1969 their readiness to recognize Israel as "a fact of life" and a reality, to end all belligerency, and to respect the territorial integrity and the sovereignty and independence of all states including Israel on condition that it withdraw from the territories occupied in June 1967.⁹⁹

On June 14, 1968, the editorialist Haikal described the erroneous Arab strategy in June 1967, and presented a picture of what their goal and their strategy should be in the future.¹⁰⁰ He first said that Arab strategy in June 1967 was not the mere repulse of Israel but its destruction. The Arabs wanted to realize an unlimited goal at a time when even the United States could not realize such a goal in Vietnam. The words that the Arabs spoke, said Haikal, went far beyond their intention and were, moreover, far above their ability. The result was that the reaction they produced in the world was favorable to Israel. In thinking of the future, he believed that a total confrontation that would use extreme force to reach a final and decisive solution in the Arab-Israel struggle was almost impossible.

VI. The Two Sides of the Coin

The story of the Egyptian revolution has been one of successful achievements as well as disastrous failures, but the failures have outweighed the successes, and these were often negative and of no real value to Egypt and the Egyptians. The revolutionary leaders, with Nasser at their head, strove to give Egypt a legitimate place among the sovereign modern nations of the world and proclaimed their adoption of the principle of non-alignment in the cold war in order to assure their freedom of independent action. They ended by bringing upon Egypt the most painful humiliation in its modern history in the war in June 1967 and made Egypt dependent militarily, economically and diplomatically on the Soviet Union, and allowed their country to become the mainspring of Soviet influence in the Arab world.

According to its first statement issued in the name of General Naguib on the morning of July 23, 1952, the revolution was a protest against corruption and government instability that influenced the army and led to its defeat in Palestine in 1948. The revolution was also, according to the ultimatum addressed to King Farouk on July 26, 1952, a protest against the king's misconduct and his tampering with the constitution, and against the lack of security for the individual's life, property, and dignity. Under the revolution, however, government was virtually by decree and the individual's life, property, and dignity were even less respected than under Farouk. The misconduct of Farouk, moreover, touched primarily his own personal reputation and extended to a few suspicious deals that brought him some extra millions to spend on his pleasures and on gambling. The misconduct of the revolutionary rulers extended to much more. Their pleasures were of a different kind, and their gambling was harmful in many ways and touched the whole country and even beyond. They spent extravagantly on foreign military adventures and conspiracies, and they wasted their time combatting internal enemies and reactionaries, real and imaginary, and holding show trials. They allowed corruption to spread in the civil and military administration. The resulting weakness and disorganization led not to one, but to two military defeats in Palestine, in 1956 and 1967, and the second of these was by far more serious for Egypt than that of 1948 because it caused the occupation of Egyptian territory and untold misery for hundreds of thousands of Egyptians.

Nasser's great achievement in the revolutionary era, according to a prominent leader of the Baath party, was to place Egypt in the main stream of Arab nationalism, and to assume the leadership of the Arab nationalist movement and "open his heart to all the Arab progressive and liberation movements and support them."[101] The movement of Arab unity under Nasser's leadership, however, has failed. The Nasserist effort to realize Arab unity and solidarity degenerated into a crusade for spreading socialism and revolution which Nasserism considered a prerequisite for Arab unity. Nasser's support for what was called progressive and liberation movements took the form of a campaign to overthrow the non-conformist regimes and ended in civil wars and internal struggles, because progressivism and liberation in the Nasserist concept meant socialism, class warfare, one party rule, and non-alignment in the Nasserist style. Nasserism could not settle for less even though some of the states subjected to these campaigns, like Lebanon and Jordan, and Syria before the Baath regime, were otherwise progressive and liberated. The Arab world under Nasserist leadership thus witnessed a cold war in which disunity, intrigue and quarrels reached a stage hitherto unknown to the Arabs since the age of decadence at the end of the Middle Ages.

The Egyptian officers under Nasser's leadership were the first among the Arab leaders of military coups since 1936 to undertake certain revolutionary actions and measures that have been imitated by others and have become an established standard of revolutionary behavior and achievement. First among these actions was the law of agrarian reform of September 9, 1952 and the destruction of big landlordism along with the political influence of the landowners. Second, the Egyptian revolutionary regime was the first among the Arab military regimes to purchase arms from the communist bloc and to begin an era of friendly relations with the Soviet Union, and of public defiance of the Western powers and their Arab allies. Third, the Egyptian revolution embarked on a policy of non-alignment to assert its political emancipation and allow itself to play a world role, and also to obtain economic and financial aid from both East and West. This policy eventually failed when it began to play the game of the Soviet Union at the expense of Arab interests and led to the miscalculations that caused the disastrous war of June 1967 and to Egyptian dependence on the Soviet Union. Fourth, the Egyptian revolutionary regime was the first to nationalize foreign interests on a large scale beginning with the Suez Canal Company and continuing with various other companies every time Egypt quarreled with a foreign country, as in the case of the Belgian interests in 1961. Fifth, the Egyptian revolution was the first to intervene openly and unabashedly in the affairs of other Arab states under the pretext of defending Arab interests everywhere and of supporting progressive and liberation movements. Intervention went to the extent of inciting people to revolt against their legitimate rulers and provoking civil wars in which Egypt intervened militarily to support one faction against another.

The sixth among the "firsts" of the Egyptian revolutionary regime was the official adoption of the socialist system, first with the socialist laws of July 1961 and then with the Charter of May 1962, and the use of distinct Marxian language in support of the inevitability of the socialist revolution. Egypt thus set the example for other Arab states and provided the encouragement for large scale nationalizations, and for the destruction of capitalism and private enterprise that became the mark of revolutionary status and the symbol of opposition to the West. It is doubtful if any Arab state, including Baathist Syria, could have imposed socialism independently without the encouragement and sometimes the pressure of Nasserism. Nasserist Egypt, moreover, introduced along with socialism those slogans that made wealth and capitalism synonymous with reaction and treason, and associated the "reactionaries" with imperialism and Zionism. The seventh innovation of the revolutionary regime in Egypt was not entirely new since it was known under other Arab regimes, but not on such a large scale. It included a series of stratagems in government such as the one party organization that served as a popular base and a source of support for the regime, the series of constitutions that were all presented by the government and approved by a plebiscite, the extensive use of referendums for presidential elections where only one candidate was presented, and finally the holding of public and often televised trials of the enemies of the regime. It must be said that most of these "firsts" were copied from the totalitarian European systems and especially from the communist regimes.

These revolutionary innovations and actions were not all beneficial to Egypt and to the Egyptians. Most of them, such as the socialist system, extensive industrialization, the liquidation of foreign interests, and non-alignment in its pro-Sovietic aspect have either remained controversial, or have proved to be harmful. The Egyptian intervention in the affairs of other Arab states has been particularly disastrous to Egypt as well as to the states involved. Some of these measures, however, have decidedly benefited Nasser personally, and have given him stature and prestige and added a short-lived popularity and lustre to his regime. Nasser succeeded in firing Arab imagination when he defied the West in the arms deal and the nationalization of the Suez Canal Company and became overnight the acknowledged leader of the Arabs. The Arabs were not as much impressed by his agrarian reform or by the building of the Aswan Dam as by the action that made of him the symbol of their freedom from Western influence. In their weakness, they thought they had found the man who would defend their dignity, satisfy their need for outside admiration, and correct their injustices and restore Arab rights in Palestine. He did not rise eventually to the level of their expectations, and many far sighted Arabs began to see in him, even in the midst of his success, the signs of a false prophet and a charlatan.

The success of the Egyptian revolution and the first victories of the Nasserist regime must be attributed to a certain extent to Nasser's great tactical skill, his courage, self confidence, cunning, and prudence that made of him a shrewd and effective conspirator. It is actually as a conspirator that he began his career. Nasser knew how to recruit his fellow free officers and how to command the obedience and loyalty of his colleagues in the Revolution Command Council, and then how to drop them one by one when they outlived their usefulness or thought of questioning his policy. He was able to prepare his plans in secret and then surprise the world with his decisions. He mobilized the right persons at the right time to act for him against his opponents and then disclaimed any previous knowledge of their action or any relation to it. He was flexible in his relations with his opponents to the extent of being alternately conciliating and friendly, or ruthless and unscrupulous, in accordance with what the circumstances required. This is how he behaved with General Naguib at home, and with King Hussein outside. He often took no initiative for action but reacted to what others did. He earned a world reputation, in fact, for his quick and offensive reaction to insults, and for hitting back promptly and with force. This is what he did when Imam Ahmad of Yemen criticized his socialism in a poem in December 1961. He immediately began the attack against the Imamate that ended with the revolution of September 1962.

Nasser usually took a defensive attitude even when he was the aggressor and the transgressor, and tried to convey the impression that he was the target of a conspiracy. The conspirators were invariably portrayed as reactionaries associated with imperialism and Zionism. This is how he attacked the Baghdad Pact and the Hashemites of Iraq between 1955 and 1958, and later King Faisal of Saudi Arabia and his so-called Muslim pact in 1966. Nasser was also constantly able to find a scapegoat for his misfortunes, economic as well as military, and to take the posture of the hero who refuses to be intimidated. In his speech of July 22, 1966, he told the Egyptians that the United States was delaying the aid in surplus food which he had asked, because of policy conflicts over Israel and frictions with Saudi Arabia. "We were told we were not following the right course," he said, "and that is why we are not receiving aid . . . .- we shall not surrender and we shall not give in . . . . the freedom we have bought with our blood we shall not sell for wheat, for rice, or for anything." The great advantage that Nasser had over his rivals was that he told the Arabs things which they like to believe, and they did believe them irrespective of the measure of truth they contained. He appealed to their passions, and he aroused their hatreds, jealousies and resentments with an air of sincerity and innocence that strengthened their faith in him.

Nasser's qualities as a master conspirator and skillful tactician were accompanied by certain vices among which the most conspicuous were his covetousness and avidity for power, his vanity, cynicism and suspicion, and his anger. It has been said of him during the crisis in May 1967 that as a good peasant, he is cunning and prudent, but anger and covetousness sometimes cancel the prudence and leave the field free for cunning alone.[102] Nasser was too aggressive and relentless in his single minded pursuit of power and in his attempt to retain it. Egypt was not enough for his ambition and its domestic problems worried him, so he shifted his activity and his interest to the Arab world, and even to the Afro-Asian world. International politics under his rule superseded internal development, and even the aspects of internal economic growth were not motivated simply by humanitarian concern, but also by considerations of status and prestige.

The Egyptian revolution has essentially produced two radical internal changes: first, the total destruction of the old ruling elite and its replacement by another, and second, the end of capitalism and private enterprise, and the concentration of wealth and economic activity in the hands of the state, that is in the hands of the new ruling military class and their supporters. The style and extent of these changes were unknown in the Arab and Eastern Mediterranean world and could not have been devised by the individualistic Arab mind, unless one supposes that the Egyptians are not as Arab and as individualistic, or as adventurous and freedealing as the rest of the Arabs, which is true to a certain extent. The two far reaching changes and the ideology and slogans that accompanied them were in fact imported from the Slavic Communist world, although certain aspects of them were known under such regimes as those of the Ptolemies and Muhammad Ali, but without the ideology and the slogans. In spite of their radicalism, these changes are among the easiest to be achieved by a revolution, because they involve the mere use of force to supplant the old ruling class and confiscate the property of the citizens and non-citizens under various pretexts. They were also the easiest to introduce to other Arab countries where the military imposed them by force. The positive changes on the other hand, were more difficult to make: to provide a stable government based on the rule of law and insure the participation of the people in it, to guarantee the peoples' civil rights and freedoms mentioned in the various constitutions, to reform the administration and improve the work of the bureaucracy, to build a strong army, to run the new economic system efficiently, to raise the standard of living among the poverty stricken ignorant masses, and to create a new moral and mental outlook that reflects itself in more efficient work, more dedication to public service, more honesty in human relations, and more patriotic feeling.

The Egyptian revolution has failed in the achievement of most of these positive goals. Experiments in government have been following one another at the rate of one every three years with nominal popular participation and with a one-party organization created and dominated by the government. Freedoms have consistently been suppressed. The essentially administrative-bureaucratic nature of the state has been left intact. A new hierarchy useful for the policies of the new regime was set up with the military stratum at the top of the hierarchy and with every other group, even professionals and intellectuals, bureaucratized.[103] The rising prosperous middle class was ruined and the old ruling elite was destroyed without bringing substantial material and moral improvement to the condition of the lower classes. Corruption has been widespread in the economic system, and the military officers and other favorites, mostly from the poorer classes, have availed themselves with impunity of the opportunity for accumulating wealth while they were executives of state-controlled corporations and projects. Economic development did not achieve what was expected, and many losing industrial projects had to be closed. The people in general, and the intellectuals, workers, and students in particular, were indoctrinated and regimented for the service of the socialist state, while the educational and academic standards have been degraded. The Egyptian revolution gave Egypt no military strength to stand in the face of Israel, and Israel was virtually the only justification for building up that strength. The Egyptian revolution produced no such enthusiasm for defending or spreading its ideals that made the French revolutionaries fight successfully against Europe after 1792 and spread the ideas of freedom, equality, and fraternity. The Egyptian revolution could not generate such enthusiasm because its ideology was artificial and imported, and it remained controversial and had to be imposed by force. The Nasserist system that followed the revolution prospered on intrigue, and by intrigue, subversion and violence it spread outside Egypt and brought with it dictatorship, instability and economic ruin.

The Nasserist regime created what a Baathist writer described as a "crisis in morals" when it attacked the arbitrary rule of the former king and proclaimed the slogans of freedom, on the one hand, and then on the other hand, it abolished all freedoms and imposed a harsh military rule in which "one half of the people spy on the other half." It is indeed a crisis in morals, said Hafez Jamali, "when the new regime proclaims that the socialist system is necessary for returning freedom to the peasant and the laborer, and fills the world with noise against the capitalist and the feudal lord because they deprived the peasants and laborers of their freedom, and then it deprives everyone of every freedom."[104]

At one time Nasser was compared to the great Muslim hero Saladin, because it was thought that he was building up the armed strength that could liberate Palestine just as Saladin had liberated it from the Crusaders in the twelfth century.[105] The comparison has proved to be unfounded. Saladin won victories and regained Jerusalem from the Crusaders. Nasser won no victories, and his second defeat in June 1967 left Sinai and the Gaza strip, as well as the Arab part of Jerusalem, in Israel's hands. Saladin unified Egypt and Syria and kept them united under his rule, and then lost no time in starting the campaign against the Crusaders. Nasser, on the other hand, consistently avoided the issue of war in Palestine for whose liberation he bought the arms from the communist bloc, as he told the Arabs. Saladin was, moreover, tolerant, magnanimous, chivalrous, and truthful, while Nasser has been known to be fanatical, covetous and vain with a predilection for intrigue and big-lie tactics.

There are those who like to draw a comparison between Nasser and Kemal Ataturk as the leaders of two famous Near Eastern revolutions in our century. The dissimilarities between the two are outstanding. Ataturk saved Turkey from the danger of dismemberment by unifying its people and preparing them for the struggle against foreign invaders. Nasser took over a united independent Egypt and then disrupted its society through class and ethnic warfare and allowed its territory to be invaded and occupied. Ataturk was dedicated and sincere in proclaiming his program to save Turkey with the help of duly elected delegates of the people. Nasser proclaimed his intention to save Palestine in threats which he had no intention to translate into action. Ataturk, moreover, abandoned the dream of the Pan-Turanists and concentrated on Turkey, while Nasser dissipated his energies outside Egypt, and under the false pretext of unifying the Arabs he fought the Arabs in order to dominate them and force on them his socialist system. Ataturk had the courage to separate church and state and to transform certain traditional aspects of Turkish society, while Nasser exploited religion and harnessed the religious leaders for propagating his socialist revolution and for destroying his enemies. He even tampered with the message of Islam to prove that Islam was a socialist religion.

Nasser has been often compared to the Egyptian pharaohs in his authoritarian rule and his absolute utilization of the resources of the state and its people. In his predatory activities, his confiscations, nationalizations without effective compensation, and the dispossession of the foreign settlers, Nasser was compared to the Mameluk leaders of Egypt in the eighteenth century. He was much like Muhammad Ali in his economic policy, his monopoly of foreign trade and his uneconomic state-controlled industrial projects, some of which had to close later because they were financially unsound. Muhammad Ali, however, founded a modern state with the beginnings of a modern administration and a strong army that won victories in the four corners of the Near East with the help of purely Egyptian material resources. In one way, Nasser can be compared to Khedive Ismail for his extravagance and external adventures, and for his large scale borrowing and bringing foreign influence to an independent country. Ismail, however, achieved certain results in his foreign conquests in the Sudan and contributed to the intellectual and cultural revival of Egypt. He also opened the Suez Canal which Nasser's blunders have caused to be closed.

It has been claimed that Nasserism differed from all the former authoritarian Egyptian regimes to which it has been compared in that its goals were different, for it sought to achieve social justice and to work for the people's welfare. One can argue, however, that dictators and despots have always tried to justify their rule by speaking of the people's welfare which they occasionally were able to serve in one way or another. In Egypt, certain measures were actually taken to achieve these goals and to rehabilitate the poor and ignorant masses with education and health programs and with efforts to expand the chances of gainful employment and landownership for them. But the concept of the people's welfare soon came to be dominated by the imported Marxian idea of class struggle. The exercise of power which was justified by the drive to achieve the initial moderate goals of Nasserism became an instrument for implementing the socialist revolution, and soon became an end in itself while everything was subordinated and sacrificed to its consolidation regardless of the harm it did. The virtue of the war in June 1967 was to demonstrate the extent of the damage Nasserism did to Egypt, its army, its people, and the Arab world by the class war and the revolutionary socialism which it imposed by force, and by its close dependence on the Soviet Union. The war also showed that a modern state cannot be run by conspiratorial and big-lie techniques, and that when the artificial Egyptian revolutionary edifice and its false facade of power was put to the test, it lamentably failed. The revolutionary establishment was not able to withstand the shock of war, and until that supreme test occurred the Nasserist regime was able to deceive the Arab world and the world about its real worth even though serious manifestations of its ineptitude had already been revealed.

In spite of the defeat he suffered and caused the Arabs to

suffer, Nasser did not lose power in Egypt and his socialist regime has survived. Although in many Arab circles he was discredited, and the defeat only confirmed the suspicions of those who never had faith in him, he has nevertheless retained a certain measure of support in Egypt and the other Arab countries. The reasons for his survival are numerous: First, he succeeded in maintaining his control over the Egyptian army and moved fast to purge it of those who were attempting to bring about his downfall. Second, his many lieutenants and agents who had vested interests in the survival of his regime have kept the masses on his side through the one party organization — the Arab Socialist Union — that he built up. Egypt, moreover, had no other organized group that could possibly take over, or that would have desired to take over power even if it could, on account of the difficult problems created by defeat and by the Nasserist system. Third, Egyptian and Arab national sentiment in general refused to give Israel the credit, or the satisfaction of bringing Nasser down because he had been for several years the symbol of Arab nationalism and of the Arab drive against Israel. Fourth, Nasser has remained in the Arab countries the symbol of the Arab revolution, as well as its moral, if not material support. The many Arab revolutionaries, radicals, socialists, and anti-Western elements everywhere who have attained positions of power in Arab government and society, could not afford, because of their ideals or vested interests, to see Nasser fall, because this would be only a prelude to their own downfall and to the end of the socialist system which they established with Nasser's encouragement. Fifth, the Soviet Union, which knew too well the danger that Nasser's fall would bring upon the socialist ideology and the whole radical anti-Western outlook and upon its own prestige in the Arab world, lost no time in giving him and his regime some of the moral and material support they needed.

VII. Egypt After Nasser: Problems of Succession and Continuity

Among the Arab revolutionary leaders and authors of military coups d'état Nasser alone was able to dominate the ruling regime of his country without interruption until his death. He was the only Arab military leader to die in his bed while he was still in power and to be succeeded by a close associate who promised to follow in his footsteps. Some of those who ruled by the sword in other Arab countries have perished by the sword a few months or years after their military takeover, while others were overthrown by their military colleagues and were allowed to live in obscurity at home or to go into exile.

Nasser died unexpectedly of a heart attack on Monday September 28, 1970 at the age of fifty-two. He had been suffering from diabetes and circulatory trouble in his legs for several years. His confidant, Muhammad Hassanein Haikal, disclosed in an *al-Ahram* article that he thought several times of resignation because of his agonizing pain but he was afraid that it would be taken as a symbol of defeat. On September 11, 1969 he suffered a heart attack that kept him one month in bed but the people were not told what the real sickness was for fear of its effect on the masses and on the army.

The people's reaction to Nasser's death showed the extent of his popularity among the Egyptian and Arab masses and portrayed the qualities of his charismatic leadership. Tens of thousands of persons from Cairo and other cities and rural areas came to al-Qubba Palace where his body lay in state to pay their respect and express their grief. In the five-mile funeral procession from the old building of the Revolution Command Council in Gezirah to the mosque named after him and in which he was buried on October 1, 1970, an estimated four million people crowded the streets and their surroundings. Reporters said that it was the biggest outpouring of grief within living memory. They also commented that despite the revolution and its Arab socialism and industrialization, the Egyptian people bid their leader farewell in a fashion very little changed since the days of the Pharaohs. [106]

The image of Nasser as a father of his people and as a popular hero was partly a creation of official propaganda and public manipulation, and partly a product of Nasser's concern in his many speeches and declarations for the rights and dignity of the laboring masses and a natural result of the benefits that his regime granted them. Nasser cultivated their loyalty and enjoyed their adulation, and they looked up to him as the man on whom they could depend even though he left them neither freedom nor initiative, squandered the meagre resources of the country on fruitless foreign ventures, and often played more to their emotions and prejudices than to their real needs.

In various cities of the Arab world processions were organized on the day of Nasser's funeral and stores and offices closed either voluntarily or by orders of Nasserist enthusiasts. The Arab masses saw in Nasser the symbol of their aspirations for unity and strength and the leader in the struggle against imperialism and Zionism even though his policies ended in defeat and in foreign occupation of Arab territory and the Arabs were left humiliated and divided, while Egypt found itself economically and financially weaker and under Soviet influence. Failure, however, did not destroy his hold on the masses because their adherence was no longer based on reality or on an awareness of the disastrous defeat but on a Nasserist legend based on memories of the recent past when Nasser successfully defied the great powers, gained international influence that was out of proportion to his inherent strength, and scored victories even in the midst of defeat. The people were not aware or perhaps did not care that he often spoke one way and acted another, or that he became a force to be contended with largely because of the circumstances of the cold war and the self interest of the Soviet Union, or that his frequently changing attitudes towards various Western and

Arab states eventually weakened their confidence in him and deprived him of their support.

In the foreign press and among foreign political figures Nasser was recognized as the most popular and controversial Arab leader in modern times. They generally felt that his death left a void that could add to the already existing chaos in the Arab area. They spoke of him as the only Arab leader who had enough strength and prestige to make peace with Israel. An Israeli spokesman even remarked that though Nasser was "our major enemy," he was also "our best hope for peace."[107] On July 23, 1970 Nasser had accepted, after deliberations with Moscow, a proposal for peace and for a ceasefire made by Secretary of State William Rogers on the basis of the Security Council resolution of November 22, 1967, and three days later King Hussein of Jordan indicated his agreement to the proposal. The Palestinian guerillas who had never accepted the Security Council resolution for a political settlement organized an impressive demonstration in Amman against the ceasefire proposal on July 27, 1970 and called Nasser a "coward" for having accepted it, while Iraq joined in denouncing the agreement. Nasser reacted at the time by placing a ban on the use of Cairo radio by the Palestine Liberation Organization, and he scornfully told the Arab opportunists who were accustomed to criticize without attempting to fight, "Those who want to fight should send us their troops and take part in our struggle."[108] The ceasefire that effectively began on August 7, 1970 ended a long period of fighting that reached its climax in the last seventy days when the Israeli Air Force conducted massive daily bombardments of Egyptian artillery and missile sites near the Suez Canal.

Nasser was also given credit as a mediator and arbiter in inter-Arab disputes and as a forceful leader who used his influence to work for stability although he had been before the sobering defeat of June 1967 the instigator of most inter-Arab quarrels and of most of the conspiracies, riots and revolts and the resulting instability within the Arab states. In the bloody clashes between the Palestinian guerillas and the

Lebanese troops in April and October-November 1969 and March 1970, and between the guerillas and the Jordanian troops in June and September 1970 he sent his personal representatives to Beirut and Amman and invited the leaders to Cairo where the quarrels usually ended in conciliation and agreement. The Cairo agreements, however, were neither sufficiently clear nor decisive and reflected the lack of clarity and decisiveness in Nasser's own attitude towards the Palestinian guerillas. He sometimes encouraged and defended them—and thereby weakened the authority of the governments of Lebanon and Jordan - in order to remain on the side of the Arab masses, and at other times he denounced their extremism especially when it interfered with his own policies and plans. Nasser's last effort as a mediator and also the last act of his eventful career occurred on September 27, 1970 when he succeeded in bringing the violent nine-day fighting between the Jordanian troops and the guerillas to an end. The leaders of the warring parties, King Hussein of Jordan and Yasser Arafat of the Fateh and the Palestine Liberation Organization, were invited to an Arab summit meeting in Cairo and were persuaded to sign a ceasefire agreement that was to be supervised by a five-man Arab commission. Twenty-four hours after the conclusion of the agreement Nasser passed away.

The two important questions that arose after Nasser's death were those of choosing his successor and deciding the future of the Nasserist system. The two questions were related because the chosen successor could use his influence to adopt or modify the inherited system, and the question of adherence to Nasser's policy was therefore a determining factor in the choice of the new president. The provisions of the Egyptian constitution of 1964 enabled Anwar Sadat to become acting president immediately after Nasser's death since he was the only vice-president after December 1969. The same provisions allowed him to remain acting president for sixty days until the election of a new president. Sadat was the closest supporter of Nasser and the most likely to continue his policy. Along with Hussein al-Shafii, he was the only member of the original revolution command council to remain in active political service. In the early revolutionary period he was in charge of the Muslim Congress for the promotion of Egyptian leadership through Muslim solidarity. He also occupied the presidency of the national assembly for several years. Sadat was of the same age and military rank as Nasser and was known to be a devout Muslim. He was also a good classical Arabic speaker and a well-known apologist for the revolution and for the officers' rule in his one-sided published Arabic work entitled "The Complete Story of the Revolution," and its English version, *Revolt on the Nile*. During the entire period of Nasserist domination, Sadat hardly ever held an executive position of great responsibility or one that required initiative and independent judgment. He was known, however, for his patriotism and intense national feeling but time will show the kind of balance he will make between the national interests of Egypt and of the Arabs, and revolutionary socialist interests and ideologies.

Sadat was in a better position to become Nasser's successor than Ali Sabri who leaned more to the left and was known for his Russian sympathies, and Zakaria Muhieddin who leaned more to the right and had a pro-Western label. Both Sabri and Muhieddin were former prime ministers. Ali Sabri later became secretary-general of the Socialist Union and in the last months before Nasser's death he was the liaison man between the Soviet military advisers and technicians, and the Egyptian authorities. He was too much identified with the Russians to be acceptable to the people and the army. Zakaria Muhieddin, on the other hand, was a moderate who had opposed the growing Soviet penetration and the economic policy of Nasser and had been in retirement since March 1968. He was unacceptable to the Russians, but he was the man whom Nasser publicly named as his successor when he presented his resignation to the people of Egypt in June 1967. Neither he nor Sadat, however, had those special qualities of leadership and command over the masses which took Nasser several years to develop under more favorable circumstances.

A struggle for power was feared among the main contenders, and at one time the rumors indicated that a presidential council or some such type of collective leadership would rule Egypt in order to avoid the struggle. The Soviet prime minister, Alexei Kosygin, who came immediately after Nasser's death at the head of a delegation to attend the funeral and confer with Egypt's leadership, stepped in to voice the Soviet Union's interest in the stability of Egypt and the continuity of Nasserist policy. In the four sessions of talks with Egyptian dignitaries he is said to have urged them to fill the vacuum left by Nasser and swiftly select his successor in order to prove that Egypt was stable and that it deserved to retain its prestige in the Arab word.[109]

Shortly after Nasser's funeral on October 1, 1970 Muhieddin's name came up strongly for the succession. The premature move to bring him back to the political leadership was evidently promoted by the information minister and editor of *al-Ahram*, Muhammad Hassanein Haikal. Reports were circulated that Nasser designated Muhieddin to succeed him while other reports indicated that Sadat was the one whom Nasser on his deathbed had nominated for the succession. The readers of *al-Ahram* were told that Anwar Sadat and Ali Sabri suffered heart attacks during the funeral, but these stories were officially denied on the following day.[110] Those who were evidently influential in deciding the succession and speeding the presidential election were a group of leftist close associates of Nasser who were supported by the army and the defense minister, General Muhammad Fawzi, and had been in contact with Kosygin's Soviet delegation. They included Sharawi Gum'a, the interior minister in charge of public security and its secret police, and Sami Sharaf, Nasser's special aide and former intelligence chief. They imposed censorship on the public discussion of political problems, prohibited demonstrations of students because they feared that the mourning for Nasser could become an excuse for political action particularly after anti-Sadat demonstrations had been reported in Cairo and Alexandria. They also arrested some 200 persons from extremist groups of both left and right. On Saturday October 3, 1970 they set in motion the nomination of Sadat in order to counteract any rival bid for the control of the regime. They also followed the procedure that the constitution prescribed for legitimizing the election of the single presidential candidate by a series of illusory democratic processes.

The recommendation to nominate Sadat president was made by the 12-member higher executive committee of the Socialist Union that included Sharawi Gum'a and the other "king makers." On October 5, the recommendation was sent to the 150-member central committee of the Socialist Union that unanimously approved it and sent it to the national assembly. On Tuesday October 6 one-third of the national assembly approved the candidacy of Sadat and on the following day he was nominated unanimously by the 353 assembly members who were present. Sadat accepted the nomination in a twenty minute speech in which he proclaimed his adherence to Nasser's policy for the achievement of the following goals: liberation of the occupied land and a settlement for the Palestinian refugees, unity of the Arab countries, nonalignment between the power blocs, support for the national liberation movements, and defense of the socialist gains.[111] The nomination of Sadat had to be approved by a nation-wide referendum. On October 15, seventeen days after Nasser's death, Sadat was accepted as president by 90.04 per cent of the votes cast by the Egyptians. About 15 per cent of the registered voters did not vote, and those who opposed his election numbered 711,252. On Saturday October 17, Sadat was sworn in before the national assembly and became Egypt's second president. In his short speech before the assembly, Sadat modestly said that he was not distressed that 700,000 persons opposed him because "our people should not place their full fate in any single person after Gamal Abdul Nasser." Observers concluded that he referred to a collective leadership to run Egypt when he said that the fulfillment of the task left unfinished by Nasser was "beyond the ability of any single person."[112]

The overriding consideration in the choice of Anwar

Sadat by the political leadership and the committees of the Socialist Union was undoubtedly his closeness to Nasser and his willingness to follow Nasser's policies. In its unanimous vote for the nomination of Sadat on October 7, 1972, the national assembly similarly stressed the fact that he was "a comrade of Nasser in all the stages of his struggle and he was chosen vice-president (in December 1969) in one of the most difficult stages of our struggle." The assembly then affirmed its determination to follow Nasser's path towards socialism, against imperialism, for liberating the occupied Arab lands, maintaining Egypt's ties with the Arab states and friendship with the Soviet Union.[113] In accepting the nomination, Sadat vowed to follow Nasser's objectives and to respect his legacy. Ten days later, in the ceremony in which he was sworn in as president in the national assembly, Sadat sat in front of a brown bust of Nasser while the assembly president, Labib Shuqair, outlined Sadat's pledges to carry on the polices of Nasser including the struggle to regain the occupied territory. Shuqair also mentioned that the referendum of October 15 proved the unity of the Egyptians and showed that there was no political vacuum after Nasser's death.[114] The mourners in the streets also indicated the popular will to carry on in Nasser's tradition as they shouted "Sadat, Sadat, do not think that Nasser is dead!"[115]

The Egyptians and the Arabs in general were agreed about at least one aspect of Nasser's policy to which they gave particular emphasis and that was the effort to liberate Arab territory occupied by Israel in 1967. In the meeting that followed Nasser's funeral on Thursday October 1, the delegates of ten Arab states - Algeria, Tunisia, Libya, Sudan, Syria, Iraq, Kuwait, Saudi Arabia, Yemen, and South Yemen - issued a statement in which they said that they would follow Nasser's policy to fight international colonialism and Zionism and would continue the struggle to liberate the occupied territory. They also pledged full support of the new Egyptian leaders and urged them to follow in Nasser's footsteps until victory was achieved. Outside this objective, the continuity of

Nasser's policy must have meant different things to different categories of people. For the laboring masses it meant the continued concern for their problems and their living standards; for the political leadership and the various official bodies such as the Socialist Union and the national assembly it meant the preservation of the existing power structure and of the socialist system; and for the younger generation including the university students it meant "loyalty to the revolution" which vaguely indicated their approval of the process of reform and change after the fall of the old regime but not necessarily the acceptance of the new authoritarian system of rule.

Among the former leaders, including Nasser's retired colleagues, and in certain intellectual and non-official circles there had always been a conviction that the Nasserist system had to be modified, but no one except those who had served with Nasser had the courage to suggest its modification. Following Nasser's death, three of his prominent former associates and fellow RCC members - Zakaria Muhieddin, Abdul-Latif Baghdadi, and Kemaleddin Hussein - are said to have tried to see Sadat to present certain proposals for the future of the Egyptian political structure but he refused. On Sunday, October 4, they sent the proposals to Sadat, and on the following day Baghdadi was able to meet him but the proposals were not accepted. They are said to have demanded, first, an open political system with at least one opposition party and a free press; second, the election of a constituent assembly supervised by an independent body and not by the Socialist Union; third, an independent judiciary with guarantees that there would be no arrests without formal legal charges; fourth, the release of political prisoners; and fifth, a collective authority at the head of the government instead of a single strongman.[116] It was the coalition of leftist Nasserist aides in charge of the security system that supported Sadat to turn back the attempt of Baghdadi and other former RCC members to modify the Nasserist system. The same coalition also proceeded to speed the nomination of Sadat and took the necessary precautions to prevent any dissenting group from making a rival bid for power.

The accession of Sadat to the presidency and his decision and that of the Egyptian leadership to continue Nasser's policy do not necessarily mean that the situation in Egypt and the other Arab countries could remain the same as in Nasser's time. The Russians will probably continue to extend full support to Egypt as Premier Kosygin promised in his radio talk in Cairo on October 1, 1970, and the Soviet Union will expect Egypt not to reject a political solution of the Arab-Israeli conflict. But Sadat would not be able to accept compromises that Nasser could have accepted because he does not enjoy the same leadership and prestige to make unpopular decisions. Nor can Sadat or any other Egyptian leader influence the Arab world as Nasser did. The Soviet position as a result would be weakened because Nasser's death has deprived it of the benefit of that influence. The Arab rulers and leaders can be expected to act more on their own without the fear of blackmail and intimidation or other pressures. Although Sadat is known to be a better speaker, and speaks with a louder voice than Nasser, it is not sure that he would choose to make speeches against Arab leaders, as Nasser did, and it is even less sure that the Arab leaders would be willing to listen if he chose to speak. Sadat, however, would perhaps make even tougher speeches against imperialism, Zionism and the United States in order to gain popularity and to leave no misunderstanding about his position.

Sadat, moreover, will not be regarded as a symbol of the Arab revolution against imperialism, Zionism and reaction as Nasser had been. The Arab leaders consequently will no longer have to outbid anyone in radicalism, as they had to do during the Nasserist era for fear of being denounced as traitors or reactionaries, or in order to prove that they were revolutionaries and socialists in good standing. Already in Syria the radical Baath leadership with President Nureddin Atassi and party boss General Salah Jedid have been swept out of office before mid- October by the defense minister, General

Hafez Asad, and the Saiqa guerillas have been recalled from Jordan and disarmed. In Iraq, the radical vice-president Hardan Takriti was dismissed and some of the Iraqi forces in Jordan have been withdrawn. In Jordan, the new prime minister, Wasfi al-Tell who was appointed on October 28, 1970 is not particularly sympathetic to Nasserism and is viewed as a foe by the Palestinian guerillas. The Palestine liberation movement that was created with Nasser's encouragement and protection to carry on the struggle for Arab rights in Palestine has increasingly directed its activities against other Arabs with the result that the number of Arabs killed by Arabs since the June War in 1967 has been ten times that of Israelis killed by Arabs according to Nasser's estimate.[117] The radical ideologists of the movement, moreover, claim that the Palestinian revolutionaries alone will achieve the genuine Arab social revolution that Nasser was unwilling to achieve because he was fearful of the participation of the masses. The guerillas have reduced their activities to a minimum against Israel even before their war with the Jordanian troops in September 1970, and they have been withdrawing from Israeli borders probably in preparation for another showdown with King Hussein's troops.

While it can be presumed that the end of the overwhelming influence of Nasserist policies on the Arab states would be welcome and beneficial to those states, the cooperation and influence of Egypt would, nevertheless, remain necessary for the solution - political or military - of the Palestine question. The serious problem which the Arabs will continue to face as part of the heavy Nasserist legacy is that Egypt has become so dependent on the Soviet Union and so indebted to it that any settlement with Israel would have to obtain the approval and insure the interests of the Soviets.

In Egypt itself, Sadat inaugurated his presidency with the appointment of the first civilian prime minister in the history of the revolution - with the exception of the forty-five days of Ali Maher in July-September 1952. The choice of the veteran diplomat and foreign affairs expert, Mahmud Fawzi, was interpreted as a sign of division and suspicion in the Egyptian leadership because Sadat sought a political non-entity instead of a strong executive and political leader. The close associate of Nasser, Hussein al-Shafii, boycotted the meeting of the central committee of the Socialist Union that approved the nomination of the prime minister on October 20, 1970. Both Shafii and Ali Sabri were later appointed vice-presidents, but Shafii evidently felt offended that he was not appointed also to the post of Secretary-General of the Socialist Union that was given to Abdul-Muhsen Abul-Nour, a former officer, cabinet minister and loyal associate of Nasser. Although Shafii was considered the least political among the former officers, he sulked at home for a few days. It was evident that Sadat did not inherit the kind of loyalty that was expressed to Nasser, and that friction and division might eventually result from the atmosphere of suspicion and the sidetracking of qualified leaders from the positions of power. On the other hand, it would seem that Sadat and his aides have been concentrating their attention and efforts on such vital domestic problems as high prices of consumer goods, crowded public transit, water and meat shortage, and · the complicated and inefficient bureaucracy. A timetable has already been drawn and allocations have been made for solving these questions. Sadat might eventually prove to be, even without Nasser's charisma, more successful than his predecessor in settling the pressing problems that touch the living conditions of the Egyptian population after these conditions had become worse than under the old regime.

CHAPTER II
NOTES

1. Abdul Nasser, *Philosophy of the Revolution*, 85-115.
2. *al-Nasr,* October 8, 23, and November 7, 30, 1961.
3. *The New York Times,* April 17, 1966.
4. *al-Hayat,* October 19, 1965; *The New York Times,* October 20, 1965.
5. *The New York Times,* May 6, 1963.
6. *al-Nasr,* January 16, 1963.
7. See a description of the book by Simon Jargy, *Orient,* no. 6 (1958, 2), 189-191. The book was published in Cairo in 1958.
8. Account given in *The New York Times,* August 24, 1965.
9. On some reasons for this shift, see Wheelock, p. 51.
10. See Anthony Nutting, *The Arabs,* 350.
11. Albert Hourani, "A Moment of Change: The Crisis of 1956," in *Vision of History* (Beirut: Khayat's, 1961), 137.
12. Nasser's speech on December 23, 1960 in *The Scribe,* January 1961, p. 9.
13. Nutting, 351-352.
14. Michel Aflaq, *Maarakat al-Masir al-Wahid* (The Battle of Common Destiny), 2nd ed. (Beirut, 1959), 108.
15. Desmond Stewart and Editor of *Life* (New York: Time Inc.), 1962, 98.
16. See the details on the formation of the United Arab Republic in Vol. II ch. 3 on Syria
17. Nasser's speech of December 23, 1960, in *The Scribe,* January 1961, p. 9.
18. See Wheelock, 55.
19. See the details on Nasser's interventions in Jordan and Lebanon, in Vol. II chs. 5 and 6 and in Yemen in this Volume, ch. 4.
20. Haikal in *al-Ahram,* March 9, 1962; *al-Nasr,* January 26, 1963 on Haikal's January article.

21. *The Charter,* 111.
22. Nasser's speech on March 26, 1964 at the opening of the national assembly as reported in *The New York Times,* March 27, 1964; quoted in *Middle East Forum,* May 1964, 7.
23. Nasser's broadcast speech on February 22, 1967 heard by the author in Cairo.
24. Open letter from Fikri Abaza to Khruschev, *al-Musawar,* March 1959. The occasion was the brief crisis between Nasser and Khruschev after Nasser's attack against the communists in his speech of December 23, 1958. The Russians had reminded Egypt of what it owed to the Soviet Union.
25. C. L. Sulzberger in *The New York Times,* March 9, 1964 said that Nasser himself told him about his admiration for Tito because he showed him the way.
26. T. Moussa, 25 ff.; see also the declaration of Akram Hourani in *al-Nasr,* June 6, 1962.
27. The story of this meeting of November 29, 1959 is related in *al-Nasr,* June 13, 1962 by Akram Hourani and it was confirmed by other Syrian witnesses like Amin Nufuri.
28. See text of Nasser's speech in *Arab Political Documents* 1965 eds. W. Khalidi and Y. Ibish (Beirut, 1965), 220-229; *Time,* June 11, 1965.
29. *al-Ahrar* (Beirut), June 3, 1965 quoted in T. Moussa, 150; the Syrian radio also attacked Nasser on June 6.
30. Haikal's article quoted in *The New York Times,* September 27, 1964.
31. *The New York Times,* December 20, 1963.
32. Rushdi al-Maluf in *al-Safa* (Beirut), quoted in *The Heritage,* September 25, 1965.
33. *al-Ahram,* May 8, 1964.
34. *Middle East Forum,* June 1964, p. 8.
35. See article in *al-Hayat,* May 24, 1964.
36. This is the stage in American-Egyptian relations that M. H. Haikal called "the attempt at containment," and it lasted from 1959 to 1963. In March and April 1967, Haikal wrote a series of weekly articles in *al-Ahram* entitled, "We and America," and he divided American relations with Egypt into four stages: 1) Stage of the attempt to

domesticate which ended in 1955, 2) Stage of the attempt to punish 1956-1958, 3) Stage of the attempt to contain 1959-1963, 4) Stage of the attempt at violence, after 1964.

37. Drew Pearson column, June 7, 1964.
38. The Lebanese press put Nasser on the spot when he criticized Lebanon's economic system and pro-Western attitude in September 1964 and asked him why he has accepted more than two billion dollars in aid from the United States, and the Lebanese newspapers volunteered the answer: 1) "to feed your hungry people," 2) in order not to fight Israel, 3) to safeguard American oil interests.
39. Discussions of the senatorial foreign relations committee, quoted in T. Moussa, 65, 69.
40. *The New York Times,* December 2-6, 1964.
41. Nasser's speech quoted in *The New York Times,* December 24, 1964; the Arabic colloquial expression "drink the sea water" was translated in the English speaking press as equivalent to "jump in the lake."
42. *The New York Times,* June 23, 1965,
43. Related by T. Moussa, 72.
44. For much of this information, see Jean-Claude Froelich, "L'Egypte et les peuples noirs," *Orient,* no. 32/33 (1964, 4; 1965, 1), 13-28.
45. Hedrick Smith in *The New York Times,* February 24, 1965 mentioned that high Egyptian officials complained in private to West German diplomats of Moscow's pressures; see also *The New York Times,* January 31, February 10, 18, 25, 1965; for more information, see T. Moussa, 155 ff.; Marcel Colombe, "Remarques sur la Crise Germano-Arabe," *Orient,* 32/33 (1964, 4 and 1965, 1), 7-12.
46. The pro-Nasserist *al-Muharrer* (Beirut), November 28, 1966 mentioned that in the meeting of the Unified Political Command in Baghdad, Egypt and Iraq agreed that "the progressive forces" are responsible for the liberation of Palestine.
47. *al-Zaman,* January 23, 1967.
48. Quoted by *L'Orient* (Beirut), December 8, 1966.
49. *L'Orient,* December 12, 1966; *al-Hayat,* December 9, 1966.
50. *al-Ahram,* March 15, 1967; *al-Hayat,* and *al-'Amal* (Beirut), March 17, 1967.
51. *The Daily Star,* (Beirut), April 22, 1967.

52. See the declarations of Lieutenant Ahmad Mustafa in *al-Ahram*, March 22, 1967.
53. *The Herald Tribune*, May 24, 1967.
54. *The Herald Tribune*, May 18, 1967; see on the crisis Randolph S. Churchill and Winston Churchill, *The Six Day War* (Boston: Houghton Mifflin, 1967), especially chapter 2 "The Straits Closed."
55. It is believed, on the other hand, that U Thant's report to the Security Council on May 19, based on UN observers' testimony, gave no indication of Israeli mobilization of troops close to the Syrian border. See Benjamin Shwadran, "Soviet Posture in the Middle East," *Current History*, December 1967, 331.
56. See the claims of Defense Minister Badran in *The Los Angeles Times*, February 25, 1958, and of Lt. General Muhammad Fawzi, Marshal Amer, and Badran in *New Outlook*, September-October, 1967 quoting *al-Hawadith* in Beirut.
57. See for these opinions *The Herald Tribune*, May 22, 1967; *The New York Times*, May 19, 1967; Shwadran, "Soviet Posture in the Middle East", 332.
58. *Le Journal de Dimanche* (Paris), May 28, 1967.
59. See *The New York Times*, September 12, 1967 for Richard H. Nolte's declaration on September 11 after his resignation. He had arrived in Cairo on May 21 and left on June 10, 1967.
60. See the assessment of *Combat* (Paris), May 28, 1967 on Soviet motives.
61. See Albert Hourani in *The Observer* (London), September 3, 1967; Shwadran, "Soviet Posture . . . . ", 333.
62. *Mideast Mirror*, June 3, 1967.
63. Drew Pearson and Jack Anderson column "Russian Doubletalk Upset Nasser," January 3, 1968 have mentioned on the basis of reliable intelligence sources that Nasser had two channels to the Kremlin, the diplomatic channel which sent him appeals to avoid war, and the KGB intelligence channel which he trusted more because it was secret. Through the secret channel Nasser received Russian approval for closing the Strait of Tiran, and a promise to prevent American intervention and to provide Soviet assistance in case of absolute need. Amer was reportedly suspicious of this double talk and wanted Egypt to attack first instead of waiting for the Israelis to attack.

64. Quoted in *Le Monde,* June 13, 1967.
65. Nasser first acknowledged his mistake in private at Khartoum at the end of August, then publicly in an article in *Look* magazine, March 4, 1968, and then in a speech to his troops on March 10, 1968.
66. See *al-Ahram,* October 6, 13, 20, 1967; *The Los Angeles Times,* October 21, 1967.
67. *al-Ahram,* October 27, 1967.
68. Muhammad Saddiq Shanshal, "After the Tragedy of Marshal Amer," (in Arabic), in *al-Anwar* (Beirut), September 29, 1967.
69. *The Los Angeles Times,* March 13, 1968.
70. See Eric Downton in *The Sunday Telegraph,* June 18, 1967.
71. See the text of the speech of resignation, withdrawal of resignation, and comments in the *Herald Tribune,* June 12, 1967.
72. See Eva Fournier in *Journal de Dimanche,* June 11, 1967.
73. *Le Monde,* June 13, 1967.
74. Drew Pearson and Jack Anderson column, January 3, 1968.
75. *L'Aurore* (Paris), June 23, 1967.
76. *The New York Times,* July 2, 1967.
77. See the reports of Eric Rouleau, correspondent of *Le Monde,* and the reports of *al-Ahram* in *The New York Times,* August 30, 31, September 5, 1967.
78. Report on the prosecutor's accusation of the defendants in *The New York Times,* January 23, 1968.
79. Excerpts from the document in *Time,* December 15, 1967; the 14-page document was allegedly obtained by the intelligence agent of another Arab state in Cairo after Amer's death. The document is described as not a forgery, but unmistakably Amer's.
80. Reports on the two attempts appeared in *The New York Times,* May 20 and July 3, 1968. The second reported attempt was based on "reliable reports reaching London."
81. See the reports and comments of Eric Pace and Joe Alex Morris, Jr. in *The New York Times,* February 29, and *The Los Angeles Times,* March 1, 1968 respectively.
82. See the article "The Secret Behind the Referendum of May 2 in

Egypt," by "A Great Egyptian Political Writer" in *al-Hayat,* April 28, 1968.

83. See George Lenczowski, "Arab Bloc Realignments," *Current History,* December 1967, 351.

84. *The Los Angeles Times,* December 25, 1967.

85. See *The Los Angeles Times,* May 9, 1968 on Atassi's visit to Nasser on May 6-8, a few days after the end of the visit of Talhuni, prime minister of Jordan.

86. See Shwadran, "Soviet Posture . . . . ", 369; *N. Y. Times,* September 9, 1968 on Richard Nixon's speech of September 8 that said "Israel was a bulwark of strength in the path of Soviet ambition."

87. See the appeal of Representative Gerald Ford for military help to Israel in *The Los Angeles Times,* December 25, 1967; see also the advertisement by "The Committee of Americans for Permanent Peace in the Middle East" and its arguments in *The New York Times,* August 10, 1967; see also the analysis of the situation in the column of Drew Pearson and Jack Anderson, January 7, 1968.

88. This last assertion was attributed to Secretary of State Dean Rusk in the one-page advertisement by 96 American Rabbis in *The New York Times,* January 5, 1968 on the eve of Levi Eshkol's visit to the United States for negotiating the sale of arms and especially planes.

89. See the thesis of General John Glubb in *The Middle East Crisis, A Personal Interpretation* (London: Hodder and Stoughton, 1967).

90. Reported by *Paris-Presse,* June 22, 1967.

91. *Le Monde,* June 20, 1967.

92. The visit was reported in *The New York Times,* July 2, 1967.

93. President Nasser admitted that there were about one thousand Russian advisers, according to *The New York Times,* March 13, 1968; see also Hedrick Smith in *The New York Times,* January 15, 1968.

94. See *L'Aurore,* June 23, 1967; Joseph Alsop's column, July 17, 1967 quoting an article in an official Moscow weekly by I. Belayev and E. Primakov; see also Drew Middleton in *The New York Times,* July 16, 1968.

95. Richard Nolte quoted in *The National Observer* (New York), January 8, 1968.
96. Haikal's article in *al-Ahram*, August 4, 1967.
97. Drew Middleton quoting an intelligence agent in *The New York Times*, July 16, 1968.
98. The speech of Bourguiba at Kef in Tunisia on August 24, 1967.
99. Declarations by King Hussein in Washington on November 5, 1967 and April 10, 1969, and Mahmud Riad, foreign minister of Egypt, in Copenhagen, in early July 1968, and President Nasser in *N. Y. Times*, February 3, 1969.
100. The article was reproduced in *al-Anwar*, June 14, 1968.
101. Munif al-Razzaz, *al-Tajribah al-Murrah* (the Bitter Experiment) (Beirut, 1967), 51.
102. Jean-Jacques Faust in *Journal de Dimanche*, May 28, 1967.
103. P. J. Vatikiotis, "Egypt 1966: The Assessment of a Revolution", *The World Today*, June 1966, 244-245.
104. Hafez Jamali, "Crisis in Morals" (in Arabic) in *al-Nasr*, July 4, 1962.
105. Actually Saladin did not liberate all Palestine; he made a treaty with the Crusaders that left several coastal cities in their hands. The Crusaders were completely forced out of Palestine about 100 years later, in 1291
106. See Joe Alex Morris, Jr. in the *Los Angeles Times*, October 2, 1970.
107. Quoted by Lawrence Mosher in the weekly *National Observer*, October 5, 1970.
108. The *New York Times*, July 25, 1970.
109. The Soviet delegation included also General Slatvei Zakharov, chief of general staff, and the deputy foreign minister Vladimir Vinogradov. See *Los Angeles Times*, October 5 and 9, 1970.
110. *L. A. Times* October 5, and *Time*, October 26, 1970.
111. *N. Y. Times*, October 8, 1970,
112. Results of referendum in *N. Y. Times*, October 17, 1970, see also *L. A. Times*, October 19, 1970.
113. *N. Y. Times, L. A. Times*, October 8, 1970.

114. *N. Y. Times,* October 18, 1970,
115. Reported in *L. A. Times,* October 1, 1970.
116. The proposals were mentioned in *N. Y. Times,* October 10, 1970.
117. Cited in Miles Copeland, "The Strategy Left by Nasser," *Life Magazine* (October 9, 1970.), 37.

CHAPTER III

THE SUDAN: MILITARY RULE AND POPULAR REVOLUTION

The Sudan was brought under military rule in November 1958, less than three years after its complete independence. In October 1964 it became the first Arab country to end the rule of the military and re-establish democracy by a popular revolution, not by another military coup. The emergence and passing of military rule can be explained by certain aspects of Sudanese history, and by some features of political and social life in the Sudan.

I. Background and Problems

The course of events in the Sudan shortly before and after the achievement of independence in 1956 was influenced by external factors relating primarily to the relations of the country with Egypt, and by internal factors bearing on the role of the educated elite, the position of the religious organizations and their leaders, the attitude of the army officers, and the problem of the southern Sudan.

The condominium agreement of 1899 placed the Sudan under the joint domination of Britain and Egypt, but it was Britain who had the upper hand. The question of the future of the Anglo-Egyptian Sudan and its relationship with Egypt was raised in almost all the negotiations between Egypt and Britain for Egyptian independence before and after the treaty of 1936. The Egyptian governments generally wanted the unity of the Nile Valley under the Egyptian crown. They were willing to give the Sudan some form of self government but in permanent union with Egypt, and they assumed that, with few exceptions, this was what the Sudanese people wanted. When the Wafd cabinet unilaterally abrogated the treaty of 1936 with Britain in October 1951, it also abrogated the condominium agreement and gave King Farouk the title, "King of Egypt and the Sudan." The British, on the other hand, refused to recognize the abrogation and opposed Egyptian ambitions and plans for the Sudan. They claimed that the Sudanese should be allowed to freely choose their future status and exercise their right of self-determination.

In the meantime, the educated Sudanese, most of whom were graduates of Gordon Memorial College in Khartoum, began to organize for national action and to make their aspirations known because both Egypt and Britain were in the habit of making decisions for the Sudanese without soliciting their opinion. In February 1938 they formed the Graduates' General Congress and engaged first in educational and social activity. They consisted mostly of civil servants, and their secretary was Ismail Azhari, a mathematics teacher at Gordon College who had studied at the American University of Beirut in the late 1920's. In April 1942 the Graduates, assuming the role of spokesmen for the people of Sudan, presented to the Government several nationalistic demands, but the British refused to recognize their new political role as well as their demands. Azhari then turned to Egypt for support and with an extremist wing of the Graduates' Congress called for the unity of the Nile Valley. His group won control of the Congress in the elections of 1943 and organized the Ashiqqa (Brothers) party, the first genuine political party in the Sudan.[1] The new party was supported by Sayyid Ali al-Mirghani and his Khatmiyya Brotherhood which had been close to the Egyptian administration in the nineteenth century and was later weakened by the success of the Mahdist movement and rule. The moderate Sudanese nationalists who opposed unity with Egypt left the Congress and organized the Umma (Nation) party.

They were under the patronage of Sayyid Abdul Rahman, the Mahdi's son and leader of the Ansar (supporters of al-Mahdi).

The two main political parties in the Sudan were thus organized by the educated elite, but each of them obtained a popular following among the masses by an alliance with a powerful religious order or brotherhood. The traditional rivalry between the Khatmiyya, that feared the return of Mahdist rule, and the Ansar was revived and became an important factor in the competition between the Ashiqqa and the Umma parties. Each of the leaders of the two religious orders sought to enhance his influence and power by his patronage of one of the two political parties. For many years, Sudan politics were dominated by these two combinations and their rivalries, the Umma-Ansar cooperating with the British and in favor of an independent Sudan, and the Ashiqqa-Khatmiyya favoring union with Egypt. When in 1944 the British Governor-General established an advisory council for the Northern Sudan in order to associate the Sudanese with the government of the country, Egypt was not consulted and most of the twenty-eight Sudanese members in the council were from the Umma party. The council, moreover, had no representatives from the Southern Sudan and was not allowed to discuss the affairs of the southern provinces, in accordance with British policy that treated the region separately in view of its ethnic, religious, and cultural differences with the north. The population of the Southern Sudan, close to one-third of that of the whole country, was Negroid by race, pagan and Christian by religion, and spoke various African languages, while the Northern Sudan was Muslim and Arabic speaking.

The Sidqi-Bevin negotiations of 1946 for abolishing the Anglo-Egyptian treaty of 1936 failed because of the controversy over the Sudan. Egypt insisted on the unity of the Nile Valley under the Egyptian crown in these discussions as well as in those that took place in 1947 at the United Nations, but the British maintained their declared policy of no change in the status of the Sudan until the Sudanese have been consulted through constitutional channels. In June 1948 the advisory council of the Northern Sudan was superseded by a legislative assembly and by an executive council, half of whose members were Sudanese. The Northern Sudanese nationalists were reassured about the unity of the Sudan when it was decided to include representatives of the Southern Sudan in the legislative assembly and the Southerners accepted, while the British ended their policy of excluding the Northern Sudanese from the South. Egypt opposed the new measures and so did the pro-Egyptian Ashiqqa who, moreover, boycotted the elections and thus left the Umma party in control of the new assembly.[2] The secretary-general of the Umma, Abdallah Khalil, who was at one time an officer of the Sudan defense force, became the leader of the assembly. The Ashiqqa demonstrations at the time of its meeting in mid-December 1948 led to the arrest of Ismail al-Azhari.

The abrogation of the Anglo-Egyptian treaty of 1936 and of the condominium by the Egyptian Wafd cabinet on October 8, 1951 was not recognized by the Sudan Government. The bill passed by the Egyptian parliament defining the relation of the Sudan to Egypt could not therefore be enforced. Britain, on the other hand, encouraged the enactment of a self government statute for the Sudan in 1952. The drafted statute was debated in the legislative assembly and was enacted on April 23, 1952. It provided for an all-Sudanese council of ministers responsible to a bicameral parliament in internal affairs. The British government waited for the government in Egypt to give its consent to the statute, prior to its implementation, but the Egyptian revolution took place in July.

The military leaders of the revolution in Cairo were anxious to solve the Sudan problem with Britain before discussing the question of the evacuation of British forces from the Canal Zone. General Naguib and his colleagues did not insist on Egyptian sovereignty in the Sudan, as the old regime did, and were ready to concede the right of self determination for the

Sudanese. Naguib, moreover, did not call the Umma-Ansar group "separatists", as they were called before the revolution, and he was an intimate friend of Sayyid Abdul Rahman, leader of the Ansar. The Egyptian officers, nevertheless, did not abandon their hope of re-establishing Egyptian influence in the Sudan. They began discussions with the various Sudanese parties in late 1952 for modifying the self government statute and obtained their consent to the proposed modifications on January 10, 1953. It was at this time that the Ashiqqa party led by Azhari and other pro-Egyptian groups formed the National Unionist Party. The ruling Egyptian junta then opened negotiations with Britain and secured her approval of the modifications. On February 12, 1953 the Anglo-Egyptian agreement was signed. It solved the Sudan problem by granting self determination for the Sudanese and maintaining the unity of their country. During a transitional period of three years, self-governing institutions, including the election of a parliament, were to be created before the people could decide the future of their country. An international commission of five members was to share power with the governor-general, and an international electoral commission was to prepare and organize the general elections.

In the elections that followed in November and December 1953, Azhari and his national unionist party won a majority in both houses of parliament. He consequently formed the cabinet on January 6, 1954 but he took no steps for union with Egypt. The Sudanese voted for his party because they sought freedom from the British, not because they desired to unite with Egypt. The Umma party did not succeed because it had cooperated with the British, but it attributed its defeat to the Egyptian propaganda compaign in favor of Azhari and the Egyptian bribery of Sudanese politicians. When General Naguib arrived in the Sudan to attend the ceremonial opening of Parliament on March 1, 1954, he was greeted with anti-Egyptian demonstrations that led to clashes with the police and the death of several persons. Azhari and his party realized that a large section of the people had no desire to unite with

Egypt. The Sudanese were, moreover, disappointed and disillusioned with Egypt on account of the crude methods it used to influence the election campaign, the suppression of the Muslim Brotherhood and the communist party in Egypt and the fall of Naguib who was respected by the people of the Sudan.

In May 1955 Aznari officially made the pledge of working for the independence and sovereignty of the Sudan. The Sudanization of the administration, the police, and the defense force was completed as Sudanese civil servants and officers replaced the discharged British and Egyptian personnel. The British and Egyptian forces were evacuated from the Sudan before the end of 1955. The Sudan was ready for a plebiscite, but as there seemed to be almost general agreement about its future, especially after the national unionist party declared for independence, it was decided that parliament would declare the country independent without holding a plebiscite. On December 19 the prime minister's resolution calling for the recognition of independence was passed by the two houses of parliament and the Sudan became officially an independent republic on January 1, 1956. The self government statute was amended to meet the new situation and became the transitional constitution. A supreme commission of five Sudanese members replaced the British governor-general at the head of the new republic.

The nature of the relation with Egypt, which was a major problem during the struggle for Sudanese independence, was thus settled but not indefinitely and continued to be a source of tensions in Sudanese politics. The other problem of the relation of the Southern Sudan with the rest of the country remained unsolved. In August 1955, shortly before the proclamation of the complete independence of the Sudan, the Equatoria province of the Southern Sudan revolted and a few hundred Northern Sudanese were killed. The Southerners resented the arrival of inexperienced and sometimes intolerant Northerners to take the place of British administrators. They were against Northern political and cultural domination and were not interested in Sudanese nationalism and unity based on Arabism and Islam. They essentially wanted some kind of autonomy. The lack of progress in solving their problem was a major cause of instability and tensions in the Sudan government.

The Sudan, on the other hand, was free of the tensions and problems created by feudalism in the other Arab countries. In the Sudan, about 90 percent of the land is owned by the state and the greatest employer and agricultural producer is the state. It owns and directs the agricultural work of the greatest part of the land it owns, and the rest is worked by managers, who obtain concessions from the government in partnership with farmers.[3] The labor movement in the Sudan began to develop before independence, and among the labor unions, the most influential and numerous was the Railway Workers' Union. The formation of a workers' trade union federation in the Sudan was opposed by the government in 1950 and it developed into an extremist ally of the Ashiqqa party and was infiltrated by communism.

The Sudan was ruled after independence by a parliamentary regime that had most of the features and defects of parliamentary rule in the other Arab countries: temporary alliances of politicians and of parties, factionalism, adhesion to personalities rather than programs, opportunism and political intrigue. As the leader of the majority party in Parliament, Azhari had been prime minister since January 1954 and continued to hold this post when the country became completely independent on January 1, 1956. He was challenged by some members of his party and at one time on November 10, 1955, he had to resign because he lost a vote of confidence, but he was reinstated a few days later when he regained a majority vote. Like other leaders, such as Quwatli in Syria and Beshara Khouri in Lebanon, whose period of rule witnessed the end of colonial domination, Azhari was popular for a short time as a champion of independence, but later was brought down when his political opponents decided that he had retained power long enough. He had first to accept a coalition government with the Umma party in early February 1956. In June, a dissident group in his national unionist party split away and formed the People's Democratic Party. It was oriented towards Egypt and was supported by Sayyid Ali al-Mirghani, leader of the Khatmiyya, whereas Azhari's NUP broke with the Khatmiyya in an attempt to modernize the party and attract the intellectuals and labor forces.[4] It had already abandoned its central ideological goal of union with Egypt. In early July 1956, Azhari was ousted, and a new coalition cabinet was formed with Abdallah Khalil of the Umma party as prime minister and with the support of the new People's Democratic party. The opportunistic alliance of these two parties that were completely different in their orientation and affiliations was evidently intended to exclude Azhari and what remained of his party from the exercise of power. This alliance lasted, and Abdallah Khalil's premiership with it, until the military takeover on November 17, 1958. In the meantime new parliamentary elections had taken place in March 1958 and the two allied parties — the Umma and the PDP — continued to rule and were supported by the two rival religious fraternities with which they were affiliated.

The coalition government under Abdallah Khalil was divided over the question of accepting American economic and technical aid. While the prime minister and his Umma party were pro-Western and felt that the Sudan was in need of aid for its development budget, his partner in the coalition, the People's Democratic party, was anti-Western and opposed his views on American aid. The aid agreement was signed, however, at the end of March 1958, and was ratified by Parliament in July in spite of the parliamentary effort to reject it and to make the rejection a sign of protest against the landing of the American marines in Lebanon in mid-July.

The coalition cabinet had also to face the demand of the leaders in the Southern Sudan for a federal regime at a time when the government was trying to obliterate the cultural and educational differences of the North and the South. In its effort to integrate the southern educational system and take full charge of education in the southern provinces, the Sudan government began the absorption of missionary schools and thereby caused Southern resentment and provoked tensions that were aggravated later by the high handed policy of the military regime.

The most serious problem for the coalition government was that of its relations with its Egyptian neighbor. The two countries had to settle the question of the Nile waters and to agree about the area of the northern Sudan which would be flooded by the construction of the High Dam. Egypt took a belligerent attitude after the formation of the United Arab Republic. While the Sudan was preparing for elections Nasser sent his troops in February, 1958 to two areas claimed by Egypt, one on the Red Sea and the other on the Nile. A small force landed unopposed at Abu Ramada on the Red Sea, while two columns left Aswan, the one to Wadi Halfa, and the other across the desert to Abu Ramada. The first column lost its way, and many men of the second died of thirst. The Sudan raised the problem to the Security Council on February 20, 1958, and Egypt withdrew its force accusing the Sudanese of exaggeration in their complaint and blaming the dispute on the "imperialists."[5] Again in mid-July 1958, Egypt attempted to create trouble in the Sudan. It was perhaps encouraged by the fall of the monarchy in Iraq. The notorious officer Ali Khashaba, who had been expelled from three Arab countries for subversion, arrived in Khartoum as a new counselor at the Egyptian embassy on July 14. Three days later, he was told to leave because he was stirring up subversion, but Egypt regretted the disregard of "friendly and brotherly relations linking the people of the two countries" by the Sudan government.[6]

In the summer of 1958 the coalition of the Umma and the PDP was about to break, as could be expected because of the differences in their orientation. Contacts began between the Umma politicians and those of Azhari's NUP to form a new coalition cabinet, but at the same time there was growing concern in Umma circles and among some superior officers about the attitude of Egypt. In October, the leader of the

PDP, Ali Abdul Rahman, who was a member of the cabinet. went to Cairo to meet Nasser without telling Abdallah Khalil Azhari and other leaders also appeared in Cairo, and they were joined later by Abdallah Khalil himself. The object of the visit was to negotiate with Nasser, but the atmosphere was not favorable and the trip of the Sudanese leaders to Cairo, especially that of Khalil, was said to have been like "going to Canossa." The Umma leader was afraid that a rapprochement between the other Sudanese leaders and Egypt might lead to the increase of Egyptian influence. This fear and mistrust was shared by some officers and contributed to the staging of the first military coup.

II. The Four Military Coups 1958-1959 and the Military Regime

Between November 1958 and the same month in 1959, the newly independent Sudan witnessed four military interventions. The first was a successful bloodless coup d'état against the parliamentary regime under which the Sudan had been ruled since 1954 and especially since its independence on January 1, 1956. The three other interventions were attempts by rival and dissident officers to seize power from their colleagues, and only one of them succeeded.

The first coup was staged on November 17, 1958 under the leadership of fifty-eight-year-old Lieutenant General Ibrahim Abboud, commander in chief of the armed forces. The capital Khartoum, was occupied by 4,000 troops, the government buildings in the capital and the radio station in neighboring Omdurman were seized, and the cabinet members were placed under house arrest. In a series of orders and proclamations based on the "Defence of the Sudan Ordinance," and on the powers conferred on General Abboud by the revolutionary Supreme Council of the Armed Forces of which he was the president, a state of emergency was proclaimed in the Sudan and military area commanders were allowed to exercise power in the provinces; the provisional constitution was suspended, Parliament and political parties were dissolved, and newspapers and news bulletins were suspended until further notice.[7]

The military intervention was primarily caused by the fear of Egyptian infiltration and the threat of the hostile Egyptian intrigues against Sudanese independence. The proclamation broadcast by General Abboud on the day of the coup made no reference to this threat and explained the military intervention in a long diatribe against the parties and the parliamentary system, almost exactly as Ayub Khan had done a few weeks earlier in Pakistan. General Abboud, however, referred to the bitter political strife between parties trying to secure personal gain by every means, lawful and unlawful, through the "utilization of certain newspapers and the contact with foreign embassies." He also said that he will spare no effort to improve relations with Egypt "to resolve all outstanding problems and put an end to the artificial strain which has hitherto subsisted between the two countries." He began his proclamation by mentioning the "state of degeneration, chaos and instability," as well as suffering in the country, and blamed them on the competition of parties for assuming power and utilizing national resources for personal gain. In a pattern similar to that of other statements that justify military intervention, General Abboud described how the officers had been watching the partisan governments hoping that public stability will be maintained, but when the situation continued to deteriorate "the Sudanese Army and the security forces had no alternative but to take over in order to put an end to this chaos." The proclamation assured the people that the military were not after personal gain and were not motivated by any hatred or malice towards anyone. "Our aim," he said, "is the stability, prosperity, and welfare of the country and its people."

The military coup was not opposed by those whom it supplanted. Neither political leaders nor the two religious leaders intervened against the coup. Sayyid Abdul Rahman, leader of the Ansar, gave his consent indirectly and with uneasiness. He died shortly after on March 24, 1959 and was succeeded as Imam by his son Saddiq who later on led the Mahdist opposition to military rule. The leader of the Khatmiyya agreed to the coup because he disliked party politics and intrigue. The coup, moreover, seems to have been made with the knowledge and consent of Abdallah Khalil, the ousted prime minister who, like Azhari, was given a good pension. It was reported that at various occasions he admitted his foreknowledge of what was going to happen, and he expressed his belief that the army was better prepared to stand in the face of Egyptian designs. It was as if General Abboud's government came by a virtual handover from the previous parliamentary regime.[8] The people were ready to give the military a chance, as they often do at the beginning, especially when the leader of the coup was the popular and respected General Abboud.

The military government that followed the coup was described in the Constitutional Order no. 1, issued on November 17, 1958. The Sudan was proclaimed a democratic republic in which sovereignty was vested in the people. The constitutional authority in the Sudan was given to a Supreme Council of the Armed Forces that consisted of twelve senior officers under General Abboud to whom the Council delegated all its legislative, judicial, and executive powers as well as the command of the armed forces.[9] General Abboud thus became the head of state and the military dictator of the new republic. The new regime appointed a council of ministers of twelve members, seven of whom were military officers who belonged to the Supreme Council, and five were civilians.

The Sudanese officers' coup was explained by the Egyptian "Middle East News Agency" in a special report that was reproduced on November 19, 1958 by the press in the United Arab Republic. It claimed that American aid was disliked, in spite of bad economic conditions, because it imposed a kind of economic trusteeship over the Sudan, and that the coup took place as the United States was preparing to bribe the members of Parliament before the opening of the parliamentary session. This claim was disproved, however, when the new military regime confirmed the aid agreement on November 29 and accepted an American loan of thirty million dollars.

The foreign minister's statement on November 30 emphasized that "this revolution is purely a Sudanese move. . . to secure and to maintain the independence of the Sudan and to provide confidence, stability, and prosperity for its people." It was also a mild revolution which was marked by its gentle treatment of the former rulers. The coup was not followed by trials of the outgoing ministers. On the contrary, the two former prime ministers received life pensions, and the other members of the cabinet received individual letters of thanks for their services, and fourteen days' pay. When the statues of Gordon and Kitchener were removed as a result of a decision of the military regime on December 11, 1958, the removal was done with due ceremony and the statues were sent to England.[10]

The military government was described as nationalistic in its emphasis on Sudanese independence, conservative in its aversion to violent change and radical reform, and discreetly pro-Western, although officially it was neutral. The most prominent and perhaps pro-Western among the military leaders was Major General Ahmad Abdul Wahab who was the second in command after General Abboud and the minister of interior in the cabinet. He was an adherent of Sayyid Abdul Rahman al-Mahdi, who allegedly secured for him the interior ministry. The military commander of the Khartoum region, General Hasan Bashir, was described as the strongman of the regime.[11]

The struggle for power between certain commanders of the military regions and the Supreme Council began in early 1959 and produced the first coup against the new military regime. The causes were political and personal. The commander of the eastern region, Brigadier Muhieddin Abdallah, and his colleague Brigadier Abdul Rahim Shannan resented the fact that they were excluded from the Supreme Council although some officers of lower grade, or younger in age were in it. They also disagreed with the Council on internal projects and foreign policy. Muhieddin Abdallah was evidently regarded as progressist and pro-Egyptian, and he was jealous of Abdul Wahab and did not like his policy. He consequently plotted with Shannan, and the two made the coup of early March in two stages.

On the very early morning of March 2, 1959, the two angry generals, Abdallah and Shannan, brought troops to Khartoum, seized the strategic points in the capital, and went at dawn to arrest General Abdul Wahab and two others in the Supreme Council. General Abboud did not try to use force against them, perhaps because he was not sure of General Hasan Bashir, commander of the capital, and therefore sought the help of mediators. The mediation efforts, in which the two religious leaders took part, ended with a compromise and a call for moderation and army unity. Abdul Wahab and the other officers were released and the troops were withdrawn. That was the end of the first stage. Two days later, March 4, the second stage began with the return of the troops because the two commanders suspected that action would be taken against them. The capital was surrounded and Generals Abdallah and Shannan asked the resignation of the Supreme Council because of the alleged dissatisfaction of the army and the people with its policy. The Council met and after a violent discussion all its members resigned except Abboud. It was reformed on March 5, but five of the original members were excluded and seven, including Abdul Wahab, were retained. The two leaders of the coup, Abdallah and Shannan, along with the commander of the central region, Maqbul al-Amin, became new members and were given ministerial posts. When the new ten-member Council met on March 9 to take the constitutional oath, Abdul Wahab refused to take the oath before the departure of the rebellious armies from the capital to their respective regions. A short communiqué appeared after the ceremony. It mentioned the disagreement among the generals as well as the decision to retire General Abdul Wahab.[12] The dissident generals were thus victorious and their coup is said to have been made under Egyptian influence. General Shannan claimed later that the coup in March was to allow General Abboud to be the real leader and prevent Abdul Wahab from becoming president, and also to solve the standing problems with the United Arab Republic and stop foreign interference encouraged by Abdul Wahab and the former premier, Abdallah Khalil.[13]

    Disagreements continued in the army and the two generals Abdallah and Shannan were dissatisfied because they were a minority in the Council. General Abboud watched them and tried to prevent a repetition of the coup of early March by giving orders that no military units should be moved except by an order from him. On May 22, the two generals attempted another coup but it failed due to bad planning, hesitation, and perhaps disagreement at the last moment. Two army units were brought from Gadaref in the Eastern region to the outskirts of Khartoum on the basis of fabricated telegrams from Army Headquarters, but the Government reacted quickly. The garrison at Khartoum sent its armored cars against them and they withdrew when they saw no support coming from the north. The conspirators in the north at Shendi were arrested by preventive measure because General Hasan Bashir was informed about their intentions. They were nine, including two brothers of General Shannan. On May 27, the interim commander of the Eastern region and eight of his officers were arrested. After an investigation, thirteen other officers and the two generals, Shannan and Abdallah, were also arrested on June 1, 1959. They were tried in open court martial where they were accused of inciting to mutiny by sending troops to Khartoum to overthrow the regime. The two generals received a death sentence which was later commuted on September 22 to life imprisonment.[14] Twenty officers were dismissed from the service, and a member of the Supreme Council was deposed because he knew about the mutinous movements and did not report them.

The sentences against the conspirators were severe, but they put an end to divisions among the senior officers. The third coup in the first year of military rule was attempted by cadets and junior officers at the Infantry Training School in Omdurman and it was a failure. Cadets and junior officers were critical of the military regime and were in contact with the students at the University of Khartoum. They evidently included in their ranks some communists and certain dismissed officers. The Government knew that some violent action was being prepared for the first anniversary of the military regime, and it warned the leaders among the young officers that severe measures would be taken against any attempted mutiny and sentences would not be commuted, but the attempt was not prevented. On November 9, 1959 the mutineers occupied the infantry school and marched on Khartoum. General Hasan Bashir easily contained their advance and had them arrested. Their leaders were tried and five of them — all majors and captains — were sentenced to death and hanged on December 2. Seventeen officers were dismissed. The reaction of the military regime was thus prompt and ruthless and it meant that no insubordination on political grounds could be tolerated. The officers were hanged and not executed by the firing squad evidently because it was feared that the soldiers would refuse to fire.[15] The executions were followed by student demonstrations and processions and the University was closed twice before and after December 5, 1959.

By the end of the first year of military rule, internal strife between military factions had ended and stability and security had been restored. On November 8, 1959 the Nile Waters Agreement was signed with Egypt and smoother relations between the two countries were inaugurated. The Sudan received fifteen million pounds from Egypt as compensation for the land near Wadi Halfa that was to be flooded by the Aswan dam. The Nile waters were reapportioned between the two countries and the quota of the Sudan was increased. The economic position of the Sudan was improved and stabilized especially after the sale of accumulated arrears of cotton which meant more revenue and increased foreign currency reserves. Hydroelectric and industrial projects were started and some were completed in the first three years of military rule such as the Managil canal and the Khartoum textile factory. The railway was extended to Wau in the far South, and merchant ships were ordered in Yugoslavia. Several banks were opened for industrial and agricultural development. Housing schemes were initiated, a new labor law was enacted, and rents and prices were restricted.[16] In contrast with Egypt and other Arab countries under military regimes, the Sudan did not attack capitalist enterprise, and the businessmen were not called "imperialists" and "exploiters." The Sudanese of the capital were shocked by the arrest of wealthy "reactionaries" in Cairo and the seizure of their property in October 1961.

The military ruled the Sudan with what was described as a "light touch," partly due to the influence of General Abboud, who was compared to Egypt's General Naguib but lasted longer. The military, moreover, did not seek to build up a hero-image for themselves and did not try to rouse the public by the spectre of foreign threats and influences.[17] Some of the military spokesmen criticized Nasser of Egypt as "too noisy, too fast, and too precipitate in his actions." As a result, "after ten years, he was still just beginning," and he did not have a democratic government. The Sudanese military hoped to do better by moving more slowly.[18] They took two steps to build "a real democracy avoiding the mistakes of the past." First, they inaugurated on July 1, 1961 the new provincial councils and gave them power and autonomy, but these councils were headed by a senior officer who acted as the central government representative. Second, they formed a constitutional commission to recommend the establishment of a central legislative council. On the fourth anniversary of the military takeover, 17 November 1962, General Abboud issued the Central Council Act that provided for a council of 72 members, 54 elected by the provincial councils, and 18 appointed by the president of the Supreme Council of the Armed Forces.

It was given the power to legislate, ratify treaties, and question the cabinet ministers. The president of the Supreme Council, General Abboud, shared with it the legislative power. It was also headed by a senior officer appointed by Abboud. Its first meeting was held in November 1963. Although most of the opposition to the military regime boycotted the Central Council, it included nevertheless some distinguished members who criticized the regime's policy in the South, spoke on the freedom of the press, and exposed scandals and corruption in the administration and helped arouse public opinion.[19]

Discontent with the military regime appeared after the abortive coup of the junior officers in November 1959 and continued in spite of the apparent passive attitude of the people. The politicians, and the Sudanese in general, missed the excitement of party politics, and along with the intelligentsia and the trade unions resented the restrictions on their activities and the suppression of their freedoms. Certain aspects of corruption were noticed in the granting of import licenses and other favors, and complaints were made about the arrogant behavior of officers. A special source of trouble and of demonstrations at Halfa in the north in November 1960 was the government decision to transfer the villagers of that area to another region in the south on the Atbara river.

The first formal petition addressed to General Abboud to end military rule and restore parliament was sent on November 25, 1960 and was signed by leaders of dissolved parties including Sayyid Saddiq Al-Mahdi leader of the Ansar and of the Umma party. It is to the credit of both the Sudanese military regime and Sudanese personalities that this petition and others to follow were sent at all. Under other military regimes, political leaders rarely had the courage to send similar petitions. The Supreme Council disregarded the petition and deprived the two former prime ministers, Azhari and Khalil, who signed it, of their pensions. The leader of the Ansar, Sayyid Saddiq, should also be credited for his refusal to use his religious influence with the troops for bringing pressure to bear on the government. He felt that the army allegiance to the state would be weakened if he were to tamper with its loyalty, and this would endanger all succeeding governments.[20]

In the summer of 1961, the military government had to face another wave of protests. The railway workers' union struck in June for a substantial wage increase and the railways were crippled for several weeks. Repressive action was taken against the union. The alleged torturing of a communist who was caught distributing leaflets against the regime gave the politicians a pretext to denounce the military government in a sharply worded telegram sent to General Abboud. The government reacted by arresting twelve of the leading party leaders who signed the telegram and transferred them to Juba in the South on July 11, 1961. They included Muhammad Ahmad Mahjub, Abdallah Khalil and Ismail Azhari, but not Sayyid Saddiq who was among the signatories. General Abboud described them as "a handful of persons who cannot but place their own interests above those of the country," and claimed that they started unwisely their opposition against the country's interests, spread rumors to mislead the simple people, and began urging students to riot.[21] In the following month on August 22, the Mahdist youth marched in a procession in Omdurman to the Mahdi's tomb on the occasion of the Prophet's birthday. The procession was deemed illegal in view of the ban on demonstrations, and the Mahdist youths were ordered to disperse. Upon their refusal they were dispersed by gunfire after they had attacked the police, and the clash left fifteen dead, twelve Mahdists and three policemen. The regime's authority was upheld after it had been tested. On October 2, 1961 Sayyid Saddiq died at the age of fifty. He was a firm believer in democracy and constitutional rule and a defender of public liberty. He was succeeded in his religious function of Imam by his brother Sayyid al-Hadi, while his political leadership of the Umma party was taken over by his son Sadeq, the young Oxford graduate. The political leaders in exile were moved back to Khartoum at the end of January 1962 and released. The government continued to be harassed by workers and student groups. The power of control over the University which the government assumed in November 1963 did not insure more order among the students. The appointment of the minister of education, General Muhammad Talat Farid, as chairman of the governing body of the University was, moreover, resented by members of the faculty.

The failure of the military regime to solve the problem of the Southern Sudan gave the political opposition another opportunity to assail the government of the military and demand the restoration of democratic rule. The Southerners resented the attempts of the military government to enofrce unity by pressing Arabization and Islamization on the South. They resisted the measures to impose a uniform system of education with an Islamic Arab orientation, and disliked the substitution of Friday for Sunday as the offical holiday, as well as the pressures to discourage the acceptance of the Christian religion and restrict the educational activity of the Christian missionaries. Demonstrations and disturbances began in 1960 when the government issued heavy sentences against those who criticized its measures. Many Southern political leaders and students began to leave the country and an organization called the Sudan African National Union was established in exile to work for a federated Sudan.[22] In February and March 1964 the foreign missionaries were expelled because they were suspected of favoring Southern separatism. Rebellion had already started in the preceding year and the rebels carried out their terrorist activities against the government whose policy of repression did not restore internal security. The Abboud regime finally announced in September 1964 that a special commission would be appointed to investigate conditions in the South, and the citizens were invited to give their opinions on the subject. Debates on the problem of the Southern Sudan were held at the University of Khartoum but the students decided in their first meeting that the government should resign before any solution could be found. This led the government to forbid further discussion, and out of the students' defiance of the government order came the popular revolution of October 1964 that ended the military regime.

III. The Popular Revolution of October 1964 and the Restoration of Democratic Rule

The revolution of October 1964 that overthrew the six-year old military rule was, along with the Lebanese revolution of 1952, the only revolutionary movement in the contemporary Arab world in which the enitre population joined forces to overthrow an unpopular regime. It was also the only popular movement to succeed in removing a military government.

It must be noted, however, that this movement was not planned for a certain date or period, and in the last months of military rule no immediate change of government was anticipated.[23] In spite of rising discontent in the ranks of the intelligentsia, the politicians, and the proletariat, there was no organized opposition and no planned action. Radical elements in the communist-infiltrated labor unions and tenant organizations, and students at the University of Khartoum who included supporters of communism as well as members of the conservative Muslim Brotherhood, were the most militant agitators against the military regime. The problem of the Southern Sudan gave them the occasion of protesting against government brutality in suppressing the rebellion in the South, and the first incident that suddenly developed into a revolution occurred on October 22, 1964 when the students held an unallowed discussion circle on that problem. In the clash that accompanied the attempt of the police to disperse them, nine students were wounded and thirty-six policemen were injured. The students used sticks, bottles, and stones in attacking the police, while the latter first used tear gas and then were reinforced by a group of policemen who carried firearms and evidently discharged them. The death of one of the wounded students on the following day produced an indignant and violent reaction. The doctors refused to treat the injured policemen. Demonstrators and rioters went through the city attacking and damaging various stores, offices, and gas stations. Other riots and pressures on the military government followed and constituted what is known as the October revolution.

In contrast with a military coup, a popular revolution does not overthrow a ruling regime, especially a military one, and announce its successor overnight. General Abboud was forced to dissolve the Supreme Council of the Armed Forces and the cabinet on Monday October 26, three days after the beginning of the riots. The new civilian cabinet was formed only on October 30, while General Abboud's resignation, which meant the removal of the last symbol of military rule, came on November 15, 1964, three weeks after the first riots began. During all this period, agitation was almost continuous and bloody clashes sometimes occurred and some people were killed, but they ended always with more concessions on the part of the military, until the revolution completely triumphed. The reason for the people's success was their unity and determination to end military rule, and the inability of the Supreme Council of the Armed Forces to agree on the use of extreme force. The Sudanese military rulers perhaps could have maintained their control by dealing ruthlessly with the riots and killing more people, but they were not prepared to go to that extent. Many officers, moreover, disapproved of military rule and favored a return to rule by the civilians. The obedience of the soldiers was also questionable if asked to fire on their countrymen in a prolonged struggle.[24] The Sudanese military, in contrast to those in other Arab areas, evidently were more sensitive to the consensus of opinion among the people, and did not in the first place destroy the various elites or subvert the popular organizations that could challenge their power. They had no special ideology or system to force on the country, and did not try to rouse hysterical hatreds against imaginary enemies and threats from outside in order to retain power. It must be said also that in no other Arab country the people's consensus against military rule was as great and their violent action to end it as determined as in this particular revolution in the Sudan.

The armed forces tried to restore order after the riots of October 23. On Saturday and Sunday, October 24 and 25, they arrested hundreds of persons, but more deomonstations took place in spite of the announced curfew, and by the fourth day of rioting on Sunday evening eight persons had been killed. The judges of the High Court closed the courts and along with other civil servants, they appealed for the termination of military rule and the cessation of sabotage acts. Government offices were closed on Sunday and civil servants stopped work. On Monday, October 26 the rail workers and the airport and radio employees went on strike and rioting continued. The minister of interior, General Muhammad Ahmad Irwa, warned that curfew-breakers would be shot down, but General Abboud had already realized the extent of popular opposition to his regime and decided to make concessions. As a result of negotiations with a United National Front that represented the various parties and dissident groups, he announced on Monday evening the dissolution of the Supreme Council of the Armed Forces and the cabinet and took full powers in his hands. He promised the formation of a new cabinet "acceptable to all citizens," and in his radio address he told the people, "On many occasions I have told you that your brave army when it took power, did not intend to hold it forever."[25]

Negotiations about the formation of the caretaker cabinet and its membership lasted several days during which doubts were raised about the good will of the army negotiators. On Wednesday October 28 a procession of impatient students marched to the presidential palace. As they reached near the gates, a shot was heard and orders were given, as a result, to the security forces to open fire on the crowd outside the palace. Fourteen persons were killed and many were injured, but no more clashes occurred in the following few days. A change in the military command was announced on October 28. The powerful General Hasan Bashir, who had reportedly warned that his troops would occupy Khartoum if he was relieved of his post of deputy commander of the armed forces, was ousted from that post and was replaced by General al-Taher al-Maqbul, former military governor of Kassala near the Ethiopian border. General Bashir, however, continued to lead a big faction of the army in support of General Abboud against the smaller faction of "free officers." The Cairo daily *al-Ahram* insinuated that it was these free officers who surrounded the supreme military headquarters in Khartoum with tanks and forced General Abboud to dissolve his cabinet and his junta or Supreme Council.[26]

Political maneuvering and the formation of various political fronts immediately followed the first events of the popular revolution. The Front of Professional Organizations was the first to appear. It included labor unions, professional associations of lawyers, engineers and medical doctors, the Gezirah tenants, the student unions and the University faculty. It was controlled by leftists because of the positions of leadership attained by communists in these organizations. Several component associations later on left the front because of its dominance by communists. The other important front was the United Front of Political Parties. It included the Umma, the national unionist party, the people's democratic party and the Muslim Brothers party. The people's democratic party eventually withdrew from this front and formed a coalition with the communist party.

A United National Front was formed during the negotiations with the military to insure cooperation between the two hostile fronts - the professional front and the united front of political parties. It was therefore a coalition that represented elements of both fronts in a committee of twelve members. The majority of members in the committee belonged to the organizations, while the parties had only one member each. The communist party, however, had more than one because its members represented various organizations. The composition of the civilian cabinet that was formed on October 30 followed the same "syndicalist" pattern as that of the committee of twelve and this is why the communist representation on the cabinet was completely out of proportion with the numeric strength of the communist party.[27]

On Friday October 30, 1964 the caretaker or transitional government, as it was called, was formed of fourteen civilians headed by Sirr al-Khatim Khalifa, deputy undersecretary in the ministry of education. General Abboud remained head of state and commander in chief. The new government ended temporarily the clashes in which about twenty-seven persons were killed since October 22 and more than one hundred were injured. The representation of the two old parties, the Umma and the national unionist party in the cabinet was small, but they held the two important portfolios of foreign affairs, and finance and economy. The small and well organized communist party had four members on the cabinet, one officially representing the party, and three representing the bar association, the labor federation and the tenant farmers. The cabinet forcibly had to be a coalition cabinet until the elections, but it was dominated by communists and leftists. One of its main tasks was to prepare for the election of a constituent assembly that would draft a constitution. In the meantime the Sudan was to be ruled by the constitution of 1956.

The new government proceeded to undo what the military regime had done and to remove the restrictions on freedom. The Central Council created by the military was dissolved, the state of emergency was ended and the freedom of speech, assembly and the press were restored. Political prisoners were released and the ban on political parties was raised. The new government significantly abandoned the strictly neutral policy that the independent Sudan had hitherto followed, and took position in support of certain movements such as the

Congo rebellion, the Yemen revolution, and the anti-Ethiopian revolt in Eritrea.

The civilian cabinet appointed a special commission to purge the civil service of inefficient and corrupt persons and of those who collaborated with the military. The communist minister of agriculture, Ahmad Sulaiman, was the secretary of the commission and naturally dismissed and retired those who were known to be anti-communist under the pretext of "collaboration," even though many of them were competent officials. The result was chaos in the administration, and also in the economy due to the dismissal of foreign technicians who directed various projects and industries, and to the indifference of the leftist rulers as long as their rivals were ousted. The communists still had one goal, the end of General Abboud's tenure. For them and for many others, he was a symbol of military power and a threat that the army might decide again to rule the country. On November 8, General Abboud gave them the opportunity to spread a rumor that the army was preparing a coup against the civilian government. What Abboud did as commander in chief was to order the arrest of seven politically minded officers who were supposedly planning a pro-Egyptian coup with Egyptian help. Abboud gave the order without consulting the prime minister and the cabinet who believed that the seven officers were arrested because they were supporters of the revolution. The communists now took full advantage of Abboud's action to engineer his resignation. They announced from the radio at Omdurman on November 9 that a coup against the new civilian government was being prepared and called upon the citizens to barricade the streets. On the following day, demonstrations and riots began while the various fronts presented a demand to the cabinet for the replacement of Abboud.

The alleged preparation of a coup by Abboud and the army was a communist invention, but the riots it caused almost paralyzed the public services. At the airport, service was suspended, cars were damaged, trees, cars and stones were dragged to block bridges and streets, and cries of death for the members of the dissolved Supreme Council were heard.[28] It is to the credit of Prime Minister Khalifa and his government that they did not act in haste under the pressure of the "street." For several days the prime minister conferred with General Abboud and senior army officers who supported him. When Abboud resigned on November 15, the agreement was reached, as Premier Khalifa said, for the General to resign "in dignity." Khalifa also complimented the armed forces because they had responded to the people's desires and feelings. General Abboud recorded his resignation speech in the presence of cabinet ministers and it was later broadcast by the state radio. It is significant that in the speech, he mentioned that he was giving up powers bestowed on him by the United National Front Government two weeks before, not those arising from the army coup of 17 November 1958. He also signed the appointment of Maj. Gen. Muhammad al-Khawad as commander in chief of the army. As head of state, he was replaced by a council of five, similar to that dissolved in 1958.

Arab and foreign commentators agreed that the end of military rule in the Sudan was more than a mere Sudanese internal event. The liberal *al-Hayat* in Beirut viewed it as a turning point between the collapse of legal parliamentary regimes in the Arab world and their triumphant re-emergence. It was "a sign of hope that the Arab states would return to normal conditions based on reason, wisdom, and noble character and not on revolutionary sophistry, arms rattling, and rambunctious broadcasts." The Sudan, because of this event, has moved to the forefront among the Arab states and observers have been watching the development and results of the Sudanese experiment as a possible example to be followed.[29] The *New York Times* correspondent, Hedrick Smith, noted that in an era when military coups d'etat have been toppling governments in Africa, Asia and Latin America, and when Westerners have been saying that the underdeveloped world was not ready for democracy, the Sudanese people "have demonstrated that, despite Western doubts they want another chance at democracy."[30] The significance of the Sudanese uprising itself in the restless Middle East and Africa was also noted, and a diplomat was quoted expressing the need to do "some new thinking" because "all of us have been saying for so long that the only thing that matters in these countries is the army. . . but the army couldn't come back here even if it wanted to." The lesson of the Sudan was also closely studied by its neighbors, and President Nasser watched with concern the public uproar in Khartoum and his government reportedly even reviewed its contingency plans lest some such incident as the killing of a university student, coupled with the widespread grumbling over food and other shortages, confront the Egyptian regime with a public outburst.[31]

The new government promised to solve the problem of the Southern Sudan by negotiation. The military regime had been unable to stamp out the revolt in spite of the ruthless efforts it made and the posting of two-thirds of its army in the South. The minister of interior in the new civilian regime, Clement Mboro, a Southerner, appealed for an armistice during his fact finding tour of the southern provinces at the end of November. The mass demonstration of several thousand Southern residents in the North to welcome his return to Khartoum developed into a riot followed by clashes between Southern and Northern Sudanese on Sunday December 6, 1964. An unknown number of persons were killed and hundreds were wounded. After several months a conference opened in Khartoum on March 16, 1965 with delegates of various Southern and Northern fronts and groups and observers from several African states. The Sudan government made concessions to the South but the extremists wanted a referendum to decide if the South wanted the government offer or preferred independence or federation. The problem of the South remained unsolved and the elections for the constituent assembly took place in April 1965 without Southern participation.

The elections were preceded by disagreements and quarrels between the leftist parties and fronts and the old moderate and conservative parties on several electoral, administrative, and economic issues and essentially on the way in which democracy was to function in the Sudan. The Communists and their allies, the pro-Egyptian people's democratic party, wanted the further postponement of the elections, even after they had been postponed from March to April. The government accepted the students' demands for the addition of fifteen seats for "graduates" in the coming assembly, lowering the age limit for voters from twenty-one to eighteen, and extending the franchise to women. The Trade Union Federation and the Tenants Association, encouraged by the communists, demanded half the seats in the assembly. The communists, as it has been said, aimed at placing the state in the hands of the workers, peasants and other revolutionary groups including those of the middle class. The power struggle between them and the old parties was a battle over parliamentary democracy or "a one party system" run by communists and pro-Nasserists.[32] Moreover, the Tenants Association proposed in its election manifesto to nationalize private cotton schemes and to convert them along with all government schemes into cooperative societies. The communists wanted to purge what they called "reactionary bureaucrats" in the civil service and to have special constituencies for "workers, peasants and nationalist intellectuals."

The civilian government dominated by leftists instituted a purge of army and police officers in early 1965 and suppressed six newspapers because they had allegedly received subsidies from the military regime. It also set up a commission to inquire into the circumstances of the 1958 military coup in the hope of incriminating Abdallah Khalil and discrediting the Umma party.

The general impression in the Sudan was that the communists were overplaying their hand. The old political parties, the Umma and its Ansar supporters and the national unionists, who counted hundreds of thousands of followers, reacted against communist influence and pressed for early elections. They also demanded changes in the cabinet and eventually asked for its resignation. On February 18, 1965 the cabinet of Sirr al-Khatim Khalifa resigned and six days later a new cabinet was formed but the prime minister was retained. The leftists lost their hold on the new government which consisted of three Umma members, three national unionists, three Southerners, and one representative of an Islamic party allied to the Muslim Brotherhood. One seat was left open for the communists and three for the people's democratic party, but it was only on April 1 that these two parties agreed to take the four seats that had been reserved for them. They possibly hoped to delay the elections by joining the cabinet. The tenants and workers organizations were not allowed to have any representatives in the new government and the old parties thus scored a victory over the leftists.

The elections began on April 21, 1965 and all the parties, including the communist, participated, but the people's democratic party decided not only to boycott, but also to "resist" the elections. They contended that the voting in the North alone would lead to the separation of the South where the unsettled conditions made it difficult to hold elections. The PDP carried out its threat to prevent the elections at Khashm al-Girba near the Ethiopian border. Its men attacked the police with sticks and swords and it was only after four policemen had been killed that the police opened fire. Ten civilians were killed. Reinforcements were sent to areas where the PDP supporters were frightening voters away from the polls, and the PDP leader, Ali Abdul Rahman, was arrested. The results of the elections showed that the people preferred the moderation and experience of the old parties and were tired of the leftist disorder that followed the popular revolution. The Umma party scored the greatest success with 75 seats in the constituent assembly out of 173 seats for the Northern Sudan. The national unionists obtained 54 seats and two graduate seats. The people's democratic party, in spite of its boycott of the elections, had three seats. The communist party as such did not succeed in having any seat, but eleven of the fifteen "graduate" seats were won by communists, among whom was the first woman deputy. The Islamic Charter party obtained three seats and two of those reserved for graduates.[33]

The two old parties now formed the cabinet after the resignation of Khalifa on June 2, 1965. Rivalry between the Umma and the national unionists over the premiership ended with a compromise. The Umma leader and former foreign minister, Muhammad Ahmad Mahjub was elected prime minister in the first assembly meeting on June 10, while the national unionist leader, Ismail Azhari, was chosen as president of the Supreme Council of five members which fills the function of the presidency of the republic. In the Sudan, as in other Arab areas, it thus became a characteristic of the restored parliamentary governments that follow a period of military rule that the old moderate parties usually come back and the old party leaders of the pre-military regime win immediate recognition. The same thing occurred in Syria after the fall of Shishakli in 1954 and after the breakup of the union with Egypt in September 1961.

The new cabinet included six ministers from each of the Umma and national unionist parties and three ministers from the Southern Sudan. The Supreme Council of five — sometimes called Council of State or Sovereignty Council — was also formed exclusively by members from the two old parties, two from each, and one Southerner. Shortly before the new cabinet took over, a Sudanese broadcast mentioned on June 8, 1965 that the government averted a coup by seizing the arms that were to be used in the planned coup and by arresting suspects. Two ministers in the outgoing Khalifa cabinet, and Brigadier General Abdul Rahim Shannan and twelve other persons were arrested on charges of conspiracy to seize power. It was found out later that the arms, that included guns and grenades, were brought on two Syrian planes and were addressed to Hafez Jamali, Syrian ambassador in Khartoum. They were destined for delivery to Eritrean leaders who were operating from the Sudan territory against Ethiopia.

On June 9, the Syrian government denied that its ambassador had anything to do with the arms, while the ambassador himself is reported to have said that the arms were brought with the approval of the Sudan government and were not to be used for interference in Sudanese politics.[34]

The constituent assembly discussed the fate of those members of the Abboud cabinet under the old military regime who were arrested during the October revolution. The High Court had ordered their release on July 3. In view of the controversy over whether the ministers should be tried or not, the assembly put the question to a vote on July 7, 1965 and the decision, supported by the Umma party, was against trying them.[35]

The restored democratic regime in the Sudan, as in many other developing countries, was characterized by frictions and clashes between parties and personalities in the coalition governments, and by the appearance of factions and new coalitions and party alignments. Shortly after the formation of the first Mahjub Cabinet in June 1965, personal rivalry between Azhari, president of the Supreme Council, and Mahjub, the prime minister, appeared and the struggle for power and prestige almost caused a crisis in September before the meeting of the Arab summit conference at Casablanca. Each of the two wanted to head the Sudanese delegation to the conference and Mahjub threatened to resign from the premiership because Azhari insisted on his right to preside over the delegation. Wisdom finally prevailed and the two left for Casablanca, but while Azhari was the official head of the delegation, Mahjub was the one who conducted the discussions. On his way back to Khartoum, Azhari stopped in Cairo and the Egyptian propaganda media made insinuations to the possibility of cooperation between the national unionist party led by Azhari and Egypt. The Umma party became suspicious of the visit, but as Azhari returned to Khartoum it became evident that his visit to Cairo had no special significance and no agreement was made with Egypt behind the back of the Umma party. In October peace was again disrupted between the two parties in the coalition and between the two leaders because of Sudanese representation in the Organization of African States conference at Accra. Both Azhari and Mahjub expressed the desire to represent the Sudan but Mahjub won and left for Accra. Azhari's resentment soon caused a split in the coalition cabinet when three national unionist ministers resigned on October 20, 1965.[36]

Mahjub retained the premiership until July 25, 1966. In the meantime a split occurred in the Umma party itself between the wing led by Imam al-Hadi al-Mahdi who supported Mahjub, and another wing of younger and more moderate elements led by Sadeq al-Mahdi, al-Hadi's nephew. In August 1966 the thirty-year old Sadeq became prime minister and replaced Mahjub in an Umma party coalition with the national unionists. The Sadeq al-Mahdi cabinet remained in office until mid-May 1967 and had its share of frictions with Azhari. Mahjub returned to the premiership after Sadeq's loss of support in a vote of confidence, and Mahjub's faction of the Umma was again allied with the national unionists. The alliance of the two old parties — the Umma with its two factions and the national unionist party — thus became a constant aspect of Sudanese politics even after the national unionists merged in the spring of 1968 with the people's democratic party to form the United Democratic party. The constituent assembly was dissolved in February 1968 before having approved a permanent constitution for the country. After the elections for a new assembly in April-May, the new cabinet was again a coalition cabinet between the faction of the Umma party headed by Imam al-Hadi to which Mahjub belonged, and the new United Democratic party, in addition to the Southern Front party that consisted of Southerners living in the North. Mahjub was in fact the one who formed the cabinet on June 2, 1968, but his faction of the Umma had only five ministers out of sixteen while the United Democratic party had nine.[37]

The restored democratic regime was also characterized by

a struggle led by the Umma party and the Muslim Brotherhood against the communists during the lifetime of the constituent assembly that was elected in April 1965. The campaign against the communist party began when a communist student defamed the Prophet Muhammad and his favorite wife Aisha. On November 16, 1965 a draft bill to ban the communist party, oust its members from the government, and consider it an offense to be a communist was introduced in the constituent assembly, but the national unionists refused to vote it and clashes occurred between pro-communist and Muslim Brotherhood members. On November 22, the assembly passed a bill allowing the government to present a draft law banning the communist party. Premier Mahjub commented that "our democracy is based on Islam."[38] The draft law was eventually presented to the assembly and the communist party was banned in December 1965; its members in the assembly had to be dismissed. Communists and Muslim Brethren held demonstrations after the constituent assembly vote, the former to express their protest, the latter their satisfaction. The assembly decision was contested by the Supreme Court which held that the communist deputies should not be dismissed, but in December 1966 the assembly overruled the court and asserted that the communist deputies were enemies of Islam and agents of the Soviet Union. On December 26 clashes between Muslim groups and communists left seventeen persons injured in Khartoum. The clashes took place when the Bar Association organized a procession to protest against the rejection of the court judgment by the government and to ask both government and assembly to apologise to the Supreme Court for having rejected its judgment.[39] The assembly, however, maintained its decision and the Umma party supported by Muslim groups thus proved its ascendancy and its ability to defend tradition, ban leftist extremism and subversion, and preserve an atmosphere of moderation under the democratic regime.

Two days after the clashes of December 26, 1966 between the frustrated Communists and their opponents, the government had to deal with an attempt to stage a military coup by leftist junior officers who were presumably encouraged by Communist elements. The attempt on Wednesday, December 28, did not prove to be serious and was easily foiled by the armed forces. The prime minister at the time, Sadeq al-Mahdi, declared on the radio that "some criminals have tried to overthrow democracy in the Sudan by usurping power with the help of new recruit units in the army."[40] The leader of the attempted coup was Lieutenant Khalid Hussein Uthman who was in charge of new recruits. He ordered two hundred of them to surround the republican palace, the radio station, and the bridges and reportedly went to sleep with his clothes on. When Premier Sadeq al-Mahdi was informed about the attempt, he went to the radio station, but was prevented by the recruits from entering until army officers arrived and orderd the recruits to surrender their arms. According to the Khartoum daily, *al-Sahafa,* some coup units occupied the radio station and the entrance to the bridge on the White Nile, but the units were evidently neither adequate in number nor well equipped and the participation of officers was very limited. This is why the attempt collapsed so quickly.

After the failure of the attempted coup, units of the Sudan Army were posted to guard bridges and public buildings. Lieutenant Khalid Hussein and two other lieutenants were arrested as well as several communist party members because of their movements on the night of the attempt. The commander of the Sudan eastern military sector and six other officers were arrested on the following day, December 29, 1966. It was said that the leader of the attempt had in his pocket the names of these seven officers who were ready to become members of the revolutionary council after the success of the coup. He had also the text of the speech he was expected to broadcast as spokesman of the revolutionary council. The rumor spread among the Khartoum University students that the government prepared this attempt, and some fifteen of them were arrested because they wanted to demonstrate against the government. The military court began the trial of those involved in the coup in February 1967 and on March

18, the Supreme Council of the Sudan approved the sentences of the military court on four of the defendants. The leader of the attempt received ten years in jail and was expelled from the army. Three non-commissioned officers were sentenced to five years.[41]

IV. The Leftist Military Coup d'état of May 1969

The democratic parliamentary regime that was restored by the popular revolution of October 1964 was ended by a military coup d'état on the morning of Sunday May 25, 1969. The coup was prepared by a group of young leftist officers under the leadership of thirty-nine year old Colonel Jaafar Numairi in cooperation with Socialist and Communist civilian elements. Leftists in the army had attempted in the past to seize power during the conservative military regime of General Abboud. The attempts were made by Generals Shannan and Abdallah on March 2-4 and May 22, 1959, and by the junior officers and cadets on November 9, 1959. In the popular revolution of October 1964 the leftist elements including the well-organized Communist party and the socialist chief justice Abu-Bakr (Babakr) Awadallah played an important role. The leftist officers opposed to the military government of General Abboud weakened the position of the regime and its military supporters and contributed to the success of the October revolution. The Communists then overplayed their hand under the restored democratic system and in the struggle for power between them and the old parties they were the losers. Their party was banned and the Communists lost their seats in the constituent assembly at the end of 1965 in spite of the support of their leftist friend, Chief Justice Awadallah, and of the Bar Association. The abortive leftist coup of the junior officers on December 28, 1966 was followed by the arrest of certain Communists and showed the presence of strong leftist influences in the army. It also showed that the leftist officers were not as yet sufficiently well organized to carry out a successful coup and seize power.

It is not certain that the civilian government grasped the full significance of the attempt of December 28, 1966, particularly the activity of revolutionary elements in the armed forces. While the ruling democratic regime was being undermined by party quarrels and popular criticism, the Communists who had been driven underground and their leftist military and civilian allies did not abandon their cherished objective of taking over the government. They profited from the disagreements between the ruling parties and exploited the people's complaints against certain aspects of incompetence and corruption. The uneasy coalition of the United Democratic party and the faction of the Umma party led by Imam al-Hadi after the elections of April 1968 was breaking up and Prime Minister Mahjub who had been in office since June 1968 presented his resignation in April 1969. His cabinet was a caretaker cabinet at the time when the coup of May 1969 took place. The Umma party had by this time succeeded in healing the split between its two factions and al-Hadi al-Mahdi, leader of al-Ansar and of one of the two Umma factions, was preparing to present his candidacy for the presidency of the republic towards the end of 1969, while his nephew Sadeq al-Mahdi head of the other Umma faction was in line to become prime minister. It was said that the direct cause of the leftist coup of May 1969 was precisely the reestablishment of unity within the Umma party and the feeling among the leftists that their presidential candidate, Abu Bakr Awadallah, would not be elected while the two other candidates of the old parties, Ismail Azhari and al-Hadi, had more chances of success.[42] The leftists also exploited the economic difficulties and pressures such as the increase in the domestic and foreign public debt, the deficit in the balance of payments, the diminishing reserves of foreign exchange, the growth of inflation, and the slow pace of development projects.

In the early morning of Sunday May 25, 1969 the forces

that had been posted by the leaders of the coup outside Khartoum under the pretext of conducting maneuvers were ordered into the capital. They consisted of some 450 men and included two paratroop units, and one armored and one infantry unit. They cut the telephone and cable lines and proceeded to occupy the radio station and the presidential palace and to arrest the army commanders and civilian rulers. In announcing the coup from the radio station at Omdurman, Colonel Jaafar Numairi mentioned that a new revolutionary council has seized power and that the council acted as representative of the sovereign people "according to a constitution which will be proclaimed later." In the series of orders and ordinances that followed the bloodless coup, the supreme council, the cabinet and the constituent assembly were dissolved, the political parties were banned, the newspapers were closed, martial law was imposed and the warning was given that strikes and hostile actions were prohibited under penalty of death. In making the usual apology for the coup, Colonel Numairi said that the country knew no stability since 1956 and that its history was a series of tragedies because of the many parties that seized power for their private interests and thus corruption and bribery prevailed. The country, he said, was opened to foreign influence and the parties served imperialist interests. The masses, according to Numairi, rejected these former governments because they (the masses) wanted the Sudan to assume its rightful place in the Arab world and in the struggle for Palestine. They also wanted a solution for their economic problems and for the question of the Southern Sudan.[43]

The revolutionary council had already agreed with its civilian partners about a new cabinet and announced its formation immediately after the coup. It was a predominantly civilian cabinet of twenty-one ministers of whom two were military — Colonel Numairi, now promoted to major general's rank, for defense and Captain Farouk Abdallah for the interior. The prime minister was the former chief justice, Abu Bakr Awadallah, who had resigned on supposedly democratic grounds in May 1967 because the Communist party was banned. He was known, however, to be a socialist disciple of Nasser and an exponent of the one-party state. He accepted the destruction of the democratic regime, the banning of parties and the restrictions on freedom imposed by the military. He nevertheless claimed that the new regime sought to establish "genuine democracy." The cabinet included Nasserist socialists like Awadallah, extreme leftists like Numairi, and four or five Communists. The secretary-general of the Communist party, Abdul Khaleq Mahjub, was excluded. Most of the Communist ministers belonged to the pro-Moscow group and included the lawyer Farouk Abu Isa who was appointed minister of state in the prime minister's office to keep an eye on Awadallah. This was viewed as an indication of Communist influence in the revolutionary council. The justice minister Amin al-Shibli, on the other hand, was known to be an independent Marxist with no official membership in Communist organizations in the Sudan.[44]

The new cabinet announced that it stood behind the Arab cause in Palestine and promised to strengthen the armed forces and to establish closer relations with Eastern Europe. This had been also the policy of the preceding regime that broke relations with the United States and Britain, played a leading role in the Arab League meetings after the June war, and sent a military delegation to Moscow immediately before the coup. The new regime, however, emphasized its leftism by such acts as the recognition of East Germany and the new revolutionary (Viet Cong) government of South Vietnam. It spoke of itself as a socialist regime and hinted at nationalizing local capital with "imperialist connections." In the days that followed the coup, the radio broadcast demands forwarded to the government by certain organizations to nationalize banks, corporations, export-import trade and newspapers.[45]

Prime Minister Awadallah claimed that the new regime was not a military dictatorship like that of General Abboud. The dictatorship, in reality, became more ruthless due to the extreme leftist fanaticism and immaturity of the leaders. The

The Sudan: Military Rule and Popular Revolution / 213

revolutionary council to which Awadallah's cabinet was responsible consisted of ten members among whom the prime minister was the only civilian. The military members were mostly young officers.[46] The new regime began by dismissing twenty-two senior officers including the chief of staff, Hamad al-Nil Daifallah, who was arrested after having eluded capture for a few hours, the commander in chief of the armed forces, Muhammad al-Khawad, sixteen brigadier-generals and four colonels. Fourteen officers were appointed to key military positions and included new commanders for the air force, armored units, and police. The head of the revolutionary council, Colonel Numairi, had been involved in attempted movements against the parliamentary regime and the Abboud military government. It was said of him that he was able and had the dedication of Nasser. On the other hand, one of his classmates in 1965 at the U.S. Army Command and General Staff College at Fort Leavenworth (Kansas) described him as an indifferent and dull student who spent much of his time exchanging ideas with other Arab soldiers studying there.[47]

The revolutionary council placed the former rulers, Azhari, Mahjub, and most of the cabinet members under house arrest. The secretary of the Umma and former prime minister, Sadeq al-Mahdi, was sent to a distant province and placed under house arrest because he was said to have incited resistance against the coup. At one time, Colonel Numairi threatened to try all three leaders — Azhari, Mahjub and Sadeq alMahdi — for high treason and execute them. Similar declarations and threats of merciless suppression of any opposition gave the new regime what was called a "ferocious image" and caused speculation on whether it was feeling secure.[48] The government admitted in a communiqué on the day following the coup that its forces clashed with the Muslim Brethren in Omdurman and dispersed them. In order to avoid demonstrations and more clashes it forbade all celebrations on the occasion of the Prophet's birthday on Wednesday May 28, 1969.

On June 9, 1969 the revolutionary council and the cabinet

decided to grant regional autonomy to the three southern provinces "within the framework of a new integral socialist Sudan." It was difficult to interpret what "regional autonomy" meant. The new regime spoke of allowing the Southerners to run their own domestic affairs but also wanted genuine socialist unity. Suspicion, however, continued between the North and the South, and Clement Mboro, the popular Southern politician, was still detained in early September. The outlawed militant movement in the South, the Anya Nya, responded to the new men in Khartoum by forming a provisional government of its own. In mid-September 1969 seventy-nine rebels were reported killed in the Upper Nile province in a battle with the armed forces of the new regime.

The new regime evidently sought to reenforce its position among Arab revolutionaries by multiplying the visits to Cairo and giving more declarations on its anti-Israeli attitude. By June 18, 1969 — in less than a month after the coup — three delegations had visited Egypt. In early September, while the Arab states that were directly concerned with Israel were holding a small summit conference in Cairo, General Numairi arrived on the third and last day of the talks. The Sudan wanted also to impress on the Arab states and on the Russians its need for more arms. The new regime took, on the other hand, a more drastic anti-American position. During his visit to Cairo "to strengthen relations with Egypt," Premier Awadallah declared on July 28, 1969 that he had "definite information that the United States was trying to sabotage our revolution." The new Sudan government had asked three American diplomats to leave because they were accused of collusion with counterrevolutionaries. The United States government had only an indirect diplomatic representation, and in an official declaration it said that it had to reduce the number of its representatives from sixteen to thirteen at the demand of the Sudanese rulers.[49]

The Sudan has remained unique among the Arab countries in ending military rule by an unarmed popular revolution in 1964. In the four and half years that followed, it succeeded in keeping the restored democratic system and the civilian rule free from military intervention. It also succeeded in defeating the designs of Communists and other leftists who probably wanted to operate a change in the economy and in society along Egyptian lines. It was thought for some time after the October 1964 revolution that the Sudanese officers had disengaged themselves from politics after six years of military rule and that they would continue to show self restraint and respect for the will of the people. The coup of May 1969, however, proved that the leftist officers who had showed their opposition to military rule and helped the people to overthrow the regime of General Abboud did so only to prepare the way for their own rule in alliance with the leftist parties. The new military dictatorship that they established has been, and is expected to remain, more intolerant of human freedom and more ruthless in the suppression of any challenge to its authority than the former mild military regime of General Abboud. The reason is that the new military leaders and their civilian facade are committed to a program of radical social and economic change which they can implement only by force.

The new rulers would probably find it difficult to operate their changes due to the expected opposition of the traditional religious and other conservative forces. These same forces, however, would be handicapped by the varied response of the masses and their expected division into those who seek certain material benefits from the rule of the revolutionary leftists and those who remain opposed to revolutionary changes. On the other hand, the new leftist regime itself would be handicapped by the latent causes of conflict among its leaders who range from left of center to Communists. In the interpretation and execution of their theories and plans, and in the conflicting ambitions of the various leftist factions and personalities differences might arise and lead to clashes as they did under the Baath regime in Syria in 1966 and in Iraq in November 1963. The Sudanese who were enraged by the oppression and corruption of the soldiers in 1964 could still become enraged by the oppression and excesses of the leftist military rulers after 1969 and might be able to find some disenchanted officers to help them force a return to democracy and freedom.

An indication of disagreement among the leftist leaders of the new regime occurred when the left-wing premier, Abu Bakr Awadallah, was dismissed by the revolutionary council on October 28, 1969 and a new cabinet under General Numairi was formed. It is supposed that the change took place following a declaration by Premier Awadallah during a visit to East Berlin that the revolutionary regime in the Sudan could not manage without the Communists who, he said, were its "vanguard". The statement by Awadallah was sent to Khartoum by a Communist aide who accompanied him and was broadcast over the radio. General Numairi reacted by broadcasting one hour later a statement in which he explained that Awadallah's remarks reflected only his personal views and that the revolution in the Sudan was for all the people, not one faction or party. Two days after Awadallah's return the cabinet change took place. It was partly the outcome of a general sensitivity to the participation of Communists in the revolutionary regime and resulted in the exclusion of Mahjub Uthman, the Communist minister of national guidance, from the cabinet.[50] The Communist minister Farouk Abu Isa, however, remained and in the meetings of the Arab League Joint Defense Council in Cairo on November 8, 1969 he was chairman of the Council. Frequent official declarations on the discovery of conspiracies to overthrow the military government, and the arrest of a large group of fifty-six persons announced by the interior ministry on December 24, 1969 indicate that the new regime is still struggling for stability and security.

CHAPTER III
NOTES

1. See Mekki Shebeika, *The Independent Sudan* (New York: Robert Speller, 1959), 479 ff.; Peter M. Holt, *A Modern History of the Sudan* (London: Weidenfeld and Nicolson, 1961), 143 ff.; Robert O. Collins and Robert L. Tignor, *Egypt and the Sudan* (Englewood Cliffs: Prentice Hall, 1967), 150 ff.

2. According to Shebeika, 479 ff., the ordinance that created the legislative assembly was prepared and agreed to by the British ambassador in Cairo and the Egyptian foreign minister, but it was rejected by the foreign relations committee of the Egyptian senate.

3. Declaration by Sadeq al-Mahdi in Beirut, in *al-Hayat,* May 16, 1965.

4. See André Ribaud, "Où en est Le Soudan," *Orient,* no. 12 (1959, 4), 37-44 on this attempt of the NUP to evolve and adopt modern political and social formulas.

5. See short account of the dispute in P. M. Holt, 176-177; **Gregory** Blaxland, *Egypt and Sinai,* (New York: Funk and Wagnalls, **1966),** 292.

6. See account in *Time,* August 4, 1958, p. 22.

7. Text of orders no. 1-3 and proclamation by Gen. Abboud in *Directory of the Republic of the Sudan* (London, 1959), 9 ff; M. Khalil, I, 359-361.

8. See opinion of A. Ribaud, 37 ff.; P. M. Holt, 182.

9. Text of the Constitutional Order no. 1 in the *Directory of the Republic of the Sudan,* p. 9.

10. See K. D. D. Henderson, *Sudan Republic*(London: Ernest Benn, 1965) 132-133. GE, 11.
For these assessments, see André Ribaud, 37 ff.

12. *Ibid.*; Holt and Henderson mentioned that General Abdul Wahab was retired on pension on May 9 with a grant of 3,000 acres of state land.

13. See Holt, 185.

14. An Israeli broadcast on June 16, 1959 claimed that the arrested officers belonged to the national unionist party and that the Egyptian government wanted to overthrow the regime in the Sudan because it was firm in defending the rights of the Sudan in the Nile waters.

15. Henderson, 135.

16. See Peter Kilner, "Military Government in Sudan: The Past Three Years," *The World Today* (June, 1962), 261; Henderson, 136; Jay Walz in *The New York Times*, December 17, 1961; *Arab News and Views*, April 1, 1961.
17. See comment by Henderson, 129.
18. See report of Jay Walz in *The New York Times*, December 17, 1961.
19. For these developments: Henderson 142-144; Peter Kilner, 266, *al-Hayat*, November 18, 1962.
20. Reported in Henderson, 134.
21. Text of Abboud's speech in *al-Nasr* (Damascus), July 13, 1961.
22. For the Southern Sudan problem see Kilner, 265; Collins and Tignor, 159-161.
23. See the study of a contemporary observer on the spot, Thomas E. Nyquist, in "The Sudan: Prelude to Elections," *The Middle East Journal*, XIX, 3 (Summer, 1965), 265.
24. For some explanations on the attitude of the military, see Henderson, 129, 203; Nyquist, 265.
25. Quoted in *The New York Times*, October 27, 1964. A report in the Beirut press of October 29 mentioned that in the evening of Monday October 26 between 7 and 9 P.M. the presidential palace where General Abboud and his cabinet were meeting, was surrounded by troops commanded by two dissident superior officers who were referred to as "free officers." They issued an ultimatum to General Abboud in which they threatened to bombard and destroy the palace if he did not dissolve the Supreme Council and the cabinet.
26. See *The New York Times*, November 30, 1964 and compare with fn. 25 on the report from the Beirut press.
27. For an explanation of these fronts and the "syndicalist" composition of the cabinet see Nyquist, 265-266. Henderson, 205 mentioned a Committee of Public Safety with whom General Abboud opened negotiations.
28. See description of the riots in *The New York Times*, November 12, 1964.
29. Article "The Sudan After One Year of Democratic Rule," by "An Old Arab Statesman," *al-Hayat*, October 30, 1965.
30. Hedrick Smith, "Upset in the Sudan", *The New York Times*, November 17, 1968.
31. *Ibid.*

32. See assessment of the situation by *The New York Times,* February 15, 1965; Henderson,214.
33. See results in *Mideast Mirror,* June 12, 1965, 5; *al-Hayat* (Beirut), May 14, 1965; Henderson, 225.
34. *Mideast Mirror,* June 12, 1965.
35. *Mideast Mirror,* July 10, 1965. The votes were 88 against the trial, and 66 in favor.
36. On these two conferences and the rivalry between the two leaders, see *al-Hayat,* October 30, 1965; *Mideast Mirror,* October 23, 1965.
37. *The New York Times,* June 3, 1968.
38. *Mideast Mirror,* November 20, 27, 1965.
39. *al-Hayat,* December 25, 1966; *The Daily Star* (Beirut), December 28, 1966.
40. Report on the attempt in *al-Safa* (Beirut), and *The Daily Star,* December 29, 1966.
41. *al-Nahar* (Beirut), March 19, 1967.
42. *al-Hayat,* May 26, 1969; *The Economist,* September 6, 1969, 33-34.
43. *Los Angeles Times,* May 26; *al-Hayat,* May 26 and 28, 1969.
44. See *al-Hayat,* May 27, 1969; *The Economist,* September 6, 1969. The leftist Beirut daily *al-Anwar,* May 28, 1969 commented that the Sudanese Communist party had a "national identity" and that the Sudanese left whether nationalist or Communist was an Arab nationalist left. Other Communist ministers were the Southerner Joseph Garang (Qaranq) for supply, Dr. Taha Jaafar for labor, and Mahjub Uthman for information.
45. *al-Anwar,* May 29, 1969.
46. *The N. Y. Times,* May 27, 1969 reported that the council included one colonel and seven majors besides Numairi and Awadallah.
47. *The Economist,* September 6; *L.A. Times,* June 6, 1969 article by Stanley Meisler.
48. Editorial, "New Broom in the Sudan," in *New Africa,* ed. H. C. Taussig, XI, 3/4 (London, 1969), 3-4.
49. *Los Angeles Times,* July 21; *New York Times,* July 29, 1969.
50. *N.Y. Times,* October 29, 1969.

CHAPTER IV

REVOLUTION AND CIVIL WAR IN YEMEN

The coup d'état of September 26, 1962 against the traditional political and social order in Yemen was preceded by two abortive revolutionary attempts with limited goals in 1948 and 1955. This is why certain contemporary Yemeni writers speak of the three stages of the revolution against the Imams of Yemen.[1] In spite of its initial success, the third and most important coup, known since then as the Yemeni Revolution, differed from all other Arab military coups in that the new regime that followed continued to be challenged by the overthrown Imam and his partisans. As a result, it did not gain immediate and unanimous recognition by the world community and led to a cruel civil war that was complicated and perpetuated by the intervention of external armed forces.

Yemen has been ruled for over a thousand years by a line of Imams that began in 898 (284 A.H.) with Imam al-Hadi Yahya, grandson of al-Qasim al-Rassi, and ended, or was interrupted, in 1962 by the overthrow of the 67th Imam, al-Mansour Billah Muhammad al-Badr. The Imams derived their authority, religious as well as temporal, from their privileged status as descendants of the Prophet Muhammad and spiritual heads of a moderate Shia sect called the Zaydis who live in the northern and central highlands of Yemen and constitute about half of the population. They carry the name of Imam Zayd, descendant of the Prophet through Hussein ibn Ali, who died as a martyr in 740. Although theoretically any Sayyid (descendant of the Prophet through Hasan or Hussein), who qualified for the post could be elected Imam, the Imamate in Yemen became hereditary and remained in the same family with the exception of four Imams who ruled between 1853 and 1890 (1269-1307 A.H.). Revolts and rebellions against the ruling Imams and struggle for power even among members of the same family were frequent, particularly in the 18th and the first half of the 19th centuries. The Imams were often forced either by rivals or by foreign conquerors to leave their capital, Sana, and retire to the northern highlands where Imamic rule originated. Tribesmen who flocked to support their Imam against foreigners or who fought the domestic wars in the rugged mountainous regions have distinguished themselves as fearless and resourceful warriors. Their greatest exploits in their wars against the Turkish rulers in the first decade of this century made of Yemen, as the saying went at the time, "the graveyard of the Turks."

I. The Coup Against Imam Yahya 1948

During the Imamate of Yahya (his full name and title is al-Mutawakkil Yahya Hamiduddin 1904-1948), Yemen first gained autonomy under Turkish rule in accordance with the Treaty of Daan in 1911, and then, when the First World War ended in 1918, it became completely independent. Imam Yahya ruled over a larger and more unified Yemen than the country had known during the greatest part of its history. In the treaty of February 1934 with Britain, he was recognized as King of the Yemen, which to him meant all Yemen including what Yemeni nationalists called "Occupied Southern Yemen," but to the British it meant the former Yemen which was ruled by the Turks. The kingdom acquired fairly well defined boundaries in the north after the Treaty of Taif with Saudi Arabia in 1934, but Imam Yahya had to recognize the Saudi expansion into Najran and Asir. Yemeni nationalist writers have viewed these treaties as surrender on the Imam's part to his northern and southern neighbors, and have attributed his failure to achieve a more complete unity of Yemen to his weakness and, in the language of more modern writers, to "the reactionary, feudal, and sectarian nature of the Imamic state which was unable to impose unity through a revolutionary war of liberation."[2]

The movement against Imam Yahya's rule began in the 1930's and gained strength in the following decade. Its leaders in Yemen or in neighboring British-occupied Aden assailed the Imam's isolationist policy, his despotic and oppressive government and administration, and his stubborn resistance to change. The Imam's fear of foreign influence and of local modernization made him reluctant to open his country to regular foreign commercial and cultural relations. Yemen thus acquired the reputation of being the most secluded land on earth.[3] Imam Yahya tried to increase his prestige, however, by signing a few treaties of "commerce and friendship" with certain governments and kept contacts with international and inter-Arab politics by joining the United Nations and the Arab League and participating in a number of Arab national conferences.[4]

As Yemeni merchants, public officials, and students became acquainted with the outside world, they felt more and more their backwardness compared to the Arab countries of the Eastern Mediterranean with their constitutional regimes, free press, modern education, progressive economy, and improving standards of living. In Yemen the Imam's religious and temporal authority was unchallenged. It was tempered only - as in the case of many medieval and modern autocratic regimes - by revolt or assassination. He appointed the members of his advisory council; his small army consisted entirely of Zaydis.[5] He depended on the support of the tribal sheikhs, in majority Zaydis, and kept their sons or other important members of the tribe as hostages to insure their loyalty. The tribesmen were by no means nomadic. They were farmers, lived in villages, and were hostile to city dwellers. High political office and important administrative positions belonged to the upper strata of the privileged class of Sayyids who numbered more than 100,000 in a total population of some five million, and to the learned Qadis (literally judges). Some of the Sayyids were wealthy landlords, but their authority and privilege rested on religious grounds and not on their wealth and large following among the farmers. The people suffered from extortion, bribery, high taxation, slow justice, monopoly of trade by the Imam's family, lack of educational and sanitary systems, lack of agricultural, industrial and financial institutions, and the absence of modern means of communication. The Sunnite Muslims of the Shafiite rite who formed about the other half of the population were bitter because they were deprived of political power.

Imam Yahya alienated certain ambitious Sayyids and princes of his own family when he secured in 1937 the recognition of Prince Ahmad, the eldest of his fourteen sons, as crown prince. Ahmad according to some writers was known for his cruelty and is said to have been the most hated among his brothers. Other writers, even among the future leaders of the revolution of 1962, praised his magnanimity, courage, patience, tolerance, generosity and wisdom.[6] Among his prominent rivals was Sayyid Abdallah ibn Ahmad al-Wazir and his cousin Ali, both of whom were related to Imam Muhammad Al-Wazir who died in 1888. Abdallah al-Wazir had served under Imam Yahya in many high posts, but the Imam grew suspicious of him and kept him in Sana. The conspiracy against Yahya was thus motivated by the struggle for power among the ruling groups who were concerned about their positions under a strong ruler like Ahmad, and by the desire for administrative and constitutional reform.

The Yemeni merchants and eminent exiles abroad, and particularly in Aden, were among the most outstanding opponents of the Imamic regime. They organized in the mid-1940's a movement of "Free Yemen" and their society, The Great Yemeni Society, issued a newspaper called *Sawt al-Yemen* (Voice of Yemen) edited by the Shafiite Qadi Muhammad Mahmud al-Zubayri, and a number of pamphlets such as the one entitled *The Plundered and Afflicted Yemen*. They maintained contacts with the secret opposition within the

Imam's circle of supporters and among leading religious dignitaries in Yemen. The Free Yemeni movement in Aden became active in 1946 and drew particular attention when it was joined in November of that year by Imam Yahya's controversial ninth son Ibrahim, who took the title of *Sayf al-Haq* (The Sword of Truth), instead of the traditional title of Yemeni princes, *Sayf al-Islam* (The Sword of Islam).[7]

The program of the Great Yemeni Society in Aden proposed to set up a limited monarchy with an elected legislative assembly and a cabinet responsible to it. The program included the reform of the administration and of the judicial system by the adoption of a code of laws based on the Sharia, the appointment of honest judges and the separation of the judicial from the executive power. It also called for the reform of the finances by establishing a clear cut budget, a national bank with national currency and a modern system of taxation, the preparation of a plan for economic reform that would improve the methods of agriculture, limit land ownership, build roads and irrigation works, exploit the mineral wealth, establish industries, abolish monopolistic commerce, and establish commercial relations especially with the Arab countries. The reformers wanted also the spread of education by opening schools, sending students abroad, and granting freedom of expression in addition to the building of hospitals and fighting disease. The program also gave particular attention to the organization of a regular army, and the expansion of diplomatic relations and cooperation with the Arab countries. It did not demand the end of the Imamate, and made sure that the consititutional regime should not conflict with, or take the place of the Sharia. The malcontents, however, hoped to end the rule of the Hamiduddin family by depriving Crown Prince Ahmad of the succession at his father's death. The candidate of the opposition for the Imamate was Abdallah al-Wazir, and he promised to rule as a constitutional monarch. The other two rivals of Prince Ahmad were his two brothers Hasan and Abdallah.

The conspiracy, or at least the maneuvers of the Great

Yemeni Society, were said to have been encouraged by the British, for they tolerated the activity of the Free Yemenis in Aden. Prince Ahmad in fact later exploited fully the idea of British responsibility for his father's assassination in order to discredit the Wazir regime and accused it of acting as the instrument of the British. It is believed, on the other hand, that the Muslim Brotherhood in Egypt agitated against Imam Yahya's rule, and that the liaison between the Brotherhood and the malcontents in Yemen was al-Fadil al-Wartalani, an Algerian businessman who established himself in Sana and was known to be the brains of the opposition.[8] The executor of the conspiracy was Colonel Jamal Jamil, an Iraqi officer who had taken part in the coup of Bakr Sidqi in 1936 and left for Yemen later when Imam Yahya asked for an Iraqi military training mission. Colonel Jamil managed to remain in Yemen as an artillery instructor after the Iraqi mission under Colonel Ismail Safwat had left, and he became involved in local intrigue against the Imam. He hoped to share power in the new regime that would follow the coup.

A few days before the coup, the *Voice of Yemen* in Aden published a report on a revolt in Sana in which Imam Yahya was killed, and mentioned Abdallah al-Wazir as the new Imam. Immediately after reading the news, Imam Yahya called al-Wazir and asked him for an explanation, but al-Wazir categorically denied the falsehoods reported by the newspaper in Aden and even wrote an article in the *Iman* ("Faith", the newspaper in Sana) asserting his loyalty to the Imam, "that loyalty which even the storms cannot shake," and recognizing Prince Ahmad as the legal crown prince "to whom the hearts even before the hands had sworn allegiance."[9] The Imam was satisfied and the rumors subsided, but Abdallah al-Wazir and the other conspirators were afraid of punishment, especially when they heard that Prince Ahmad was on his way from Taiz in the south to Sana to take charge of public affairs, for the Imam was then about eighty years old and was partially paralyzed, and conditions in the capital, where al-Wazir was most powerful, were uncertain. The conspirators consequently precipitated action against the Imam and his son Ahmad. Their last meeting was held in al-Wazir's house on the eve of the coup and the persons who were to commit the assassination were chosen.

On February 17, 1948 Imam Yahya left Sana as he often did in the late morning for a village called Haziz, about ten kilometers to the south of the capital. He was accompanied by his prime minister, Abdallah al-Amri, and four grandsons, three of whom left on the way. The Imam's carriage was first stopped by the assassins who used a covered truck that had been supplied by al-Wartalani, and then the Imam and his party were shot to death by a machine gun that had been given by Colonel Jamil. It became known later that the old Imam died gallantly trying to shield his young grandson. His body was pierced by some fifty bullets. Two of his sons, Princes al-Hussein and al-Muhsin, were killed later at Saada Palace by order of Colonel Jamil who had proceeded to the Palace to seize the Imam's treasures.

After the assassination, the Free Yemenis in Aden left for Sana with Prince Ibrahim, while Abdallah al-Wazir was proclaimed the ruler in the capital. The notables and religious leaders and even certain princes declared their allegiance to the new Imam. Some of them had no other choice - such as two of the Imam's sons and Muhammad al-Badr, his grandson. The "Sacred National Pact" or program of reform agreed upon by the Yemeni exiles and the former opposition was then announced. Abdallah al-Wazir appointed a legislative assembly of sixty members under Prince Ibrahim, and a cabinet under his cousin Ali al-Wazir with Hussein al-Kibsi - who used to be Imam Yahya's adviser and envoy on various diplomatic missions - as foreign minister, and Muhammad Mahmud al-Zubayri as education minister.

Crown Prince Ahmad, known for his fearlessness and strength, was still in Taiz when the coup took place. The conspirators had planned for his assassination either in Taiz or in the port city of Hodeida. But Ahmad was able to escape to

Hodeida unharmed and from there to reach the northern fortress of Hajja five days after the assassination. He took with him some soldiers and a good deal of money - some 100,000 dollars and a sack full of gold - and began to assemble the tribal forces, particularly those of the Hashid and Bakil confederations. He made the inevitable payments to the tribal chiefs and incited the tribesmen against the dwellers of Sana and vowed to punish the city that killed its Imam by declaring that its gates would be open for plunder. After having proclaimed himslef Imam in Hajja, he started the march on Sana accompanied by his two brothers, al-Hasan - who was promised succession to the Imamate after him - and al-Abbas. Abdallah al-Wazir sent forces against Prince Ahmad, but they were defeated. He appealed to the Arab League for help, but Ahmad warned the League against intervention. His forces stormed Sana on March 13 after a three days' siege during which some of al-Wazir's soldiers and supporters deserted him and joined Ahmad. The capital city was ruthlessly plundered by the victorious tribesmen with the blessing of al-Abbas who commanded some 20,000 warriors. Ahmad moved to Taiz and made it his capital, thus refusing to live in the city that killed its Imam. He was officially proclaimed Imam with the title al-Nasir li-Din Allah (The Upholder of the Religion of Allah).

Imam Ahmad dealt severely, as he was expected to do, with the leaders of the coup. Among those who were put to death after their trial at Hajja were Abdallah al-Wazir, his foreign minister al-Kibsi, and Colonel Jamal Jamil. Those who were imprisoned included some of the prominent leaders of the coup of September 1962 and of the republican regime that followed: Colonel Abdallah al-Sallal, Brigadier Hammud al-Jayfi, Colonel Hasan al-Amri, Qadi Abdul Rahman al-Iryani, and Ahmad Muhammad Numan. Prince Ibrahim was sent to jail where he died of "heart attack" on Imam Ahmad's orders. Some leaders managed to leave the country and included al-Wartalani, Abdallah ibn Ali al-Wazir, and al-Zubayri.

The coup against Imam Yahya was not strictly speaking a military coup. It was prepared and carried out by the joint efforts of civilian and military malcontents and conspirators. The army was too ineffective to support the new regime, while the tribal forces mobilized by Prince Ahmad proved their superiority and dealt a decisive defeat to the twenty-five-day regime of al-Wazir. Certain Yemenis who wrote later under the influence of the 1962 coup, have insisted on calling the 1948 coup a popular revolution. They have also explained its failure by the people's disappointment and consequent refusal to support it when they realized that the Imamate would continue to be the ruling institution under a different line of Imams.[10] It is believed, however, that the fall of the Imamic regime was not envisaged in 1948 and that the people's apathy and indifference, particularly among the Zaydis, was caused by the brutal murder of Imam Yahya that shocked also the tribal chiefs and supporters of al-Wazir and caused them to withdraw their support.[11] Imam Yahya was respected as a pious and learned spiritual leader, and in Arab circles he was known for his patriotic stand for Arab independence. He was, moreover, an old and disabled man, and considerations of old age, gallantry, and loyalty had their weight in the scale of Arab values before the era of revolutionary military violence of the late 1950's. The people expected al-Wazir to punish Imam Yahya's murderers but instead he appointed the conspirators and other participants in the plot, some of whom were young and inexperienced, in important posts. He executed several members of the Imam's family and thus failed to inaugurate his rule with a regime of order and justice as he had promised. The Waziri regime was also weakened from the very beginning by dissensions and suspicions between Zaydi and Shafii leaders.

The regime that followed the coup failed for two other causes. First, the lack of funds because al-Wazir either failed to secure the Treasury, or perhaps tried to keep much of Imam Yahya's wealth for himself and did not spend enough on the influential chiefs and partisans.[12] Second, the hesitation of al-Wazir to move immediately against Prince Ahmad and his tribesmen before they could prepare to take the offensive. The

Waziri regime was concerned about its recognition and support by the Arab League, and had claimed that the Imam died naturally. The Arab League sent a commission of seven to inquire and advise on the status of the new regime.[13] But the commission never reached Sana, for Prince Ahmad had begun his offensive against the capital. In Riyad, where the commission stayed in early March, Ibn Saud made very clear his opposition to the new regime because it usurped power by assassination. Ibn Saud thus gave Prince Ahmad his moral support; it is believed that he also supported Ahmad materially. The commission asked both al-Wazir and Ahmad to send representatives to Riyad to submit their differences. Moreover, when al-Wartalani arrived in Riyad at the head of a delegation representing al-Wazir, he asked the League to send a few planes and tanks to defend Sana, and he proposed a referendum to determine the succession. Ahmad sent no representatives. The opinions were divided in the League commission and remained so until the news came that Ahmad entered Sana. The Arab countries recognized him as the Imam of Yemen in an Arab League meeting in Beirut on March 21, 1948.

The coup of 1948 is significant because, in the recent history of revolutions and military coups, it marked the first successful act of violence against a head of state in the Arab countries. It was a deliberate revolutionary act against certain practices of the Imamic system prepared by a military and civilian elite, but it did not go to the extent of seeking the end of the Imamate. It is also significant because for the first - and so far the last - time in the history of Arab coups, the regime that followed the coup pleaded for recognition and material support by the Arab League as a body, and did not seek support from one particular Arab state or group of states.

The coup of 1948 succeeded only in eliminating an Imam. The reformists who were now in jail or in exile, did not give up hope of achieving their goals and again resorted to conspiracy under Imam Ahmad.

II. Abortive Attempts Against Imam Ahmad

Imam Ahmad ruled Yemen for fifteen eventful years (1948-1962) as a fearless autocrat. Like his father he had a firm belief in the divine mission of the Zaydi Imamate. He also had no desire for introducing political and administrative changes that would weaken his power. He continued to have the full and free use of the state revenues that were kept in the *Bait al-Mal* (The Treasury) and to spend as little as possible on public services. He also refused to stop the practice of employing his sons or his brothers in lucrative government positions, partly because he wanted to keep them under his authority and prevent them from plotting. He accepted to abolish Imamic monopolies and certain restrictions on trade after the Egyptian revolution of July 1952, but he did not take immediate action in that direction.

Imam Ahmad, however, did not and could not keep Yemen as isolated as in the days of his father. He lived in an age of vast and violent developments in the Arab countries and the outside world, and the means of communication and information, especially by radio, were continuously spreading new and progressive ideas. He and the obligarchy of Sayyids with him naturally opposed any modernization of the political and social organization out of self interest because it could destroy their privileged position and prestige. Yet, paradoxically, the Imam at various times since 1951 agreed to employ Egyptian teachers and military instructors as well as Soviet technicians, and to send scores of Yemenis to Egypt and Western as well as Communist-Bloc countries. On their return, the trained young men were not given their due share of responsible positions in the administration.[14] The feeling of resentment and frustration among the intellectuals was sometimes expressed in poetry, and among the best known poems were those entitled "Challenge", and "We And The Rulers" written by Abdallah al-Barduni.[15]

Imam Ahmad responded, for political reasons, to Yemeni

public opinion and to the arguments of close advisors in the field of economic development. Under the influence of his progressive brother Abdallah, and his own son al-Badr who was in charge of the foreign aid program, he discussed certain economic projects and agreed to several concessions for the exploitation of the country's natural resources. But it is believed that he was not really disposed to implement what he discussed or planned, and that his contacts and plans were intended for propaganda purposes. His problem was that he disliked to spend money and to employ foreigners.[16] The only substantial projects were carried out by foreign governments and by foreign money: the Hodeida port by the Russians, inaugurated in June 1962, the Hodeida - Sana road by Communist China, inaugurated in January 1962, and the Mocha-Taiz-Sana road by the United States, still unfinished.

Imam Ahmad's troubles and the constant menace to his life derived from three main sources, namely, the opposition of the discontented Free Yemenis, the classical struggle for power among brothers in the Imamic regime, and the problems with the British in Southern Arabia. These three factors, individually and collectively contributed to the creation of a more serious threat to Ahmad and the Imamate, namely, the Egyptian involvement in Yemeni and South Arabian affairs. Ahmad's continuous disputes with the British in the protected southern areas and his irredentist hopes for regaining what he called "Southern Yemen" led to discussions in January 1954 between the British and the Arab protected chiefs for the formation of the South Arabian Federation. Imam Ahmad resented the formation of a federation in the South dominated by Britain and immediately appealed to the Arab League. Since then, the future of Southern Arabia became an all-Arab national cause which Egypt sponsored and exploited with the help of her great propaganda machine. Although Nasser in Egypt denounced the British and thus acted as a friend of Yemen, he soon became the champion for the liberation of Southern Arabia, while in Yemen itself he came to be regarded by the discontented elements as their savior from the

Imam's conservative regime. The Egyptian concept of "national liberation" was adopted by the Arabian South, and Egyptian agents established contacts with the nationalist movement in Aden and with the Free Yemenis in and outside of Yemen. They also interfered in the dynastic rivalries between the Imam and his brothers and even participated in the conspiracies against Imam Ahmad.

Several plots were organized to put an end to Imam Ahmad's rule, but only a few reached the stage of execution and none of them succeeded. In February 1950, Prince Ismail, Ahmad's brother and minister of education, was arrested on the pretext that he was implicated in a plot against the Imam. He was jailed, but as the charge against him was evidently not serious, he was soon released. In September 1953 another plot was discovered and a few arrests were made in Sana and among the Imam's bodyguard, but no great details were made public. The most serious conspiracy that came very close to removing Imam Ahmad was carried out in the coup of April 2, 1955. It was organized by Prince Abdallah, the seventh of Imam Yahya's fourteen sons, and Lieutenant- Colonel Ahmad al-Thalaya (sometimes called also al-Thala'i) supported by six officers and some 600 soldiers.

Abdallah was generally recognized as an enlightened prince, but he was not popular on account of his money-grabbing activities which brought him a fortune of some eight million pounds sterling.[17] He had been minister of defense and governor of Hodeida, and had traveled in the Arab countries, Europe and the United States. He promoted economic development and favored a change in the political structure of the state. He soon became the central figure in family rivalries and the candidate of certain Yemeni elements for the Imamate. His progressive program was discussed in 1952 by his brother the Imam, but no action was taken. The Free Yemenis in Cairo, according to a writer who knew them personally, did not like Abdallah because he "glorified the British and the Americans and was in favor of defense pacts."[18] The Free Yemeni leaders Numan and Zubayri were favorable to Prince al-Badr after he met them in Cairo in early 1955 and accepted their conditions which were the granting of a constitution with civil liberties, abolishing the system of hostages, and ending the isolation of Yemen. This is why they were not in favor of the coup against Imam Ahmad. Prince Abdallah was able to establish contact with some reform minded officers, and in early 1955 decided, with their approval, that a movement should be undertaken on the first occasion against his brother, the Imam, who was preparing to declare his son al-Badr crown prince. The highest ranking among those officers was Lieutenant-Colonel Ahmad al-Thalaya who had been a colleague of Abdallah al-Sallal at the military academy in Iraq in 1934, and had been jailed for two years after the assassination of Imam Yahya. Imam Ahmad released him and put him in charge of training in the Yemeni army as a sign of reconciliation, but the Colonel continued his intrigues among the officers and with Prince Abdallah.

It is ironic that the occasion chosen for starting the coup was one in which Imam Ahmad was defending the poor people against the excesses of the soldiery. On March 28, 1955 a dispute developed between a group of Yemeni soldiers and the residents of a village in the region of Huban, north of Taiz, in which one or two soldiers were killed. Before punishing the offenders, Imam Ahmad told al-Thalaya, who commanded the garrison at Taiz, that an investigation should be made, but the soldiers, probably with al-Thalaya's tacit approval, went to the village on March 30 to commit revengeful acts of destruction and murder. According to a Yemeni writer who claims to have been a witness of the events,[19] al-Thalaya profited of the occasion and persuaded his troops to support him in removing the Imam by force because he was incompetent, and replacing him by Prince Abdallah. On the following morning, the Imam's palace was attacked by artillery and machine gun fire. Prince Abdallah, as related by the narrator, asked the Imam's permission to go to the barracks with some officials in order to restore order and examine the army's demands, and Imam Ahmad accepted. Colonel Thalaya then called the leading state dignitaries to the barracks and asked them to pledge allegiance to Prince Abdallah, but while some of them accepted, the others refused because they had already given their *baya* (sworn allegiance) to Imam Ahmad. It was finally agreed after a violent discussion to send a delegation to Ahmad to ask for his abdication on the basis of the army's demands. Imam Ahmad, after some hesitation wrote down an ambiguous formula in which he agreed to abandon the exercise of power, but the army refused this trick and ordered the delegation to return and obtain a clear abdication or else they would attack and destroy the palace. The Imam consequently wrote and signed a clear act of abdication in favor of his brother and asked those who came out to support him to go back to their homes.

The leaders of the coup trusted in Ahmad's good faith, as the narrator said, and began their work on the reorganization of the state. Imam Ahmad, however, did not take his abdication seriously, and although he was closely watched, he sent messengers in secret to his supporters around Taiz, and asked his son, al-Badr, in Hodeida to leave for Hajja to mobilize the tribesmen. He also took secret measures to defend himself at the appropriate moment. Colonel Thalaya, it is said, was suspicious of the Imam's intentions and would have eliminated him if Prince Abdallah had not objected. Three days after the abdication, the Imam succeeded in introducing some of his supporters and loyal guardsmen to the palace. He distributed generous sums of money among them and similarly sent gifts to the artillery men in various points around Taiz and told them to begin their attack on the barracks as soon as the fire signal was given from the palace. When the signal appeared, the fire of artillery, machine guns, and rifles began pouring on the barracks and continued for thirty-six hours. The revolutionary forces and the army were unable to resist and dispersed while Prince Abdallah surrendered along with some officials. Colonel Thalaya was caught east of Taiz and was brought to the Imam who had him beheaded at once, along with the other officers and with Princes Abdallah and al-Abbas, without trial.

Although this narrative, written by a supporter of the present republican regime, contains many exaggerations that contradict the known facts, it has nevertheless a general foundation of truth. The Imam was forced to abdicate on April 2, 1955 after an armed force had besieged his palace. He was not killed possibly because Prince Abdallah was mild-mannered and did not want to begin his reign by shedding blood, as al-Wazir had done. But it seems that in abdicating, the Imam agreed only to hand over his executive powers. He ordered that everyone should return to his work and that "our brother Sayf al-Islam Abdallah, may God save him, should come and take charge of the nation."[20] Imam Ahmad, however, did not hand over the Imamate to his brother and was thus able to create confusion and hesitation among the revolutionaries. It is said that after his abdication, the Imam refused orders to leave for Egypt or even to move from his palace to another one, and the army consequently cut off water and electricity from the palace and shelled it for three days.[21] In the meantime, al-Badr prepared for decisive action against the coup. He gathered supporters from among the Hashid and Bakil tribesmen and as he advanced from Hajja to Taiz, the revolutionaries began to disintegrate. When the tribal forces marched from the extremities of Taiz and surrounded the army forces, Imam Ahmad left the palace on a horse with a sword in his hand, and rode through the besieging forces who were caught by fear and panic and fled. On April 5 the movement collapsed.[22]

Prince Abdallah evidently did not surrender in the barracks but was arrested on April 7 while attempting to escape to Saudi Arabia. Lieutenant-Colonel Thalaya and six other supporting officers were publicly beheaded in Sana on April 10, while Prince Abdallah and his brother al-Abbas - who supported Abdallah's claim from Sana - were tried and beheaded at Hajja on April 14. Prince al-Hasan was in Cairo and was not involved in the coup. Colonel Thalaya apparently was given a public trial in the Imam's own way. He was called to the Training Square near the palace in presence of the army, the Ulama, the notables and the people. The Imam reminded him that twice he ordered his release from imprisonment, and then scolded him for preventing his physician from seeing him during the siege of the palace, and for other unhuman acts, and then asked him, "Is this how you reward the kindnesses done to you?" Then the Imam turned to the army and the Ulama and said, "I take God as my witness, if you think that this officer does not deserve death I will forgive him." But the Imam's supporters shouted that he did deserve death, and so he was beheaded.[23]

In many ways this serious attempt against Imam Ahmad resembled that of 1948 against his father. The motives in both cases were desire for reform in addition to the presence of rivals anxious to take the place of the ruling Imam, but the grievances of the army were among the important causes of this second attempt by al-Thalaya, for the army felt it was neglected and scorned, and its members received low salaries and bad treatment. In both cases there was no plan to abolish the Imamate. Similarly the failure of the two movements can be attributed to the same factors, namely, the inadequacy of the armed forces at the disposal of the usurpers as compared with the overwhelming tribal forces that supported the legal ruler, and the wavering allegiance of the dignitaries to the new regime on account of its illegality and weakness, in addition to the absence of popular participation and support for the coup. In this coup against Imam Ahmad, the army was responsible for the attempt from beginning to end. Its failure was received by the people of neighboring Aden with joy and the raising of Yemeni flags, because Imam Ahmad always claimed the British-protected areas in the South as part of Yemen.

A significant account has been given in connection with this coup on the double role played by the notorious Abdul Rahman Baidani who later became deputy prime minister after the coup of September 1962. Baidani was born and brought up in Egypt, of Shafiite Yemeni parents. He became a friend of Nasser and Anwar al-Sadat, and married Sadat's sister. During his many trips to Yemen as an Egyptian agent, he is said to have participated in preparing the coup against Imam Ahmad by procuring the arms and the money needed to pay the men.[24] At the same time he became the Imam's informer about the coup in order to gain his complete confidence, for this would facilitate Baidani's future subversive activities. After the coup, he persuaded the Imam to appoint him minister in Bonn and succeeded in becoming Imam Ahmad's confident and counselor and a close friend of his son al-Badr.

Imam Ahmad committed the same mistake that his father had done when he proclaimed his son, Muhammad al-Badr, crown prince soon after the failure of the coup, for the Zaydi Imamate is elective in principle and many Zaydis thought that Prince al-Hasan was a better candidate. Al-Hasan preferred under the circumstances to leave the country and became the head of the Yemeni delegation at the United Nations. Al-Badr was known as a good soldier and was generally well liked, but he was credulous and confused. He was impressed by Baidani's reform program and by Nasser's foreign policy. He persuaded his father to join the Jidda Pact in April 1956 for mutual defense with Egypt and Saudi Arabia. In July 1956 al-Badr visited the Soviet Union and other Eastern European countries with his father's consent and Nasser's blessing, and in January 1958 he visited Communist China. He signed several agreements of cooperation for the economic development of Yemen, and the Russians promised to send arms. The agreements were soon followed by the arrival in Yemen of Russians, Czechs, Bulgars, and Egyptians for development projects and for military training.

On March 8, 1958 Imam Ahmad unexpectedly joined the United Arab Republic - which had been formed in the preceding month - in a federation known as the United Arab States. He hoped that the federation would bring him support against the British in the South, and at the same time would conciliate Nasser as well as the Free Yemenis outside Yemen and prevent them from attacking his regime. For Nasser, however, the federation was in harmony with his expansionist projects in Southern Arabia and a good step for the liberation of the Yemenis themselves. The federation created such organs as the federal council, the defense council, and the economic and cultural councils, but their activity was restricted by the negative, non-cooperative attitudes of the Imam.[25] The formation of the federation scared the Southern Arabian chiefs who feared Egyptian intervention and thus hastened the establishment of the South Arabian Federation in February 1959 under British protection. At the same time the nationalist agitation of the trade unions in Aden was strengthened by the federal link between Yemen and the United Arab Republic, while the Aden Trade Union Congress and its leader Abdallah al-Asnag soon became Nasser's principal instrument of attack against the British. The Egyptian technicians and instructors who were sent to Yemen created more hostility to the Imamic regime, and it was essentially during this federal period that Nasser chose the Yemenis who were to act as the instrument of his policy, in addition to the many Yemenis who were being trained in Egypt since the mid-1950's as officers and technicians.

Imam Ahmad was worried by the presence of too many strangers - Communists and Egyptians - in his territory and by the conduct of his radical-minded son al-Badr. The discovery of pamphlets signed by "Free Yemeni Officers" and directed against the Imam was for many Zaydis and for the Imam a warning that there was conspiracy against the regime. In the midst of these worries, the Imam fell sick and had to leave for Rome in April, 1959 for the treatment of his heart trouble and drug poisoning that had arisen from his use of morphine against the pains caused by his arthritis. He had called his brother al-Hasan from New York to help counterbalance his son, but al-Hasan followed him to Rome and al-Badr was left behind to rule Yemen as regent. Free Yemenis were generally satisfied with al-Badr's modernizing activities, but Zaydi traditionalist elements felt that Nasser was using al-Badr to establish his control over Yemen especially when al-Badr appointed Egyptians in such key positions as the Directorate of Public Security. Under the regency of al-Badr, unrest increased and certain areas inhabited by Shafiite Sunnis were out of control. The troops in Sana revolted against one of their officers and burned down his house for having taken disciplinary action against some guards. They also resented their hard living conditions, and al-Badr promised to increase their pay by 25 per cent. Disturbances occurred in Taiz and were followed by placing the governor under house arrest while the army took over. The allegiance of the Hashid and Bakil tribes had to be bought to restore order, and a number of officers were executed.[26]

Imam Ahmad returned unexpectedly in August and quickly set out to deal with the disturbances. An unknown number of persons were beheaded or jailed. At the end of 1959 he summoned Ibn al-Ahmar, chief of the Hashid tribe that was in revolt in the north, and had him beheaded.

In January 1961 the Imam was saved from a car accident and the rumors spread that it was an attempted assassination. The most serious attempt to eliminate Imam Ahmad, however, occurred two months later in the hospital of Hodeida where the Imam arrived in the evening of March 26, preceded by his royal guards, for an X-ray examination. The executors of the plot were three: Lt. Muhammad al-Alafi, who was in charge of the internal order in the hospital, and two other officers, Abdallah al-Liqya and Muhsin al-Hindwan. The royal guards were prevented by Alafi from going inside the hospital under the pretext that the patients should not be disturbed by their presence.[27] The Imam, accompanied by some princes and four bodyguards, had finished visiting certain sections of the hospital and was going down to the X-ray room when al-Alafi opened fire at him from one angle and the two other officers fired from another. The Imam's surprising presence of mind saved him. He threw himself on the ground and the assassins thought he was dead, and escaped. At least five bullets hit the

Imam and several members of his retinue were wounded.[28] The guards outside the hospital opened their fire on the three assassins as they fled but missed them. Alafi ended by shooting himself when he was surrounded by the royal guards and was ordered to surrender. The two other officers were arrested and beheaded. Five other participants in the plot were discovered and executed. Official sources in Yemen gave no details on the plot and charged that the attempt was financed by some Yemeni residents in Aden supported by colonialism. The secrets remained little known until the overthrow of the Imamate in September 1962. It was learned then that several military and civilian personalities prepared the plot. Among them was Colonel Abdallah al-Sallal, who was eventually transferred from his command in Hodeida to Sana, Captain Muhammad al-Ruaini, director of the Hodeida airport, and Hussein al-Muqadami, director of the hospital. The last two were imprisoned until the coup of 1962.[29]

Imam Ahmad did not recover completely from the effect of his wounds, and rumors on his abdication were persistent during the period that followed the attempt on his life. He reluctantly delegated more power to al-Badr, but he recalled his brother al-Hasan from New York, and al-Hasan again became the candidate of the traditionalist Zaydis and the conservative Sunnis who feared al-Badr's pro-Nasserist policies. Imam Ahmad's common sense, as it was said, made him incline to his brother al-Hasan, but his paternal feelings made him decide for his son al-Badr. In September 1961 he made an appeal on the Sana radio to support him.

The last year of Imam Ahmad's reign was troubled by external and internal agitation that contained warnings of the explosion that was to follow. Yemeni conspirators in the plots against Imam Yahya and his son Ahmad had hitherto aimed at the elimination of despotic and conservative monarchs and the appointment of constitutional reform-minded ones. In the late 1950's their objective changed. They now worked for the overthrow of the Imamic regime altogether and the establishment of a republic. Egypt could not incite the Yemenis openly to revolt against their monarch in the way it had done in Iraq and Jordan, as long as the federal link existed. In December 1961 Imam Ahmad gave President Nasser the opportunity to break this link. The Imam was encouraged by the Syrian coup of September 1961 and the end of the United Arab Republic to reveal his hostility to Nasser's socialist system and to the abuse of King Hussein of Jordan and Saud of Saudi Arabia by the Voice of the Arabs in Cairo. In mid-December 1961 he wrote - or perhaps ordered a young Yemeni poet to write for him - a poem of the *urjuzah* type of sixty-four verses addressed "To the Arabs" in which he criticized those who "shout over the microphone with every incongruous voice," and adjured the Arabs "to a unity founded on accepted principles and whose law is the Sharia of Islam, sacred in its qualities and precepts, free from the defect of innovation that permits what Islam has prohibited, such as taking away the property of the people and what they have lawfully earned on the pretext of nationalization and equalization, for this has no justification in religion, nor is it permitted by logical reasoning."[30]

The Imam's poem was published and broadcast over the radio. Nasser reacted by announcing the termination of the federation of the United Arab States on December 27, 1961. He stated in his announcement that "the United Arab Republic believes that unity and federation cannot be erected on sound foundations unless there is agreement among the parties concerned on the solution of the problems of social change." His government had been hopeful, he said, that the federation would be an instrument for serving the Yemeni people and their just cause, but "the experiences of the past years had proved beyond doubt that the Yemeni people did not profit from the experiment." Two days later the Cairo radio broadcast the call for revolution in Yemen. This was followed regularly by other broadcasts that identified the Imam with imperialism and appealed to Yemenis to revolt and "to join the battle for Arab liberation, unity and socialism." The Voice of the Arabs was often used by Yemeni leaders living in Cairo for announcing their revolutionary program and making fiery attacks on the Imam and his regime. The Yemenis in Egypt included Muhammad Mahmud al-Zubayri who was introduced on the radio as "the leader of the Yemeni liberation movement in Cairo," Muhsin al-Ayni who had been deported from Aden for his role in trade union agitation, and Dr. Abdul Rahman Baidani who had been a confident of Imam Ahmad and al-Badr and Yemen's minister in Bonn.

It is believed that while he was in Yemen in 1959, Baidani chose Abdallah al-Sallal to lead the future coup against the Imamic regime. At the same time Baidani persuaded the unsuspecting Prince al-Badr to put the same Sallal under his protection.[31] Sallal was thus in a better position to plot against his protector. It has been recalled in this connection that when Imam Yahya gave his approval for sending Sallal to the military college in Baghdad in 1936 he thought he would be a loyal and harmless officer, for he was a Zaydi son of a blacksmith and belonged neither to the ambitious Sayyid class nor to the turbulent tribesmen. Sallal was then nineteen years old.[32] After his return, three years later, he developed an inclination for opportunist revolutionary action and was imprisoned for spreading subversive ideas. In the early 1940's he was imprisoned for three years in Sana for distributing leaflets against the Imam. He later spent seven hard years in the dungeons of Hajja for his involvement in Imam Yahya's assassination in 1948, and was still in the Hajja prison when the coup of 1955 against Imam Ahmad occurred. He was released at al-Badr's request and appointed chief of his guards. In 1959 he was put in charge of Hodeida harbor and became involved in the attempt on Ahmad's life at the hospital. Imam Ahmad dismissed him, but al-Badr still trusted him and made him an inspector of the military aerodrome in Sana. The Egyptians believed he would be useful for their future plans for several reasons: He was a revolutionary, he was unscrupulous, and al-Badr trusted him as a fellow reformer. Baidani thought that it would be easy to remove

Sallal after the coup, but the events later proved that he was mistaken.

Baidani left Yemen in 1959, perhaps after Imam Ahmad had received sufficient warnings about the role he was playing, and returned to live in Cairo. In 1962 Nasser pushed him to the front as his future key man in Yemen and allowed him to broadcast the program of the planned revolution over the Voice of the Arabs. On May 12, 1962 Baidani broadcast a plan for a complete change in Yemeni adminstration and gave details on the proposed establishment of a Yemeni republic. He gave later a series of talks entitled "The Secrets of Yemen," on a Cairo radio program called "The Enemies of God." He described the specific aims of the revolution in Yemen and made a a violent attack against the Imam to inflame the population. To make sure that these broadcasts were heard by the people of Yemen, Nasser's agents provided them with transistor radios.

The radio propaganda campaign from Cairo proved effective in increasing the tension and disorder in Yemen. Imam Ahmad at times acted with extreme severity and caused villages that sheltered agitators to be destroyed. At other times he tried to conciliate the army and appealed to the people to respect the principles of Islam and condemn Nasser's socialism. He issued in June a decree establishing a development council under al-Badr for new agricultural projects, but the appeal of the Cairo radio remained strong, especially among the youth. Demonstrations were organized by Yemeni students in Sana against the alleged Imam's approval of American bases. The demonstrators carried Nasser's picture and the flag of the defunct United Arab Republic as they marched on the ministry of education. The police had to open fire and several students were killed. Again in September the students demonstrated in both Sana and Taiz, and pictures of the Imam and his son al-Badr were trampled under foot.

III. The Coup d'État of September 1962 and The Yemeni Arab Republic

On September 19, 1962 the Voice of the Arabs in Cairo spoke of the coming revolution and warned the Imam about the difficult challenge he had to face and the account he had to give to the people of all the promises for modernizing Yemen. The Imam did not live to face that challenge. He died peacefully at the age of seventy-one in his bed on Tuesday September 18 at 9 p.m., a few hours before the last warning of the Cairo broadcast. The Sana radio announced Imam Ahmad's death and the succession of his son Muhammad al-Badr, on the following day (September 19). The new Imam, who took the title al-Mansour Billah, prepared to face the gathering storm, and he faced it with courage. In his first speech, he explained his goals and plans to make the country prosperous and raise its political, economic and cultural standards, and promised to secure for the citizens their rights in conformity with those recognized in the modern world. His first reforms showed his determination to work for a better Yemen. He began by expressing in formal decrees his opposition to his father's oppressive regime. He declared a general amnesty for all political prisoners and exiles, lifted all taxes for the remainder of the year, abolished the hostages system and the feudal mortgage laws and increased the pay of the army. He decreed the establishment of a Shura (advisory) Council of forty members, half to be elected and half nominated, the formation of elected municipal councils, and appointed himself prime minister in order to speed the development projects. Soon after his accession he appointed the very man who was preparing his destruction to the highest military post: Abdallah al-Sallal became the army chief-of-staff.

The reactions to Badr's succession and announced reforms, and the opinions about his good faith and his competence to implement the reforms have differed. According to a report from Yemen on September 24, based on a Sana radio broadcast, Imam al-Badr received a message from the leaders of the Yemeni Liberation Movement in Cairo expressing their readiness to support him if he followed a progressive policy.[33] A foreign service officer and observer of Yemeni affairs similarly expressed the belief that many of the present supporters of the Republic were prepared, before they were caught up by the coup against Badr, to give him an opportunity to try his hand at reform.[34] The same observer believes that Yemen would have experienced drastic changes had Badr succeeded in maintaining his control over the country, and that a clash between him and the conservative Sayyid oligarchy "would almost certainly have occurred had he retained his throne for any length of time." A Yemeni republican, evidently very much under the influence of revolutionary events, has stated, on the other hand, that al-Badr's announced goals and promises were received by the majority of the army and the people with indifference and scorn because they already knew his inability to lead the country on the path of reform and progress, and they realized that the plans and the promises he announced were only similar to those that his father had made under critical conditions to deceive and mislead the people. The Yemeni author added that the people of Yemen were anyway tired of the Imamate and of personal rule regardless of whether al-Badr could have implemented his plans and promises or not, because national consciousness demanded a popular democratic rule that would sufficently make up for the complete deprivation imposed by autocratic rule, and that would destroy feudalism and the antiquated foundations of the Imamic regime.[35]

In discussing the attitude of Egypt towards al-Badr's accession one should remember that al-Badr had placed himself since 1955 in the Cairo camp and fell under the spell of Nasser and his modernistic activities and foreign policies. He also established friendly relations and cooperation with the Soviet Union and Communist China. The Egyptian press and radio constantly praised his progressive liberal policies before and after the federation between the United Arab Republic and Yemen. Al-Badr followed the Nasserist line to the extent of urging Jordanian officers to make a coup against their king when he visited Jordan in 1957. It is even reported that after his accession, he sent a telegram thanking President Qudsi of Syria for his congratulations and he included in the telegram a word of advice to Syria to cooperate with Egypt at any price.[36] It is believed, on the other hand, that Egypt did not do much for Yemen in the course of the eight years of friendship with al-Badr (1954-1961). Egyptian officials and agents among whom the most prominent was Baidani intrigued against the Imamate and distributed Nasser's pictures, while the Free Yemenis received protection and encouragement in Cairo. Nasser's condolences for the death of Imam Ahmad reached al-Badr on September 21 after most of the world leaders had sent theirs. Nasser's message to al-Badr included wishes of success for achieving his people's aspirations. It soon became evident that Nasser had already decided not to allow al-Badr to try his hand at achieving these aspirations. On the day Nasser sent his condolences, the Cairo radio broadcast an attack on the two Arab kings Saud and Hussein who, it said, were "just as dead as Ahmad but not yet buried." Baidani resumed his series of broadcasts on "The Secrets of Yemen", attacked al-Badr's succession to the Imamate and repeated what he had already said in August on the plans of reform and the establishment of a republic. He also accused al-Badr, his old friend and benefactor, of having announced that he would pursue "the enlightened policy of his defunct father." The accusation was believed and caused disappointment among those who trusted in al-Badr.[37] Baidani's last broadcast from Cairo ended with the ominous phrase, often used in the language of the revolutionists, "the appointment with fate has arrived."

Imam al-Badr ruled Yemen for eight days only after his father's death. On September 26, 1962 he was overthrown by a coup d'état under the leadership of his trusted aide Abdallah al-Sallal and with the cooperation of seven other officers.[38]

The communiqué No. 1 issued by the General Army Command mentioned the causes of what became known officially as the Yemeni revolution. It reminded the revolutionaries in the various parts of Yemen, the soldiers, the merchants, and the Yemeni exiles of the tyranny, greed, and crimes of the Imams and the humiliation and sufferings of the people. It said that the revolution was that of the entire people, and that it believed in God, and in Arab unity and Arab nationalism, and it condemned the divisions between Zaydis and Shafiis, and Hashimis and Qahtanis.[39] The Sana radio proclaimed officially the fall of the monarchy and the establishment of a Yemeni republic. The fate of the Imam was revealed in another communiqué which said that the Army Command had given orders to the Free Officers to besiege the royal palaces. Tanks and armored cars were brought to the Imam's palace and al-Badr was asked to surrender, but he tried to defend himself. His resistance lasted only a few hours for the artillery opened fire and "the tyrant was buried under the ruins of his palace," and several supporters of the past regime and other reactionaries were arrested.[40]

The communiques from Sana and the reports from Cairo persisted in relating the story of al-Badr's death under the ruins of his palace because the success of the revolution required that al-Badr should be believed dead. Other reports, sometimes contradictory in nature, were circulated to make al-Badr responsible for the timing of the coup. A report from Cairo on October 1 alleged that al-Badr asked Sallal to prepare the defense of the palace and the city of Sana because he feared that his uncle al-Hasan - who had actually sent a declaration of loyalty to his nephew on September 23 - might come from New York to contest the succession. Sallal, while pretending to obey, seized the opportunity to start the coup against al-Badr instead of defending him. He brought troops from Hodeida to Sana and moved the tanks into position around the palace. The troops seized the radio station and then directed their fire on the palace.[41] Another report of about October 22 made by Colonel Abdallah al-Dabbi, who had been appointed by al-Badr Director of Security in Sana, related that the revolution had been planned long before September 26, 1962, but the conspirators had to act on that date because they learned on that very day that al-Badr's Intelligence discovered the plan and the names of its organizers. Sallal consequently decided to begin the revolution immediately in order to avoid the failure that met the two former revolts of 1948 and 1955 and to save his own life.[42]

When on October 3 some Westerners who left Yemen reported that the Imam was still living and that his palace was not totally destroyed, Cairo and Sana had to modify the story of the Imam's death in the palace. The Cairo report of October 1 had said that al-Badr was entertaining friends in his reception room when he heard gunfire and realized that the royal guards would not defend him. As he tried to escape, the roof collapsed on him and his friends, and he died. After October 3, Cairo and Sana fabricated a story about two soldiers who said that they shot al-Badr in the palace. Another story mentioned how al-Badr escaped dressed as a soldier, while a soldier dressed in the Imam's robes was found dead in the palace and was mistaken for him. Still another report that gained credence at the time related that the Imam escaped wounded and died of his wounds in a hospital in Saudi Arabia.[43]

On October 15, 1962 - less than three weeks after the coup - al-Badr sent letters to the heads of Arab states informing them that he was alive. Several accounts have been given on how he saved himself from an almost certain death during or after the shelling of his palace. A Yemeni republican author wrote that the armed forces consisting of units of tanks and armored cars moved from the command headquarters in the barracks to the Bashair Palace where al-Badr lived and blew it up with heavy artillery. The Imam was able, with the help of some aides, to escape from a back door of the palace and reached the outskirts of Sana after going through some unknown areas. He then went to the villages in the neighborhood of Hajja and asked the tribesmen to support him but they did not respond. He was surrounded by a company of the garrison of Hajja, but finally succeeded in escaping to Jizan in Saudi Arabia.[44] Another republican account by Colonel Abdallah al-Dabbi mentioned that the revolution met no resistance even among the palace guards. The Imam, he said, escaped while tens of his guards were surrendering to the revolutionary forces. He put on a soldier's uniform and went from a garden behind the palace through a *sirdab* (tunnel) until he reached the Hamadan tribe, but they refused to defend or join him. He then moved to another tribe and still another until he was near Hajja. He resorted to the stratagem which his father had used in 1948 in order to win over the tribesmen: He declared Sana and Hajja open for the tribes. The tribesmen as a result attacked Hajja but were repulsed and al-Badr was finally carried wounded to Saudi Arabia.[45] According to these two reports the Imam received little or no support from the tribesmen once the revolution had been proclaimed, and he could find safety only within the borders of Saudi Arabia.

Another story was told by al-Badr himself and it became known only in early November 1962. The Imam said that during the evening of September 26, his cabinet met in the palace until 11 p.m. When he left for his private quarters, an officer of the guards tried to shoot him. The officer was arrested and al-Badr went to bed, but thirty minutes later a soldier told him that he heard the noise of tanks. The lights went out after a few seconds and the palace was shelled by the tanks. The shelling lasted all night and the two top floors were demolished. Al-Badr decided to leave on the following day at noon. He had his ordinary clothes and was not wounded. As he walked outside the palace a woman recognized him and gave him a soldier's uniform. He left Sana at night with five men and by morning, he said, he had fifteen hundred. As he moved northward, more men joined him.[46]

The Imam was thus able to leave his palace, probably disguised as a soldier, and must have received some tribal support on his way to the north. His successful escape was a hard blow from the very beginning to the Yemeni revolution, for it helped strengthen the opposition of the elements attached to the Imamate. Yet, even in the absence of Imam al-Badr, the Imamic regime was not expected to end without a struggle. The Imam's family was very numerous and many of its Zaydi followers were too fanatic to accept the change peacefully and fade away. The revolutionaries were probably aware of the fact that in the long history of the Imamic state, one of the reasons for its survival for over a thousand years was the presence of a great number of eager Hashemite Sayyids each of whom considered it a duty to assume the Imamate, in addition to the firm religious belief of the Zaydi sectarians in Imamic rule. This is perhaps why the revolution was eager to eliminate as many members of the Imam's family as possible in the first days of the revolution.[47]

The first candidate for the succession, after al-Badr had been presumed dead, was his uncle al-Hasan. On September 27 al-Hasan left New York and on his way declared in London that the leaders of the revolt were a small army group with no popular support. He was recognized Imam by his followers and before October 14, he was reported to be at the head of the royalist forces in northern Yemen. When al-Badr's survival was established, al-Hasan again recognized him as Imam and was appointed prime minister in the new government formed by al-Badr on October 17. Al-Hasan has since then commanded one of the major royalist armies in Yemen.

In the meantime Sallal had become the commander-in-chief of the army after the coup and ruled Yemen with the other seven members of the military junta that came to be known as the Revolution Command Council. On September 28, 1962 he formed a cabinet in which Baidani was vice premier, Muhsin al-Ayni minister of foreign affairs, and Muhammad Mahmud al-Zubayri minister of education. All three had been living in Cairo before the coup. The Revolution Command Council proclaimed on September 27 the general policy of the new Yemeni Arab Republic and the goals and programs of the revolution. Internally the goals were: 1) The revival of the true principles of the *Sharia* (Islamic Law) "after the tyrannical corrupt rulers had discarded them," and the removal of all ethnic, sectarian, and tribal hatreds and divisions. 2) The organization of the masses in a united popular body that would participate in the build up of the revolutionary edifice and control the organs of the revolution and prevent them from deviation. 3) Reorganization of the army on a modern basis in order to make it a force capable of protecting the people and the revolution. 4) Initiating a cultural and educational revolution that would destroy the remains of the defunct regime which deepened ignorance and caused intellectual backwardness. 5)The achievement of social justice through a social system that agrees with the conditions of our people and the spirit of "Islamic Law" and national traditions. 6) Encouragement of national capital provided it does not become monopolistic and exploitive. 7) Appeal for the return of the emigrants and profiting from their experience and wealth. In the national Arab field, the goals were described as: 1) Faith in Arab nationalism and effort to realize complete unity in one Arab state on a democratic popular basis. 2) Complete solidarity with all Arab countires in what national interest requires. 3) Support of the Arab League and increasing its effectiveness. 4) Development of economic relations with all the Arab states. 5) Establishment of stronger ties with the "liberated" Arab states to achieve Arab unity. The international policy of the revolution was described as: 1) Commitment to the policy of non-alignment. 2) Resistance to imperialism and all forms of foreign intervention. 3) Respect for the United Nations Charter. 4) Establishment of friendly relations with all the states that respect our independence and freedom. 5) Acceptance of external aid and loans that impose no conditions and do not touch the independence and freedom of the country.[48]

On October 31, the Revolution Command Council proclaimed a provisional constitution of eleven articles for a transitional period of five years during which an electoral law would be prepared and the permanent constitution presented by the government would be voted upon. The goals of the revolution mentioned in the first article were almost identical with those proclaimed after the coup. The other articles mentioned the people as the only source of authority, guaranteed the various liberties including respect for property "in accordance with the provisions of the law," proclaimed Islam as the official state religion and Islàmic Law as the source of all legislation, and asserted the independence of the judiciary. The constitution also stipulated that the Revolution Command Council was the supreme sovereign power in the country and could appoint and dismiss the cabinet ministers. The RCC and the cabinet together formed a national congress for discussing general policy as well as the affairs of each ministry. The constitution created a defense council that consisted of sheikhs with the rank of state ministers who would be in charge of the protection of their respective regions when the council was not in session. The last article mentioned the appointment of Brig. Gen. Sallal by the RCC as president of the republic, prime minister, and commander-in-chief of the armed forces.[49] Sallal formed a new cabinet in which Baidani remained vice premier and acquired the portfolio of foreign affairs, while Ayni was sent to the United Nations as head of the Yemeni mission. The cabinet consisted of military and civilian members, and some new ministerial departments were created following the Egyptian pattern such as the ministry of municipal and rural affairs, and that of national guidance. A new revolution command council was formed at the same time, and it now consisted of eighteen military and civilian members. The provisional constitution, and the changes in the cabinet and the RCC were the result of a visit by Field Marshal Amer of Egypt towards the end of October. The cabinet changes were interpreted as the strengthening of Nasser's grip on Yemen because the ministers who did not cooperate with Baidani were excluded.[50] President Sallal was promoted to the rank of Field Marshal on December 14, 1962. He had been promoted from colonel to brigadier general immediately after the coup.

Among the measures and changes introduced in the first

few months after the coup to modernize Yemen and provide it with the needed institutions were: The establishment of a National Construction and Development Bank on October 29, 1962 to finance industrial and commercial enterprise, the raising of the salaries of military officers and government officials by 100 to 150 per cent on November 24, the passing of the first military service law on January 6, 1963, and the establishment of the Supreme Council for Tribal Affairs on January 3, 1963. The outstanding social and administrative development was the removal of the Sayyid oligarchy from office because it was identified with the tyranny of the Imamate and its many devious ways of extortion and embezzlement. The most oppressive taxes were abolished, and troops were no longer to be quartered on villages. The courts were placed in the hands of the people's representatives, and the extensive lands owned by the Imam's family were nationalized.[51]

The Yemeni coup was thus followed by the standard type of political and social changes that had become a common pattern in the Arab revolutionary movements: The establishment of a republic, the removal of the old ruling class, the end of big landlordism, the creation of the public sector and the transition towards a socialist economy. Old, backward, and isolated Yemen was thus suddenly omitted from the list of reactionary states and was reclassified among the "liberated" Arab states who, moreover, were expected to follow a policy of non-alignment accompanied by cooperation with "the friendly nations" (i.e. those of the Communist Bloc), and must raise the banner of struggle against the "old and new imperialism" in order to qualify for the title.

Like most other revolutionary movements, the Yemeni coup was followed by executions after summary trials usually conducted in what is called a "people's court." The Sana radio broadcast every day the names of high ranking officials of the Imamic regime who were executed for having served feudalism, reaction and tyranny. In the first two days, twenty people were executed and included the foreign minister Hasan ibn Ibrahim, and a former delegate at the United Nations called

Abdul Rahman Abu Taleb. Thirty-eight sharifs and important members of the Ulama (religious scholars) were reported executed in early November. The people's court began its sessions on November 21 for the trial of Muhammad Abdallah al-Shami, governor of Sana, for having signed a treaty with Britain and plotted against state security. The octogenarian Ali ibn Ahmad Ibrahim, who had been chief-of-staff for forty years, was tried for high treason on charges of corruption and weakening the army. Both were sentenced to death.[52] The executioner's sword that was used for chopping off heads was soon abandoned for the more modern method of execution by firing squads! Many high ranking royalists who were not in custody were tried in absentia and condemned to death. The fourteen royalists who were thus sentenced on October 18, 1962 included Prince al-Hasan and several other princes. Shortly before June 16, 1963, the Sana radio announced the discovery of a plot to overthrow the republican regime and as a result many Yemenis were executed outside the prison of Hajja.[53]

IV. Characteristics of the New Revolutionary Regime
A. The Civil War and the Egyptian Involvement

Several special characteristics have distinguished the Yemeni coup and the revolutionary republican regime that followed it from other military coups in the Arab countries. The outstanding feature which explains all the others is the fact that the forces that led the coup were not strong enough to insure the acceptance of the republican regime and the other changes that followed its proclamation. In contrast with those who led the Egyptian revolution of 1952 and the Iraqi revolution of 1958, the Yemeni leaders were neither able to eliminate or keep away the old ruling family, nor to destroy the opposition of those who stood for the former regime. They could not elicit a sufficiently strong popular backing for their movement. The result was a civil war which would have probably lasted a little longer than the internal strife that followed the coups of 1948 and 1955, but would have ended in favor of al-Badr and Imamic rule if it were not for the intervention of the Egyptian military forces to support the republic. Instead of being restricted to a local struggle between royalists and republicans, or conservatives and radicals, or moderate reformists and socialist revolutionaries, the Yemeni civil war thus became an international military and ideological conflict in which the Egyptian military effort on the republican side was approved or supported by radical socialist Arab regimes with the Soviet Bloc and China, while the Saudi aid in funds and arms to the royalists was supported or approved by the Arab monarchies and certain western powers.

The troubles and challenges that confronted the republican regime can best be explained by the nature of the forces that led the coup and the special conditions of the Yemeni environment. The Yemeni coup was made by the revolutionary officers supported by the little commercial bourgeoisie and the radical intellectual youth. The Yemeni army was small and weak. In spite of some training by Egyptians and Russians, and some arms shipments from Russia, it was still ineffective against the large tribal forces that viewed the military with distrust. The Yemeni officers, moreover, had not developed an awareness of public interest and had no sufficient education, experience, and modern concepts of reform, and were thus unable to lead the revolution. The coup was made in a tribal armed society where the people were ready to fight against each other, and where many were still attached to the Imamate. The break which the leaders of the coup made with the past in proclaiming a republic and abolishing the Imamate was too sharp, and the traditionalist and hitherto almost isolated country was not ready for it. The coup, moreover, was not supported by an organized party, and there was no preparation for it among the popular urban and rural masses. The Free Yemenis, some of whom were in exile, knew about the possibility of a revolution but did not participate in it. Most of them were bourgeois reformists, not revolutionaries, and formed the old traditional opposition; they would have accepted reform under the Imamate. They joined the republican regime after having been overtaken by the revolution, but disputes ultimately arose between them and the leaders of the coup. These disputes are sometimes explained by the fact that they were jealous of the leaders of the revolution who had been beneath them in position and prestige.[54] The revolution also, it must be remembered, occurred in a strategic area adjacent to Aden and the South Arabian Federation - the two merged on August 16, 1962 - and to oil-rich Saudi Arabia whose monarchical rule resembled that of Yemen but was more modernistic and enlightened. Neither Saudi Arabia, nor the South Arabian Federation and its British allies, nor the Western oil interests could remain indifferent, as a result, to Egyptian intervention.

The role and motives of Egypt in preparing the coup led inevitably to the Egyptian deep military involvement in Yemen and to the many local and international complications it created. Without Egyptian encouragement, the small group of Yemeni officers and their small ineffective army probably would not have staged the coup against al-Badr and announced the radical changes in the political and social order. It is believed that Egypt prepared to subvert the Imamic regime and overthrow it since the formation of the federation of the UAR and Yemen in 1958, and some even go beyond that date.[55] It is certain, however, that Nasser began his open call for a revolution in Yemen in the broadcast from Cairo immediately after the break-up of the federation in December 1961. His plans and those of the Yemeni radicals for the revolution were not canceled by the death of his foe, Imam Ahmad, and the accession of Nasser's former friend and disciple al-Badr, because what was intended was not a mere change of Imams but a sweeping change that would open the way for Egyptian influence. Open incitement to revolt thus led, for the first time in the history of the Egyptian revolution, to open and direct military intervention. Egyptian open calls for revolution against the Hashemites of Iraq did occur, but when the Iraqi revolution took place in July 1958, it succeeded by its own means. The many appeals of Egypt for overthrowing Hussein of Jordan never succeeded in stirring a revolt, but when an outside attack against Jordan was feared in 1958, Britain sent paratroopers at Hussein's invitation and Nasser did not react except orally, as he most often did. An open Egyptian campaign against President Chamoun of Lebanon succeeded in fomenting a rebellion in May 1958, but Egypt did not send troops to help the rebels even when the American marines landed near Beirut. It did send arms and recruits from Syria, but this was done in a clandestine way and was continuously denied by Nasser. The flow of recruits even decreased after the American intervention.

In Yemen, Egyptian intervention was not only open but it was on a large scale and consequently very costly. The Egyptian aid to the Algerian revolution is said to have cost about five million dollars yearly in arms and ammunition. The cost of supporting the rebellion in Lebanon is sometimes estimated at some sixty million dollars, but the operations of the Egyptian army in Yemen have cost Egypt an estimated half a million dollars a day. Egypt was evidently prepared for intervention and was prompt in arriving on the scene. The first ship to reach the Yemeni port of Hodeida on September 27, one day after the coup, was an Egyptian vessel. It carried "technicians and medical supplies."[56] In early October three Egyptian warships came to Hodeida. They unloaded tnaks, mortar bombs, greandes and troops. On October 20, Sallal declared, "Brother Gamal Abdul-Nasser has ordered a few moments ago the dispatch of a great striking force to help us."[57] Yemeni units were often commanded by Egyptian officers, while the number of Egyptian units multiplied. On October 23, it was reported that all the forces that attacked Maarib in the east of Yemen were Egyptian, and those that occupied Saada in the north consisted of 1500 Egyptians, mostly paratroopers. By the middle of November, the

Egyptian forces were about six to seven thousand in republican-held territory; in December they reached 13,000 troops equipped with tanks and guns.[58] Egypt had to send also a considerable number of doctors, teachers, engineers and administrators. Each Yemeni minister in Sana had an Egyptian adviser with a number of aides. On November 10, Sallal signed a defense pact with Egypt. Eleven days later a republican delegation to Moscow was able to secure arms and Russian technicians.

The royalist forces consisting of warlike tribesmen fought bravely for their Imam and prevented Yemeni republicans and Egyptians from conquering more ground than they had secured at the very beginning. On November 11, 1962 Imam al-Badr spoke to journalists in northwestern Yemen of two royalist armies, one under his uncle al-Hasan in the east, and his own army in the northwest. The tribesmen who supported the Imam were now motivated by their hatred of the Egyptian invaders, particularly after the casualties inflicted on the tribal elements. On October 20, Sallal sought to dissipate the apprehensions of the Yemenis about the presence of Egyptian troops. He told the worshippers after the Friday prayers in Sana not to believe the deceitful men "who tell you that the Egyptians came to rule over the Yemenis." As the Egyptian forces gradually increased to about 70,000 and Egyptian administrators in Yemen and policy makers in Cairo dominated the affairs of Yemen, Sallal's words became more difficult to believe. The Yemeni manpower that Sallal could use was very limited and he had to recruit sometimes urban schoolboys between the ages of fourteen and sixteen.[59] By the end of December 1962, the Egyptian forces had not made much progress despite their tanks and their unopposed air force. The republicans held Sana and part of the center, Taiz and the south, Hodeida and the west, while the Imam controlled about half of Yemen particularly in the north, east, and part of the center.

The Egyptian intervention was as unpopular in Egypt as in Yemen, especially after the rise in the number of casualties and the arrival of the wounded and the mutilated to Egyptian hospitals. Certain press reports mentioned demonstrations in Egyptian villages of the Delta when the bodies of the victims were returned, others spoke of mutinies among Egyptian officers in Yemen and also indicated that Nasser sent the undesired Free Officers to Yemen.[60] Stories were told about ambushes by royalist warriors, the annihilation of entire Egyptian units as in the battles of Sirwah and Maarib at the end of October, the cutting of the noses and ears of Egyptian soldiers, and the killing of prisoners out of hatred for the Egyptian invaders and their indiscriminate bombing of villages and their use of napalm bombs and other modern methods of destruction.

The official explanation given by Egyptian as well as republican Yemeni sources for the open intervention in Yemen was simply that Egypt responded to Sallal's appeal for help to protect the republic against its enemies. According to these sources, the Imam and his forces were not the only foes of the new regime and would not have dared to engage the struggle against it without the encouragement and support of the Saudi Arabian and Jordanian monarchies in the north and the British in the south, or - in the modern language of the Arab revolutionaries - without "the alliance of reaction and imperialism" against the revolution. The two Arab monarchies, they said, were frightened by the prospects of revolution in their own countries; they therefore brought Prince al-Hasan from New York, and as soon as he reached Riyad, he was given considerable funds, arms and men and was sent to Najran in order to oppose the revolution and regain the throne.[61] The Saudis thus began their infiltration and on October 7, Cairo and Sana reported that the republicans were fighting Saudi forces on the northern border. Jordanians also were said to have attacked from the north, and the sherif of Beihan, encouraged by Britain, from the south because British colonialism feared the effects of the revolution on the future of the

South Arabian Federation. With so many enemies on its various fronts, Yemen had to call for help and Egypt answered the call.

The immediate response of Egypt according to this explanation was dictated by her position of leadership in the Arab revolutionary countries and her belief in the necessity of backing the Arab struggle for independence and liberation. The Yemeni revolution was regarded as a movement of liberation from tyranny and backwardness, and in supporting it, Egypt was only implementing one of the provisions of its socialist charter of May 1962 which says, "The United Arab Republic, believing that it is a part of the Arab nation, finds it inevitable to forward its call and the principles that it contains so that they might be placed at the disposal of every Arab citizen. In so doing, it is not necessary to be stopped one moment by the old and worn out argument which might regard this action as intervention on its part in the affairs of others."[62] Nasser and his aides have often referred to this self imposed mission of supporting revolutionary movements in their speeches and declarations. On April 23, 1964 Nasser told a mass rally in Sana, during his first visit to Yemen, that Britain must evacuate Aden and added, "on this blessed ground we swear by God to expell Britain from all parts of the Arab world."[63] In a speech in the National Assembly on February 26, 1965, Marshal Amer asserted that by its quick response in Yemen, the United Arab Republic has been able to affirm that "It was in fact, not in words, the base of the Arab revolution and its fortress." The inevitability of the revolution, he said, has been confirmed as a solution for the problem of Arab underdevelopment which was imposed by imperialism and reaction and their alliance.[64] Sallal also made his own declaration along that line. On December 27, he said in a parade in Sana that "The Yemeni National army would liberate the entire Arabian Peninsula!"

The claim that Egypt was invited by the Sallal regime to support the revolution has not been contested. The agreement on sending Egyptian military and technical aid to Yemen must have been a part of the general agreement about staging the coup and a calculated condition for the maintenance of the republican regime. But the claims of Cairo and Sana about the presence of Saudi and Jordanian forces fighting in northern Yemen has not been confirmed by any eye witness or account. It is commonly known, however, that the Saudi government has given moral and material aid in arms and funds to the Imamic cause, but the motive was not the mere fact that the coup overthrew the Imam and established a republic. Saudi Arabia was concerned about the association of the coup makers with Egypt. It was challenged by the presence of an Egyptian army in Yemen and feared the danger of exporting revolution and expanding Egyptian influence into Saudi Arabia and the rest of the Peninsula, and overthrowing their monarchical regimes. On the other hand, it is commonly held that the implementation of the Egyptian revolutionary creed by backing Arab liberation movements was not the only motive that decided Egypt to send its men to fight in Yemen. Egyptian action in Yemen has been viewed as the beginning of an attempt to dominate the Arabian Peninsula and benefit from its strategic position and its oil resources. It has been regarded as the revival of that traditional Egyptian policy of expansion in Arabia which Mameluk Sultans, Ottoman governors, and particularly Muhammad Ali had followed, but with the one difference that Egypt was now operating under the cover of liberation and revolutionary missionary zeal.[65] The Egyptian campaign in Yemen had also been explained as an effort to regain the prestige that Nasser lost in the break-up of unity with Syria followed by the violent Syrian attacks against the Nasser regime particularly in the Arab League Conference at Shtura in August 1962. Marshal Amer himself has described the situation in the Arab countries before the Yemeni coup and referred to the campaign "organized by imperialism and reaction at Shtura" and the criticism directed against socialism by King Saud, and then added that the Yemeni revolution was "a turning point that returned the initiative to the Arab revolutionary movement."[66]

It became evident as the civil war continued that the Egyptian leaders made a serious miscalculation in committing their government to the support of the republican regime in Yemen. Their ignorance of the complications and peculiar conditions in various Arab countries - as proved by their policies, interventions and mistakes in Syria, Lebanon and Iraq - was revealed again in their involvement in Yemen. Rumors have indicated the opposition of some close aides of Nasser to the Yemeni adventure, but Nasser and his officers evidently did not expect the royalist Yemeni struggle against the Sallal regime and the Egyptian occupation to be so determined, and thus had to witness another setback in their Arab and international policy.

B. Problems of Recognition of the Republic

One of the many special features of the new Yemeni regime was the controversy about its recognition by the world community. The problem was only a corollary of the state of civil war in Yemen and the presence of Egyptian troops, for Egyptian intervention became the main obstacle to the Western recognition of the Yemeni republic. The first states to recognize the new republic were Egypt and the USSR. Other Arab and Eastern Bloc states followed and by October 15, twenty-one states had announced their recognition. One of them was Syria, but although its recognition came in the first week after the coup, it was not followed by diplomatic relations because Nasser, who conducted Sallal's diplomacy, was hostile to the "separatist" Syrian regime and Egypt herself refused to exchange diplomatic representation with Syria after the break-up of unity. It was only on May 24, 1966, when a rapprochement occurred between the new radical Syrian regime and Egypt, that Nasser lifted his veto and allowed diplomatic relations to be established between republican Yemen and Syria.[67]

The two great powers, Britain and the United States,

whose recognition of the new regime meant a great deal to the Yemeni republic, waited several weeks because the new republic had not assured effective control and stability in Yemen, and the former sovereign Imam was still leading the struggle to recover his authority. At the end of October, Britain continued to have doubts "about the control of the Yemeni government over the whole country," and in the first week of February 1963, it still held that the situation "was not sufficiently clear to justify recognition," on the basis that a government is only recognized when it is in effective control of a country. On February 10, 1963, Sallal's government gave a week's notice to Britain to recognize the new regime, and when no favorable response came, the British legation in Taiz was closed on February 17.[68]

The United States was warned by Vice-Premier Baidani on October 7, 1962 that its delay in recognizing the republic would jeopardize American interests. Four days later, al-Ayni threatened in New York that his government would turn to the Soviet Union for aid if the United States did not recognize the new regime. On November 21, the U.S. chargé d'affaires in Yemen, Robert Stookey, declared with optimism that the republican government had "full control" of the country except for some border areas. For twelve weeks after the coup, the Kennedy administration studied the situation and conducted negotiations with the neighboring countries involved to reach a suitable settlement. Letters were sent, during the third week of November, by President Kennedy to Presidents Nasser and Sallal, and to Kings Saud and Hussein for the purpose, but al-Badr was left out. In the meantime the Imam had asked in mid-November for a meeting of the Arab League to discuss Yemeni affairs, but he received no answer.[69] In late November the royalists circulated an appeal to the members of the United Naitons against Egyptian aggression. A week later, on December 4, Prince al-Hasan sent a message to Kennedy in which he warned that recognizing the Yemeni republic "would amount to the support of a seizure of power in Yemen by the United Arab Republic."[70]

On December 19, 1962, the United States Government extended its recognition, with its "best wishes for success and prosperity," to the republican government of Yemen. On the following day, the committee on credentials at the U.N. accepted the delegates of republican Yemen as the official delegation of Yemen, whereas previously both royalist and republican delegates were present. The U.S. recognition was granted in the hope of disengaging the external forces involved in the war in an effort to quarantine civil war before it engulfs the Arabian Peninsula. While fighting continued on the northern and eastern borders of Yemen, the American recognition was apparently made as a result of two promises given by republican Yemen and Egypt. Sallal's government promised to honor its international obligations, including the treaty of Sana in 1934 with Britain, and the preservation of the status quo in Arabia. This meant that Yemen would be limited to its present boundaries and would not interfere in the affairs of the Aden Protectorate. Nasser's government promised that it would withdraw its troops gradually from Yemen with the understanding that Saudi Arabia and Jordan would stop helping the royalists with arms and funds. The U.S. recognition also expressed the inclination of American policy in favor of the modernizing trends and the belief that the Arab countries should rather "ride the wave of social change that had been sweeping the Arab world than be submerged in the waters of civil war and rebellion." The *New York Times* editorialist, a few days later, commented favorably on U.S. recognition by declaring naively that the revolution was won and the republicans were in firm control of most of the country. He also believed that the republican government in Yemen represented the modern democratic progressive forces and that the revolution was a warning to the other monarchies to continue their program of reform.[71] Recognition, for the United States, was thus an instrument of policy and was based on utilitarian considerations, not on the principles of international law. Three months after the United States had recognized the republican regime, Mr. Heath, the

Lord Privy Seal in Britain, declared on March 20, 1963 that the question of the fulfillment of the criteria for recognition was being kept under consideration. It was not a question of how long the regime had lasted, he said, as of conditions in the country and the degree of control over it.[72]

Recognition by the United States was acclaimed in Egypt as a full vindication of the coup that overthrew the Imam and of Cairo's support of the regime. King Hussein, on the other hand, declared that the United States was undercutting her friends and encouraging the subversion of other legal governments and intervention in their affairs. Imam al-Badr believed all the time that Nasser was deceiving the Americans as he and Sallal had deceived him.[73] American recognition did not lead to the disengagement of external forces or to reducing the fighting. Egypt continued to build up her forces, and at the end of December and early January it conducted bombing attacks against Najran in Saudi Arabia. This led to a note from the State Department deploring the attack, and the American Ambassador in Cairo, John Badeau, expressed concern over the bombardment.

Certain Arab authors have viewed American recognition as a sign of approval of both the Yemeni coup and the Egyptian expedition to Yemen. The Kennedy administration, it is held, aimed at undermining and destroying British influence in the Arabian Peninsula after it had been destroyed in the Eastern Mediterranean following the Suez crisis. Kennedy relied on Nasser's leadership in the Arab area to implement his policy, and gave him full support in loans, grants and food supplies. Kennedy, moreover, is said to have believed that the Arab countries were bound to fall under the domination of revolutionary socialism, but he thought that this Arab revolutionary socialism or national communism would stand in the face of Soviet international communism. Another sinister motive of the alleged American approval of Nasser's involvement in Yemen was to keep the Egyptian army occupied in Arabia and away from the borders of Israel. Of all these aims, only this last one - the guarantee of the safety of Israel - was realized. The other aims in this Machiavellic plan were not reached because the Egyptian expedition was not successful in destroying the resistance of the royalists and thus, after two years, the United States felt that its partnership with Egypt for dominating the Peninsula did not give the expected results. The death of Kennedy also was another reason for the failure of the "plan", for his successor evidently did not believe that British influence should be removed from the Peninsula and probably did not accept the common misconception that revolutionary, or Arab socialism was a fortress against Soviet or Chinese communism.[74]

C. *Experiments in Government and Republican Dissensions*

The successive changes and experiments in government that usually follow a coup, and the struggle for power among the leaders of the revolutionary movement have occurred in Yemen as in all the other Arab countries in the aftermath of military seizure of power. This common feature, however, assumed a special character in Yemen owing to the presence of an external force that played its own role in government changes and influenced the struggle between the leading republicans. Yemeni leaders often won power and lost it by Egyptian approval or disapproval, and the changes in government were made usually on Egypt's recommendation. The provisional constitution of October 31, 1962 was proclaimed after Marshal Amer's visit to Sana, and the new Sallal cabinet that was formed at the same time retained the Egyptian-born Baidani as vice-premier and excluded those who could not cooperate with him. A few months after the coup, rivalry developed between Sallal, the Zaydi native of Yemen, and Baidani, the foreign-born and foreign-educated Sunni. In Mid-January, 1963, Baidani arrived in Cairo and it was said that Sallal thwarted an attempt by Baidani to oust him.[75] The

Yemenis feared Baidani as a potential puppet of Nasser, although Nasser was probably not involved in Baidani's attempt. Egypt evidently recognized the problems that Baidani's continued presence in Yemen could create and accepted his dismissal, but at the same time Sallal was made to understand, when Amer visited Sana again at the end of January, that it was Cairo who commanded. Baidani remained for some time in Cairo, but later in the year he was arrested on September 22, after his return from Aden, for "suspicious contacts with the British during his presence in Aden."[76]

The new Sallal cabinet of February 18, 1963 - the third in less than five months - confirmed Baidani's dismissal. It also indicated the interest of Cairo and Sana in "Southern Yemen" by the creation of a cabinet post for Southern Yemeni Affairs. On April 18, 1963 a new development in government, that followed the Egyptian pattern, took place. The Revolution Command Council was replaced by a "presidency council" under Sallal with eighteen members, of whom five were chosen from among the tribal sheikhs. The cabinet was now called the "executive council" and it had a chairman or president instead of a prime minister, and one or more vice-chairmen.[77] A further constitutional development was announced on January 7, 1964 when a "political bureau" was established as the highest authority for political and legislative affairs, and a "national security council" responsible for military and civil defense was set up. No mention was made of the remaining powers of the presidency council that had been created on April 18, 1963. The executive council (cabinet) was to continue for administrative and executive affairs. As in most other revolutionary regimes, the same persons were appointed and reappointed to the various organs of government, sometimes in more than one at the same time. On January 9, 1964, Hasan al-Amri, and Ahmad Muhammad Numan, for example, were appointed in the political bureau, and a month later when a new executive council was formed, al-Amri became its chairman and Numan its vice-chairman. On February 10, 1964 a decree was issued for the formation of a Yemeni

Progressive Union to serve as a popular base for the government along the pattern of the Arab Socialist Union in Egypt.[78]

The series of constitutional changes continued after Nasser's visit to Yemen on April 23, 1964. On April 28, a new constitution was announced and the Yemeni republic was declared "an Islamic Arab state, independent and sovereign." The new constitution abolished the "political bureau" and provided for the creation of a consultative council whose appointed president was Ahmad Muhammad Numan, but the members were to be nominated by a nine-man supreme committee which was set up later in May. The executive council was abolished and the regular cabinet was formed on May 3, 1964 under Hammud al-Jayfi, one of the leading senior officers of the revolution, to whom Nasser transferred most of Sallal's administrative powers. Most of the members of the former political bureau and the executive council were given positions in the new cabinet. Hasan al-Amri was appointed vice-premier.

On July 13, 1964 an agreement was signed between Egypt and Yemen for the coordination of their policies in "the political, military, economic, social, cultural and propaganda fields as a step towards complete unity."[79] The agreement was along the lines of that signed between Egypt and Iraq on May 26, 1964. Any attack or threat against either country was considered directed against the other. A Coordinating Council of Presidents Nasser and Sallal with three ministers from each government and three part-time members from each country was created with headquarters in Cairo. The agreement would have seemed superfluous, as long as Egypt dominated the affairs of Yemen, but it could have been designed to keep Yemen closer to Egypt after the end of the civil war, or to strengthen the position of Egypt in view of the emergence of a republican "third force" that was critical of Egyptian policy in Yemen.

Republican dissidents were encouraged to speak openly against the Sallal regime and its Egyptian backers after the breakdown of the cease fire of November 8, 1964 that had been arranged in a meeting of republicans and royalists at Erkwit in the Sudan. On December 12, 1964 prominent republican leaders like Numan, Iryani, and Zubayri resigned from their cabinet and other high posts and denounced the government under Sallal as "corrupt, impotent, and bankrupt." A delegation of dissident republicans headed by Ibrahim Ali al-Wazir arrived in Beirut on December 28 and explained their viewpoint about Egyptian withdrawal from Yemen and allowing the Yemenis to choose their own regime. At the same time, about sixty republicans fled to Aden under the leadership of Colonel Taha Mustafa, former secretary of Sallal, in protest against Egyptian influence. Nasser did not sacrifice Sallal to satisfy the expressed wishes of the dissident republicans and to make peace with the royalists but, on the contrary, he backed him following Sallal's visit to Cairo. When the Jayfi cabinet resigned on January 6, 1965 after most of its members had left, it was replaced by another under Hasan al-Amri, the very man whose dismissal along with that of Sallal was asked by the dissidents. A state of emergency was then declared by Sallal, and the new prime minister, acting as military governor, prepared to try the dissidents of the Jayfi cabinet. On January 25, 1965 Sallal published a law for establishing the Yemeni Arab Union in which all the popular forces in the country would be incorporated. At about the same time, al-Zubayri, founder of the new moderate republican "Party of Allah", called for Islamic, republican, consultative rule "that would be neither Imamic nor military rule." He was assassinated in early April by an unknown person.

Experiments and innovations in government continued under the Sallal regime. In early March 1965 Sallal appointed by decree a 25-member committee to draw up a national charter.[80] This was probably a response to the announcement of a national charter by the royalists on February 3, 1965 in which al-Badr promised to submit to the authority of a legislative assembly if the Egyptians withdrew. An important change occurred on April 22, 1965 when the first cabinet to be headed by a civilian prime minister replaced the Amri cabinet. Ahmad Muhammed Numan, who only a few months earlier had denounced the Sallal regime in Beirut and asked for the withdrawal of the Egyptians, was the new prime minister. His 15-man cabinet included two officers only. It is believed that Numan accepted the premiership on condition of creating a presidency council that would replace the post of president of the republic. The presidency council of six members was immediately created "to plan, direct, and supervise the execution of state policies." The government also invited the people of all persuasions to meet in a conference at Khamr, twenty miles north of Sana, to achieve peace for the nation. The conference met on May 2, under the presidency of Sheikh Abdul-Rahman al-Iryani, but no royalists attended. The purely republican conference resulted in a new interim constitution that replaced the constitution of April 1964 and was designed to limit Sallal's power. The significance of the new constitution announced on May 8, 1965 was that it was the first one to be made by the Yemenis themselves. It called Yemen an "Islamic Arab Yemeni republic" and provided for a republican council of three members and a consultative assembly of ninety-nine members. The assembly was given the power to nominate the president of the republic and withdraw confidence from the cabinet and the republican council by a two-thirds vote.[81] It mentioned the creation of a popular political organization called "the popular congress", a national defense council, and a supreme Sharia court.

The Numan cabinet was evidently too independent minded to survive. Its young educated elements, including some Baath party members, criticized the Egyptians, while pro-Egyptian circles in Taiz issued pamphlets against the Numan cabinet accusing it of connections with the imperialists.[82] The power struggle between the independent republicans and Sallal was again opened. Sheikh Iryani, member of the republican council, complained that Sallal's creation of a Supreme Council of the Armed Forces in late June was unconstitutional. On July 1, Premier Numan resigned and flew to

Cairo. Sallal arrested some ministers of the Numan cabinet as well as members of the "Party of Allah" founded by Zubayri. He attempted to form his own cabinet, but Cairo ordered him to cancel his plans. He then left for Cairo on July 8 and emerged as the victor in the power struggle. On July 20, the pro-Egyptian general Hasan al-Amri formed the new cabinet. Sallal proclaimed a national pact to preserve the republic and "to crush rebellion and the enemies of the people." In the meantime the dissident republicans formed a Popular Forces Front and broke with Sallal. More than thirty republican leaders and many more of their supporters crossed the border to Beihan in the South Arabian Federation. The Interior Minister in the Numan cabinet appealed to the Arab League and the U.N. Secretary General to insure the withdrawal of the Egyptians from Yemen.[83]

The Jidda agreement of August 24, 1965 between President Nasser and King Faisal of Saudi Arabia for ending the civil war in Yemen was followed by a reconciliation of republican leaders, and both Numan and Sallal went to the Third Arab Summit Conference at Casablanca in September 1965. A new republican council of six members under Sallal was formed on September 4 and it included Numan, Iryani, Amri, and Jayfi. Iryani was placed at the head of the republican delegation to the Harad conference that opened on November 23 for selecting the interim coalition government by both the republican and royalist delegates in accordance with the Jidda Agreement. When the Harad Conference failed and it became evident that the Egyptians would not withdraw their forces from Yemen, the Popular Forces Front - also known as the Yemen-First republican faction - became bitter and began to study the possibility of a purely Yemeni settlement after direct talks between them and the royalists. Nasser consequently sent Sallal back from Cairo in mid-August 1966, after an absence of ten months, to destroy the republican scheme and reassert Egyptian influence. Yemeni resentment against the heavy-handed Egyptian presence was increasing and Premier Hasan al-Amri himself had recently returned irritated from Egypt because he was rebuffed in his attempt to assert more control of Yemeni affairs. As a result, al-Amri moved to the position of the Yemen-First republicans.[84]

Premier al-Amri was not consulted about Sallal's return from Egypt in mid-August and tried to block it by sending troops to gain control of the Sana airport and the radio station before Sallal's arrival. But a superior Egyptian force rallied by the Egyptian ambassador, Ahmad Shukri, forced the Yemeni troops to abandon their plan. Sallal's home was guarded by Egyptian tanks and the conflict between him and al-Amri persisted. Under these conditions, some forty members of the Yemen-First republicans left for Cairo to ask for Sallal's recall from Yemen because he was too dictatorial and too pro-Egyptian. They were also ready to accept the peace plan presented by Kuwait, which would have replaced Egyptian forces by a pan-Arab force in Yemen, created a transitional government of all factions for ten months and conducted a plebiscite to determine the form of government. The republican delegation was refused an audience with Marshal Amer, and on the evening of Friday September 16, 1966 its members were arrested by Egyptian intelligence officers while they were meeting in Numan's apartment. Among them were several members of the republican council, including Premier al-Amri, Numan, Jayfi, and Iryani. In Yemen it was claimed that the Amri cabinet resigned, but its members were in reality under arrest while Sallal himself formed the cabinet contrary to the provision of the constitution which did not allow the president to be prime minister.

The coup made by Nasser on September 16, 1966 against the republican delegation in Cairo was described as a cynical strongarm move, and it meant that Nasser intended to keep his army in Yemen until after the British withdrawal from Aden in January 1968. It also meant that Nasser crushed a genuine republican peace faction and ruled out evacuation based on a purely Yemeni settlement.[85] The Nasserist coup or purge increased the ferment against Sallal's regime. Shooting and grenade throwing incidents became nightly occurrences. Sallal, on the other hand, dismissed thirty-five officers along with some high officials, and arrested many supporters of Numan and al-Amri. Among those dismissed was al-Ayni who left his United Nations post for Beirut to form an anti-Egyptian front. Sallal also prepared treason trials for the leaders who were arrested in Cairo and for other opponents. On October 25, 1966, after a brief trial, seven former officials including a veteran republican minister were executed by a firing squad. They were convicted of treason for trying to overthrow Sallal. The Egyptian military authorities in Yemen, in attempting to break the opposition movement, arrested some 2,000 persons in San. nd 1,000 in Taiz. At the end of 1966, the leader of the Popular Forces Front, Ibrahim al-Wazir, declared in Beirut that the question in Yemen was one of Egyptians and Yemenis and no longer one of republican or royalist regimes. Executions of dissident republicans continued while Sallal, backed by Egypt, remained president and prime minister, but in reality he was a figurehead for whom Egypt could no longer find a substitute.

While constitutional and other changes succeeded each other in republican Yemen, the royalists tried to reorganize Imamic rule along democratic lines. The basic aspect of Imamic government during the civil war was the sharing of power between the Imam and his cabinet and other royalist leaders, and the delegation of authority to certain members of his family. The Imam promised in the charter of February 3, 1965 to accept the establishment of a legislative assembly if the Egyptians left. Influence and leadership, however, belonged to the Imam's close relatives - uncles and cousins - who commanded the royalist armies. After the abortive Jidda agreement of August 1965, al-Badr remained in Hejaz for treatment. An important development occurred during this period and was announced by the Imam's headquarters in northern Yemen at the end of November 1966. It was the creation of an Imamate Council under the presidency of al-Badr with his cousin Muhammad ibn al-Hussein as his deputy, his uncle al-Hasan as vice-president, and seven members. The Council was authorized to make the important appointments with the Imam's approval and after consultation with the cabinet. It was also given political, administrative, and military authority and had to present reform and development projects. The decree creating the council was issued after meetings between the royal family and the heads of tribes and commanders of the various regions.

V. Inter-Arab Tensions and Attitude of the Great Powers

One of the most significant special features of the Yemeni revolution was its impact on the growth of inter-Arab tensions, on the one hand, and its repercussions on the policies and attitudes of the great powers, on the other. The Egyptian presence in Yemen on the side of the republican forces was viewed as an attempt to export revolution and socialism to the rest of the Arabian Peninsula in order to overthrow its traditional governments and ultimately gain control of the Arabian oil resources. Saudi Arabia reacted defensively by supporting the royalists, without fighting on their side, to safeguard its security. The resulting clashes between Egypt and Saudi Arabia were ideological and political. For Nasser, the Yemeni war was a struggle to insure the success of the Arab socialist revolution and gain influence in the Arab world, while for the Saudi monarchy it was a struggle for survival in the Peninsula. Egypt and Saudi Arabia became so much involved in Yemen that negotiations and mediation efforts to end the civil war were addressed to them rather than to the original contending parties, the Yemeni republicans and royalists.

Saudi Arabia had first to meet the Egyptian challenge by reorganizing its government and announcing some needed reforms. On October 17, 1962, three weeks after the Yemeni coup, Crown Prince Faisal replaced his incompetent brother King Saud as prime minister and acceded in his policy statement to a long standing demand for internal reforms.[86] One of them was the abolition of slavery and the emancipation of slaves. Eventually, Faisal was given the title of Viceroy, and all the powers of his royal brother were transferred to him by a formal decision of the Ulama supported by the majority of Saudi princes on March 31, 1964. On November 2 of the same year, King Saud was dethroned and Faisal was declared King of Saudi Arabia.

Clashes between Egypt and Saudi Arabia took the form of cold war accusations and hostile announcements by the powerful Egyptian propaganda machine at the beginning. Cairo and Sana accused Saudis and Jordanians of invading Yemen, and then began broadcasting the news of Saudi and Jordanian pilots who defected to Egypt. In early October they gleefully reported that three Saudi pilots left for Egypt with their planes and their arms cargo. Later in November, three Jordanian pilots were said to have preferred to defect to Cairo rather than fight against the Yemeni republicans. The pilots produced no evidence that they had orders to go to Yemen, and the Saudi government protested to the Egyptian Embassy in Jidda against Egypt's incitement of Saudi pilots and its open encouragement of treason by receiving the pilots officially at the airport and appointing them in the Egyptian Air Force. Egypt then began on November 6, 1962 its attacks on Jizan and the Saudi border, or on what it called "the bases of aggression" in Saudi Arabia. The Saudi government reacted on the following day by breaking diplomatic relations with Egypt. The bombing attacks were renewed, this time against Najran in Saudi Arabia in early January 1963, and the United States reacted by sending a note to Cairo deploring the attack. President Kennedy made public on January 8 a letter he had written to Prince Faisal on November 25, 1962 giving him assurances of friendship, cooperation and support for protecting the security and maintaining the integrity of Saudi Arabia.[87]

The United States was now in the difficult position of wanting to maintain friendly relations with Egypt, and at the same time guaranteeing the integrity of the pro-Western Saudi government. The United Nations Assistant Secretary-General, Ralph Bunche, visited Yemen on March 1, 1963 on a fact-finding tour, but he met the republicans only and refused the invitation of the royalists. During his visit, Egyptian warships shelled the Saudi port of Jizan on March 3 and 4. A month later, the mission of the American retired diplomat Ellsworth Bunker to Saudi Arabia and Egypt ended with apparent success, for both countries accepted the stationing of U.N. observers to make sure the end of Saudi support for the royalists and the withdrawal of Egyptian forces estimated then at about 28,000 soldiers. The agreement was thought to be a face-saving device for Nasser in view of the high financial cost of the war which he could not afford, and the heavy casualties approximating five thousand Egyptians. But after the return of the first units of troops to Egypt in May, it became evident that Nasser was not withdrawing, but only rotating his forces. Before the U.N. truce team arrived in Yemen in early July 1963 under the direction of the Swedish Major-General Carl Van Horn, Nasser and his generals had already made it clear that Egyptian forces "will be there until it becomes certain without any deception or doubt that the reaction that hates the Yemeni revolution is forced by defeat to contain that hatred in its own heart."[88]

The United Naitons observation operation began on July 4, 1963 and ended on September 4, 1964. It was almost decided to end it ten months earlier because no success had been registered in the disengagement agreement, but it was extended several times, and in vain. The United States government was disillusioned, but while it denounced Nasser's bombardments of Saudi border towns, it continued its 432 million dollar program of aid to Egypt.[89] Its occasional interventions for ending the civil war were ineffective partly because it refused to recognize the royalists as a party that should be consulted.[90] Nor did the world organization show any concern when the Saudi ambassador to the U.N. presented to the U.N Secretary-General a letter in March 1967 with proofs on the

1. King Farouk (1920-1965) and Winston Churchill in 1942 (From Barrie St. Clair McBride, "Farouk of Egypt", Robert Hale, London 1968).

2. Mustafa al-Nahas Pasha (1879-1965), leader of the Egyptian Wafd party until its dissolution in January 1953 (From "The New York Times", August 24, 1965 — AP photo 1950).

3. King Farouk and Mustafa al-Nahas Pasha, Egyptian prime minister and leader of the Wafd party, May 1951 (Keystone Press Agency, from Harry Hopkins, "Egypt the Crucible", Secker and Warburg, London 1969).

4. General Muhammad Naguib (born 1901) and Lt. Col. Gamal Abdul Nasser (born 1918).

5. Lt. Col. Abdul Nasser, Secretary of State John Foster Dulles, and Gen. Muhammad Naguib in Cairo, May 1953 (Keystone, from Harry Hopkins "Egypt the Crucible").

6. Field Marshal Abdul Hakim Amer (born 1919) in Moscow, early December 1960 (From "The Scribe", January 1961).

7. Advertisement in "al-Ahram", July 23, 1964 conveying the congratulations of a state-owned corporation to President Nasser on the 12th Anniversary of the revolution and mentioning twelve achievements under Nasser's leadership.

8. The Nile diversion ceremony at the Aswan High Dam in mid May 1964 showing from the left: President Nasser, Nikita Khruschev, Abdul Salam Aref of Iraq, and Abdallah al-Sallal of Yemen (Keystone, from Harry Hopkins, "Egypt the Crucible").

9. President Nasser in Moscow with Soviet leaders, Alexei Kosygin, Leonid Brezhnev, and Anastas Mikoyan, late August 1965 (from "The New York Times", August 29, 1965).

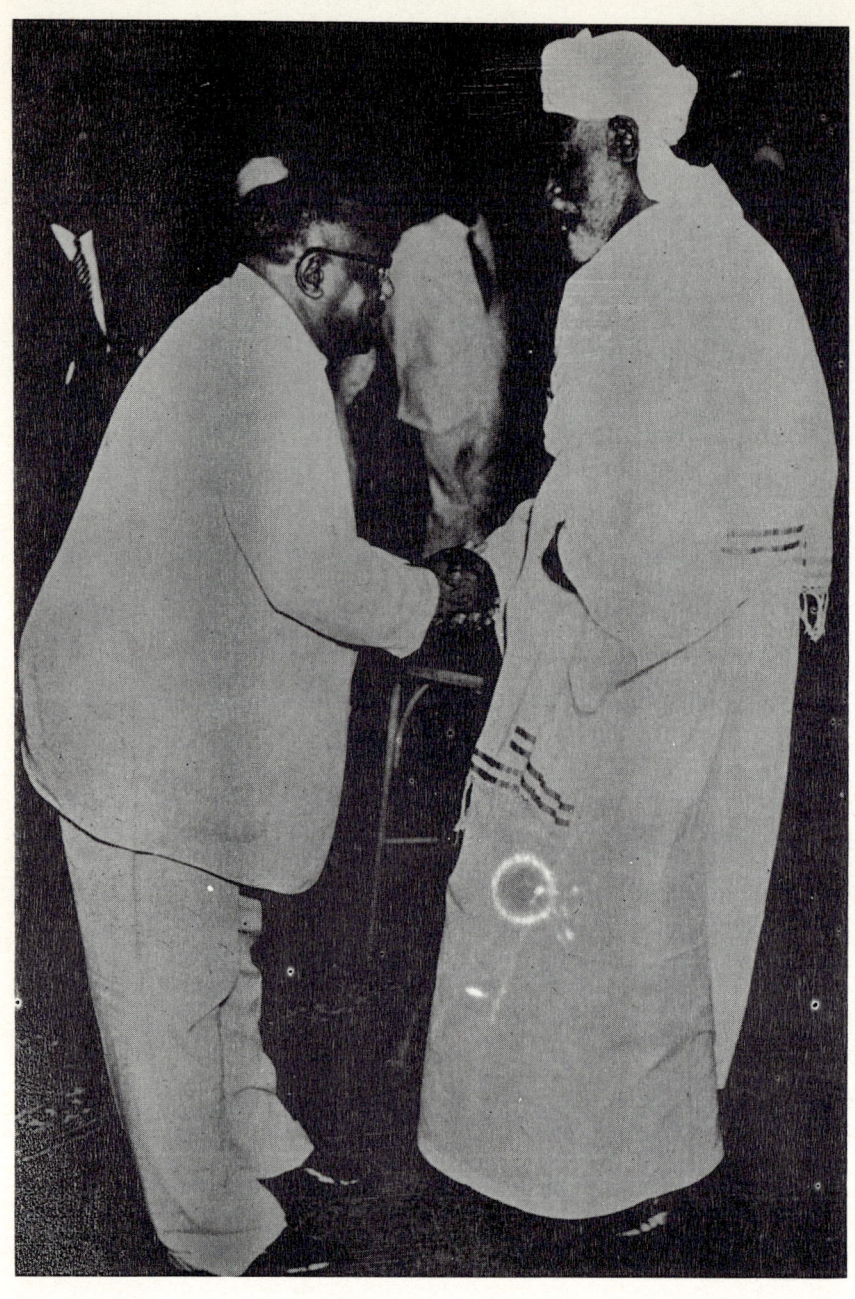

10. Ismail al-Azhari (1900-1970) leader of the National Unionist party greeting al-Sayyid Abdul Rahman al-Mahdi (1885-1959), son of the Mahdi, head of the Ansar religious brotherhood, and patron of the Umma party (From P.M. Holt, "A Modern History of the Sudan", Grove Press, New York 1961).

11. General Ibrahim Abboud (born 1900), head of the Sudanese State after the coup d'etat of November 17, 1958 (From P.M. Holt, "A Modern History of the Sudan.")

12. Colonel Jaafar al-Numairi, leader of the coup d'etat of May 25, 1969 in the Sudan (From "al Anwar" — Beirut — May 28, 1969).

13. Imam Yahya Hamiduddin of Yemen, ruled 1904-1948 (sketch made by Ameen Rihani was only known portrait of the Imam; from Harold Ingrams, "The Yemen: Imams, Rulers and Revolutions", John Murray, London 1963).

14. Imam Ahmad 1891-1962 (Photo Planet News Ltd., from Harold Ingrams, "The Yemen, Imams, Rulers and Revolutions").

15. Imam Muhammad al-Badr, born 1926 (The Central Press Photos Ltd., from Harold Ingrams "The Yemen: Imams, Rulers and Revolutions").

16. General (later Marshal) Abdallah al-Sallal (born 1917?) chief of State in Yemen after the coup d'etat of September 26, 1962 (from "Time", September 13, 1963).

17. Imam Muhammad al-Badr (center seated) and his royalist warriors in the Yemen civil war.

18. Sayyid Muhammad Idris al-Sanusi (born 1890), King of Libya 1951-1969 (From Henry Serrano Villard "Libya, The New Arab Kingdom of North Africa," Ithaca: Cornell University Press, 1956).

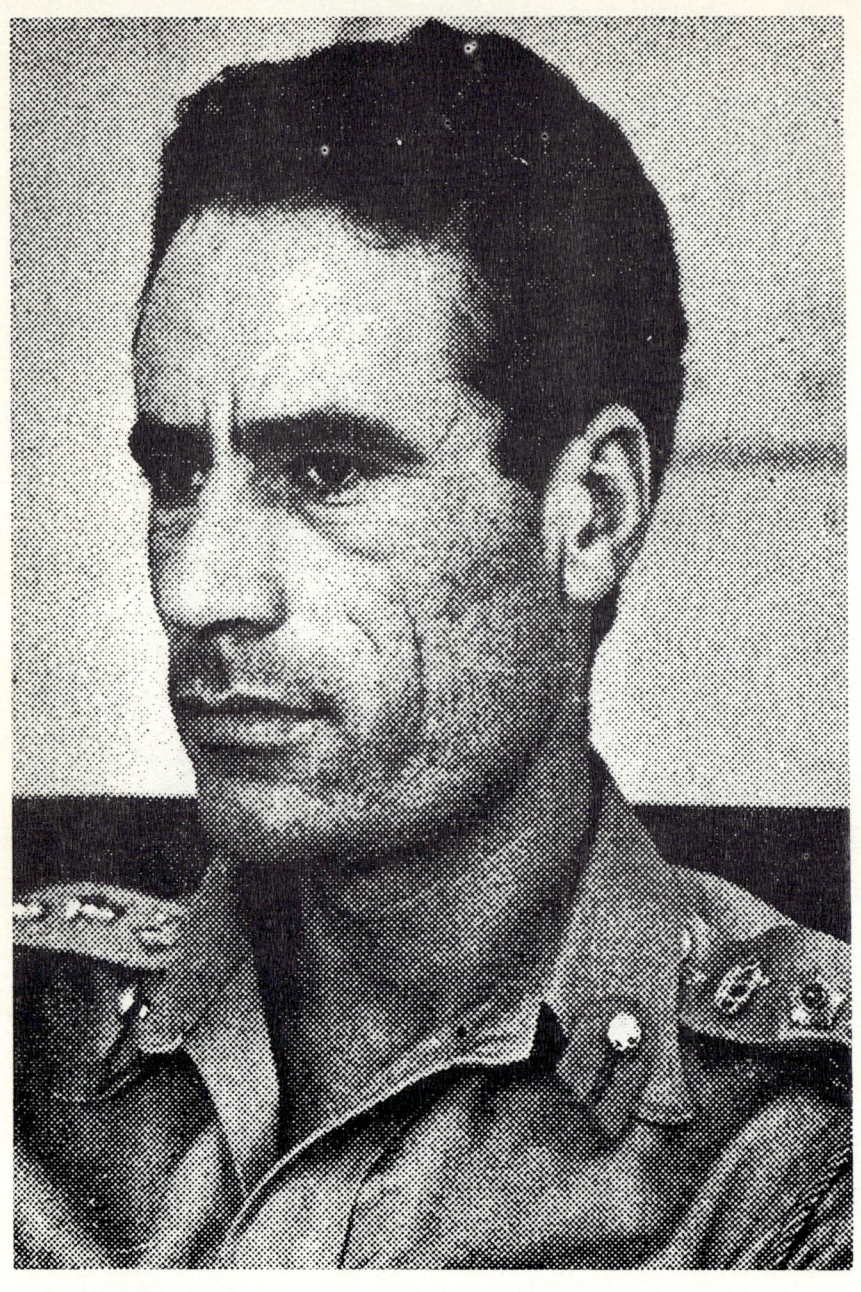

19. First Lieutenant (later Colonel) Mu'ammar al-Qadhafi (born 1942?) leader of the junior officers' coup of September, 1969 in Libya (From "The Economist", December 20, 1969).

use of poison gas by Egyptian bombers in the attack of January 5 against the village of Ketaf near Saada.[91] Details were known later about the widespread use of poison gas by the Egyptians in an effort to terrorize the royalists into submission.[92] One of these bombardments occurred in May 1967, at a time when Egypt and other Arab states were mobilizing their forces to meet the danger of war with Israel. In late July 1967, the American Department of State issued a statement saying, "We continue to be deeply disturbed by the many reports concerning the use of poison gas against civilians in the Yemen," and expressed its support for international action to deal with the problem.[93] But by then, even Saudi Arabia was not prepared in the aftermath of the Arab-Israeli war of early June 1967 to request the consideration of this problem by the Security Council because of its concern about Arab solidarity and the critical situation in Egypt.

The Arab countries, divided as they were between militant socialist revolutionary states, and anti-revolutionary and neutral states, took no decisive action to end the civil war or investigate the use of poison gas by Egypt. The war only increased the polarization in the Arab world while the Soviet Union promoted Arab division and disagreement. The Arab revolutionary governments and the various conferences they patronized were ready to protest against any unhuman acts or foreign intervention in Vietnam and the Congo or elsewhere, but remained silent about the horrors of the civil war in Yemen that was prolonged by the Egyptian presence.[94] The other Arab states did not officially take sides or denounce the atrocities by fear of hurting their relations with Egypt. The free press in some of them, and particularly in Lebanon, condemned the wasting of Arab lives and resources in a struggle between Arabs instead of devoting their efforts for the Israeli challenge. "Keeping the Egyptian army engaged in the colonization of Yemen," said one writer, "and sending it away from the borders of Israel is an act of national treason."[95] According to Nasser's logic and that of the Arab revolutionaries, Israel's turn was to come after they had gained more power by "winning more people from imperialism and reaction and getting rid of Kings Saud and Hussein."[96] Even the ultra-Arab nationalists of the Baath ruling party in Syria never denounced Nasser for keeping his forces in Yemen and killing fellow Arabs. For them and for the other revolutionaries, Arab socialism and revolution took precedence over Arab nationalism. Imam al-Badr, on the other hand, in complaining in early December 1962 about the Egyptian raiding of pro-royalist towns "as if they were in Israel," told Nasser, "the way to Israel is Sinai, not Yemen!"[97] The Yemenis living in Aden appealed to Bourguiba of Tunisia during his visit to Saudi Arabia in late February 1965, to save Yemen from "bloodshed and misery never experienced by any people before," and then added, "the rightful and honorable war should be fought in Palestine not in Yemen."[98] Observers in various parts of the world noted that "Israel feels safer while Egyptians fight in Yemen," and that the U.A.R. was too involved in Yemen to do more than talk about war with Israel.[99]

The Arab feeling of the need for unity in order to deal with Israel, particularly after its diversion of the Jordan waters in 1963-1964, led to two attempts to end the civil war and provided Nasser with a breathing spell in his fruitless effort to subdue the royalists. The first attempt was made after the first and second Arab summit conferences of January and September 1964 when tensions were relaxed and diplomatic relations between Egypt and Saudi Arabia were restored. During this period Jordan decided to recognize the republican regime in Yemen on July 22, 1964. Nasser was apparently ready to accept peace without achieving victory. His summer offensive in 1964 failed, and for the first time he recognized the royalists as a party to the dispute. On November 9, 1964 a cease fire began after the meeting of republicans and royalists at Erkwit in the Sudan, but the Yemeni national congress of republicans and royalists, which was expected to meet in late November to lay down the principles for ending the war and deciding the future form of government, never met. This was the end of the first attempt. Egyptian forces were increased to

50,000, and later in the spring of 1965 to 60,000, but they again suffered heavy losses and their offensive failed in March and April 1965, while their units were isolated in certain areas.

The second attempt to end the war occurred in the summer of 1965 before the meeting of the third summit conference at Casablanca in September. The peace talks between President Nasser and King Faisal in Jidda led to the Jidda Agreement of August 24, 1965. The Egyptian press explained the factors that paved the way for the talks. It mentioned the dangerous development in the situation with relation to Israel and the need "to serve the most sacred causes of the Arab struggle instead of engaging in a side battle."[100] The semi-official *al-Ahram* disclosed later that Nasser had scheduled an attack on Saudi Arabia as "the base of aggression" for September 7, 1965, but orders were given to cancel it after the Jidda Agreement.[101] A long transitional period of fifteen months was provided by the agreement for ending the civil war, and it was to be in three stages. First, a conference of fifty republicans and royalists would meet at Harad in Yemen after three months to appoint a caretaker or interim government; second, the Egyptian troops would withdraw in the following ten months; third, a national Yemeni plebiscite would be held two months later to determine the form of government. The agreement was viewed by the Arabs as "a triumph of reason over emotions," but the radical Baath in Syria accused Nasser of betraying the Yemeni revolution. The conference of republicans and royalists met at Harad on November 23, 1965 to nominate the interim government, but it soon became deadlocked over several issues including the composition of the interim cabinet, and the mention of the "republic" in the interim legislation. The Jidda Agreement as well as the summit spirit of solidarity became a dead letter after the adjournment of the Harad Conference on December 24, 1965. It looked as though Palestine in whose name many Arab representatives met was less important than the spreading of the socialist revolutionary gospel.

Between the ill-fated Jidda Agreement of August 24, 1965 and the Israeli war of June 1967, inter-Arab tensions increased and the Egyptian campaign against Saudi Arabia and the Arab "reactionaries" reached its climax. It was generally felt that the Soviet Union played its role in the failure of the Jidda Agreement and in "keeping the pot boiling" in Yemen. By writing off some of Cairo's debt to Moscow for the equipment used in Yemen, and giving 200 million dollars in financial aid as a result of Nasser's visit to Moscow at the end of August 1965, the Soviet Union encouraged the Egyptians to continue their occupation.[102] In his speech of February 22, 1966 on the anniversary of the defunct union between Egypt and Syria, Nasser declared that his forces were ready to stay for many years in Yemen. Egypt actually followed a new strategy during the long ceasefire that followed the Jidda Agreement. It pulled its troops back from exposed positions, consolidated its hold on key cities and prepared for a long occupation. In early 1966, King Faisal sought to strengthen his air defense system against possible Egyptian attack and made a 400-million-dollar order of jets and air force equipment from the United States and Britain. Four months later, towards the end of April, he negotiated the building of an airport near the Yemeni border and the purchase of twelve new jets. Nasser answered these defensive arrangements with contempt and in his May Day 1966 speech to a mass rally at al-Mahalla al-Kubra he threatened to occupy the two Saudi frontier towns of Jizan and Najran, and then said addressing King Faisal, "We tell him we can destroy his twelve planes and his airport in five minutes." Nasser also made Saudi Arabia responsible for the American arms shipments to Israel because, according to him, the United States used the arms deal with Saudi Arabia as a screen to provide Israel with arms.[103]

King Faisal's effort to strengthen Muslim solidarity in a series of visits to Muslim countries in December 1965 and the first four months of 1966 infuriated Nasser and made him react violently against what he called a "Muslim pact," or an imperialist plot for a reactionary alliance against the Arab socialist revolution. The Egyptian press and radio, as well as the Egyptian-subsidized newspapers in the Arab world conducted a continuous violent campaign against the so-called Muslim pact and its sponsor until the Israeli War of June 1967. Premier Kosygin's visit to Cairo in May 1966 helped in bringing together the two hitherto hostile leaders of the Arab revolution, Egypt and Syria, and in hardening the lines between the Arab revolutionaries in general, and the so-called Arab reactionaries and their Western friends. Saudi Arabia was accused by Egypt of backing financially the Muslim Brotherhood whose plot against the Egyptian regime was discovered at the end of August 1965. In the trial of the Brethren in April 1966, the chief prosecutor said, "This case was one of the battles against reaction and imperialism which had hatched the plot in Saudi Arabia in cooperation with fugitive collaborationists."[104] Egypt also claimed that there was contact between King Faisal and the twenty officers who were arrested in April 1966 for plotting a coup. Yemen, as it has been said, thus became a microcosm of the Middle Eastern struggle between socialist and conservative forces.[105] Endless embarrassment, moreover, was caused to neutral states, like Lebanon, who still enjoyed freedom of speech and of the press, by the injurious declarations and insulting attacks of the Egyptian-sponsored newspapers against Saudi Arabia.[106] Even as great a power as the United States had to be careful, on the occasion of King Faisal's visit in late June 1966, to make the royal visitor feel welcome without annoying rival Arab leaders.[107]

Egypt sought to undermine and discredit the Saudi monarchy and to stir revolt in Saudi Arabia by publishing provocative news in the state-controlled press between January and March 1967 on explosions and sabotage in the palaces and government buildings in Saudi Arabia, and on the activity of a revolutionary organization called "The Union of the People of the Arabian Peninsula." On March 17 the Saudi minister of Interior announced that those who had been committing sabotage, murder, and destruction in Saudi Arabia were not

Saudi revolutionaries but Yemeni infiltrators trained by the Egyptians in Cairo and Taiz. Those of them who were arrested were tried in the great Sharia Court in Riyad where they confessed their crimes. Seventeen persons were condemned to death on March 12, and five days later they were executed. In Egypt and the other socialist Arab countries, and in the pro-Egyptian press elsewhere, the executions were called "The Riyad massacre." In Lebanon certain mosques held prayers for what they called "the martyrs of Yemen."[108] On March 19, a dynamite explosion rocked the Saudi Embassy in the capital of Lebanon. On the same day, the Maronite Partiarch denounced severely in his Sunday sermon those who disturbed the security of Lebanon. The reaction against Egyptian subversion was also echoed on March 28, 1967 by the leaders of three major Lebanese parties who met President Charles Helou to call his attention to Lebanon's deviation from its traditional non-alignment policy in Arab disputes.[109] At the United Nations, the Saudi Ambassador presented a memoir to Secretary-General U-Thant in answer to protest messages that the UN received against the executions from anti-Saudi sources. The memoir told the story of Egyptian-sponsored sabotage in Saudi Arabia and the dispatch of explosives even in fruit-juice cans. It gave assurances that the trials were made according to the Muslim Law and by competent judges.[110]

Egypt also exploited the sojourn of deposed King Saud in Cairo to embarrass his brother, King Faisal, and draw support for the republicans in Yemen. It was considered bad taste and hypocrisy on Egypt's part to give so much publicity to Saud, who had been previously insulted and ridiculed by Nasser and had opposed the republican regime in Yemen, and to extract from him declarations in favor of the Yemeni republicans. Former King Saud was taken on a visit to Yemen on April 23, 1967 in the company of Amer and Sadat, and in a speech in Sana he announced his recognition of the Yemeni republic and its president, his "brother Abdallah al-Sallal." On April 27, Saud talked from the Voice of the Arabs to the people of Saudi Arabia and told them that their rulers were allies of imperialism. He also appealed to the Saudi army on the border of Yemen to stop its skirmishes.

Throughout the period of the civil war in Yemen, Cairo had been backing and organizing terrorist campaigns against British political rule in the South Arabian Federation. When the British government announced its decision to grant independence to the Federation and withdraw from Aden on January 9, 1968, Egypt became more inclined to keep its forces in Yemen in order to help install pro-Nasser nationalists in the area and particularly in strategic Aden. The apprehension that Egyptian forces might attack from Yemen to support the South Arabian revolutionaries led the government of the Federation to send a delegation to London in June 1966 to insist on keeping a British force in the South as a security guarantee. Again in May 1967, a South Arabian delegation asked for British protection for four years after independence, but Britain promised only nine months.[111] Modern Arab history thus witnessed for the first time this curious phenomenon of a national government that was begging the colonialist power to stay after the grant of independence because of the threat of revolution from within and intervention from without. The two nationalist revolutionary organizations in South Arabia, the Egyptian-supported Front for the Liberation of Occupied South Yemen (FLOSY) led by Adbul Qawi Makawi, and the more independent National Liberation Front (NLF) led by Qahtan al-Shaabi, wanted the end of the Federation and of the Sultanates of which it was formed. The NLF proved more powerful outside Aden, while FLOSY operated mainly in Aden. By the end of August 1967, the government of the Federation had practically collapsed. The NLF rebels kidnapped Sheikh Ali al-Keladi, chairman of the Federal Council on August 28. His successor, Sheikh Ali Babakri, resigned one day later because the officers of the Federal Army refused to respond to his singular appeal asking them to take over the government. The officers felt that the Army was favorable to the rebels, and they were pressed by the NLF leaders to reject the appeal. The forces of the NLF, moreover, controlled thirteen out of the seventeen states of the Federation. The British government, aware of the collapse of the federal government, preferred to establish a new government under the National Liberation Front and declared that it would not negotiate terms for independence with the Federation. In early September, civil strife began in the suburbs of Aden between the two contenders for power, the NLF and FLOSY. The authority of the South Arabian Federation thus vanished before the date fixed for complete British withdrawal and at a time when Egypt was preparing to withdraw its forces from Yemen as a result of its serious losses in the war with Israel in early June 1967.

VI. The Coup Against Sallal and Other Results of Egyptian Withdrawal

In Yemen the tensions caused by the civil war were temporarily relaxed as the Arabs, and especially Egypt, prepared to meet the new challenges and repair the losses created by the successful Israeli invasion. In the Arab summit conference at Khartoum, at the end of August 1967, President Nasser and King Faisal agreed on a plan for settling the Yemeni conflict, after preparatory negotiations had been conducted by the prime minister of the Sudan, Muhammad Ahmad Mahjoub. Like the Jidda Agreement of August 24, 1965, the new agreement of August 30, 1967 was based on the withdrawal of Egyptian troops, and the cessation of Saudi support to the royalists. A committee of three members consisting of an Iraqi chosen by Egypt, a Moroccan chosen by Saudi Arabia, and Premier Mahjoub of Sudan as a balancing personality, was to supervise the implementation of the agreement and sponsor an alliance between Yemeni factions.[112] No clear terms were mentioned about an interim government or a plebiscite. President Sallal in Yemen reacted angrily and denounced the agreement as "an injurious encroachment on the sovereignty of Yemen and its people." Sallal's concern stemmed from his fear that the republicans would be overwhelmed and the royalists would dominate the situation when the Egyptians would leave. He rejected the mediation of the three-member Arab committee and declared that he would ask Russian and Chinese help to protect the borders of his country if Egypt enforced the decision to withdraw its forces. When the committee arrived in Sana on October 3, 1967 to arrange for peace terms and supervise the Egyptian withdrawal, the leftist supporters of Sallal organized demonstrations against it, and in the riots that followed nine Egyptian soldiers were killed and seven disappeared, while five Yemeni rioters lost their lives. The members of the committee took refuge in the Egyptian Headquarters and left on the following day after Sallal refused to meet with them. Sallal later sentenced to death and executed his interior minister, Colonel Khatri, because his police fired on the mobs that were demonstrating outside the Egyptian Headquarters and attacking an Egyptian command post in Sana.[113]

Sallal's only remaining hope was the Yemeni army which he tried to satisfy by appointing three of its officers in the cabinet that he formed on October 12, 1967. He held the portfolio of foreign affairs in addition to his titles of president of the republic, prime minister, and secretary general of the Popular Revolutionary Union. He sent to jail hundreds of his former supporters, and his love of Nasser turned to hatred. In Cairo, Nasser released three highly respected republican leaders who wanted peace with the royalists, and towards the end of October a group of republicans led by Iryani left Cairo for Yemen in order to arrange a "national conciliation conference" among tribal leaders. Sallal agreed with the republican leaders returning from Cairo to call a meeting of opposing factions in Yemen, not in Khartoum.

On November 1, 1967, Sallal left Yemen to attend the fiftieth anniversary of the Bolshevik Revolution in Moscow. On his way he stopped in Cairo where it is said that Nasser gave him a cold reception and advised him to resign and go into exile.¹¹⁴ Sallal then left for Baghdad where he expected help from the Arab socialists. While he was in Baghdad, the dissident republican officers staged a bloodless coup and announced the removal of Sallal "from all positions of authority." The communiqués mentioned that the vanguards of the people and the armed forces, including the republican guard, took power from Sallal and occupied the presidential palace without any resistance. The coup was described as "an extension of the revolution of 1962" that overthrew the Imam.¹¹⁵ A presidential council of three members presided by Sheikh Abdul Rahman Iryani as a provisional head of state was formed. The other two members were Ahmad Muhammad Numan and Muhammad Ali Uthman. The cabinet was formed by Muhsin al-Ayni who, with Iryani and Numan belonged to the "third force" that had opposed the Egyptians and Sallal.

The coup against Sallal was led by four dissident officers among whom were Lt. Cols. Muhammad Iryani and Ahmad Rahumi. They said they had to stage the coup because the republican high command could not persuade Sallal to form a government that would realize unity on Yemeni soil. In one of the communiqués it was mentioned that the original plan was to oust Sallal before his departure on Wednesday November 1, but the leaders decided to take power in his absence to avert violence. The riots that broke out in Taiz on November 7 and 8 were quickly ended. They were attributed to "subversive elements" that supported Sallal. Egypt considered the coup a purely Yemeni domestic matter. The Egyptian troops estimated at about 27,000 soldiers had already started to withdraw in mid-September, and most of them were at the time of the coup gathered at Hodeida and ready to leave. It is even said that when Sallal left Cairo on his way to Baghdad, Nasser sent a cable to Sana instructing the remaining Egyptian troops not to block a coup in case it occurred. The coup actually occurred three days after the end of the four-day visit of the Egyptian vice-premier, Hussein Shafii, to Saudi Arabia on November 2, where he had talks with King Faisal. It is likely that both the Egyptian and the Saudi sides were aware the coup would take place and they gave their preliminary approval.

Sallal thus remained in office as long as the Egyptian troops were in Yemen, and his fall must be considered an indirect result of Egyptian defeat in early June which led to the agreement in Khartoum about the withdrawal of troops and the payment of Saudi subsidies to Egypt. Sallal was described by Iryani, the new head of state, as a man who was concerned only about keeping his position. He is said to have attacked and complained against the military whenever he received the civilians, and did the same against the civilians when he received the military. He attacked the conservatives to please the intellectuals of the younger generation, and did the same against the young intellectuals when the conservatives were in his audience. He also provoked rivalries between Zaydis and Shafiis. Iryani and other high ranking republicans have also claimed that Sallal plundered the Treasury and withdrew half a million *reals* before leaving the country.[116] According to the former interior minister, Brigadier Abdallah al-Dabbi, Sallal asked for asylum in Egypt after the coup but Nasser refused, and Sallal thus remained in Baghdad.

The new prime minister, Muhsin al-Ayni, declared after the coup that Yemen would follow a "good neighbor" policy with the sister states, including Saudi Arabia. The new regime declared that its goal was "to correct the situation in Yemen," and Iryani spoke of establishing contacts with the pro-royalist tribes to bring them to the republican fold. The prime minister flew to Cairo after the coup to establish "brotherly relations" that had been cool since the October 3 riots. He also wanted the continuance of Egyptian financial, technical, and cultural aid. He obtained a pledge from Nasser that the ten million dollar budgetary aid for the Yemeni army would continue until June 1968, but the one hundred Egyptian teachers had left Yemen and many schools were closed at the time of the coup.

The coup against Sallal did not bring peace to Yemen

because the new regime was not ready to compromise with the royalists. On November 8, three days after the coup, Premier Ayni declared that the new regime would talk to the royalists but not to the royal family, and that the republican form of government would not be put in question in a referendum. On the other hand, the dissenting member of the presidential council, Ahmad Numan, who had left Cairo for Beirut "for medical treatment" instead of going to Yemen, declared that he favored talks with all royalists, including the royal family, and that the form of government should be decided by the people of Yemen. He also favored the mediation of the three-member committee, whereas the other members of the council in Yemen thought that the committee had served its purpose. The new regime thus took the initiative away from the committee and followed a policy that differed little from that of Sallal. On November 19, Numan presented his resignation from the presidential council because of its refusal to cooperate with the committee. He believed that this lack of cooperation would lead to the resumption of war "of which I want no part," as he said. It is interesting to note that Numan, who represented the majority of the Shafiite Muslims, was more inclined to compromise on the form of government than Iryani, the Zaydi leader. The three-man peace committee on Yemen held its last meeting in Beirut on January 19, 1968 and sent back the Yemeni problem to Egypt and Saudi Arabia because it was unable to fulfil its main objective of reconciling the republicans and the royalists, or even arranging for talks between them.

The royalists had completed the occupation of the northern, eastern and central regions of Yemen after the withdrawal of Egyptian troops and began preparing the offensive against Sana since the time of Sallal, but called it off when the coup happened. The tone of the declarations by Ayni and Iryani evidently were not encouraging, and the tribal leaders who wanted to see what the new regime had to offer were probably disappointed. On November 17, the royalist radio in northeastern Yemen said that the royalists under Muhammad ibn al-Hussein, cousin of al-Badr and vice-chairman of the Imamate council, began their offensive against Sana and closed the Hodeida-Sana road. Ten days later, the royalists announced that they were outside Sana. The royalist leader, Muhammad ibn al-Hussein, offered amnesty to those who opposed the Imam, and reassured the Yemenis that the theocratic Imamate in its old form and with its oppressive features would not be restored. The royalists asked for a national conference to appoint an interim regime for holding a referendum. They believed that the tribesmen wanted an imamate of some kind, but constitutional and limited by an elected legislature. The republican rulers did not respond to the royalist appeal. On December 7, 1967 Muhammad ibn al-Hussein, who commanded the royalist forces around Sana, gave the republicans a forty hours ultimatum "to surrender or be destroyed." Already on December 2, the dissident republican leader, Ahmad Numan, had predicted in Beirut that Sana would be pillaged and sacked, but this, so far, has not occurred. The republican leaders at the time, however, were shaken and Iryani left for Cairo on the same day as the ultimatum, for "medical checkup," while the republican foreign minister, Hasan Makki, arrived in Cairo one week before the scheduled meeting of a conference of Arab foreign ministers. The families of Soviet technicians and almost all diplomatic missions left the capital as the battle of Sana began. The royalists tried to damage the airport in order to prevent the arrival of Soviet supplies by plane, and the road to Sana was cut off to prevent Russian heavy equipment that was being landed in Hodeida from reaching the capital.[117]

The new republican rulers after Sallal made the royalist attack inevitable when they refused to negotiate arrangements for an interim government and to hold a referendum that could put the republic in question. King Faisal probably rejected the overtures of the new regime because of its refusal to submit to a popular vote and its determination to maintain the republican system and ignore the three-member peace committee. It might be assumed that, in taking this attitude, the new regime was expecting to impose peace on its own terms on the royalists, and it was prepared to receive Soviet military support in men and equipment. Before the Egyptians ended the evacuation of their forces on December 7, 1967, Soviet technicians and MIG 19 fighter bombers were already arriving in Sana to replace Egyptian technicians and planes, and Soviet pilots were flying bombing missions for the republicans. On November 17, Premier Ayni announced the arrival of Soviet planes, and a sense of urgency was noticed at the Sana airport where forty Soviet technicians were working while certain foreign correspondents were expelled probably in search for privacy.[118] As the royalists encircled Sana at the end of November, the presidential council called on the people to defend the republic against "mercenaries and other enemies of the revolution," and Iryani sent an urgent message to Premier Kosygin for assistance. The first royalist ultimatum on December 7 was followed by the formation of militia units or a popular resistance force, and arms were distributed to the people of Sana. On December 5 the royalist radio announced the shooting down of a military aircraft piloted by a Russian north of Sana. The pilot allegedly was a captain and had identification papers including his pocket assignment card from Russia and his Yemeni instructions on the targets.[119] The republicans, on the other hand, claimed that King Faisal was helping the royalists, and Hasan al-Amri, the commander in chief of the republican armed forces and acting president during Iryani's absence, believed that the first step to peace in Yemen was to end outside aid to the royalists.

On December 18, the Ayni cabinet resigned and a war cabinet was formed five days later by Lt. Gen. Hasan al-Amri. Sana was now a besieged city where food and gasoline had to be brought by military convoys. Travel to Taiz and Hodeida had to be done by plane. Royalist guns in the hills around the capital struck especially at night. The streets and school playgrounds were full of armed civilians and militia volunteers. Royalists and republicans claimed victories in the battle for Sana, but as time passed, it became evident that the position of the republicans improved and they were able to repulse the royalist attacks and defeat their attempts to capture the capital city. The balance was tipped in favor of the republicans because of the emergency airlift carried out by the Russians. It was estimated that in the three weeks between the end of November and mid-December, close to one hundred flights of transports arrived from Russia bringing planes, crews, technicians, and ammunition. The promised twenty-four MIG 19 fighter bombers were delivered, their ground crews were Russians, and some of the pilots were, according to certain reports, Russians or Syrians.[120] The republican air power inflicted heavy casualties on the royalists and by mid-January 1968, about fifteen strong royalist attacks on the capital had been beaten back. In early February a republican armored column was able to break through on the road from Hodeida to Sana, and gradually the royalist threat to the capital began to peter out.

In Saudi Arabia, the broadcast from Mecca accused Russia of intervention in the civil war in early January 1968. Later in February, King Faisal warned that he would resume aid to the Yemen royalists because of intervention on the part of Syrians, Russians, and Southern Yemenis in favor of the republicans. These interventions were denied by Muhsin al-Ayni at the United Nations in late April, when he was able also to declare that the siege of Sana by the royalists had been raised.[121]

The new Yemeni regime, whose leaders were once members of the "third force" that favored a Yemeni peace formula without Egyptian intervention, was thus unable to reach a peace settlement with the royalists in spite of the withdrawal of Egyptian forces. In their determination to preserve the republic, they have been encouraged and supported generously by the Soviet Union, which has replaced Egypt as the political patron of republican Yemen. Already during the Egyptian presence in Yemen, the Russians had played an important role to insure the success of the revolution. They were not prepared to abandon that role after the Egyptians had moved out. Shortly after the royalist threat to Sana had been relaxed, the Russians were accused of inciting the leftist extremists of the popular resistance movement to overthrow the government of al-Amri in an attempted coup on March 22, 1968. The popular resistance group was formed in December 1967 and consisted of dedicated republican workers and students who contributed to al-Amri's success in holding the capital against the royalists. They apparently began to receive arms and money from a similar leftist faction of the National Liberation Front in Aden and were falling under communist control. On March 22, the popular resistance group attempted to take over Hodeida and to intercept a large shipment of Soviet arms that included fifty tanks. They sealed off the port of Hodeida, but they were defeated in a short gun battle during which al-Amri shelled their headquarters and arrested forty of their men. They were soon released because the popular resistance movement countered with a strike and al-Amri felt obliged to seek the end of the strike.[122] This is only one example of how revolutionary regimes often help create extremist forces that become a threat to them and attempt to take their place once the danger to the revolution is removed.

In other developments in royalist ranks, a peaceful bloodless coup d'état occurred against former Imam al-Badr in May 1968 in a meeting attended by princes and tribal leaders at Saada in northern Yemen. The royalist strongman Muhammad ibn al-Hussein, cousin of al-Badr, was named commander in chief of the royalist forces and head of the new six-man Imamate Council. He thus replaced al-Badr in these two positions in which he had been acting as deputy for the former Imam, who had been living in Saudi Arabia since 1966 after having effectively led the royalist forces for four years from the caves of northern Yemen. The coup was considered a part of the preparations for a new offensive against the republicans after the winter offensive had failed to storm the capital.[123]

In Southern Arabia, the British announced in early November 1967 that they would withdraw from Aden at the end of that same month instead of the formerly fixed date (January 9, 1968). The fighting immediately resumed between the two rival national groups, the Front for the Liberation of Occupied South Yemen and the National Liberation Front, but the latter was victorious and it was supported by the 9,000-man army of the South Arabian Federation. On November 26, the British pulled out from Aden and two days later, the British High Commissioner, Sir Humphrey Trevelyan, pronounced South Arabia independent and left wishing the new state "every happiness and a peaceful and prosperous future." The South Arabian Federation was thus replaced by a new republic called the People's Republic of South Yemen, and its capital, al-Ittihad, near Aden was renamed Medinet al-Shaab (The People's City). On November 30, the NLF leader, Qahtan al-Shaabi, was proclaimed president of the republic and a 13-man high command council consisting of NLF members became the policy making and legislative body.

It is ironic that the British left Aden and South Arabia as the Egyptians were withdrawing from Yemen. Israel's success in the war in June 1967 thus prevented Nasser from keeping his forces in Yemen until after the British withdrawal from South Arabia and also put an end to his support of the FLOSY and doomed its chances for taking over the government of the new independent state. The Egyptian presence in Yemen since 1962, however, must be given due credit for encouraging and supporting the nationalist anti-British movement in the Arab South where the struggle began earnestly in 1963 with hand grenades in the towns, especially Aden, and ambushes in the country. On the other hand, the Egyptian withdrawal from Yemen must be given due significance because it allowed the transition to independence and the setting up of a government in South Arabia to be done smoothly and without the interventions and possible civil war that would have been certain between FLOSY and NLF had the Egyptians stayed in Yemen.

The NLF militant rulers of the new republic of South Yemen have attempted to extend their revolutionary movement to all southern Arabia, and they have partly succeeded in doing what Nasser was probably preparing to do if the June war had not upset his plans. Between September 17 and October 15, 1967 even before South Yemen became independent, the NLF were able to dominate the three states of the Eastern Aden Protectorate - the Quaiti, the Kathiri, and the Mahri sultanates. The sultans of these states as well as those of the former South Arabian Federation have been living mostly in Saudi Arabia and scheming to return. The NLF regime has also spoken of backing a revolution in the Sultanate of Muscat and Oman.[124]

An extremist leftist faction of the NLF in the republic of South Yemen has challenged the official NLF government under al-Shaabi in the same way as the popular resistance extremists in republican Yemen have challenged the rule of al-Amri. On March 20, 1968 the South Yemen army averted an extreme leftist coup in Aden by arresting several hundred left wing NLF members who were trying to take over the government. President al-Shaabi proceeded to purge the army and the civil service of these extremists who also were trying to build up influence in Yemen and support the extremist popular resistance. The South Yemen leftists were particularly strong in the three eastern former sultanates where they carried out reforms and nationalized companies without authorization by the central government.[125] Party differences within the NLF began in February 1968 and led to rebellions that the central government had to fight. President al-Shaabi described the dissident NLF leaders of the rebellion as opportunists and deviationists. In mid-May, his army was able to recapture three towns in the eastern region from which the rebels had launched their revolt. The leftist extremists nevertheless succeeded one year later in removing President Shaabi on June 22, 1969 in a bloodless coup and replaced him by a presidential council.

It is worth noting that while the South Yemen guerillas have succeeded in establishing an independent republic after four years of struggle against the might of Britain, the republican regime established by the revolution of 1962 in Yemen has not succeeded in ending the civil war after five years of active Egyptian support, followed since November 1967 by extensive Russian aid. The republic, however, has been more secure since the failure of the great royalist offensive against Sana in January 1968. The fighting has been reduced to a few isolated engagements at a distance from the capital. The royalist commander Muhammad ibn al-Hussein was criticized for trying to concentrate power in himself, and a reaction in favor of Imam al-Badr, who had been living in Taif in Saudi Arabia since 1966, was noticed and resulted in the return of the Imam to the political scene. It was said that certain tribes in northwestern Yemen threatened to defect to the republicans if the Imam's authority were not restored. This is why Saudi Arabia forced a reconciliation between the royalist leaders, and al-Badr was returned to northern Yemen in mid-September 1968. A new royalist offensive was prepared against Sana, and General al-Amri, the republican prime minister who had visited Moscow in September for more arms, commanded the forces around Sana in person and was able with the help of his tanks, MIG fighters, and rockets to frustrate the royalist attack in mid-October 1968. The royalists had neither the air cover nor the armor with which the Russians provided the republicans, and Saudi Arabia could not give its royalist allies this decisive equipment without openly breaking its engagement not to help the royalists. Moreover, the mercenary-minded tribal leaders and commanders on whom ibn al-Hussein had depended in the offensive against Sana were not all reliable. In December 1968, the royalist commander, Qasim Munassar, who participated in the siege of Sana in early 1968 and claimed that he killed more republicans than anyone, joined the republican side and brought with him several trucks of arms and ammunition and the loyalty of thousands of tribesmen who had been fighting for the royalists. He claimed that he had fought against the republicans not because of his love for the Imamic regime, but because he felt that the republicans were controlled by "outsiders"-Egyptians and then Russians. The resistance of Sana, he said, impressed him because there was no foreign support and he became convinced that the republican regime was purely a Yemeni affair.[126]

The republican government of General al-Amri continued to be threatened by dissension among the republicans. On August 30, 1968 radio Sana announced the failure of an attempt to overthrow the government by rebellious officers and the formation of a state security court to punish "the intruding destructive elements who disturb public safety". The rebellion under the leadership of a former chief of staff and a leftist extremist called Abdul Wahab al Raquib was evidently caused by the dismissal of some officers of the Shafii sect and consequently it took the aspect of a sectarian quarrel in the Yemeni army. On August 27 and 28 the mutineers seized some government buildings and even kidnapped some cabinet ministers. Premier al-Amri suppressed the rebellion and formed a committee to reorganize the army.[127] On September 15 he formed a new cabinet—his sixth since the revolution of 1962— with seven Shafiis and nine Zaydis. The resignation of his last cabinet and the formation of a new one was intended to bring closer together the two sects. Tension, however, rose again when Lt. Col. al-Raquib was slain and it was said that troops loyal to al-Amri killed him. In late January 1969 goverment troops and tanks ringed Sana the capital as a result of a reported plot to assassinate President Abdul Rahman Iryani, but the plotters were arrested and it was said that they also intended to kill the commander of the armed forces, General Hamoud al-Jayfi.

In March 1969 the republican government felt sufficiently secure to begin its first experiment in a restricted parliamentary democracy. An assembly of forty-five members — fifteen appointed and thirty elected — met on March 17 to elect the three-man republican council. The assembly included representatives of the tribal chieftains, the intelligentsia, the military personnel, and the business leaders. On March 29, the reelected Abdul Rahman Iryani was sworn in as president of the presidential council and he asked General al-Amri to form his seventh cabinet.[128]

The republic of Yemen has thus survived after seven years of civil war, and the republican leaders have refused to put the republican form of government in question in any proposed negotiation with the royalists that would provide for a popular referendum. Although the civil war has not ended and the Imam and his supporters have not been reconciled, the royalist challenge to the republic has been weakened by the changing attitude of the tribal leaders and of Saudi Arabia itself that provided the material and moral support for the royalists. The decisive factor in the change of attitude was the withdrawal of Egyptian forces from Yemen in accordance with the Khartoum agreement of August 1967 because it reassured the royalist partisans that Yemen was no longer subject to foreign control, and it convinced their Saudi allies that Yemen would not be used as a center of Nasserist revolutionary subversion against Saudi Arabia. The republic has also survived partly because of the massive Soviet military support in heavy military equipment and technical aid that supplemented and followed the massive Eqyptian support which initially allowed the republic to stand on its feet. The royalist side could neither obtain nor use the heavy war material that was placed at the disposal of their adversaries, and they were also weakened by dissension and by the fluctuating loyalty of the tribal leaders who sometimes found more prospects of gain in joining the republican side.

The civil war could possibly regain its former activity and violence if the republican government were to submit to foreign influence, or if it resorts to measures that might alienate the unstable allegiance of the volatile tribal forces and that of their leaders. In the meantime, the coup d'état that established the republic in 1962 has been followed by the inevitable struggle for power among the republican leaders and by more conspiracies and coups d'état . The republican leadership, however, has demonstrated its determination to preserve the republic and has been forced, on the other hand, to challenge and overcome the attempts of the Soviet-backed leftists to seize power. It can be concluded with certainty that no matter what the future brings—the survival of the republic or the restoration of the monarchy- Yemen would not be returned to the same political, economic and social conditions and institutions that prevailed under the Imamic regime.

CHAPTER IV
NOTES

1. See for example, Ahmad Hussein Sharaf al-Din, *Al-Yemen Ibr al-Tarikh* (Yemen in History), (Cairo, 1964), 316 ff.

2. See Muhammad Ali al-Shahhari, *Tariq al-Thawrah al-Yemeniyah* (The Road of the Yemeni Revolution), (Cairo: Dar al-Hilal, November 1966), 41-43.

3. Harold Ingrams, *The Yemen: Imams, Rulers, Revolutions,* (London: John Murray, 1963), 6 ff.

4. The Imam signed treaties with Italy in 1926, the Soviet Union in 1928, the United States in 1946 and established the first Yemeni legation in Washington in 1947. He adhered to what is known as the Arab Baghdad Pact with Saudi Arabia and Iraq in 1936, joined the Arab League in November 1945 and the United Nations in 1947, and sent delegates to several Arab conferences on Palestine.

5. For a description of the Imamate and conditions in Yemen, consult al-Shahhari, 53 ff; Muhammad Said al-Attar, *al-Takhalluf al-Iqtisadi wal Ijtimai fil Yemen* (Economic and Social Underdevelopment in Yemen), (Beirut, 1965), 62-126; J. Heyworth-Dunne, *al-Yemen: A General Social, Political and Economic Survey* (Cairo, 1952), and "Témoignage sur le Yemen," *Orient,* no. 31 (1964, 3), 21-30; Robert Surieu, "Problèmes Yemenites," *Orient,* no. 7 (1958, 3), 43-53; William R. Brown, "The Yemeni Dilemma", *The Middle East Journal,* XVII, 4 (1963), 349-367.

6. See, Ahmad Muhammad al-Shami, *Imam al-Yemen Ahmad Hamiduddin* (Beirut, 1965), 11-21 quoting Ahmad Muhammad Numan who wrote the introduction to the book in 1953; also pp. 178 ff. quoting Qadi Zubayri's letter to Numan praising Imam Ahmad in 1950; for an estimate of the causes of the coup against Imam Yahya, see al-Attar, 37.

7. On the coup against Imam Yahya and the controversy about Prince Ibrahim, see Majid Khadduri, "Coup and Counter-Coup in the Yemen 1948", *International Affairs,* vol. 28 (January, 1952), 59 ff., 61 n. 1; see also Sharaf al-Din, 318 ff.; Ingrams, 75.

8. Khadduri, 61-62.

9. Sharaf al-Din, 219-220; Khadduri, 62-63 mentions almost a similar version of the story with a broadcast from Sana denying the news; Ingrams, p. 75 and Heyworth-Dunne, "Témoignage Sur le Yemen", 33 mentioned an unsuccessful attempt on the Imam's life in Sana on January 17, 1948 - one month before the assassination. It failed due to the vigilance of the Imam's faithful slave, Anbar, who surprised the would-be assassin before he could penetrate to the Imam's apartments.

10. Sharaf al-Din, 317.

11. Khadduri, 67-68; Heyworth-Dunne, "Témorgnage sur le Yemen", pp. 35-36; Ingrams, 75.

12. Ingrams, 75; this conflicts with the uncertain statement of Sharaf al-Din, 321, where he says that the first act of al-Wazir was his order to open the warehouses and treasury and arms depots in the palace of Sana and distribute money and arms to all those who came to support him, and thus the people flocked from all over the country to profit from the distribution.

13. For details about the Arab League commission and its activity in this affair, see Khadduri, 64-66; Heyworth-Dunne, "Témoignage," 36.

14. For figures on Yemeni students abroad in 1961 and the feeling of those returning to Yemen, see William Brown, 354-55; on Egyptian teachers and the efforts of Ahmad Farid Rifai before 1952 for cultural and economic development of Yemen, see Heyworth-Dunne, "Témoignage. . . ", 44 ff.

15. See the text in Sharaf al-Din, p. 326-330. The Arabic titles of the poems are *Tahaddi*, and *Nahnu wal Hakimun*.

16. See Heyworth-Dunne, "Témoignage. . . ", 57, 63 on his own experience and the plan he was asked to elaborate in 1954 with British help, and on the concessions for exploiting salt mines to a German firm in 1953, and for oil and mineral resources to an American firm in 1955.

17. See a description of his character in Ingrams, 24; Sharaf al-Din, 366 ff.

18. See Ahmad Muhammad Zein al-Saqqaf, *Ana "Aaed Min al-Yemen* (Returning from Yemen), 3rd ed. (Beirut, 1962?), 21-24. The first edition was published in 1955 right after the coup.

19. The writer is Ahmad Hussein Sharaf al-Din, 366 ff.; the events leading to the coup begin on March 25 in this book. See also the version of Ahmad al-Saqqaf, 30 who says that Imam Ahmad ordered the arrest of Thalaya after scolding him for his weak command, but the soldiers released him from prison and started the revolt.
20. See Ingrams, 90; Heyworth-Dunne, "Témoignage. . . ", 60. The dates are those of the *Middle East Journal*, IX, 3 (1955), 321.
21. al-Saqqaf, 33 ff.
22. *Ibid.*, 44. In another story it is related that Ahmad, in spite of being in his sixties, audaciously seized a gun from a careless guard and overwhelmed his captors. See Ingrams, 90.
23. al-Saqqaf, 45.
24. See the account of Heyworth-Dunne, "Témoignage. . . ", 59-60; the author also mentions that Baidani approached him in February 1954 and asked him to make a secret arrangement with his party - that of Abdallah and al-Abbas - for a loan for developing Yemen in exchange for a treaty that would guarantee British power in South Arabia; Baidani also asked that Britain furnish arms, munitions and money to kill Imam Ahmad.
25. For the constitution and organs of the federation, consult *Basic Documents of the Arab Unifications* (New York: Arab Information Center, 1958), 21-25; for the functioning of the federation, see Sharaf al-Din, 346 ff.
26. For the regime under al-Badr, see Ingrams, 109-110.
27. This version is given by Sharaf al-Din, 273; the pretext given by Alafi, according to Ingrams, 112, was that the Imam himself did not want the guards inside the hospital.
28. Ingrams, 113 mentioned five bullets; Sharaf al-Din 374 speaks of more than 20 bullets fired, out of which twelve hit the Imam.
29. For these details, Sharaf al-Din, 372-73.

30. The text of the poem is in Sharaf al-Din, 349-352. I have almost adopted, with slight modification, the translation of these verses as given in Ingrams, 115-116. Sharaf al-Din relates that the Imam wrote the first part of the first verse, "Advice given to all the Arabs," and told the poet to complete it with an appeal to the Arabs to unite and cooperate; when the poet finished this part of 23 verses, the Imam told him to make it 40 verses with a condemnation of the disputes among Arabs and the abuse by radio attacks. Then he asked him to make it 60 verses and to include in it the real political object of the Imam which was an attack on socialism and nationalization as practised in Egypt.

31. Heyworth-Dunne, "Témoignage. . . ", 71; Ingrams, 119 simply says that Sallal was discovered in 1959 by Nasser's Egyptians.

32. Sallal was born in 1917; another date of his birth is 1922. For Sallal's career before the coup, see Sharaf al-Din, 372-73; Ingrams, 119ff., 130 ff.

33. Reported by *al-Hayat,* September 25, 1962.

34. William R. Brown, 358, n. 13.

35. Sharaf al-Din, 379-380.

36. These reports have appeared in an article in *al-Hayat,* October 21, 1962, signed by "An Old Arab Politician."

37. Ingrams, 128-129 believes the accusation was false; al-Attar, 289 relates it as a fact and says that as a result, the revolutionary council in Sana prevailed on the entire revolutionary committee to overthrow al-Badr.

38. The seven other officers who cooperated with Sallal and were mentioned at the time of the coup were: Colonel Hammud al-Jayfi, Major Abdallah Juzailan, Captains Abdul-Latif Daifallah, Muhammad Qaid Saif, Muhammad al-Makhidi, and Lieutenants Ali Abdul-Mughni, and Muhammad Mufrih. See Sharaf al-Din, 381; Attar, 299 says out of 400 officers in the entire army, only 40 belonged to the revolutionary committee.

39. "Hashimis" refers to the descendants of the Prophet and relates to Hashim, the Prophet's clan in Mecca, while the "Qahtanis" are Southern Arabs and original inhabitants of Yemen but ruled at this time by the privileged Hashimis.

40. Extracts of the first and other communiqués in *al-Nasr* (Damascus), September 28, 1962.

41. This report was related by Ingrams, 130.
42. This report was given to the Middle East News Agency in Cairo and was quoted by *al-Hayat* (Beirut) October 23, 1962.
43. On these stories, see Ingrams, 131.
44. Sharaf al-Din, 382.
45. Related by Dabbi to the M. E. News Agency and quoted by *al-Hayat*, October 23, 1962.
46. This story was related by Ingrams, 129-130.
47. Cairo mentioned sixty members of the family killed by September 27, 1962. See the *Middle East Journal*, XVIII, 1-2 (1963), 141; Ingrams, 132 mentions that the republican regime offered L.1500 reward for every member of the royal family killed or captured; see Sharaf al-Din, 242 for an explanation on the long duration of the Imamic state.
48. Translated from the Arabic text in Sharaf al-Din, 383-385.
49. Text of provisional constitution in Sharaf al-Din, 385-387.
50. For these changes and their interpretation, see *al-Nasr*, November 1, 1962; Ingrams, 133.
51. For some of these reforms and particularly the wrath against the Sayyids, see Brown, 352.
52. *The New York Times*, September 29, 1962; *al-Bayan* (New York), November 13, 1962; *al-Hayat*, December 6, 1962.
53. *al-Hayat*, June 16, 1963.
54. For an explanation of these factors and conditions, see al-Shahhari, 94, 101.
55. See *al-Nasr*, October 10, 1962; Heyworth-Dunne, "Témoignage. . . ", 70-71.
56. Jay Walz in *The New York Times*, October 10, 1962.
57. *al-Hayat*, October 21, 1962.
58. *Le Figaro*, November 16, 1962; Ingrams, 135.
59. As reported by Dana Adams Schmidt, in *The New York Times*, December 10, 1962.
60. Reported in *al-Nasr*, October 30, and November 20, 1962; December 4, 1962 mentioned a demonstration against the war in Yemen in the town of Beni Sueif in which fourteen persons were killed.

61. Details on this explanation in Sharaf al-Din, 388-392; al-Shahhari, 82.
62. *al-Mithaq* (the Charter), (Cairo: Department of Information, 1962), 111. The Charter was presented by President Nasser to the National Congress of Popular Forces on May 21, 1962.
63. *Mideast Mirror*, April 25, 1964.
64. *al-Hayat*, February 28, 1965 quoting the statement of Amer published in *al-Ahram*.
65. For these other motives of Egyptian intervention, see Jubran Shamiye, Ya Uqalà al-Arab Ittahidu (O Thoughtful Arabs Unite!), Vol. 3 (Beirut, 1965?), 376-383; also R. B. Serjeant in *M. E. J.*, XX, 3 (1966), 401.
66. *al-Hayat*, February 28, 1965, quoting Amer's speech in the Egyptian National Assembly.
67. *al-Nahar* (Beirut), May 24, 1966. The ambassador of Yemen in Lebanon presented his credentials also to Syria.
68. See Ingrams, 138-143 on the question of recognition and his criticism of the United States action.
69. *al-Nasr*, November 16, 1962.
70. *The New York Times*, November 28 and December 8, 1962.
71. *The New York Times*, editorial, December 24, 1962; see also December 20, 1962.
72. Ingrams, 142-143.
73. See the confessions of al-Badr to Colonel McLean, British M.P., about the plan of close alliance between Egypt and Yemen in 1958, when al-Badr was in Damascus with Nasser and Tito, in order to use Yemen as a base for disrupting Saudi Arabia and undermining the British position in the Persian Gulf, and weakening the link between Arabia and the West so that Nasser might profit; see Ingrams, 142.
74. For this explanation of the American support of the Yemen coup, see Jubran Shamiye, 386-390.
75. *The New York Times*, January 28, 1963.
76. *M. E. J.*, XVIII, 1 (1964), 108.
77. *The New York Times*, April 19, 1963.
78. For these developments, see *M. E. J.*, XVIII, 2 (1964), 238; *al-Hayat*, February 11, 1964.

79. *The New York Times*, July 14, 1964.
80. *Mideast Mirror,* March 6, 1965, p. 15.
81. Details on this constitution in *al-Hayat,* May 11, 1965; *Mideast Mirror,* May 15, 1965.
82. Hedrick Smith in *The New York Times,* June 29, 1965.
83. For these developments, *Mideast Mirror,* July 10 and 24, 1965.
84. *The New York Times,* August 14, 1966. According to Hedrick Smith in the *N.Y. Times,* September 21, 1966, al-Amri broke with Cairo because he was prevented from importing armored cars directly from East Germany and had to receive them from the Egyptians; he was also irritated over the control of currency notes and the payment of the Yemeni army and tribes by Egyptian advisers; al-Amri also felt he was snubbed by Cairo during the visit of Kosygin in May, 1966.
85. See *The New York Times,* September 21 and October 2, 1966.
86. Faisal had been dismissed from the premiership by his brother Saud in December 1961; King Saud appointed him in March 1962 deputy prime minister and minister of foreign affairs. See *al-Nasr* and *The New York Times* November 8, 1962 for the internal reforms.
87. *The New York Times,* January 9, 1963.
88. Nasser's speech on May 21, 1963 at Republic Square, Cairo; see *The New York Times,* May 24, 1963, and *Time,* March 15 and May 10, 1963.
89. This was the three year contract made under President Kennedy in 1962 and that expired on June 30, 1965.
90. See the letter of Bushrod Howard, Jr., advisor to the royalist government of Yemen, in *The New York Times,* November 21, 1964.
91. Saudi ambassador Jamil Baroody presented the letter, and Secretary-General U-Thant took no action and said that the U.A.R. denied the allegations, and that he had no means of ascertaining the truth; see *The Egyptian Gazette* March 1, 1967.
92. These details were mentioned in an article in the *U.S. News and World Report,* July 10, 1967, including the report of the International Red Cross which investigated and confirmed the use of gas against the village of Gahar on May 10, 1967 where seventy-five people were killed.
93. *The New York Times,* July 28, 1967.

94. See for example the indignation expressed by the Arab writer Umar Haliq in his article in *al-Hayat,* August 21, 1965 entitled "Failure of the Socialist Revolutionary Movement in Yemen, A Lesson to All the Arabs."
95. See Tewfik Moussa, *al-Ishtirakiya al-Misriya wal Qadiya al-Falastiniya* (Egyptian Socialism and the Palestinian Question), n.p. n.d. (1966?), 90.
96. Speech of Nasser in Port Said, December 1962.
97. Quoted in the *Santa Barbara News Press* December 3, 1962.
98. *Mideast Mirror,* March 6, 1965.
99. Drew Middleton in *The New York Times,* May 3, 1965.
100. *al-Ahram,* August 15, 1965.
101. *al-Ahram,* May 6, 1966.
102. See Tewfik Moussa, 90, who believes that the Egyptian presence in Yemen was since then based on the demands of the Soviet Union, was financed by it and implemented its plans; see also *The New York Times,* April 30, 1966.
103. *al-Ahram,* May 27, 1966.
104. *Mideast Mirror,* April 16, 1966.
105. *Time,* April 22, 1966.
106. The Beirut newspapers *al-Sharq, al-Muharrir, al-Anwar* and some weeklies copied Egyptian reports on Saudi Arabia so much that the Saudi permanent under secretary for foreign affairs, Umar al-Saqqaf, gave a declaration on February 18 that was considered by *al-Ahram* a warning to Lebanon on publishing disturbing incidents. Ambassador Baidani made a speech at the Arab University in Beirut, accompanied by applause, against King Faisal and the kingdom of Jordan; see *al-Ahram,* February 19, and March 8, 1967. Lebanese leaders denounced these actions because they hurt the interests of Lebanon.
107. *The New York Times,* June 21, 1966.
108. *al-Anwar* (Beirut), March 25, 1967.
109. The three Lebanese personalities were former President Camille Chamoun, leader of the National Liberal Party, Pierre Gemayel, leader of the Kataeb (Phalanges), and Raymond Edde, leader of the National·Bloc.

110. *al-Hayat,* April 1, 1967; Baroody said that the U.A.R. caused the protest messages to be sent in order to divert attention from its use of poison gas against the Yemeni royalist villages.
111. *The New York Times,* June 16, 1966; *The Daily Telegraph,* May 17, 1967.
112. *The New York Times,* August 24 and September 1, 1967.
113. *al-Anwar,* October 6, 1967; *Time,* October 20, 1967.
114. *Time,* November 17, 1967.
115. See Eric Pace in *The New York Times,* November 6-8, 1967 for an account of the coup; *Time,* November 17, 1967.
116. Reported by the correspondent of *al-Anwar* after an interview with Iryani; see *al-Anwar,* November 18, 1967.
117. Events reported by *The New York Times,* November 18, 28, December 8, 1967.
118. See account by Thomas Brady, N.Y. Times correspondent, who was expelled from Yemen along with Reuter's correspondent; *The New York Times,* November 23, 1967.
119. *The New York Times,* December 6, 13, 1967. A report from Washington said that the United States received reliable reports on Soviet pilots flying combat missions for the republicans.
120. See report of Hedrick Smith in *The New York Times,* December 15, 1967; *Ibid.,* February 29, 1968.
121. *al-Anwar,* April 24, 1968.
122. *Ibid.,* on the denial by al-Ayni at the UN that there was any tension between republican Yemen and the Russians for inciting extremists to disturb national unity; see the account of Dana Adams Schmidt on the abortive extremist coup in *The New York Times,* April 16, 1968.
123. The anti-Badr coup was mentioned in a dispatch from Beirut in *The New York Times,* June 3, 1968.
124. See the account of Dana Adams Schmidt in *The New York Times,* December 13, 1967 on the NLF domination of the eastern sultanates.
125. Dana Adams Schmidt in *The New York Times,* April 16, 1968.
126. *N.Y. Times* report, January 11, 1969.
127. *al-Anwar,* August 31, 1968.
128. *Ibid.,* March 16, 1969; *L.A. Times,* March 31, 1969.

CHAPTER V

THE JUNIOR OFFICERS' COUP D'ETAT AND THE NEW REPUBLIC IN LIBYA

The military coup d'état of September 1, 1969 replaced the Sanusi monarchy that had been established eighteen years earlier by a socialist republic. It added an eighth radical Arab republic dominated by the military to the already existing seven — Egypt, Syria, Iraq, Yemen, Southern Yemen, Sudan, and Algeria. The action of the Libyan junior officers in a country that had been experiencing rapid economic and social progress after the discovery of oil illustrates once more the preeminence of radical ideological considerations involving the orientation of foreign policy in the staging of Arab military coups. The Libyan military intervention came only a few months after the radical coup of May 25, 1969 in the Sudan. The two interventions occurred in two Arab countries that were among the least involved in the Arab-Israeli conflict.

I. State and Society Under the Sanusi Monarchy and the Oil Producing Revolution

Libya became an independent kingdom in December 1951. It had been a part of the Ottoman Empire until 1911 when it was occupied by Italy. The resistance against Italian domination was led mainly by the Sanusi Brotherhood that was concentrated in Cyrenaica in the eastern part of Libya where it exercised political and religious influence since the middle of the nineteenth century. The Sanusis were a mystical order that sought to restore the purity of the Muslim faith. Their leader in the anti-Italian struggle since the end of World War I was Sayyid Muhammad Idris, born in 1890 and grandson of Sayyid Muhammad Ali al-Sanusi who established the revivalist movement and began to spread it in Cyrenaica in the 1840's. The Sanusi resistance was broken by the Italian Fascist regime and Muhammad Idris went to live in Egypt in 1922, but during World War II he cooperated with the British, and his tribal forces in Cyrenaica joined in the war against the Italians and the Germans. British military rule replaced that of Italy in the regions of Cyrenaica and Tripolitania after the expulsion of the Italians and Germans in 1943, while the Free French ruled the arid region of Fezzan in the southwest. In November 1949 the United Nations General Assembly decided that Libya should be granted independence not later than January 1952. A constitution was drafted with the help of a UN commission and approved in December 1951, and the independent United Kingdom of Libya thus came into being with the Sanusi leader Muhammad Idris I as its constitutional monarch.

The new kingdom was a federation of three provinces: Tripolitania in the west, Cyrenaica in the east where the king had his main support, and Fezzan in the southwest. The federation had two capitals of equal status, Tripoli in the far west and Benghazi in Cyrenaica, in order to satisfy the two main provinces. The Tripolitanians would have preferred a unitary state in which they felt they could play the leading role. They were relatively more sophisticated than the people in Cyrenaica, and their province was more urbanized and had a larger population. The orientation in Tripolitania was more towards Egypt while Cyrenaica was more pro-British and more loyal to King Idris whom the Sanusis regarded as their religious and political leader. Pessimists at the time feared that the federal union might not last on account of these differences. In the elections of the federal parliament in February 1952, the opposition National Congress party centered in Tripolitania proclaimed pro-Egyptian and pan-Arab slogans in addition to its well known advocacy of a unitary state. It attracted the support of Communist, labor nd xenophobic elements but it won only a few seats in Parliament while the overwhelming majority of successful candidates supported the government. The elections were followed by violent rioting that led to the dissolution of the National Congress party and the exile of its leader, Bashir al-Saadawi, who went to live in Egypt.[1] The federal union lasted until 1963 and was replaced, after the necessary constitutional amendment, by a unitary state that was divided into ten centrally governed administrative districts. In the meantime Libyan national consciousness had been growing with a sense of national unity as a result of living together under a sovereign independent state.

Besides the suspicions and the differences between the Libyan provinces that raised doubts about their continued union during the first years, Libya suffered from two major handicaps: the lack of economic assets, and the absence of educated and trained personnel for the administration. Libya was a poor, largely arid and very thinly populated country. With an area of 680,000 square miles — the fourth largest in Africa and eleven times the area of Tunisia — its population was a little over one and a half million in 1964 or one-third that of Tunisia with 85 per cent of the inhabitants concentrated in seven per cent of the area. The overwhelming majority of the people lived in towns and settled communities and the percentage of nomads was less than ten per cent. The amount of arable land per person was higher than in certain other Arab countries because of the low density of population and in spite of the desert areas. Libya nevertheless had one of the lowest living standards in the world. Its per capita annual income in the early 1950's was less than forty dollars. It rose to 1018 dollars in 1967, seven years after the commercial production of oil began, and the total value of exports rose from eleven million in 1960 to 1168 million dollars in 1967.[2]

Libya's important asset before the discovery of oil in 1959 was its strategic position facing Europe for a distance of one thousand miles along the southern coast of the **Mediteranean**. It depended on foreign aid for balancing its budget and on technical assistance for its development projects. Its population was largely illiterate — between 90 and 80 per cent in the early 1950's — because Italian colonial rule neglected education and was reluctant to employ Libyans except in the lowest government positions. United Nations agencies as well as American and British commissions and experts were active providing technical assistance or administering their own aid. The economy and the finances were bolstered by the activities of foreign employers, the spending by foreign communities mostly Italian, American and British, and especially by the rental of military bases leased to Britain and the United States and the spending by the American and British forces. According to the twenty-year treaty with Britain in 1953 Libya accepted annual grants and services from the British and allowed them to have access to bases for the air force and ground forces mainly near Tobruk in the east and Tripoli in the west. In 1954 the United States entered into a seventeen-year agreement with Libya for the use of Wheelus air field near Tripoli as a training base for NATO and refueling station and the payment of an annual rental in addition to providing certain services to Libya.[3] The base had been abandoned in 1945 but was reactivated in 1948 and became the largest air base outside the United States.

Libya was thus able to survive largely through foreign grants and assistance before oil was discovered, and its foreign policy during these first years depended largely on its need for subsidies. Credit should be also given to the wisdom of King Idris and to the experience which he had gained as leader of the Sanusi campaign and ally of the British in the second world war. He now encouraged agricultural development and improvement in education and health with the help of foreign agencies and a local development council. In 1957 the cabinet was expanded to include a new portfolio for agriculture and another for labor and social affairs. Between 1960 and 1963 after the discovery of oil, the new ministries of industry, petroleum affairs, information and development were created. In 1958 the University of Libya opened with colleges in Benghazi and Tripoli. Many Egyptians were employed in the teachers' training college and other schools, and the educational program, as in the case of the civil and commercial legal codes, was based on the Egyptian system. The rights of minorities were guaranteed in the constitution. The Italians lived mainly in Tripolitania and engaged in agriculture and business. Their number was between thirty and forty thousand. Those of them who had to leave Cyrenaica during the war did not return.

The king dealt firmly with the members of the royal family when they attempted to create trouble. Most of them did not belong to the ruling branch. In 1954 the queen's nephew, who was a member of that rival branch, assassinated the king's counselor and controller of his royal household, Ibrahim al-Shalhi, because he supposedly restricted the activities of the Sanusi leaders. King Idris reacted strongly by sending seven princes to exile in a desert oasis and divested all other princes who were not in the direct line of succession of their titles and of the right to hold public office.

The government of King Idris, as a result of its policy of stimulating investment and petroleum development, witnessed what can be described as an economic revolution in the last ten years (since 1960) after the discovery of oil. Between 1955 and 1959 some eighty-four concessions were granted to sixteen companies on a competitive basis that obliged the companies to begin exploration and production as quickly as possible or else they would risk losing their concession. The law of 1955 indeed gave the concession on condition that one-fourth of the concession plot would be given up by the company after five years and another one-fourth after another three years. The result was a faster rate of expansion in oil production than that of Kuwait and Saudi Arabia. Oil was discovered in June 1959 and by July 1960, thirty-five oil wells were in production. In 1966 there were more than one thousand oil producing wells and the exports rose from eight million tons in 1962 to seventy-two million in 1966.⁴ Government oil revenues increased from forty million dollars in 1962 to about 800 million in 1968, and a record number of thirty-eight foreign companies - including twenty-four American - were involved in 136 concessions.⁵ Among the causes for the fast rate of expansion of the oil business, besides government oil policies, were the low cost of production and of transportation and the high quality of the crude oil produced. Libyan oil was 4,000 miles nearer to European consumption centers than the oil of the Persian Gulf and allowed the saving of Suez Canal dues and of twenty-one days in round trip shipping - or thirty-eight days in shipping around Africa after the closing of the Suez Canal following the June 1967 war.⁶

One of the results of the oil-producing revolution was that Libya was no longer dependent on foreign aid that subsidized 58 per cent of its federal budget in 1959-60, nor was its foreign policy based any longer on the sole asset of its strategic position. Libya began to extend aid to other countries instead of receiving aid. After the June war of 1967 it agreed to contribute L30 million out of the L135 million which the rich oil producing countries — including Kuwait and Saudi Arabia - gave to support Egypt and Jordan. Its balance of trade deficit was eliminated and it began to have a capital surplus instead of a capital deficit. Its per capita gross national product increased more than 25 times between the early 1950's and 1967, and in one year (1967) it increased by 42 per cent over the preceding year. Unemployment was reduced as laborers found work in the oil industry, but the new industry could absorb only a small fraction of the labor force and it could not find adequate skilled labor. The standard of living certainly advanced but so did inflation and the cost of living. The five-year plan of 1963-68 financed by a substantial percentage of the oil income began to build the infrastructure for the modernization and economic growth of Libya. Various allocations were given in the plan for agriculture, public works, communications, education, industry, low income housing and other aspects of social welfare. Between 1964 and

1966 the rate of increase in the value of production was eight per cent in agriculture, 22 in manufacturing, 37 in transport, and 138 in construction.[7] The Idris Housing Project envisaged the construction of 100,000 dwellings in the five-year period. By the spring of 1968 some 3,000 miles of roads were constructed, port facilities were built or improved at Derna, Tobruk, Benghazi and Tripoli, electric power increased three times above the 1962 level, pure water was extended to twenty urban centers, 2,000 classrooms were added annually, and fifteen hospitals were built. The enrollment in schools increased from 45,000 in 1951 to 300,000 in 1968 and came to include 85 per cent of the children of school age while illiteracy declined from 81 per cent in 1954 to 65 per cent ten years later. In the petro-chemical industry the construction of the world's largest natural gas liquefaction facilities was completed at the Esso Standard Libya plant at Marsa al-Brega.[8]

The question arose after the oil boom whether the Libyan government would remain pro-Western and follow policies condoned by the West or it would feel free to pursue a more purely national Arab policy. On the one hand it was thought that the economic and financial independence brought about by the oil income would not necessarily change or liberate Libyan foreign policy because Libya remained suspicious of the Soviet Union and the Communists and, as a wealthy but weak country, it had to be more careful in its relations with its powerful Arab neighbors who might be tempted by her wealth. Moreover, it was supposed that it was essential for Libya to be on good terms with the West in order to develop her new resources because only the West could aid in that development. Oil, therefore, according to this reasoning did not free Libya from Western ties but bound her more closely.[9] On the other hand, it was argued that the government would be forced by the younger educated elements and by the masses to loosen its ties with the West. The younger generation after ten years of independence and with better education had become restless and wanted their country to assume its rightful place in the Arab community. Those of them who were sent abroad by their government to become engineers and technicians returned with new ideas and refused to remain silent in society. They viewed oil as a liberator that should allow their government to follow a more Arab and less pro-Western policy. The people's minds were also stirred by the talk in the radio and the press in Egypt and elsewhere on Arab nationalism and unity and by the vision of Libya's role in the Arab world, while Nasser's Egypt encouraged political and social unrest. Foreign policy, therefore, was expected to change not because the discovery of oil allowed it to change but because the response of the educated younger generation to the discovery of oil and the popular unrest that followed that discovery were forcing the change. The government of King Idris recognized what was happening and while it tried to retain its friendship with the West it also had to make concessions to popular feelings.

Oil, furthermore, was not an unmitigated blessing for Libya for it contributed to the creation of tensions and social unrest. Farmers and agricultural laborers drifted to the cities for work and high wages in the oil companies, and the large farms were often unable to find seasonal labor. The government itself could not secure engineers and technicians for its development projects because of the competition of the oil business. The oil workers from the desert oases and rural communities as well as those of the little towns were affected by the social unheaval that followed the oil boom. When they were no longer needed in their jobs in the various districts they often did not return to their homes and village plots but congregated in the cities and their tin can slums waiting to be hired and adding to the social unrest. The oil boom, moreover, did not and could not benefit all people in the same way. The benefits of health and education were shared by the poorer classes, and ordinary Libyans generally were doing better than before, but the gap was also widening between them and the growing wealthy elite of contractors, professional men and certain corrupt government officials and officers. Libyans also began to react against the commercial freedom that allowed foreign businessmen to make fortunes. The oil discovery eventually changed the Libyan attitude towards foreign business investment. Already in 1959 a law required that commercial agencies should be given only to Libyans or to firms that were fifty per cent owned by Libyans. In 1960 foreigners were forbidden to buy land and property except with specific government consent. Stricter emigration laws were made to insure employment for qualified Libyans, and work permits were required from foreigners. Citizenship was given to non-Arabs after ten years' residence and to Arabs after five years. The Italians were encouraged to leave and new commercial enterprises were thus discouraged.[10] In July 1969 a government order directed all non-Libyan agents to liquidate their business by the end of August. The purpose of these measures was naturally to let the Libyans derive benefits from the oil boom.

King Idris and his government were able to guide Libya through the years of prosperity and rapidly increasing income as they had guided it through the preceding years of dependence on foreign aid. Although the country was a constitutional monarchy with an elected lower house of parliament to which the cabinet was responsible, the king was the strongest source of power and the cabinet was effectively responsible to him. The executive power was vested in the king and he also exercised legislative power in conjunction with the two houses of parliament. He applied his power wisely and played with skill his role of mediator between the politicians. The prime ministers were appointed and removed by the king, and some of them ruled for relatively long periods of three or more years during which they reshuffled their cabinets several times. They sometimes clashed with the king or with such important members of his court as Busiri al-Shalhi who was an important force in guiding the king's policy before his death in 1954.[11] There were times, however, when the cabinet had to resign because it failed to win a vote of confidence of the lower house as in the case of the Abdul-Majid Ku'bar cabinet that fell in October 1960 over the Fezzan road construction scandal that involved a few ministers but the house insisted on the collective responsibility of the cabinet in accordance with the constitution.

As in the other Arab countries under constitutional rule, Libya suffered from ministerial instability. In thirteen years after independence it had over twenty cabinet changes under seven prime ministers involving some sixty-five ministers.[12] The changes naturally did not allow the ministers sufficient time to develop insight into the problems of their respective departments, but the continuity of policy was guaranteed by the king's presence, and the civil service kept the administration functioning. Cabinet changes were caused, neither by the rivalries of parties and lack of party support — because parties in Libya were banned after the experience with the National Congress party in 1952 — nor necessarily by the incompetence of the ministers. They were caused by maneuvering for power among the active elite that consisted of representatives of old influential families, tribal chiefs, wealthy businessmen, and professional people. Libya had no recognized political leaders who derived their influence from their party position or from some kind of popular or mass leadership. There were signs of wider political participation of the citizens such as the extension of the franchise to women in 1963 and the election of some younger educated individuals and of the general secretary of the national federation of trade unions to the lower house in October 1964. The channels for the expression of popular interests, however, were few and the ties between the public and the politicians needed to be increased. On the other hand the tribal influence was decreasing with the disintegration of the tribal system, and the Sanusi order that was an active political force in the period of colonial rule practically lost its influence. The king was generally respected and his sincerity was not doubted. He was old and frail in his seventies in the decade that preceded the coup. His five marriages had given him no offspring. His brother, Muhammad al-Rida, died in 1956 and his nephew, Hasan al-Rida (born in

1928), consequently became the crown prince but nobody expected much from him and the fate of the monarchy was uncertain after the king's death.

II. Tensions and Pressures and the Army Officers

The pressures that were brought upon the government of King Idris and the resulting tensions in the 1960's were mainly related to the problem of the Libyan position on issues affecting the Arab world as well as Libyan relations with the Western powers. Pressures and tensions were encouraged by external, mostly Egyptian, stimuli. King Idris whose will usually prevailed in foreign affairs exercised great caution in his relations with the Arab countries and avoided involvement in their problems. Libya naturally expressed its solidarity with such Arab national causes as those of Algeria and Palestine. In 1956 it requested Britain not to use its Libyan bases for the Suez campaign. At the same time a plot against King Idris was discovered and the Egyptian military attaché was expelled for distributing arms. Nasser was popular in Tripolitania but the king and the Sanusis in Cyrenaica were afraid of Egyptian penetration. Libya nevertheless allowed more than 500 Egyptian teachers to remain because they were needed in spite of the fear that their continued presence would be a form and a potential instrument of Egyptian influence.[13] During the Iraqi revolt and the crisis in Lebanon and Jordan in the summer of 1958 little tension was felt, but the government was already in the difficult position of having to ensure enough funds to meet the budget deficit by depending on Western aid and accepting the Western military presence, and of trying at the same time to convince the people of Libya that it was following an independent foreign policy.[14]

The government of King Idris came increasingly under pressure in the early 1960's to assert its independence from Western influence and to follow a more active Arab policy because it was no longer dependent upon foreign aid to balance its budget after the discovery of oil. The Libyan and non-Libyan critics of the government resented particularly the presence of the British bases at Tobruk and al-Adem, east of Benghazi, and of the American Wheelus air base outside Tripoli, and asked to have them closed. The government was reluctant to end its alliance and close friendly relations with the Western powers at a time when it felt it had to guard against the inroads of neighboring revolutionary regimes and when it depended on the West for the development of its oil resources and for several other services including the training of its defense forces. King Idris and his ministers, however, had to respond to the public and its demands and to make concessions whenever they realized that popular feeling was particularly strong on certain issues. The rulers of Libya, nevertheless, made their concessions and reached their decisions with great caution. They moved slowly and, as it has been said, they acted long after they spoke.[15] They were careful not to yield easily to popular pressure and not to allow the events to move quickly for fear that they might lose control.

On January 22, 1964 the Libyan prime minister, Dr. Muhieddin Fekini, resigned following sporadic student demonstrations at Benghazi and Tripoli since January 16 in protest against the "conservatism of the regime" of King Idris and in solidarity with pan-Arabism preached by President Abdul Nasser. One month later, on February 22, President Nasser made a speech in which he allowed himself — as he often did - to interfere in the internal affairs of other Arab states. He called this time on Libya to liquidate American and British military bases on her soil because they were "a threat" to Egypt. On the following day the Libyan government of Premier Mahmud Muntasir issued a statement which said that it did not intend to renew the treaties under which the foreign military bases were maintained and that it supported other Arab governments in the resistance to imperialism. One day later, the Libyan ambassador in Cairo delivered to Nasser a memorandum and the text of a cabinet decision to terminate the agreements for the British and American bases when they run out. On March 16, 1964 while several hundred students marched through downtown Tripoli demonstrating their support for the removal of the bases, the lower house of parliament went a step farther than the cabinet in its response to Nasser's and the students' demands and authorized the government, in a unanimous vote, to open negotiations that would lead to the liquidation of the bases and the evacuation of British and American troops.[16] Talks between Libya and the representatives of Britain and the United States began in the third part of April on the future of the bases, and the Libyan press often spoke of their impending removal, but the negotiations were not urgent and the bases were not removed until after the fall of the monarchy.

In the meantime Libya participated as a member of the Arab League in the summit conferences on Palestine in 1964 and 1965, and it enforced the ban on exporting oil to Britain following the six day war until the ban was lifted in September 1967. In the Khartoum summit conference at the end of August 1967 it agreed to contribute thirty million pounds for the support of Egypt and Jordan but Libya remained, in the eyes of the revolutionary regimes and of its own awakened younger generation, outside the mainstream of the Arab struggle. Many Libyans resented their own vulnerability to charges of complicity in the Western support of Israel as a result of the Western military presence.[17] The government call for the evacuation of foreign bases continued to be an item in the policy statements of the various Libyan cabinets and it appeared in the statement of Premier Wanis al-Qadhafi (on September 4, 1968), who was destined to head the last cabinet under the monarchy. Another important item was the call for a fair solution of the Palestine problem.

Dissatisfaction with the foreign policy of the Libyan regime or with its general "conservatism" was largely unorganized. Political parties were banned but sympathizers with revolutionary parties and regimes did exist and their activities were secret. The leaders of the small Communist party that existed before independence were expelled from the country at the end of 1951. Supporters of the Baath socialist party were not allowed to spread their propaganda. On February 4, 1962 eighty-seven of them were sentenced to jail by a court in Tripoli on charges of carrying on subversive activity to overthrow the economic and political system. Baath cells that were known to the government were dissolved and their papers and funds were confiscated. Those of the Baath supporters and members who were not Libyans were deported.[18] The pro-Nasser elements were not organized into an action movement but sympathy for Nasser's goals and pan-Arab ideas was widespread. The press sometimes praised Nasser but the government was always cautious in its relations with him. The students were an important political force and wanted their country to be more involved in Arab and world affairs. They were impatient with the cabinet ministers and believed, as many young people did in other Arab countries, that they (the ministers) were concerned mainly about their position and political maneuvering and gave little attention to the country's welfare. The labor unions were a potential instrument of pressure on government policy. In July 1953 they organized themselves into a national federation of trade unions. The general secretary of the federation, Selim Shita, who at one time in December 1961 was sentenced to several months in jail for incitement to strike, was elected to the lower house in October 1964. Students and labor unions generally respected the king and supported him, but their support of the crown prince and even the monarchy were not certain after the king's death. The government discouraged the dissident elements and brought them to trial on the ground that they were dangerous to the country as in January 1968 when 106 persons were accused in Tripoli of subversive activities and acts of terrorism against the state.

Before the coup of September 1969 against the monarchy the army officers were not openly active in Libyan politics. They were generally believed to be inexperienced and unprepared for political adventure and their commanders seemed to be loyal to the king. But the number of officers trained outside the country was growing and their future behavior and attitude were uncertain. There were also cases of politically active young men who joined the army with the sole purpose of making a coup, as it was later revealed. There were occasional reports of tension in the army, however, as in June 1962 when seven officers were dismissed by royal decree in Tripoli after earlier changes in the post of chief of staff had been made. The regular armed forces were formed slowly after independence. In the late 1950's they counted no more than 3,000 men and by 1965 they had increased to 6,500. The treaty of 1953 with Britain provided for the training of the army by the British, and in 1957 an American military aid program was started for training units of the army and the air force. An Iraqi officer commanded the army until 1958 when a Libyan superior officer became available. Before the creation of the regular army Libya had a militia for police and security duties that had been formed and trained by the British in Cyrenaica and Tripolitania. The Cyrenaica defense force was created before that of Tripoli and consisted of those who had fought as allies of the British in the Second World War against the Germans and Italians. The British transformed them at the end of the war into a gendarmerie and police force and later expanded their number to more than 6,000 and gave them modern equipment and training. The Cyrenaica defense force included tribal levies and was particularly loyal to the king. It was the strongest force in Libya and received special favors from King Idris. It continued to exist side by side with the regular army and so did the Tripolitania police force. The king kept these militia forces of Cyrenaica and Tripoli separated from the regular army and wanted the powerful Cyrenaica defense force to remain unexposed to political influences and to act when needed as a defender of the monarchy and as a counterbalance to the regular army.[19]

Government allocations for the defense budget increased tremendously in the middle 1960's and particularly after the six day war in order to satisfy the people's national pride in their army and possibly to show more enthusiasm for the Arab cause. In April 1968 the cabinet ordered from the British Aircraft Corporation a missile and radar system for air defense for about L130 million and other equipment and war material such as tanks from the British government. Premier Wanis Qadhafi was proud to declare more than a year later, in August 1969, that the government "provided an ample budget to make our army rank with the best in the world in training and equipment." It was explained at the time of the air defense sale that Libya, short of manpower for a conventional army, needed a defense system that could be run by relatively few specialists, but many Libyans attacked the sale and believed that the expensive air defense system was intended to defend the country against Egypt or Algeria and at the same time to defend American and British oil interests.[20] One of the last decisions taken by the royal government was the urgent demand addressed to the oil companies in Libya to increase the posted prices of oil. Negotiations on this question were to begin in September, 1969 but the officers' coup occurred and the affair was taken up later by the revolutionary government.

The tensions in Libya and the pressures on the Libyan rulers were thus related primarily to the questions of the foreign bases and the participation of Libya in more direct action in favor of the struggle for Palestine. Libya otherwise was in the summer of 1969 a respected Arab state and its king was a revered and sincere Arab national figure whose presence guaranteed internal stability and whose wise foreign policy secured independence and external support as well as prosperity for his country. The agreements with the United States and Britain on the foreign bases were due to end in 1971 and 1973, respectively. Libya was contributing a part of its large oil income to the support of Egypt and Jordan, the two direct neighbors and enemies of Israel, and it was building up its own army and military strength. The successive governments of Libya were trying to improve the people's standard of living and to increase the benefits from the oil resources by pressing the foreign companies to increase the posted prices of oil. The country was progressing as a result of the special plans and efforts devoted to the various aspects of its development. In 1968 a young lawyer called Abdul Hamid Bakkush was appointed prime minister and initiated a program of social reform which the radicals found inadequate.

The opponents of the monarchy, and the radicals and their military disciples who were coveting power could still criticize and exploit for their special purposes the unequal participation of the various categories of people in the benefits of the oil boom, and the profiteering activities of such powerful tribal families as the Shalhi family (in the Beida district east of Benghazi) and their influence with the king.[21] They could still claim that the development or reform program was not moving far enough or fast enough. But their easiest target was above all the king's friendly relations with the Americans and the British, and the presence of the foreign bases that brought Libya into disrepute with some of its neighbors. In the gospel of the Arab radicals, friendship with certain Western powers whatever might be its motives or the national interests that it could serve were taboo and incompatible with the radicals' special brand of Arab nationalism. The reason for this attitude was not only the Arab conflict with Israel but also the commitment of the Arab radicals to the socialist revolution, their hostility to the capitalist and imperialist West and their close relations with the Soviets. King Idris and his government — and other Arab rulers as well — could no longer take decisions and make agreements in the light of national interest as they saw it. Their decisions and relationships had to conform to the ideals and plans of the radicals or else they would be branded as reactionaries. Therefore, no amount of reform and progress achieved under King Idris could satisfy the radicals because their objective was a complete change in orientation and personnel that would include the removal of the king himself and his aides. The king and the legally appointed or elected rulers and legislators naturally could not be expected to atone for their policies and for the political structure under which they governed by destroying that structure and removing themselves from the political scene. Nor was it certain that the radical change was desired by the Libyan people. The young officers, however, decided what was desirable for the entire population in virtue of the means of violence they possessed, and imposed their decision by force on the country.

III   The Coup d'Etat of September 1, 1969

The military coup of Monday, September 1, 1969 against the Sanusi monarchy occurred while the 79-year-old and frail King Idris was recuperating in Bursa in Turkey from a long illness. It was an unexpected coup in so far as no signs of recent conspiratorial military activity were noticeable and no serious agitation or discontent was apparent besides the general bitterness that followed the June war of 1967 and the resentment of the British and American presence in the military bases. In the Libyan jails there were some political prisoners, including members of the Arab Nationalist Movement, who had plotted against the monarchy in 1967. In the same year following the Arab-Israeli war an oil strike was led by a Syrian-born Libyan lawyer called Mahmud al-Maghribi and resulted in the arrest and trial of several persons including Maghribi himself. In the army, a Sandhurst and Cairo-trained colonel by the name of Saadeddin Abu-Shweirib was involved in anti-royalist activity and was retired in 1967. Both Maghribi and Abu-Shweirib were destined to hold important positions after the coup two years later. The leftist officers who led the coup, however, were young with an average age of twenty-seven and with the rank of lieutenant or captain. They called themselves "the free unionist officers" and their organization was said to have been formed in 1966.[22] They prepared their coup with the utmost secrecy, and it would seem that in the excellent planning, thorough organization and rigorous execution of the coup the young and inexperienced officers might have received expert advise and help from external sources. Libyan exiles in neighboring Egypt were also in contact with the coup leaders. One of these exiles was Saleh Buwaysir, a former vice-president of the Libyan Chamber of Deputies who had clashed with the king's advisers.[23] The size of the Libyan army at this time was between 6,500 and 8,000 but only 500 officers and men were reportedly involved in the coup.[24]

On the early morning of September 1, 1962 at about 2 a.m. troops and tanks converged on Tripoli and surrounded the major military and civilian installations including the army and security headquarters, the royal palace and the radio station. At the same time the leaders of the government including Crown Prince Hasan al-Rida were placed under arrest. At 5 a.m. the leaders of the coup were in effective control of the city. A very strict twenty-four hour curfew was imposed and the borders of Libya and its seaports and airports were closed. According to the general pattern of military coups a proclamation was issued by the anonymous Revolution Command Council announcing the creation of the Libyan Arab Republic and justifying the end of the monarchy in inevitably exaggerated terms. The people were told that the revolution was made "to execute your free will, to realize your precious aspirations, truly to answer your repeated call demanding change and purification." The armed forces therefore, in response to the alleged demands of the people "destroyed the reactionary, backward and decadent regime whose putrid odor assailed one's nose. . . The idols collapsed and the graven images shattered. . . The darkness of ages — from the rule of the Turks to the tyranny of the Italians and the era of reaction, bribery, intercession, favoritism, treason, and treachery — was dispersed."[25]

The coup leaders seemed to claim in their declarations that their action was unopposed and that the old regime fell "with one blow from your heroic army." The unprecedented rigor and duration of the curfew, however, and the week-long closing of ports and ten-day long closing of airports meant that there was resistance or extreme fear of resistance. The curfew was lifted for only three hours on the second day and for five hours — from noon to 5 p.m. — on the fourth day. On the eighth day after the coup the curfew was still from 7 p.m. to 7 a.m. and on September 30 it was reduced to be from 10 p.m. to 5 a.m. More than two months after the coup, on November 10, 1969, there was still a curfew from midnight to 5 a.m. There were reports, moreover, of shooting in the streets of Tripoli on the first two days (Monday and Tuesday) while the military takeover was proceeding, and a call was heard on the radio for all doctors and nurses to report to the Tripoli central hospital. In Cyrenaica in the eastern part of the country there were indications of some fighting. Tanks and troops were moved to Benghazi in the east, but the resistance of the Sanusi tribesmen and of the Eastern region in general was not what could be expected. The collapse of the Cyrenaica defense force, which was thought to be loyal to the king and was more numerous and tougher than the entire regular army, was even more puzzling. The revolutionary leadership claimed that the Cyrenaica defense force dropped its traditional loyalty to the king and sided with the revolution. Key officers in that force could have changed sides or were persuaded not to resist because they received promises of promotion or cash payments from the authors of the coup. According to one report the duty officer who was in charge of the strike force on the night of the coup "was in league with the revolutionaries and stood down the guard."[26] Many of the higher officers of the Cyrenaica defense force were arrested or retired and those in the lower ranks were later absorbed in the army. The coup leaders arrested the chief of staff of the regular army, Maj. Gen. Hamdeddin al-Sanusi, and some 250 majors, lieutenant-colonels and colonels. They also arrested former cabinet members and ambassadors and over 200 leading businessmen. Crown Prince Hasan had to renounce his rights to the throne of Libya and even to declare his support for the revolution.

The young officers' speedy and comprehensive arrests and

their stern enforcement of the curfew and other strict measures were effective in paralyzing the key royalist forces that were caught by surprise. The king himself could not believe what happened and when he arrived in Greece from Turkey on September 3 he said that he would return soon to Tripoli. He probably expected a counter coup by the Cyrenaica defense force or perhaps foreign intervention and support. He evidently sent his adviser to London immediately after the coup and is said to have asked for British military intervention to restore him to power but the British refused on the ground that the treaty of 1953 provided for aid against external aggression not internal revolution.[27] The British had about 2,500 well trained soldiers in Tobruk and Adem and stocks of arms and would have been able to challenge with success the weak Libyan army, but Britain chose to continue the friendly relations with Libya and the understanding that existed under the monarchy. The speedy international recognition of the new revolutionary command helped to discourage the Libyan royalist opposition and reassured the new regime. The king abdicated officially and before the end of October decided to retire in Egypt. The Western powers — Britain, the United States, France and Italy — recognized the new regime on the sixth day after the coup. The Arab countries and the Soviet Union had already extended their recognition. An important factor in the Western attitude towards Libya was the Libyan wealth in oil, the production of about 85 per cent of it by American companies, and the sale of 92 per cent of it to Western Europe. In its very first proclamation of September 1, the revolutionary council gave the reassurance that its action was not directed against any foreign state or foreign commitment. In other declarations the council made it clear that it would be making no attempt to nationalize the oil industry. Libya's income from oil at the time was close to one billion dollars and the first order to the oil terminals on the morning after the coup was to "keep the barrels going over the jetties."[28]

On the first day of the coup, the Revolutionary Command

Council made a five-point declaration on the government structure and the guidelines of its policy.[29] First, it abolished all the constitutional institutions of the old regime such as the ministerial and legislative councils (cabinet and Parliament) and threatened the old politicians with violent action if they should attempt to show hostility against the revolution in any way. Second, it placed the affairs of the Arab Republic of Libya "firstly and lastly" within the authority of the Revolutionary Command Council that became the sole authority in the country. Third, it declared that it was determined to "build the Libya of revolution, the Libya of a socialism which springs from the heart of our nation. . . and believes in the inevitability of irrevocable historical development" that will transform Libya from a backward to a progressive country. The RCC expected that, as a progressive country, Libya would naturally oppose colonialism and racism and strive to liberate oppressed peoples affected by the same problems of backwardness and social oppression. Fourth, the RCC announced its belief in the unity of third-world causes and in the efforts of that world to end social and economic backwardness. Fifth, the RCC wanted to reassure the traditional society in Libya about its attitude toward religion in a world of socialist revolution. It declared its belief in the sanctity of religions and in the value of the spiritual precepts of the Koran as well as its continued support of those precepts.

During the first few days after the coup while the anonymous RCC assumed complete control of the administration, the state seemed to be run by radio. The orders announcing the purges and the appointments in the various administrative services were communicated to the interested persons by an announcer who read the names or gave the instructions over the radio, and the persons obeyed without knowing the source or the cause of their dismissal or appointment. This is how the coup was called by one writer "a textbook coup."[30] Of all the officers who participated in the coup or were otherwise connected with it, only one was mentioned and for a few days he was thought to be its leader and the chairman of its revolutionary council. This was Colonel Saadeddin Abu-Shweirib who was probably used as a front man because he was better known than the others and he had a more advanced rank — the real leaders were all captains and lieutenants. The Middle East News Agency (MENA) explained on the third day of the coup that Abu-Shweirib was just the new chief of staff and that the real chairman and members of the RCC preferred to remain anonymous. Abu-Shweirib was allowed to keep his post for less than three months, and on November 18 he was appointed ambassador to Egypt.

On September 8, 1969 the RCC appointed a cabinet that was expected to work under its supervision. All the cabinet members were new and except for the two colonels who held the important portfolios of defense and interior, the cabinet was a civilian one. The prime minister was Mahmud al-Maghribi, the Syrian-born lawyer who had been arrested and tried under the monarchy for leading an oil workers' strike after the June war of 1967. The two recently promoted colonels, Adam Hawaz for the defense and Musa Ahmad for the interior were, with Abu-Shweirib, the only officers with more than first lieutenant's rank in the revolutionary movement but they were not members of the RCC. Both were from Cyrenaica and they were perhaps appointed in the two key posts because of the importance attached to their influence in a region that was loyal to King Idris.[31]

Before the middle of September the identity of the officer who led the military coup and became the chairman of the RCC was disclosed. Colonel Muammar Qadhafi revealed himself as the leader and commander-in-chief when he thanked the Libyan armed forces for supporting him in the coup. He was a twenty-seven -year- old first lieutenant when he led the coup on the first day of September. In an interview with the *Figaro* he mentioned that his parents still lived in a tent in the Sirt area and that the parents of some of his colleagues lived in huts. He was trying to explain why the RCC included officers only and no civilians. His reason was that the "officers truly have the conscience to represent better than anyone else the demands of the people" because of their humble origins.[32] It was said that Qadhafi entered the military college in 1963, after his graduation from the Libyan university, with the intention of preparing and participating in a military coup against the old regime. He graduated as an officer in 1965 and four years later he carried out the coup.[33] Qadhafi, like other leaders of military coups, later insisted in his speeches, but without good reason, that the revolution was a popular revolution and that "what happened on the first of September is as far as could be from being a military coup." His explanation was that the people were the teachers and the pioneers who inspired the armed forces and that these forces were an indivisible part of the people and nothing but its vanguard.[34]

The "free unionist officers" who made the coup had proclaimed in their first communiqué that their revolution was dedicated to the principles of "freedom, socialism, and unity." Because these principles were the same as those in the Baath party slogan, "unity, freedom, socialism" - but differently arranged — it was supposed that the leaders of the coup were Baath party members. The supposition, however, was not necessarily correct because the three components of the Baath slogan became a symbol for the various Arab revolutionary movements regardless of affiliation, and in the words of a Libyan RCC member, these principles "are not imported and are not inspired by a specific group." Moreover, it seems that among the underground political groups in Libya, the Baath was not as strong as the Arab Nationalist Movement that was inclined to Nasser.

IV. Characteristics and First Results of the New Military Regime

The leaders of the coup painted an unbelievably dark picture of the royalist regime under King Idris, and Colonel

Qadhafi used an old cliché when he spoke on September 22 of the old rulers as "the enemies of the people." The pre-revolutionary rule was described by a member of the RCC on November 4, 1969 as "corrupt, reactionary, backward, practically at the beck and call of the foreign British and American forces." Libya also was said to be "isolated from the decisive causes of the Arab nation."[35] As a proof, the RCC member cited the failure of Libya to take any positive action or to participate effectively when the "setback" of 1967 occurred. In order to legitimize their coup, the Libyan officers, therefore, had to prove that they were pursuing a different internal and foreign policy in the best interests of Libya and its people as well as the Arab nation. The following characteristics of military rule can consequently be mentioned in describing the attempt of the revolutionary republican regime to reach its goals, consolidate its power, and win the people's support.

The first and most obvious characteristic of the new Libyan military government was its increased involvement in Arab affairs and in talks on Arab unity, and its readiness to support the Palestine cause. The leaders of the RCC spoke out against provincialism and its failure to protect Palestine or to provide a positive solution to the problem of the Arab nation. The ministry of foreign affairs was now called "ministry of unity and foreign affairs." The defense minister, Colonel Hawaz, declared in mid-November 1969 in Cairo that the Arab armies should be unified, and in his talk about cancelling the $312 million order from Britain for an air defense system he said that the order was intended for defense against a possible threat from Egypt, whereas Libya now wanted to use the money for building up its armed forces in preparation for "the destiny determining battle" (with Israel). In mid-October already, Colonel Qadhafi had declared that his regime was not contemplating the construction of a modern regional armed force for Libya alone. The armed forces, he said, were being built "on the basis of unity and integration with the rest of the armies of the Arab nation, especially the liberated ones."³⁶ The Libyan military leaders turned to Cairo for support and inspiration in their Arab policy. They began by seeking Nasser's close friendship in order to defend their revolution and then they began to talk of union. On December 25, 1969 Colonel Qadhafi returned from the Arab summit conference at Rabat in the company of President Nasser and Colonel Numairi of the Sudan, and after two days of talks in Tripoli, the three Arab African leaders signed an agreement to coordinate their activities in military, economic and cultural matters and to hold periodic meetings for working out the details of the coordination and cooperation. Meetings were held in April 1970 and agreements were signed in Tripoli for educational and cultural affairs, in Khartoum for agricultural coordination, and in Cairo for transportation, trade and industry. Each meeting was attended by representatives and ministers of the departments concerned in the three countries. The two youngest Arab revolutions — those of the Sudan and Libya - were gratified by the December agreement because Nasser thereby helped establish their credentials. The Libyan officers were particularly satisfied because Nasser granted them the support and approval they needed.³⁷ Nasser naturally drew some satisfaction from the mass rallies and wild cheers that accompanied his visits to Tripoli and Khartoum, and from the continued recognition of his leadership and that of Egypt in various Arab quarters. He also hoped that the vast oil wealth of Libya would be placed in the service of the militant Arab camp.

Three days after the tripartite agreement in Tripoli, the British Aircraft Corporation announced on December 29, 1969 that its contract for providing Libya with an air defense system was canceled. The revolutionary government had been unhappy with this contract that it inherited from the old regime, but it signified its interest in retaining the order of 200 British Chieftain tanks. In the meantime the new Libyan leaders were associating themselves more closely — but mostly orally - with the Arab-Israeli war and with the support of the Palestinian resistance movement to which they contributed one-quarter of a million dollars at the end of 1969. When they reached an agreement with France to buy one hundred Mirage planes on January 21, 1970 certain observers consequently concluded that the balance of security and peace in the Middle East would be disturbed on the ground that the planes would be used by the new Libyan regime, or possibly by Egypt, against Israel. The government of President Pompidou of France was attacked by pro-Zionist forces while the French government explained that the planes were to be delivered in 1972-73 and it would take several years before the Libyans could be able to maintain and use them. France also made it clear that it was in her interest that Libya should buy arms from her and not from the Soviet Union.[38] The Libyan Mirage deal naturally added to the popularity of France among the Arabs and to the prestige of Qadhafi and his colleagues who proved to themselves and to their people that they could make independent decisions without listening to British or American advice.

The second important feature of the new military rule was the change of its orientation from a pro-Western to a non-aligned regime, and the liquidation of the British and American bases in order to strengthen the sovereignty of Libya, remove all aspects of foreign influence and satisfy the people's national pride. The issue of the foreign bases served at first as a justification for the officers' coup. It was used later to consolidate the precarious rule of the revolutionary leaders and to help them score a useful and easy national victory. Already on the third day after the coup the American and British commanders at the bases were told by the Libyan revolutionary council to cease combat training activities. The Libyan leaders made declarations in press conferences and speeches that the agreements pertaining to the bases would not be renewed and that the country will accept "no bases, no foreigner, no colonialist, no intruder."[39] Yet, for two months after the coup they made no formal demand for withdrawal from the bases, before the time defined by the agreements. They were probably studying the possible reactions of the foreign powers involved and receiving the advice of the more experienced Egyptians while their own power was being strengthened. On October 29 the Libyan government formally requested the withdrawal of British troops and the liquidation of British bases "with all due speed." On the following day the same request was made with regard to the American Wheelus air force base. The chairman of the RCC, Colonel Qadhafi, then began a tour of major Libyan cities including Tobruk and Tripoli where he addressed mass rallies and pressed for a favorable reply on the evacuation. He referred to colonialism that created and supported thrones and reactionary rulers, and he asserted that the people of Libya were not content to live in the shadow of foreign bases. He warned that no compromise or postponement would be accepted and that the people were ready for martyrdom in order to liberate their territory.[40]

The Libyan pressure for the evacuation of the bases was not motivated simply by considerations of national pride and by the notion that independence would be incomplete as long as the foreign bases remained unliquidated. It would seem that Colonel Qadhafi and other Libyan leaders spoke so passionately of evacuation because they were fearful that the Anglo-American forces in the bases might turn sooner or later against them and their revolution on the basis that these forces were there to protect the monarchy. Observers noticed, for example, that the Libyan officers and the Libyan military posts were easily alarmed by any unusual movement such as an extra delivery of groceries at Wheelus air base, or by any rumor on Tobruk.[41] Libyan military police and customs officers guarded the gates at Wheelus and decided who and what went in and out.[42] The British troops in Cyrenaica, moreover, were in a sensitive part of Libya that could become the source of opposition to the revolution. Yet, neither the British nor the Americans opposed the revolution, and before the end of December 1969 both had agreed to withdraw from their respective bases after negotiations and agreements with the Libyan government. The British withdrawal from Tobruk and Adem began on December 15 and ended on schedule at the end of March 1970. The Americans agreed to withdraw by the end of June 1970, and they completed their evacuation on June 11, nineteen days ahead of schedule. The evacuation from Wheelus, like that from Tobruk and el-Adem, was completed in an orderly and dignified manner. To mark the end of the foreign military presence on Libyan soil, the government opened ten days of celebrations with a military parade at Wheelus base to which Arab heads of state were invited. The celebrations were attended on June 20 and after by the presidents of Egypt, Yemen, Syria, Lebanon, and Iraq, the king of Jordan and six personal envoys of other Arab kings and presidents. The celebration turned into an Arab meeting in which the Arab-Israeli conflict was discussed in its military and diplomatic aspects and a joint plan was charted for liberating Arab territory occupied in June 1967. The Wheelus base was renamed the Uqba ibn Nafi base after the Muslim general who conquered part of North Africa in the seventh century.

Several reasons were mentioned by analysts for the American decision to accept the liquidation of Wheelus air base. Perhaps one of the most important was the recognition of the fact that for the Libyans it was a matter of intense national pride to regain possession of the base and see the end of foreign influence. One Libyan officer later compared the Wheelus base to a poisoned dagger in the back of the Arabs. American diplomats, moreover, saw that the lease was due to expire anyway in 1971, that the Air Force training that was done on Wheelus could be done elsewhere, and that the base can be given consequently without great loss but with tremendous potential gain that includes the establishment of a good working relationship and understanding with the new rulers.[43]

While the official policy of the new regime was based on nonalignment, the revolutionary leaders made it clear that their relations with other states would be on the basis of the position of these states on the Palestine question. This is why they declared the Soviet Union to be "among the Arabs' best friends" and described its aid to the Arab states and especially to Egypt as "tantamount to aid for the Libyan revolution." This is also why they considered France a friendly state but on the other hand warned against the deterioration of American-Libyan relations and called for a unified Arab stand against the attitude of the United States on Palestine.⁴⁴ The Libyan regime also committed itself to the support of liberation causes, and in the militant and emotional rhetoric of Colonel Qadhafi it asserted that "the freedom of the Arab in Libya is imperfect as long as every Arab in every place in the vast Arab nation is not liberated."⁴⁵ Libya similarly expressed interest in the efforts of Arab revolutionary regimes to combat counter-revolutionary activity as it did when it sent its deputy prime minister to accompany the Egyptian vice president, Anwar al-Sadat, to Khartoum to find out the extent of the Mahdist attempt against the Numairi regime at the end of March 1970 and to announce Libya's readiness to help the Sudanese revolution against its enemies.

The third outstanding feature of the military regime was the adoption of socialism and the extension of state control over the various institutions and activities in the country with the help of Egyptian professional and technical experts. The Libyan leaders borrowed from the Egyptian and other revolutionary movements certain slogans and theories that proclaimed the inevitability of the revolution, the realization of the "society of equality and justice" (in Egypt the formula was "sufficiency and justice") through socialism, the solidarity of the "working forces of the people - workers, farmers, non-exploitative capitalists, intellectuals and soldiers" - for building socialism, the idea that socialism is an economic necessity for the liberation of the individual from poverty and backwardness, and the notion that capital and the unlimited income from individual ownership are tools of domination and oppression. The Libyan leaders also insisted, as those of the Egyptian revolution had done, that "our socialism is the socialism of Islam," and they repeated the same fallacies that protrayed Islam as a socialist religion, and alms giving (zakat) in Islam as an instrument of dissolving differences among classes.[46] Premier Maghribi gave assurances two weeks after the coup that "we will not imitate any foreign system, and nationalization has no relevance for us since we have plenty of land and a few farmers." He also said that there will be no spectacular changes in Libya's oil policy. The ministers of petroleum and of foreign affairs both affirmed that "Libya does not intend to nationalize the oil industry at the present time." The petroleum minister however mentioned that the posted price of $2.21 a barrel was not a fair price, and he spoke of the need for more effective control of the oil companies in order to insure priority of employment to Libyans, then to Arabs, and then to others on the basis of their qualifications.[47] Observers have noted that in spite of these assurances the spectre of future nationalization has prevented the oil companies and other business interests from making new capital investments in Libya since the military coup, and oil exploration has come to a halt.[48] But at the end of 1969 the thirty-eight oil companies, mostly-American, continued to pump an estimated 3.7 million barrels a day and Libya held the third rank (after Venezuela and Iran) among the oil exporters.[49] Libyan exports doubled after the closure of the Suez Canal in June 1967 because the high grade oil of Libya lies closer to Europe than the oil of the Arabian Peninsula.

In their adoption of the socialist system, the revolutionary leaders intended to realize social justice, enable the people to share in the country's wealth, and destroy the disparities between the rich and poor. They also wanted to devote a large part of the oil income for the creation of a public sector in the economy to promote development projects that would lead to an increase in the national income.[50] What they actually did, however, was to bring the already existing national development program to a standstill, and to stop private business activities. This action and the economic stagnation and increased unemployment that followed can be explained by several factors. First, the officers dismissed hundreds of government officials, arrested some of them and threatened to bring them and the leaders of the former regime to trial on charges of treason and corruption. Some businessmen were arrested, others had their bank accounts frozen and banking operations were restricted. Commercial activity as a result was almost paralyzed. The officers needed time to sift the contracts and records for evidence of waste or graft. Second, the officers were young, inexperienced and unprepared to handle a complex national economy. In addition, they did not trust their aides and were afraid to delegate responsibility. While the money was pouring without interruption from the oil royalties no one knew what was happening to it. Third, the leaders of the new regime were under the impression that "The foreigner was the master" in Libya, and they believed that unqualified foreigners were employed by the former government as experts for the simplest jobs. In their resentment and suspicion of foreign residents they asked some of them to leave the country immediately after the coup, and they dismissed or investigated a number of others in order to terminate their services. The alarmed foreigners also began to leave voluntarily as Libya became gradually a police state and a new secret police department was created to investigate their activities. The few Jews who were living in the country left immediately after the coup. The Italians were the largest foreign community with some 35,000 persons. They provided most of the technical and professional services and controlled much of the commerce. Many of them were forced out of their work and had to leave Libya and abandon their possessions, but their exodus hurt the economy. When, for example, the skilled Italian workers were ordered by the government to leave their construction jobs, the Libyan unskilled laborers who were employed on the sites were thrown out of work. The inexperience of the ruling officers, and their suspicion and resentment of foreigners and former local officials consequently slowed down the economy. Development sites were deserted, construction of medical clinics, schools and new roads stopped, imports dropped, dockworkers and other workers became idle and unemployment rose to 12 per cent of the labor force[51]

The socialist system brought with it relatively little

nationalization because there was not much to nationalize. The important projects were state projects since the time of the monarchy, and the big business was state business. Nationalization was consequently directed at foreign establishments and especially banks. On November 14, 1969 the Libyan government nationalized all foreign banks and gave them new names. The Barclays Bank with its nineteen branches, the Banco di Roma, Banco di Napoli, and the Arab Bank were the most important. Some small private foreign and local concerns were taken over such as a private Libyan hospital in Tripoli, two Italian Catholic schools, and the American Adventist hospital in Benghazi.[52] The labor unions and students' federations had to be reorganized and to submit to state control. Qadhafi explained that they should not be controlled by "parasites and those who love power" and that they should truly represent their groups with a revolutionary spirit. He also spoke of a popular organization that would be created later and would embrace and bring together all "the working forces of the people." The establishment of unions representing students', teachers' and laborers' groups would be within the framework of that popular organization. The new leaders were, however, in no hurry to set up the popular organization or to form the various unions. Nor were they willing to restore parliamentary life to Libya except "through selection of the people's true representatives," and with the understanding that "he who engages in party activities commits treason."[53] The press was strictly watched and five newspapers were closed by decree after the coup. On October 15, 1969 the RCC issued an official daily called *al-Thawrah* (the Revolution).

The new republican regime depended particularly on Egypt for the organization of its various services and for replacing the European technicians and advisers, although it also employed other Arabs. Many Egyptians who served under the monarchy left and those who came after the coup were more numerous and their functions were more varied. In addition to the hundreds of Egyptian physicians and nurses who came to serve in Libyan hospitals, Egyptian experts in industry and land reclamation were employed and others came as financial experts to run the foreign banks that Libya had nationalized. An Egyptian became the president of the Libyan supreme court, while more Libyans went to study in Egyptian universities and at the Egyptian military academy and police college. The growing Egyptian influence and cooperation were particularly noticeable in the presence of Egyptian intelligence men, security policemen on patrol in the Libyan towns, and even Egyptian troops stationed outside Tripoli and Benghazi to help Libya guard against counterrevolutionary activity.[54] The number of Egyptian technicians and professional people with their families was put around four thousand persons in addition to about two thousand soldiers (two to four battalions of Egyptian troops) on duty in the country. Some Libyans evidently resented the arrival of the Egyptians and as they began moving into the country, posters sarcastically proclaiming "Welcome to the Conquerors" were put up on the walls in Tripoli but Libyan soldiers tore them down.[55]

The fourth characteristic of the Libyan military regime is a corollary of the first two and is related to what has been just mentioned on the attitude towards foreign residents. It is the emphasis on the Arab identity of Libya and the exclusive use of Arabic in the various aspects of public life. The replacement of foreigners by Libyans and other Arabs in government positions and the encouragement of foreign residents to leave the country were expressions of demographic and administrative Arabization. The teaching of the English language in elementary schools was at the same time discontinued because, according to Premier Maghribi, it was done at the expense of the Arabic language, but it was to continue at the post-elementary levels. To those who demanded the early study of English because it suited technological progress the prime minister said that China developed nuclear weapons with only one language.[56] On September 19, 1969 the revolutionary regime decreed that all signs, placards, tickets, stamps, cards, street directions, and advertisements should be only in Arabic. Signs that were written in English or Italian including names of banks and hotels, "stop" or parking signs in streets, directions in the post office, "up" and "down" elevator signs, "push" and "pull" signs on doors were either torn down or painted over or scratched or covered by tape with the resulting inconvenience and confusion for the foreign residents, workers and tourists. Menus in restaurants had to be written in Arabic only and waiters and hotel clerks were reluctant to speak in a foreign language especially when other people were around. To those who thought that this was unfair for the foreigners the answer was that "signs were not written in Arabic for our benefit in New York City".[57] The new regime wanted also to stress its austerity and its allegiance to the precepts of Islam by the prohibition of alcoholic drinks and the closing of the gambling casinos. Exception was made later for the foreign non-Muslim oil workers in the use of liquor.

The attempt to Arabize Libya by decree through the exclusive use of Arabic was sometimes carried to a ridiculous and absurd extent. The same procedure with its exaggerations and absurdities was often followed temporarily by newly independent countries in a spirit of self assertion and for a feeling of national satisfaction after a long period of colonial rule. But in Libya which had been independent for eighteen years, in spite of the presence of foreign bases, the procedure was a chauvinistic and demagogic device on the part of the young officers to outbid the former regime in nationalistic and religious devotion and to play on the emotions of the masses and gain their confidence and support. These procedures were usually harmful in the long run because they conveyed to the masses a superficial and false sense of nationalism. The former rulers under the old Arab regimes were neither less nationalistic nor less Muslim than the new leaders but they were more mature, more confident of their national identity and therefore more tolerant and liberal. They issued no decrees on Arabic signs and they did not prohibit the use of liquor. They were brought to power by national elections not by military force and therefore they did not have to be chauvinistic and xenoplobic in order to convince the people about their true nationalism.

The fifth and last characteristic of the new Libyan regime was that it had its internal quarrels followed by the attempt of its dissenting officers to stage a new military coup, exactly as under other revolutionary military regimes. The controversy within the ruling circles centered at the very beginning on the degree of control by the civilian ministers because the young officers in the revolutionary council did not know how to delegate authority. The civilian members of the cabinet complained that they were treated like clerks and before the end of the first month after the coup some of them wanted to resign. The first largely civilian cabinet under Maghribi lasted four months and a half until January 16, 1970 when Colonel Qadhafi became the new prime minister in addition to his chairmanship of the revolutionary council. Another controversy that created division and friction between the revolutionary leaders centered on the question of the orientation of Libyan policy and the extent of the involvement of Libya in Arab problems and in pro-Egyptian policies. Some officers like Colonels Adam Hawaz and Musa Ahmad, ministers of defense and interior, were evidently in favor of more concentration on Libyan interests and less involvement with, or dependence on Egypt. They were the only officers above the rank of first lieutenant among those who actively participated in the coup and they were not members of the RCC. They were both from Cyrenaica that was known to be loyal to the old regime and their influence in the region was no longer needed after the success of the coup. They naturally disliked the preeminent policy-making role of the RCC and of the former Lieutenant (now Colonel) Qadhafi who dominated it and who favored full cooperation with Egypt. Qadhafi, on the other hand, disliked the self assertiveness of Defense Minister Hawaz and his declaration on the air defense contract with Britain during his visit to Cairo in November 1969.[58] Friction and disagreement between officers led evidently to the preparation of a coup against the RCC and the government dominated by Qadhafi.

On December 10, 1969, a little over three months after the Libyan coup, it was reported that thirty officers, including Colonels Hawaz and Ahmad, were arrested on charges of plotting to overthrow the government and the plot was to be carried out on December 7. It was also learned that Colonel Hawaz was receiving medical treatment as a result of his attempt to commit suicide following his arrest.[59] A special military tribunal was formed for the trial of the accused officers. It consisted of a captain and two lieutenants who were all members of the RCC. Armed units were placed around foreign embassies in Tripoli because of the demonstrations that followed the discovery of the plot. The demonstrators were demanding the death penalty for the conspirators in accordance with the law for the protection of the revolution. It was thought that there were "hidden foreign hands" behind the attempt and certain observers believed that it was the result of the demands by the RCC that the United States and Britain liquidate their bases in Libya.[60] The British later agreed on December 13 to evacuate their bases, and the United States gave its approval on December 23 - in both cases shortly after the failure of the conspiracy. The law for the defense of the revolution prescribed the death punishment for armed rebellion and for other acts hostile to the revolution or harmful to the republican regime. This law, however, was not invoked, and when the investigation was completed and the public prosecutor made his statement on March 15, 1970, he only asked for prison terms for the thirty officers.

The cabinet that was formed by Colonel Qadhafi on January 16, 1970 showed the same trend as in the Sudan where the military leader of the coup, Colonel Numairi, became prime minister after the forced resignation of the civilian premier who had been appointed directly after the coup. The number of officers in the new cabinet was four instead of two, in addition to Colonel Qadhafi, the prime minister. The officers now held not only the portfolios of defense and interior, but also those of education and guidance, economy, and housing. The RCC continued to consist exclusively of officers and in December 1969 their number was eleven. The provisional constitution that replaced the Libyan constitution of 1951 immediately after the failure of the conspiracy of December 1969 gave the RCC supreme authority and emphasized the objectives of Arab unity and an economy free of foreign control.[61] The Libyan regime tightened its control against conspiracy, and in the appointments to high positions Colonel Qadhafi declared that "we shall be more careful and will not confer our confidence except upon those who are worthy of it." Libya was becoming a military police state with permits required for everything and issued in the last resort by the military, tapped hotel telephones, and continuously emerging watchdog committees and special investigating offices in addition to a new secret police department created in February 1970 to investigate the activities of foreigners and local organizations with subversive ideas dangerous to state security.[62]

V. The Meaning of the Libyan Coup

The Libyan military coup of September 1, 1969 was hailed by the Arab military socialist regimes as a "victory for all socialist revolutionary Arabs" and as "a great step towards freedom and Arab solidarity." In Cairo, the editor of *al-Ahram* called it "the most important event in the Arab world during the last few years." The event was indeed important if measured by the regular Arab revolutionary standards. It replaced the monarchy by a republic and brought to power young militant nationalists of humble origin and lower military rank to take the place of the older moderate upper class politicians and high ranking officers. This is why it was described as the revolt of "the young and the thin against the old and the portly, the idealist against the worldly, and the righteous against the corrupt." It was also a coup of the captains, or rather the lieutenants against the colonels.[63] The new leaders immediately indicated their active interest in Arab solidarity and liberation, and within their own country they succeeded in obtaining the liquidation of foreign bases, and they declared their adoption of a socialism that leads to social justice.

The Libyan military rulers, however, have been cautious in moving towards revolutionary action in spite of their emotional declarations. In fact their professions of faith in the Palestine cause and their more frequent meetings with Arab leaders in conferences and rallies have served only to justify their coup against the old regime and to consolidate their own position. But on the positive side they have neither placed their vast oil wealth in the militant Arab camp, nor have they sent their soldiers to fight on the Suez Canal front. Their financial support for the Palestine guerillas has been very modest. Their army has not expanded in number and it is not known when they would be able to handle the planes ordered in France. Their contribution for the financial support of Egypt has not increased beyond the pledge made by King Idris in spite of the moral support that Nasser gave them and which they consistently, but not unanimously, sought at a time when Nasser himself had become a symbol of diplomatic and military failure except for the faithful enthusiasts. The one positive action of the new leaders was the end of the foreign presence in their country. It certainly satisfied the national pride of the Libyans and gave the military regime some prestige and justification. The new regime nevertheless realized that the oil wealth and its exploitation by Western companies has imposed on it a certain standard of friendly relations with the Western nations which it has been able to maintain in spite of the emotional declarations and warnings. The new military regime has also been careful to avoid the advocacy of extreme ideologies, or the dependence on Communist powers. Its weapons have been ordered in France and Britain, not in the Soviet Union. In its economic and social policy the development and the progress that were being achieved under the monarchy have been reduced by the subordination of the economic interests of the people to the political interests and prestige of the new leaders. For Libyan rulers as for other Arab military rulers the main consideration in their internal and foreign policy has been and is expected to remain the preservation and strengthening of their own power and prestige, and not the interest and power of the country and its people.

About a week after the Libyan coup of September 1, 1969 it was revealed that a similar coup had been prepared to overthrow the Saudi monarchy, and it was perhaps scheduled to take place at the same time as in Libya.[64] The plotting was probably carried out by branches of the Arab Nationalist Movement that was partly responsible for planning the Libyan coup, while some revolutionaries had contacts with Nasserists in Cairo. The Arab Nationalist Movement was linked with the Marxist Popular Front for the Liberation of Palestine which believed in the revolutionary change of the political and social order in all the Arab countries. The plot, however, failed; it was discovered in time because of the extensive presence of the Saudi security system. King Faisal also was popular as a reformer before and after he became king in 1964.

The lesson that can be drawn from this abortive attempt in Saudi Arabia and from the successful revolutionary attempts in Libya and the Sudan is that the Arab revolutionaries did not care to move against those socialist leaders who were involved in the war of June 1967 and who lost it because of their ineptitude. They rather revolted against those who were least involved in the war under the pretext that they should be more involved, but in reality because they were moderate or so called reactionary rulers. What really counted then was the revolutionary change itself in the country's social and economic system and in its orientation and ruling elite, not the effective participation of the new revolutionary regime in the struggle. The revolution thus became an end in itself in the Arab countries, and provided the emerging military regime satisfied the requirements of the class struggle and placed the "sons of the people" in the place of the middle class bourgeois rulers and made inflammatory speeches against Zionism and imperalism, the purposes of the revolution were satisfied. This is one of the reasons why the revolutionary leaders and their regimes have been so ineffective in meeting the challenge of Zionism and in achieving the progress and power needed to face it successfully.

CHAPTER V
NOTES

1. See I. William Zartman,*Government and Politics in Northern Africa* (New York: Praeger, 1963), 96; "Libya: Seven Years of Independence" by F. S. in *The World Today* (February, 1959), 65; for more detail consult Majid Khadduri,*Modern Libya: A Study in Political Development* (Baltimore: The Johns Hopkins Press, 1963).

2. See Ragaei el-Mallakh, "The Economics of Rapid Growth: Libya," *M.E. Journal* (Summer, 1969), 308.

3. See the text of the treaty with Britain and the agreement with the U.S. in Khadduri, Appendix IV and V, respectively.

4. *The Middle East and North Africa 1968-69*. 15th ed. (London: Europa Publications, 1968), 459; see also J.C. Hurewitz, *Middle East Politics: The Military Dimension*, 239.

5. Ragaei el-Mallakh, 308.

6. *Ibid.*, 310.

7. For these and other figures quoted from the *Statistical Abstract* of the Ministry of Economy and Trade see El-Mallakh, *Ibid.* 313-319.

8. *Ibid.*, 319.

9. For a good discussion of these issues and attitudes see Charles O. Cecil, "The Determinants of Libyan Foreign Policy," *M.E. Journal* (Winter, 1965), 24 ff.

10. *Ibid.*, 25-27.

11. Khadduri, *Modern Libya,* 289; Cecil, 28-29.

12. Cecil, 29; Zartman, 90 ff.

13. Zartman, 100; F.S. in *The World Today,* 66; Cecil, 32.

14. F.S. in *World Today,* 66.

15. Cecil, 34.

16. *M.E. Journal,* (Spring and Summer 1964), 226 and 335, respectively.

17. *The Economist* (September 6, 1969), 13.

18. Cecil, 31.

19. See Hurewitz, 236-237.

20. See the *Economist* (September 6 and November 15, 1969), pp. **13 and 32**, respectively.

21. *The Economist* (December 6, 1969), 26.
22. See *New Africa* (London) no 56 (1969), 12.
23. *N.Y. Times,* September 9, 1969; *The Economist* (Sept. 13, 1969), 32.
24. See "Libya" by Douglas Kiker in *The Atlantic* (June 1970), 30.
25. Quoted from the first proclamation of September 1 in "Document: The Libyan Revolution in the Words of its Leaders", *ME Journal* vol. 24 no. 2 (Spring, 1970), 203 (Referred to later as *MEJ Document).*
26. *The Economist* (December 6, 1969), 26.
27. *Ibid.* (September 6, 1969), 13.
28. *Ibid.* (Dec 6, 1969), 91; Kiker in *The Atlantic,* 33.
29. The following five points are quoted or summarized from *MEJ Document,* 205, 207, 210, 211.
30. *Time,* September 12, 1969.
31. *The Economist* (December 20, 1969), 28; *The New York Times,* September 9, 1969.
32. See the text of Qadhafi's statement in *MEJ Document,* 204.
33. *al-Hayat* September 14, 1969 quoting a statement by a colleague of Qadhafi to the *Stampa* of Turino.
34. Speeches and statements by Qadhafi on September 22 and November 28, see *MEJ Document,* 204, 205.
35. See statements in *Ibid.*
36. Declarations of Hawaz and Qadhafi in Ibid, 216-219; *N.Y. Times* November 8, 1969.
37. *The Economist* (January 17, 1970), 29; *Los Angeles Times,* December 27-29, 1969.
38. *N.Y. Times,* January 22, 1970.
39. See declarations of Premier Maghribi and of Col. Qadhafi on September 18 and October 16, respectively, in *MEJ Document,* 212-213.
40. See Qadhafi's addresses in Tobruk, and Tripoli on November 7 and 28, 1969, respectively, in *Ibid.,* 213.
41. *The Economist* (Dec. 6, 1969), 26.
42. See Kiker in *The Atlantic,* 33.

43. *Ibid.,* 32.
44. See various declarations by Qadhafi and others in *MEJ Document,* 214-215.
45. *Ibid.,* 215-216 from Qadhafi's address in Tripoli on October 16, 1969.
46. *Ibid.,* 207-209 for statements by Qadhafi on socialism between mid-September and mid-October, 1969.
47. *Ibid.,* 209-210; *ME Journal* (Winter 1970) 62-63 for declaration of Maghribi on September 17, 1969.
48. Reported by Kiker, 33.
49. *Time,* December 26, 1969.
50. See declarations of members of the RCC in *MEJ Document,* 208.
51. See Kiker, 34-38; *The Economist* (December 20, 1969), 28; *Time,* December 26, 1969.
52. *The N.Y. Times,* November 15, 1969; *The Economist* (Dec. 20, 1969), 28.
53. Qadhafi's declarations in October and November, in *MEJ Document,* 206-207 1969.
54. See Kiker, 38; *The Economist* (6 December, 1969 and January 17, 1970), 31 and 32 respectively.
55. See Kiker in *The Atlantic,* 38.
56. See Maghribi's declaration of September 18, 1969 in *MEJ Document,* 210; *Los Angeles Times,* October 3, 1969.
57. See Kiker, 32; *L.A. Times* October 3, 1969; *Time,* December 26, 1969.
58. *The Economist* (December 20, 1969), 28.
59. *al-Hayat,* December 13, 1969.
60. *N.Y. Times,* December 15, 1969.
61. *Ibid.; L.A. Times,* January 17, 1970.
62. Kiker in *The Atlantic,* 36.
63. *The Economist* (December 6, 1969), 26.
64. See *The New York Times,* September 9, 1969.

CHAPTER VI

CONCLUSION: MOTIVES, CHARACTERISTICS AND RESULTS OF ARAB REVOLUTIONS AND MILITARY RULE

The military rulers and their radical civilian supporters have dominated the eventful history of the emerging independent Arab states since 1949. Their motives, methods of rule and achievement have been a subject of controversy, but the chapter they have written remains rather disturbing, if not sad, in spite of the record of occassional·success. The present concluding section of this long study will perhaps help clarify the meaning of the revolutionary socialist military action through a comparative and analytical review of the motives of those who staged the military coups and the characteristics and results of their tenure. It will also provide some comments on the controversial question of liberal democracy and its restoration after the return of the military to their barracks.

I. General Remarks on Arab Revolutions and Coups d'état

The fifty-nine revolutions and coups d'état described in this and the preceding volume were almost all planned and staged by military officers with or without the support of political parties. They were generally called *Inqilab* (upturn or coup), but some of them were called *Thawrah* or revolution. The only two popular revolutions in which the people almost unanimously called for a change of government were those of Lebanon in September 1952 against President Khouri, and of the Sudan in October 1964 against the military regime of General Abboud. The seven military coups that were called "revolutions" were, first and foremost, the Egyptian revolution of July 1952 against King Farouk and the monarchy in Egypt followed by the six "revolutions" of July 1958 in Iraq against the monarchy, September 1961 in Syria for withdrawal from the United Arab Republic, September 1962 in Yemen against the Imamic regime, February 1963 in Iraq against Kassem, March 1963 in Syria against the semi-constitutional "secessionist" regime of President Qudsi, and September 1969 against the monarchy in Libya. They were all called "revolutions" immediately after their success in usurping power from the previous government, except in the case of Egypt where the coup was first known as "the army movement." The military plotters wanted to give the impression that their movement was made by the people or at least in the people's name and in response to their wishes. They also liked to emphasize the magnitude of the change produced by their action.

In addition to the fifty-nine revolutions and coups d'état certain popular demonstrations and riots succeeded at times in producing a change in government and in policy. Among the best known were the Iraqi riots that followed the signature of the draft treaty of Portsmouth with Britain in January 1948 and led to the resignation of the Saleh Jabr cabinet and the repudiation of the treaty; the Iraqi leftist riots of November 22, 1952 that prompted the Iraqi regent to ask the army chief of staff, Nureddin Mahmud, to form a cabinet and re-establish order; the riots of mid-December 1955 in Jordan against the Baghdad Pact that ended with the resignation of the four-day old cabinet of Hazza'al-Majali; the February 1968 riots in Cairo against the Nasserist regime that led to the proclamation of a program of reform and a change in cabinet in March; and the riots of April 1969 in Lebanon in sympathy with Palestinian guerilla activities that caused the resignation of the Karami cabinet and the beginning of a seven-month ministerial crisis. Several plots were discovered generally under the military ruling regimes and in monarchical Jordan before they reached the stage of execution or clashing with the government, and it is possible that other plots were uncovered but were not publicized by the rulers.

Among the fifty-nine revolutions and coups d'état that were analyzed, thirty-seven were successful and led to a change in government or regime while twenty-one were abortive, and one — the rebellion that took the aspect of a civil war in Lebanon in 1958 — ended in a compromise. The abortive coups were included in this work because of their significance in illustrating various aspects of military rule. The majority of revolutions and coups d'état — thirty-three out of fifty-nine — were carried out against military governments by military officers except in the single case of the Sudan in October 1964 where the anti-military revolution was the work of the people. The military coups against military regimes, however, were all succeeded by other military regimes except in four cases — one in Iraq and three in Syria — where the military restored civilian rule. The second military coup of August 11, 1937 against Bakr Sidqi in Iraq restored civilian government. Similarly a return to civilian constitutional rule was effected by the second Syrian military coup of August 14, 1969 against Zaim, the fifth coup of February 25, 1954 against Shishakli, and the seventh coup of September 28, 1961 against the United Arab Republic. In all four cases, however, the military who restored civilian rule watched the civilian constitutional rulers closely, intervened indirectly in government affairs and ended by overthrowing the civilians or ruling unofficially with them. The great number of military coups d'état directed against military regimes has meant that the military have had as much disagreement with each other as with the civilian politicians. It has meant also that the military regimes were at least as unstable as the civilian ones and that their rule often degenerated into a struggle for power and the struggle was sometimes of extreme violence. The officers, however, were not as successful in their coups against their military colleagues as against civilian regimes because the military rulers were obviously better prepared than the civilians for

Conclusion: Results of Arab Revolution and Military Rule / 355

meeting the challenge of military force and intrigue. This is why the majority of abortive coups — fourteen out of twenty-one — were those attempted by the military against the military, while the abortive attempts against civilian regimes were only one-third of all unsuccessful coups.

In the various Arab countries important differences could be seen in the proportion between successful and abortive coups, and also between coups carried out against civilian and against military rulers. In Iraq, out of seventeen military coups six were against civilian regimes and they were all successful, while eleven were against military regimes and five of them were abortive. Among the seventeen military coups in Syria, six were against civilian regimes with one failure, while eleven were against military governments with three failures. In Jordan and Lebanon no military regime has ever been established but the attempts of the military to plot and to carry out military coups were more persistent in Jordan. In Egypt, out of five military coups, one was against a civilian regime — the monarchy under Farouk — and four were carried out by the military against the military with three successes, and one failure under Marshal Amer in August 1967. The three successful coups were the product of the struggle for power between General Naguib and Colonel Nasser and two of them had only temporary success — that of February 25, 1954 against Naguib and the counter-coup of the following day in Naguib's favor — until the second anti-Naguib coup of March 29, 1954 that destroyed Naguib's power. Egypt did not experience the alternation of civilian and military rule that occurred in other countries, particularly in Syria. The Egyptian military regime, in a more or less civilianized form, has continued to prevail since the first coup of July 1952. In the Sudan three out of seven coups were against civilian governments with two successes, while four were carried out against military regimes and only one of them — the popular revolution of 1964 — was successful, but the three others led by military officers failed. Among the seven military coups in Yemen, four were directed against the civilian Imamic government but only two were successful. The success of one of those two that killed Imam Yahya in 1948 was short-lived, while the success of the other against Imam al-Badr in September 1962 was doubted for some time on account of the civil war that followed it. Three of the Yemeni coups were attempted by the military against the standing military regimes and only the one against Sallal in early November 1967 was successful while the other two, in March and August 1968, that were leftist-oriented failed.

With the exception of Yemen, which was already a sovereign independent state in 1919, the Arab countries under consideration became independent, completely or by treaty, between 1932 and 1956. Military coups d'état did not occur shortly after independence or within two or three years, as it has been asserted, except in three of the seven countries — Iraq, Syria and the Sudan. Iraq's first coup was in October 1936, four years after independence by treaty and admission to the League of Nations. Syria's first coup was in March 1949, three years after complete independence, and Sudan had its first coup in November 1958, less than three years after complete independence. On the other hand, the first coup in Yemen was in February 1948, twenty-nine years after full independence. In Egypt the coup of July 1952 came sixteen years after the independence treaty of 1936, and in Libya eighteen years passed since independence before the first coup occurred. Lebanon had no successful military coup, but there was a weak attempt by the dispersed para-military forces of a doctrinal party that were doomed to failure in early July 1949, three years after complete independence. In 1952 Lebanon witnessed the first successful popular revolution in the modern Arab world. In Jordan the first military attempt to seize power came in April 1957, eleven years after the independence treaty of 1946 but only one year after the dismissal of the British commander of the Arab Legion. The Arab military officers naturally attempted to seize power only when the restraint imposed by foreign domination was removed but their attempts were made at various intervals in the various countries

Conclusion: Results of Arab Revolution and Military Rule / 357

after the removal of the restraint. Within each country, the military coups did not follow a regular cycle and they occurred sometimes at very irregular intervals. In Iraq seven military interventions took place between 1936 and 1941, and the other ten all occurred in the ten years between 1958 and 1968. In Syria three successive coups d'état took place in 1949 and four in 1963 but none occurred in the eventful four-year period that preceded the merger with Egypt in 1958. Between November 1958 and November 1959 the Sudan witnessed four military coups, three of which were abortive, and then none occurred until the popular revolution of October 1964. The explanation of these different occurrences will become clear in the coming sections on the motives and characteristics of coups d'état and military rule.

II. Motives of Military Coups d'état

In the military interventions against civilian governments, the officers usually implied that they had been watching the government and they claimed that they intervened because they had no other alternative in order to save the country from the blunders or selfishness of its rulers. In the very first coup in Iraq, General Bakr Sidqi calling himself "chief of the national reform force" told "the noble people of Iraq" that "the patience of the Iraqi army, comprising your sons, has been exhausted as a result of the situation from which you have been suffering owing to the conduct of the Government, whose sole object has been to promote its own personal interests without paying any attention to the welfare of the public."[1] Colonel Zaim, leader of the first Syrian coup of March 31, 1949, mentioned the corruption of the leaders and the violation of the constitution as his motives. In Egypt, the first communiqué of July 23, 1952 showed the officers' concern about the situation in the army. It spoke of bribery, corruption and government instability that had a great influence on the army and contributed to the defeat in Palestine. General

Naguib said that the officers could no longer endure the humiliation to which they and the rest of the Egyptian people were subjected.² In the Sudan the leaders of the first coup of November 1958 claimed that the country was in a "state of degeneration, chaos and instability." The officers said that they watched the competition between parties while the situation continued to deteriorate until they finally found no alternative but to take over power in order to end the chaos.

The motives of the officers' coups d'état against the legitimate civilian rulers were internal and external, but the two were closely related and the alleged internal causes of the coup often seemed valid precisely because of the pressure of such external issues as the Palestine question and the problem of orientation towards other Arab states or towards the foreign powers. The officers' internal motives have been in most cases the alleged incompetence of the rulers, including the politicians, and their corrupt self-seeking practices, the ineffectiveness of the democratic parliamentary system with its frequent change of cabinets, rivalry between parties and the resulting instability, and the occasional violation of the constitution or the abuse of power by the rulers. The officers also revolted against such conditions in their own military establishment as the incompetence of their senior colleagues and the need for modern arms and equipment and against the entire political structure which, in their view, was responsible for the weakness of the army.

From the very beginning of their military interventions, the authors of coups referred to the need for social reform and for paying attention to the welfare of the people. This was illustrated in the first Iraqi coup of 1936 which was the outcome of a partnership between the officers and the reformist *Ahali* (People's) group. Social reform as a motive was emphasized particularly when a radical civilian party cooperated with the military. But the emphasis became particularly strong and civilian cooperation with the officers became more frequent in the second or ideological phase of military interventions after 1955 when the doctrinal parties with the encouragement of the Egyptian revolutionary regime began to agitate for a change in the political and social order. Socialism in its Marxist aspect became a lively issue in the staging of military coups after 1961-1962 and the forces of Nasserism and of the Baath party were mobilized to support it. The moderate ruling class and the wealthy individuals who opposed socialism and radicalism were then viewed as reactionaries and the so-called reactionaries were represented as agents of imperialism and traitors and therefore had to be swept away. Military coups came to be partly the expression of ideological contests between more or less radical groups particularly after 1966 and in these contests powerful internal class and sectarian interests as well as external pressures played their role.

In spite of the importance of internal motives that were related to the officers' impatience with the political structure and to the question of social reform, it was the external factors that were really preeminent as motives of the majority of military coups. The officers and even their civilian partners rarely revolted, except in Yemen, because of the existing political system or on account of prevailing economic and social conditions. Their motives were rather related to nationalistic considerations and to the controversies on Arab unity, inter-Arab policy, and the attitude towards the great powers. In the first or pre-ideological phase the officers were often moved by a desire to make their respective countries completely independent and free. In Iraq, for example, three coups — the fifth, sixth and seventh — between January and April 1941 were the outcome of opposition to the treaty of 1930 and the Iraqi alliance with Britain and to those who stood for it. The four influential colonels therefore attempted to impose a cabinet under Rashid Ali al-Gailani who was known for his opposition to the treaty. The seventh coup of April 1, 1941 that brought Gailani back to the premiership led to a short war with Britain in May and to an outburst of radical Iraqi and

Arab nationalist hostility to the ruling dynasty because of its cooperation with Britain and its revengeful hanging of the four colonels who led the coup. In Egypt the free officers' coup of July 23, 1952 was largely motivated by their desire to end the British occupation of the Canal Zone and obtain complete independence, or as Abdul Nasser said to "decide our own future and free the nation." The overthrow of Farouk and the monarchy along with the ruling elite were viewed as steps in that direction because the monarchy failed to obtain the liberation of Egypt, and the Muhammad Ali dynasty was regarded as the symbol of subservience to foreign rulers. The officers' pretexts contained historical inaccuracies, but they wanted to portray themselves as the real leaders of the struggle for independence although independence had been virtually achieved by the efforts of civilian popular leaders who made it possible for the previously silent and foreign-dominated officers to feel free after the local armies had become independent national armies.

External factors were remarkably influential in the Syrian coups d'état. The second coup of August 1949 under Hinnawi was largely intended to put an end to the anti-Hashemite policy of Colonel Zaim, while the third coup of December 1949 under Shishakli was in the opposite direction to prevent the formation of a union with Iraq. During the ideological phase after 1955 the question of Syrian alignment with Egypt or with Iraq included also the choice between radicalism, Soviet friendship and hostility to the West and the Baghdad Pact on the one hand, and moderation in internal policy and in the attitude towards the foreign powers on the other. The policy of alignment with Egypt and all that went with it triumphed with military support, and the officers made the sixth coup of January 1958 that led to the unity of Syria with Egypt. The officers also broke that unity in the seventh coup of September 1961. Until the thirteenth coup of July 1963, most of the Syrian coups were dominated by the question of whether to restore or not to restore unity with Egypt and on what basis the restoration should take place. Socialism during this period became a factor in foreign policy and in the plans for the achievement of Arab unity because Nasserism made the adoption of the socialist system a prerequisite for membership in an Arab union on the basis that only "liberated" Arab states could become members, and the only "liberated" states were those who proclaimed socialism as their system and who chose the Soviet Union and the other "friendly nations" as their closest friends.

The Iraqi coup or revolution of July 1958 against the monarchy is an outstanding illustration of the preeminence of nationalist and ideological motives related to the orientation of foreign policy. Iraqi membership in the Baghdad Pact, the external campaign from Egypt and Syria against the Iraqi rulers and the feeling of the officers that the dynasty was isolating Iraq from the Arab nationalist movement were the basic causes for the coup. Three coups out of nine after the 1958 revolution had pro-Nasserist motives — the ninth coup of Colonel Shawaf in March 1959, and the fourteenth and fifteenth coups of Aref Abdul-Razzaq in September 1965 and June 1966 — and all three were abortive. The rebellion in the summer of 1958 in Lebanon was basically motivated by the controversy over the orientation of Lebanese foreign policy. In Jordan, all the riots, the conspiracies, and the abortive coup of April 1957 were the outcome of attempts to change the pro-western orientation of the government and to impose radical ideologies and the Nasserist system. The first coup of November 1958 in the Sudan was largely motivated by the fear of Egyptian infiltration although the officers' communiqué referred only to the "state of degeneration, chaos and instability." The abortive junior officers' coups of November 1959 and December 1966 and the seventh coup of May 1969 under Numairi were influenced by radical ideological considerations involving a change in the orientation of Sudanese foreign policy. The same applies to the fourth coup of September 1962 in Yemen under Sallal's leadership and to the coup of September 1969 in Libya.

In all these coups where external factors were more or less

preeminent, the coup makers were often encouraged, incited, financed and in a few cases reinforced by other Arab states. In the pre-ideological phase Iraq supported the second Syrian coup of Hinnawi against Zaim and the fifth coup of February 1954 against Shishakli, while the Saudi Arabian and the Egyptian governments gave their support to Zaim and Shishakli in their anti-Iraqi orientation. After 1955 Iraq attempted to change the pro-Egyptian orientation of Syrian policy and until 1957 it financed pro-Iraqi activities, but Saudi payments were more generous and Nasser's appeal was greater. The Iraqi monarchy consequently failed in Syria but was able to help Jordan maintain its regime. Saudi financial support for anti-Iraqi activity in Syria and for anti-Hashemite action in general ended in 1957 when King Saud became the ally of King Hussein against the Nasserist revolutionary inroads. Nasser's Egypt since then played the principal role of inciting revolts in Iraq and Jordan before and after the formation of the United Arab Republic. From its base in Syria and through Sarraj as its agent, Egypt sent money to its Jordanian agents and sometimes men to attempt the coup of April 1957, and to organize such conspiracies as the one that killed Premier Majali in August 1960. The revolution of July 1958 in Iraq was partly a product of Nasserist incitement and so was the abortive coup of Shawaf against Kassem in March 1959. The Egyptian duel with Kassem between 1959 and 1963 was one of the most notorious episodes of the age of military revolution in the Arab world. In Lebanon the rebellion of 1958 was encouraged and financed by Nasser and it was reinforced with recruits and arms sent across the border from Syria. The abortive coup of December 1961 was largely a reaction by certain Lebanese officers and civilians against the Egyptian influence under President Shehab. The Yemeni coup of September 1962 against Imam al-Badr was organized in Cairo and was followed by a civil war in which the republic was able to stand on its feet only through Egyptian support in men, arms, and funds. Saudi Arabia then had to defend itself against Nasserist conspiracies and had to stop the tide of revolution in Yemen by supporting the royalists until Egypt withdrew from Yemen after the war of June 1967.

The question of Palestine and the emergence of Israel have often been an indirect cause of military coups throughout the Arab world. As early as the first seven Iraqi coups of 1936-1941, the officers expressed their dissatisfaction with the British alliance partly because of British policy in Palestine. When the Grand Mufti of Palestine, Haj Amin al-Husseini, established himself in Baghdad in October 1939 he became the ally and the instigator of the influential colonels who mounted the three coups of 1941 on account of their hostility to Britain and its allies in the ruling dynasty and among the politicians. After the Palestine war of 1948 the frustrated officers in Syria resented the criticism of the politicians for their conduct of the war. At the same time they were tempted by the emergency powers under martial law that were given to them by the government to deal with the riots incited by the radical parties after the defeat, and their leader, Colonel Zaim, thus staged his first coup of March 1949. The officers also looked for a scapegoat for their defeat and put the blame on their superiors in the command and on their government as in the case of the young free officers who made the Egyptian coup of July 1952. During the ideological phase after 1955 the continued presence of the Israeli challenge and the consequent Arab purchase of arms on a large scale from the Soviet Union brought with them closer relations with the Communist world, more militancy among the Arab radicals, and more hostility to the West and to its Arab friends and allies. The Suez crisis of 1956 and the participation of Israel on the side of Britain in the war against Egypt made the position of the Iraqi dynasty and its cooperation with Britain untenable and led eventually to the coup of July 1958, while the diplomatic victory won by Nasser allowed him to expand his offensive against the Arab rulers who refused to follow his leadership. The Arab state of belligerency with Israel enhanced the position and importance of the officers and made of them the defenders and potential saviors of their respective countries, but it did not inspire them with the need for discipline and unity in order to play their genuine role of defenders and saviors. On the contrary, the arms they received were used against their own governments and even colleagues to make more coups and to incite rebellion in other Arab countries. The radical doctrinal parties and military strongmen tried to spread the idea that revolution and socialism should prevail as preparatory conditions for success in the struggle against Israel, and that the revolutionary Arab socialist countries were alone responsible for that struggle. These considerations have evidently motivated the leftist military coups of May 1969 in the Sudan and September 1969 in Libya in spite of the resounding failure of the revolutionary socialist regimes in the war of June 1967.

The motives of the dissident officers who carried out their coup d'état against the ruling military regimes were somewhat different from those that dictated their action against legitimate civilian rule. The dissident officers were often disappointed with either the excesses or the moderation of their military colleagues, and sometimes harbored grudges against them and acted out of personal jealousy. They denounced the tyranny of the military rulers and at times accused them of treason. The most commonly mentioned reason for military action against military rulers was the alleged deviation from the original goals of the coup or revolution. The deviation could mean the acquisition of personal power by the leader of the coup and the arrest or dismissal of his former supporters as a result of suspicion and fear of a new coup. It could also mean disagreement between the military factions about the implementation of certain programs of internal reform or foreign policy. The dissident officers usually spoke of the need for correcting the deviation and their coup was sometimes called a "corrective movement" as in the case of the fifteenth Syrian coup staged by the radical Baath under General Jedid against the national Baath rulers led by General Hafez in February 1966. The coup was often the outcome of a mere struggle for power between rival strongmen or military factions colored by

Conclusion: Results of Arab Revolution and Military Rule / 365

ideological and even sectarian differences as in the various quarrels and coups of Baath officers in Syria and Iraq. A major reason for quarrels among the military after their success in staging a coup is that the coup makers and their civilian partners often consisted of disparate elements that were united only by the desire for overthrowing the former regime but whose goals differed as in the case of the authors of the Iraqi coup of July 1958 against the monarchy and of the eleventh Syrian coup of March 8, 1963. The coups in these cases were carried out without sufficient agreement on the future structure of power and on the exact orientation of foreign policy. The result was that the associate leader of the Iraqi coup, Colonel Aref, ended in jail and the author of the Syrian coup, Colonel Hariri, ended in exile a few months after their coups. The situation was complicated in these two cases by the ambitions of participating leaders and parties, by the unpredictability of the officers and their shifting alliances, and by external pressures. Naturally major unexpected developments sometimes could disrupt the cooperation between military leaders and turn a man like Marshal Amer against his friend of thirty years, President Nasser, to the extent of preparing a coup in August 1967 against him as a countereffect of the defeat in the June war.

In almost all the military coups d'état, whether they were directed against the legitimate civilian government or against military rulers, there was a certain degree of encouragement and cooperation on the part of civilian politicians and parties. The free officers' coup of July 1952 in Egypt was perhaps unique in the absence of that kind of cooperation. The Egyptian civilians later on plotted, conspired and demonstrated against the revolutionary regime but the political parties that were destroyed in 1953-1954 were never able to regain power. In the other Arab countries the military rulers did not deal so categorically with politicians and parties and these as a result continued to come back to the political stage. In Yemen from the first coup against Imam Yahya in 1948 until the seventh coup in August 1968 political personalities and groups were involved. In Iraq the first coup of October 1936 was made in cooperation with the Ahali group, and in July 1958 the various opposition parties cooperated. Among the nine Iraqi coups staged after the fall of the monarchy in 1958, three were made by military and civilian Nasserists, one was attempted by Communists in early July 1963, and five involved the Baathists and were staged either by them or against them or within their own ranks. In Syria the Arab socialist leader Akram Hourani gave his support to the leaders of the first six coups and quarrelled with them all. The People's Party was involved in five coups three of which were carried out against the regimes of Zaim, Shishakli and Nasser's UAR, and two were directed mainly against the party by Shishakli. The Baath party in Syria was involved in four successful coups against military and civilian rulers between February 1954 and July 8, 1963; one coup was later directed against the Baath rulers by Nasserists on July 18, 1963, and four other coups — the fourteenth to the seventeenth between December 1965 and March 1969 — were carried out by Baath civilian and military factions against each other. In Jordan the attempted coup of April 1957 was encouraged by opposition parties allied to the military members of the conspiracy. In Lebanon, the first and fourth coups of July 1949 and December 1961 were attempted by a political party with paramilitary forces, and the rebellion of 1958 was entirely the work of local civilian groups with external financial and military support.

The motives of the civilians were largely similar to those of the officers whom they encouraged or supported except where the army acted in defense of its particular interests or where the coup assumed the character of a personal struggle for power. The politicized officers were generally influenced by the same ideologies and doctrines that prevailed among the civilians particularly in the second phase after 1955, and the struggle for power among military factions often reflected the factionalism that existed in political circles. The army ranks, however, included officers and men who wanted, but were not always allowed, to remain neutral and politically inactive. In one significant case, that of the fifth Syrian coup of February 1954 against Shishakli, all three military leaders of the coup represented the interests of three separate civilian groups that desired Shishakli's fall: the Druze Colonel Amin Abu-Assaf represented the Druze hostility to Shishakli; Lt. Col. Faisal Atassi represented the People's Party in which the powerful Atassis of Homs held influence; and Captain Mustafa Hamdun, the disciple of Akram Hourani, acted in favor of his radical mentor and his group. Officers as well as political leaders, moreover, often confused their personal and their national motives and grievances and attempted to carry out coups under the influence of their whims and ambitions as in the case of Colonel Nahlawi and his clique who resented the restoration of power to the political leaders after the secession of Syria from the UAR in 1961 and mounted the coup of March 1962. He later returned with his fellow officers from diplomatic exile in Europe and attempted to mount a coup on January 13, 1963 because the Qudsi-Azem regime refused their reinstatement in the army, but they were careful to invoke the need for a referendum on the question of union with Egypt which they had helped destroy in the coup of September 1961.

In all these cases of military coups and revolutions one can always wonder if they were really necessary and inevitable, and if the situation that led to them was really so critical in each case as to warrant the imposed change. The answers will always differ depending on the evaluation of the seriousness of the situation and on the ideas and convictions of those who do the evaluation. One can argue that the military authors of the coups, in their attempt to justify and legalize their action, have given a false or at least an exaggerated picture of the conditions that preceded the coup and that their intervention was therefore unwarranted and far from inevitable. The military coups in effect were neither the result of a national emergency or foreign danger in any of the countries under consideration, nor the product of a serious internal crisis in government or a breakdown of authority.

There was neither a threat to the recently acquired independence or a danger of dismemberment of the country, nor was there internal chaos. Where there was a breakdown of authority, as in Lebanon after the proclamation of the general strike against President Khouri's regime in September 1952 or during the rebellion of 1958, the army did not take advantage of the situation to usurp power and the parliamentary regime survived. There were demonstrations in Syria in December 1948 incited by the Baathists and other radicals following the defeat in Palestine and also against the proposed Tapline agreement, but the government was able to restore order after it did what governments usually do under similar conditions, namely, ask the armed forces to help. It naturally did not expect Colonel Zaim to make a coup after he had restored order by means of the authority that martial law gave him. Zaim certainly did not carry out his coup of March 1949 because of his concern about Palestine. Moreover, one can hardly establish the responsibility of the Quwatli regime in Syria and even that of King Farouk's government in Egypt for the failure in Palestine in 1948 when the military regimes themselves with all their equipment, their nationalist revolutionary indoctrination and their preparations over thirteen years suffered a far more disastrous defeat in 1967. Nor can one justify a coup and a change in government as a result of the defeat in 1948 when the military regimes that suffered, and were directly responsible for, a much greater defeat in 1967 have remained standing.

It is true that there were conservative Imams in Yemen and there was a corrupt king in Egypt, but the king of Iraq and his aides, and Presidents Quwatli, Atassi, and Qudsi of Syria and their aides were neither corrupt nor incompetent nor reactionary rulers. In Yemen, the Imam against whom the coup was mounted in September 1962 only one week after his father's death was a modernist, and many leaders who later joined the republican regime had agreed to his program of reform, but he was not given a chance. In Egypt the king was not the entire government and in the Nile Valley as well as the Fertile Crescent countries there were liberal leaders who tolerated opposition and criticism with a relatively free press, an independent judiciary and a rule of law, and there was social, economic and cultural progress.

The officers in reality acted at times out of rashness and false personal pride, and at other times they were used by the local politicians as well as by external forces to operate a change in political orientation. The radicals were more successful than the moderate politicians in infiltrating and using the officers. The Arab radicals were moved by a mixture of selfish opportunism and impatience to reach power and by ideological convictions on the need for radical change. Their nationalistic revolutionary motives included an arrogant contempt and envy of the ruling elite and a determination to break its power by subverting the economic and social order. Their program of subversion and change, however, could not be accomplished by due democratic process because the people or the voters did not respond to their ideologies and never gave their candidates a majority in the elections, not because the rulers made it difficult for them to be elected. They consequently made their contacts with the officers and accelerated their infiltration taking advantage of the freedoms accorded by democratic constitutional rule. The succession of coups d'état became really inevitable once the officers were in power because personal and doctrinal differences plagued their rule and divided them in the same way as their civilian supporters into conflicting factions. The Palestine problem continued to give them a pretext to stay in power although some of their most serious blunders and the resulting damage they did to their countries were related to their handling of the Palestinian problem.

III. Patterns of Military Coups d'état

In the preparation and execution of the Arab military coups certain general patterns can be recognized along with some differences in the details. The first set of patterns bears on the preparation and planning of the coup. The period of preparation varied between a few months and several years but it was usually longer and the preparation was more elaborate when the coup was directed against a well established civilian regime, and it was shorter when the officers decided to overthrow a military ruler. Sometimes secret societies such as those of the Egyptian or Iraqi "free officers" were formed and included those who were determined to force a change in government and institutions. Other organizations, particularly among the civilians, were not secret as in the case of the "free Yemeni society". The opposition parties themselves such as the National Democratic and the Independence parties in Iraq before 1958, the Baath party after 1955 in Syria, Iraq and Jordan, and the Communist party in various countries, were ready to subvert officers and civilian leaders in as much as the coup was a seizure of power primarily through the subversion of the military and civilian state apparatus. Secret and non-secret organizations had to study the motivations of officers and civilians as they recruited them. They also watched the popular reactions to public problems, led a campaign of criticism against government policies, and took advantage of anything that could discredit the rulers and weaken the people's confidence in them especially after defeat or difficulties in war or as a result of instability under the parliamentary regime. This is how the frequent cabinet changes in Egypt, the scandal of the defective weapons, and the guerilla war in the Canal Zone followed by the riots of "Black Saturday" in January 1952 helped the "free officers" plans by neutralizing the people and the parties.

The planning for the coup was not always as long and elaborate as in the case of the Egyptian coup of July 1952, nor was it accompanied by the formation of a society of free officers although the designation of "free officers" was applied after 1955 to all those who were critical of, or conspired against their governments without necessarily belonging to a formal organization. In most of the coups, particularly in

Syria, the planning consisted of contacts between concerned officers and sometimes between them and certain political personalities or parties a few months before the coup although in certain cases the idea of forcing a change developed earlier. Subversion of officers by the Baath party in Syria, for example, began while they were still cadets at the military school, and even their admission to that school was at times influenced by the intervention of the Baath or of Akram Hourani. It has even been reported that the Libyan coup d'état of September 1, 1969 was made by officers who had joined the army with the sole purpose of mounting a coup against the monarchy. The chairman of the Council of Revolutionary Command in Libya, the twenty-seven year old Colonel Muammar Qadhafi, was first a student of history and graduated from the Libyan University, but he soon entered the military college in 1963 in order to prepare for and participate in a military coup.[3] He graduated in 1965 and four years later he became the strongman and prime minister after the coup that destroyed the monarchy.

The choice of a leader was an important part of the planning for the coup. The leader was often the highest in rank among those who engaged in preparing the coup as Colonel Zaim in Syria, and Generals Kassem and Abboud in Iraq and the Sudan. In some cases the leader was the chief of staff or commander in chief of the army. Where the conspiring officers were young and of lower rank they usually chose a front man of higher rank who was well-known and more mature such as General Naguib in Egypt in July 1952 and Colonel Aref in Iraq in the Baathist coup of February 1963, but the choice ended after the success of the coup in disagreement and serious trouble between the front man and the younger officers. The leader was chosen at times by the numerous groups preparing for the coup because he was an independent opponent of the ruling regime and, as in the case of Colonel Hariri in the Syrian coup of March 1963, had many friends, who were former colleagues and classmates at the military academy, in key military positions. Colonel Hariri was thus able to obtain the cooperation of the directors of military intelligence and military police and the commanders of posts around Damascus and he naturally gave them promises of promotion in rank and position. The coup sometimes had no acknowledged leader and the communiqués about the coup were signed by an anonymous "supreme Arab revolutionary command of the armed forces", as in the Syrian coup of September 1961 against the UAR or by a "revolution command council" as in several others. The anonymity of the members of the council and the avoidance of naming any one of them as leader was not only a protective measure in case of failure but also a precaution against the ambition and claims of the person who would have been called the leader of the coup.

The leaders of the coup had to make sure that the recruited officers included commanders of combat troops and not only staff officers. The tank regiment and its commanding officers were of particular importance and had to be won over. The dismissal or transfer of the officers of the armoured or tank regiments by the ruling regime meant that a coup was expected, but the transfers often came too late and were not obeyed and then the coup followed. The officers who took active part in the coup or allowed it to take place did so because of ideological convictions or as a result of bribery in the form of expected promotions or cash payments. Previously retired or dismissed officers often participated in the coups, particularly in those carried out by the Baath party in Syria and Iraq where they were ordered by the coup leaders to join their former units as soon as the action began. Funds were often provided by foreign instigators of the coup through the agents of some great power or certain Arab countries to insure a desired orientation in foreign policy or a favorable agreement on an important issue. Sometimes it was difficult to ascertain who paid or for whose account the coup was made. The coup of Hinnawi in 1949 and the anti-Shishakli coup of 1954 in Syria were presumably supported by Iraq, those of July 1958 and March 1959 in Iraq were provoked or financed by the UAR, the Egyptian coup of July 1952 was supposedly encouraged by the United States, and that of September 1961 in Syria against the UAR was said to have been financed by Saudi Arabia. The coup leaders had to secure at least the neutrality of external powers but in some cases they needed their financial support. Beirut bankers claimed that the movement of money on the free money market of their city was an indication of what was about to happen. When a country's currency was in strong demand for no apparent reason, the Lebanese experts in Beirut concluded that someone was buying it up to send it back home in order to finance a coup. This is what happened just before the Iraqi coup of 1958. At the same time money flowed into Lebanon whenever the wealthy people in a particular Arab country were worried by an impending radical coup, and it so happened that the "flight" money arrived on the Beirut market as agents started buying the same currency to finance a coup. The two operations canceled each other out and the rate of exchange thus remained steady.[4]

The ruling regime normally found it difficult to predict a coup or to know the timing of a vaguely expected coup, but it usually took certain measures in order to weaken the position of the suspected leaders. The suspects reacted immediately by deciding the date of their coup. The timing was thus determined by the officers' fear of being arrested if they failed to strike after their identity had been discovered. This is how the Egyptian "free officers" decided to act on the night of 22-23 July 1952 when they knew that a cabinet was formed on July 20 in which the king's brother-in-law was defense minister and that he was planning to deal with them. In Syria, the General Command issued orders on February 22, 1963 for the transfer of Colonel Hariri from his post on the southern front to that of military attaché in Baghdad because he was suspected of preparing a coup and was expected to march on Damascus on the preceding day according to the rumors. His transfer and that of other officers were postponed as a result of various pressures and on March 8 he carried out his coup.

Three years later, on February 21, 1966 the Bitar cabinet in agreement with the Baath national command decided after a month of discussions and hesitation to transfer some of the dangerous Baath officers who were allied to General Jedid against the ruling Baath strongman General Hafez. The Damascenes expected a coup that same night by Jedid's forces and began buying food in preparation for the curfew that ordinarily accompanies a coup. On February 23 the forces of Jedid struck and ended the Hafez regime. On the other hand, the ruling regime was at times powerful enough to avert a coup by initiating action against a suspected leader. This is how the Baath cabinet under Bitar dismissed or transferred twenty-seven officers who were known to be supporters of Hariri on June 20, 1963. Hariri was then defense minister in that same cabinet and chief of staff and he refused to agree to the transfers. In early July he was expected to carry out a coup against the ruling Baath but he evidently found his force inadequate and he was deported to France on July 8, 1963.

In addition to this first set of patterns related to the preparation and planning of the coup, a second set bears on the execution of the coup. The officers generally carried out their coups in the capital with the help of units brought from camps that were situated at a relatively short distance from the scene of action. This was important in countries that had a centralized system of government. Only in very few cases the coups began outside the capital as in the successful Syrian coup of February 1954 against Shishakli that began in Aleppo and ended in Damascus, the abortive Nasserist coup of April 1, 1962 in Aleppo, and the two abortive Iraqi coups of Shawaf in March 1959, and of Abdul Razzaq in June 1966. The first began and ended in Mosul, and the second began in Mosul and ended in failure in Baghdad.

The officers sometimes forced a change in government by a mere threat of military action and did not have to move forces to the capital. This was particularly true of the five Iraqi coups between December 1938 and April 1941 where the plotting officers asked the prime minister to resign or sent an influential civilian to give the regent the name of their nominee for the post of prime minister. The officers' action was naturally accompanied by certain preparations in the military camps near Baghdad. The sixteenth Iraqi coup of July 17, 1968 was made by a simple telephone call at 3 a.m. to President Aref asking him not to resist and by firing some mortar shells in the direction of the Palace to reinforce the demand. The leader of a coup did not have to use force when he was confident of his strength and was already sharing power with the civilian government as in the case of the fourth Syrian coup — the second by Shishakli — on November 29, 1951 against the parliamentary regime.

The forces that participated in the coups varied in number between a few hundred and a few thousand troops. They were usually supported by artillery and tank units. It was only in Iraq, where the coups were particularly violent in the second ideological phase, that aircraft was used. The very first Iraqi coup of October 1936 used the royal air force to drop proclamations over Baghdad, and later to drop a few bombs as a warning that the time limit of the ultimatum for the change of cabinet had expired. After 1958 the air force was used freely either against an attempted coup or by the leaders of a coup. Kassem was the first to use aircraft on a relatively large scale to destroy Shawaf and his attempted Mosul coup in March 1959. The Baath officers later sent their planes to destroy the Kassem regime in the coup of February 8, 1963, and President Aref used the air force in destroying the Baath and their national guard in the coup of November 18, 1963. Even in badly prepared attempts of an adventurous nature, planes were used to raid the presidential palace as in the abortive coups of Wandawi against the moderate Baath on November 13, 1963, and of Abdul-Razzaq against the second Aref on June 30, 1966.

The military leaders began their operations in most cases between midnight and daybreak when the streets were empty and the rulers were unprepared for the surprise action. This is how most of the successful coups against the established civilian governments were carried out after a relatively long preparation and many of them were later called revolutions. The best known were the July 23, 1952 and the July 14, 1958 revolutions in Egypt and Iraq against the monarchy, the September 28, 1961 revolution in Syria against the UAR, and the September 26, 1962 revolution in Yemen against the Imamate. Certain successful coups were also made by the military opposition against military rulers before dawn as in the case of the Hinnawi coup of August 1949, the anti-Shishakli coup of February 1954, and the radical Baathist coup of February 1966 in Syria, as well as the Aref anti-Baath coup of November 1963 and the anti-Aref coup of 17 July, 1968 in Iraq. Most of the military versus military coups in Iraq, however, were mounted during the day, and they were badly prepared and ended in failure after a few hours. Such were the Shawaf coup in March 1959 and the two Abdul Razzaq coups in September 1965 and June 1966. Similarly the Nasserist coup of July 18, 1963 and the Hatum coup of September 8, 1966 in Syria were attempted against the military rulers in broad daylight and ended in failure. The only successful Iraqi coup directed by the military forces against a military regime in the daytime was that of February 8, 1963 against Kassem and it was the result of more careful preparation.

In the execution of their coup, the military leaders had to move fast once their forces were in the capital and to accomplish simultaneously several objectives that included first, the occupation of the radio station, other important centers of communication, the army headquarters, the presidential or royal palace and other government buildings; second, the arrest of the head of state, his cabinet and the leading military and civilian supporters of the regime; third, closing the border and the airport and cutting off communications with the outside world; and fourth, broadcasting a proclamation on the purpose of the coup reassuring the people in most cases that the officers were acting in the people's interest and would eventually return to their barracks, and warning the citizens against participation in any hostile demonstrations.⁵ In other proclamations or military orders, the leaders of the coup sometimes announced the imposition of martial law and of a curfew, suspended the publishing of newspapers and dissolved political parties, although this last measure was not taken in the first phase (before 1955) except several months after the coup. As a part of the ritual on the first day of the coup, the text of telegrams of support received from the various commanders outside the capital was read over the radio. The intention was to impress the people with the degree of military acceptance of the coup and to decide the wavering commanders to rally to it.

The military leaders were generally reluctant to identify themselves in their initial broadcasts with any particular party, but in the second or ideological phase, they sometimes betrayed their affiliations in the language and slogans used in the communiqués. The proclamations that announced the coup were usually signed by the leader or front man such as Bakr Sidqi in Iraq, Zaim and Hinnawi in Syria, Naguib in Egypt, and Abboud in the Sudan. But in the second phase the leaders avoided in most cases disclosing their identity and used the collective name of the revolutionary council or the supreme military council of which they were members. The officers never appealed to the people to join them in the operations of the coup against the ruling regime except in the two Iraqi coups of July 14, 1958 against the monarchy and February 8, 1963 against Kassem. In the first, Colonel Aref told the people over the radio to join the attack against the Rahab Palace where the royal family lived, and in the second the same Aref and the Baath leaders with whom he cooperated asked the people to "come to the streets to see that the criminal deception had been killed along with his tyrannical supporters." But when the leaders of the coup saw that the mob was cheering Kassem instead of attacking him they imposed a curfew. After their success in the coup or following their victory over an attempted coup, the officers at times were unable to prevent their supporters from taking the law into their own hands and disposing of their opponents. This is how mob action followed the two Iraqi coups of July 1958 and February 1963, as well as the attempted Shawaf coup of March 1959.

The twenty Arab coups in the pre-ideological phase until 1955 were generally described as bloodless coups. They were mostly made against civilian regimes and rarely encountered any resistance. They involved, however, the death of a few military guards in public establishments or the assassination of one or more personalities of the overthrown regime. This is how Jafar Pasha al-Askari was killed in the first Iraqi coup of 1936 and Bakr Sidqi and his air force commander were killed in the second Iraqi coup of August 1937. In Syria the leader of the first coup, Husni al-Zaim, and his prime minister were executed in the second coup of August 1949, and in Lebanon the leader of the Syrian Social National Party was executed a few days after his abortive coup of early July 1949. In Yemen, Imam Yahya and some members of his family were killed in the first coup of February 1949, and several persons were victims of the attempted coup against Imam Ahmad in April 1955. More persons, however, lost their lives following the ultimate failure of the two attempts than during the execution of the coups. In the second or ideological phase after 1955 thirteen out of thirty-nine coups were accompanied by violence — four in Iraq, three in Syria, two in Lebanon, and one in each of Jordan, the Sudan, Libya and Yemen. Among the thirteen cases, one was a rebellion that took the aspect of a civil war in Lebanon in 1958, another was a popular revolution against the Abboud military regime in the Sudan in 1964, and one ushered in a civil war in Yemen in 1962. The rebellion and civil war in Lebanon and Yemen were extended and violent particularly on account of external causes and involvements. Of the remaining ten cases, six coups d'état were carried out by the military against military rulers in Iraq and Syria, and four were directed against civilian regimes. The bloodiest and those that left the greatest number of casualties were the six in which the military fought among themselves — the Shawaf coup of March 1959, the anti-Kassem coup of

February 1963, and the Aref anti-Baath coup of November 1963 in Iraq, and the two Nasserist coups of April 1962 and July 1963, as well as the Baath versus Baath coup of February 1966 in Syria. The four violent coups against civilian rulers were the Iraqi coup of July 1958, the abortive Abu Nawar coup against King Hussein in Jordan in April 1957, the SSNP coup in Lebanon against the Shehab regime in December 1961 that ended in failure, and the coup against the monarchy in Libya in September 1969.

The military regimes, in sharp contrast with civilian ones, neither surrendered easily when a coup was attempted against them, nor did they forgive easily those who made the attempt after its failure. This is why the anti-Kassem coup of February 1963 in Iraq and the anti-Hafez coup of February 1966 in Syria were so violent. This is also why Kassem of Iraq dealt so severely with the participants in the abortive Shawaf coup and ordered at least thirty-four persons, mostly officers, to be shot in three groups between March and September 1959 after their trial in the People's Court. General Hafez in Syria acted similarly after the failure of the Nasserist attempt of July 18, 1963 and sent twenty-seven military and civilians to the firing squad in the following three days. Until then those Syrian officers or cooperating civilians who attempted and failed in a coup were either pardoned — and sometimes sent to diplomatic posts — as in the case of Nahlawi and his group, or were tried and sentenced to death, but the sentence was never executed. This is why the action of Hafez and of the Baath rulers generally was described by foreign correspondents as one of "un-Syrian harshness".

IV. Characteristics of Military Rule
A. The Nature of Political Change

In spite of the officers' claim, expressed in their communiqués, that they had no designs of their own and that they intended to establish a "sound democracy" within the framework of constitutional government and elected assemblies, they ended sooner or later by imposing their own rule after introducing the necessary changes in the government structure and in the entire political order. They almost always continued to hold power until they were ousted by force. The first characteristic of military rule therefore bears on the processes by which the officers destroyed the old political order with its parliamentary system and its ruling elite and substituted a system of their own creation to consolidate their own rule. There was a time when the military coup consisted of replacing a cabinet by another while the system of rule remained intact as in the third to seventh coups in Iraq between December 1938 and April 1941. In four rare cases the officers even went into action to put an end to a military regime and restore constitutional rule.[6] In most other cases they proceeded to suspend the constitution, dissolve parliament, ban political parties and proclaim a new system of government under a provisional constitution. The trend was to replace the monarchy by a republic as in Egypt, Iraq, Libya, and Yemen, and to establish a one party organization to provide mass support for the new regime. The authors of the coup sometimes ruled directly as Zaim, Kassem and the Baath officers did, and at times indirectly through a civilian parliamentary facade as in Syria after the first Shishakli coup in December 1949. The change of the form of government was in certain cases gradual as in Egypt between 1952 and 1953, and in others it was announced suddenly on the first day of the coup as in Iraq in 1958 and Yemen in 1962. The same military leader sometimes moved from indirect to direct rule as Shishakli did in early December 1951, or from a transitional military period during which the new government institutions were created to a sort of civilianized pseudo-constitutional period as in Egypt in 1956. In certain cases the transitional period was extended continuously and a permanent constitution and elections were repeatedly promised by the military ruler but they never materialized as under the Aref brothers in Iraq between November 1963 and July 1968.

Under the direct rule of the military during the transitional period, the legislative and decision-making powers were exercised by a supreme military council or a revolution command council consisting entirely of officers, but the Baath regimes in Syria and Iraq included civilians in the national revolutionary council. The cabinet was the executive arm of the military rulers and its prime minister as well as many of its members were high ranking officers. Egyptian cabinets until 1967 included an average of forty to fifty per cent officers or former officers. In Iraq only one civilian prime minister, Abdul Rahman Bazzaz, has been appointed since the coup of 1958.

In the first phase until 1955 the change in government was usually gradual and, with the exception of Egypt, it did not mean the complete transformation of the old system and the total uprooting of the old ruling elite. The officers tried to act within the legal constitutional practice and found some devious ways to legalize their action. After the fifth coup of January 21, 1941 in Iraq, Gailani could not maintain himself as prime minister because of the opposition of the lower house of parliament. The officers tried to obtain the regent's approval to dissolve the house but when they could not, due to his absence from the capital, Gailani resigned on January 31. In the seventh coup of April 1, 1941 the Iraqi officers again were determined to appoint Gailani prime minister after they had obtained the resignation of Hashimi, but as the regent who usually issues the official letter of appointment had escaped they formed a government of national defense under Gailani and convoked the lower house by a call of its second vice president. The regent Abdul Ilah was then deposed and the new regent who took his place issued decrees accepting Hashimi's resignation and appointing Gailani prime minister. In Syria, Colonel Shishakli allowed the entire parliamentary structure to function after his coup of December 1949. He certainly weakened it by his constant pressures and interventions but he could not prevent the members of parliament from directing their criticisms and sarcasm against him. He promoted himself to no more than brigadier general in April

1950 and took no post except that of chief of staff. When he dissolved parliament in early December 1951 and began to rule directly after his second coup, he evidently profited from the experience of Colonel Zaim and did not promote himself immediately to the presidency. He waited until July 1953 and then submitted a new constitution of the presidential type as well as his own candidacy for the presidency of the republic to a popular referendum and became the president of Syria. Parties were abolished in April 1952 but when elections to a new parliament took place three months after the vote on the constitution, the elected members did not represent exclusively the Arab liberation movement that he had launched in August 1952. In Egypt, the free officers were less patient in their drive to seize power and were more radical in their determination to change the entire political order. They remained in the background for only forty-five days during the civilian cabinet of Ahmad Maher. Their front man General Naguib then became prime minister and they began their fight against the powerful Wafd and issued the agrarian reform law to undermine the power of the ruling elite. Parties were dissolved six months after the coup of July 1952 and the monarchy lasted eleven months and was abolished in June 1953.

The second phase after 1955 saw more sudden and radical changes whenever coups d'état took place. The officers were not as patient or modest in promoting themselves to higher rank or to positions of power. Republics in Iraq and Yemen were proclaimed in the first communiqué about the coup. The former rulers under the monarchy were brutally disposed of and the authors of the coups were proud of their brutal action. Political leaders of the old regimes were tried in special tribunals in order to discredit the regime that they represented and to justify the officers' revolutionary changes. Egypt had set the example for these trials, in 1953, but no political leaders were tried elsewhere in the first phase. Except for Kassem of Iraq who remained prime minister until his fall and never took the title of president, most other military leaders of coups were appointed presidents immediately or a few months after their coups as in the cases of General Abboud in the Sudan in 1958, Colonel Aref in Iraq in 1963, and General Hafez in Syria who became chief of state through his presidency of the national revolutionary council. Nasser became deputy prime minister eleven months after the coup of 1952, and in 1956 he became president and since then his term has been always renewed. Most of the colonels who participated in the coups became major generals overnight, and whereas Colonel Zaim was ridiculed in 1949 for taking the rank of field marshal, several others since then — such as Aref of Iraq in 1963, Sallal of Yemen in 1962 and Amer of Egypt much earlier — also became field marshals without encountering the same criticism by their colleagues and people.

The military leaders have experimented in the second phase with various kinds of provisional constitutions and governments, and the constitutions were invariably made by them, not by elected constituent assemblies. The favorite method for obtaining the approval of the constitution and the election of the sole military candidate to the presidency has been the popular referendum. The kind of democracy established by the various provisional constitutions was a totalitarian democracy in which a single party organization was established and controlled by the military regime and the candidates to the legislative assembly had to be acceptable to the military rulers.

In order to consolidate their rule and destroy completely the power of the old ruling class, the ruling officers have not only abolished political parties and kept only their exclusive one-party organization, but they have also denied the members of those parties and of the old ruling class the right to hold public office and confiscated their property. They have restricted the freedoms of press and assembly and depended on elaborate spying and intelligence networks to watch and control the people's activities. They resorted to arbitrary arrest and held political trials. Some regimes as those of Kassem of Iraq and the Baath in Syria and Iraq have established popular resistance forces or a national guard for their own protection.

They have also spread their revolutionary ideology in society through the nationalized or state controlled press, radio and television and through indoctrination in schools and in the armed forces. They organized frequent mass rallies and invented slogans for the benefit of the military regime and in some cases created a cult of the military ruler, while the officers were given various privileges and promotions in order to keep them contented.

B. Reform and the Socialist System

The second important characteristic of military rule in the Arab countries was radical economic and social reform that reached its climax in the imposition of the socialist system by force. The authors of the coups generally sought to legitimize their seizure of power by introducing reform measures which in their view served the interests of the people and strengthened the country. Until 1955 the reforms were moderate and tended to increase efficiency and prosperity by reorganizing the administrative, legal and economic services, and concentrating on public works in irrigation, communications, urbanism, and on education and the settlement of nomads. Progress in all these aspects had already been achieved under the legitimate civilian regimes in Egypt, Syria and Iraq and the military rulers were only more vigorous in extending that progress. After 1955 the ruling officers in Egypt began to mention the establishment of the "democratic, socialist, cooperative society" and to emphasize the notions of social justice and of a classless society. They had already imposed the agrarian reform in September 1952 and they introduced it into Syria in the fall of 1958 following the merger of the two countries. They also undertook the building of the Aswan dam and the expansion of the cultivated areas in Egypt by reclamation and irrigation works. Military rulers in the other Arab countries followed the Egyptian example in agrarian reform but were more cautious in adopting the socialist system which Egypt imposed through the socialist laws of July 1961 and the "national charter" of May 1962. Private enterprise in industry and foreign trade was destroyed and the Marxian arguments against capitalism and in favor of the inevitable social revolution were reproduced in the official Egyptian writings. When the Baath party came to power through military action in Iraq and Syria it decided to implement the socialist principles of its constitution but its leaders disagreed about the extent of that implementation and the disagreement was partly responsible for the end of Baath rule in Iraq in November 1963. The Syrian Baath rulers hesitated in their adoption of the socialist system and introduced the socialist measures gradually between 1963 and early 1965 in spite of the repeated assurances they gave to the important middle class industrialists and businessmen after every nationalization decree that it would be the last one. In Iraq Aref issued his socialist decrees in mid July 1964 although a few days earlier he and his prime minister had denied any intention to nationalize industries and businesses.

The socialist system and the agrarian reform were not adopted for the sole purpose of enhancing the economic development of the countries under military rule or for improving the condition of the masses. Their adoption assumed the aspect of a class struggle of the lower middle class officers and their supporters against the businessmen, landlords and the wealthy bourgeois class in general in order to break its political power and its social prestige. The destruction of the social-economic order went hand in hand with that of the political order because the officers, particularly in Egypt, were afraid that the survival of a prosperous middle class might be a threat to their power. They therefore portrayed the members of the well to do class and the former ruling elite as reactionaries and allies of imperialism in order to better destroy them and consolidate the military dictatorship. In Syria the Baath rulers were encouraged primarily by the Egyptian example and sought to gain Nasser's favor or to prove that they were no less revolutionary and radical than the rulers in Egypt.

Radical Baathists also used their radicalism as a weapon against their moderate opponents within the party, and in some cases sectarian considerations played their role because the influential Alawi officers representing the underprivileged rural elements wanted to ruin the Muslim Sunni urban elements. In Iraq, Aref's adoption of socialism was without conviction but it was a result of the agreement about a unified political and military command between Egypt and Iraq in May 1964, and a friendly act that expressed Aref's gratitude for Nasser's support. External and internal political considerations and frivolous disputes for power thus decided the adoption of the socialist system with its nationalizations, accusations, and slogans that led sometimes to demonstrations and riots and to disastrous results for the economy of the countries under military rule.

C. Arab Nationalism and Arab Division

The third characteristic of military rule was its expressed interest in Arabism and Arab unity and in restoring Arab rights in Palestine. In most of the military coups d'état , the Arab officers sought to justify their action by claiming that the rulers of the old regime were either allies or agents of Western imperialism and were consequently unwilling or unqualified to meet the Israeli challenge. Relations between the military rulers of the pre-ideological phase and the Western powers were generally friendly or at least correct, and the same was true of their relations with Arab states allied to the West. Under the influence of Nasser's neutralism and his hostility to the Baghdad Pact, the Egyptian military regime opened its offensive against the West and the Arab friends of the West after 1955. With the rise in Nasser's prestige after the Czech arms deal and the nationalization of the Suez Canal Company, the Arab nationalists in such countries as Iraq, Jordan, Lebanon and Yemen rallied to him against their own governments, and the result was a new wave of revolutions and coups d'état and an increase in the number of military regimes. Nasser's Egypt, with the blessing of the Soviet Union, thus assumed the role of "liberator" of the Arab people from their "reactionary" pro-Western rulers and attempted to extend its social-economic revolution to the various Arab countries. It was aided by such doctrinal Arab nationalist and socialist parties as the Baath party in Syria, Iraq and Jordan, and also by the Communist party. The new criterion that was supposed to distinguish a genuine "liberated" Arab nationalist state — that could be also a candidate for membership in an Arab federation — from a "non-liberated" state was whether or not it accepted the Nasserist system with its revolutionary socialism, its close friendship with the Soviet Bloc, its offensive against Western interests and its hostility to democratic parliamentary rule.

The Arab world was thus divided, under the influence of radical military rule into hostile camps, and the emphasis of the radical military rulers and their civilian supporters shifted from the realization of the goals of Arab nationalism and unity to the spreading of socialism and revolution and the maintenance of the military rulers in power. The arms that were bought from the Soviet Union by the revolutionary governments were often used against other Arab governments or against dissident factions within the same Arab revolutionary state. The military rulers thus failed to achieve Arab unity or even cooperation and were unable to meet the Israeli challenge. Their problem was that they spent too much time on political and doctrinal disputes and on trying to remain in power at any price, and did not appreciate the need for internal concord and for concentrating their efforts on the improvement of their military institution in order to serve and defend Arab national interests.

D. Instability and Military Anarchy

The fourth characteristic of military rule was its lack of

stability manifested in the rapid succession of coups and conspiracies, changes in government structure and cabinets, and the frequent purges of army officers and civilian officials. The instability had its damaging influence on the various aspects of the people's life and activities, and on the military strength of the countries concerned. In Syria, for example, seventeen coups were made or attempted and many other plots and conspiracies were uncovered in the space of twenty years from 1949 to 1969. In seventeen years of direct or indirect military rule — from March 1949 to October 1966 — Syria had forty-three cabinets and ten heads of state, whereas in the preceding seventeen years between the implementation of the republican constitution in 1932 and the first military coup of 1949 it had twenty-three cabinets and four heads of state. The military rulers, contrary to what several writers have claimed, have not been a force for stability in the Arab world. Military coups in one country generated a chain of coups and the contagion spread to other areas. In spite of the privileges given to the officers by the military rulers in housing, exemptions and reduced prices, their loyalty to the military regime was not always secured. They were tempted to revolt either because of personal ambition and jealousy or under the influence of rival radical doctrines and various kinds of affiliations. Sometimes they were tempted by generous cash payments from external sources or by all these factors combined. Those who supported a military leader in a coup sometimes turned against him shortly after his success to support another leader. In March 1949 Major Adib Shishakli helped Colonel Zaim in the first Syrian coup but he was retired on August 6, 1949. When Hinnawi removed Zaim, he reinstated Shishakli as commander of the First Brigade, but on December 19, 1949 Shishakli made his own coup and arrested Hinnawi. In February 1966 Captain Hatum cooperated with General Jedid against their fellow Baathist colleague General Hafez in a most violent coup. In the following September Hatum attempted a coup against Jedid and then fled to Jordan when the attempt failed. In Egypt arrests of officers for plotting

Conclusion: Results of Arab Revolution and Military Rule / 389

against the revolutionary regime were made six months after the revolution of 1952 beginning with Colonel Rashad Muhanna and twenty-four other officers on January 16, 1953. In the Sudan two disgruntled generals, Shannan and Abdallah, directed two coups against the military regime of their colleague General Abboud in March and May 1959. The eastern Arab world witnessed in 1958 three military coups — in Syria, Iraq and the Sudan — and a rebellion in Lebanon and they were all partly influenced by the Nasserist revolutionary regime in Egypt. In 1963 two coups occurred in Syria and three in Iraq; four of them were interrelated.

The various military regimes and rulers that appeared and then disappeared as a result of the successive coups made constant changes in the structure of government and even sometimes issued new constitutions. They promoted new teams of civilian and military non-entities to cabinet posts and sent the former teams to retirement. Even under the same regime as that of Nasser in Egypt several constitutional experiments were made and three mass organizations were formed — the Liberation Rally, the National Union and the Socialist Union. Under the same Baath regime, the ambitions of various party members and factions had to be satisfied and the cabinets therefore had to be reshuffled under the same prime minister as in the case of the three Bitar cabinets between March and November 1963 and the three Zuayyen cabinets (February 1966 to September 1967). In Yemen Sallal formed three cabinets (September 1962 to February 1963) in about five months and Hasan al-Amri was the head of seven cabinets between January 1965 and March 1969. Under the military regimes the revolution brought forth leftist elements that were more radical than the first military rulers and were a threat to them and this added to the instability of the revolutionary countries. This is how the leftist elements in Yemen's "popular resistance" attempted a coup on March 22, 1968 when al-Amri was prime minister. Two days earlier the left wing of the "national liberation front" in the recently independent South Yemen republic had tried to stage a coup.

The South Yemeni president Qahtan al-Shaabi then purged the army and the civil service of extremists and "deviationists" but he was finally overthrown by these extremists in a bloodless coup on June 22, 1969. The same developments occurred in the Baath party in Syria and Iraq. In the eventful week of November 11-18, 1963 the Baath leader Ali al-Saadi and his radicals lost in the struggle for power and gave President Aref the opportunity to overthrow the Baath regime. On the other hand, the Syrian Baath radicals took over more than two years later (February 1966) with General Jedid while the once radical founding fathers of the Baath, Aflaq and Bitar, and the military strongman General Hafez had become relatively moderate and were even described by their opponents as old-fashioned reactionaries.

Among the activities that absorbed much of the time of the military rulers after a coup was the purging of officials and officers of the old regime or of the previous military rule and satisfying the lust of their partisans for important positions in the administration and the army. The purges were often of such colossal proportions that they wrought havoc in the government and weakened the military forces especially when inexperienced officials replaced the old ones in key positions, and young officers were promoted to much higher rank and assumed political as well as military responsibilities. This is what happened in Iraq after the coup of July 1958 against the monarchy and in Libya in September 1969 after the overthrow of the Senousi dynasty. In Egypt some 1500 officers were assigned to leading political, administrative and economic positions between 1952 and 1964[7] while scores of other officers were arrested or dismissed after every conspiracy or attempted coup. In Syria the Baath rulers replaced the officials in the superior positions of director-general after the coup of March 1963 by their own partisans and called many reserve officers, mostly Baathist teachers, to become active officers without the necessary training. In order to consolidate their power they started by purging the army, first, of the so-called "separatist" officers, second, of the Nasserists, and third, of the partisans of General Hariri who made the coup that brought them to power. In early May 1963 forty-seven Nasserist officers were dismissed, pensioned or transferred to diplomatic posts, and General Hariri who was chief of staff and defense minister helped in the operation. On June 20, 1963 the Baath military leaders, Generals Hafez and Umran, dismissed or pensioned twenty-seven officers who were supporters of Hariri while he was on a mission in Algeria without consulting him. The perversion of the standards of discipline and decency was never as complete as under the Baath who treacherously profited of the absence of a military chief on official duty to strengthen their own position and confront him with a fait accompli. This is what the Baath did later in Iraq on July 30, 1968 to General Ibrahim Daoud, the minister of defense and the former commander of the presidential guard who had brought the Baath to power two weeks earlier. He was dismissed while he was on official duty inspecting the Iraqi contingents in Jordan.

The Iraqi Baath leaders, like all military leaders, have lived in the constant fear of military coups and have had to purge, arrest, and try officers who had been at one time their allies. The attempted coup of January 20, 1970 against the Baath regime of General al-Bakr led to the execution of thirty-four Iraqi officers and civilians and seven others on charges of spying, including General Rashid Muslih, who had been interior minister and martial law executor after the Baath victory over Kassem in March 1963. The Sudan lived in the same constant fear of coups and its continuous purges and arrests certainly did not contribute to stability. In mid-December 1969 the Sudanese rulers arrested fifty-six persons accused of conspiracy to overthrow the Numairi regime that took over power in May 1969. One month later the Sudan announced that it foiled the fifth attempted coup since May 1969. In South Yemen, the extremists who forced the resignation of President al-Shaabi on June 22, 1969 purged no less than one thousand officers and men from their relatively small armed forces.

Egypt has presented a contrast to the other Arab countries in that it was not shaken by as many military coups and it did not experience the alternation of military and civilian regimes since the fall of the monarchy in June 1953. From the very beginning the Revolution Command Council took drastic and decisive measures to destroy the political parties and uproot the politicians of the old regime. The ruling officers subordinated the civilian to the military bureaucracy but they performed the functions of government as the non-military rulers had done.[8] In other countries the officers continued to cooperate with the politicians and parties in preparing the coups and in the governments that followed. The Baath party in Syria and Iraq had never been able to solve the problem of the relation between its military and its civilian wings in the exclusive rule it imposed on the two countries. Among other factors that contributed to more stability in Egypt were its homogeneous, submissive and docile population, its higher degree of organized group life, and the fact that its free officers worked independently of political parties and ideological groups and were not as divided into conflicting factions as in such countries as Syria and Iraq.[9] Their cohesiveness and unity were achieved after long preparation and lasted longer than in other Arab revolutionary states. Egypt nevertheless had its conspiracies and purges as well as its personal rivalries, and although the continuous presence of Nasser and some close collaborators assured greater stability it did not bring a corresponding degree of loyalty and efficiency. Moreover, while Nasser's Egypt kept its people and its officers under control, it was largely responsible for the instability of the other Arab countries by its revolutionary propaganda, its incitement to violence, its direct intervention and its subsidies to the dissident and mercenary elements. The mere example of the changes imposed by the officers in Egypt accompanied by the initial success of Nasser's challenges to the great powers and their Arab allies also produced an unsettling effect on the various Arab states.

V. Results of Revolutions and Military Rule
A. Those Who Ruled by the Sword

One of the characteristic results of revolutions and military rule in the Arab states was that the military leaders who often obtained the satisfaction of becoming heroes overnight after the success of their coups d'état were discredited after a few months or a few years by their mismanagement of public affairs or by their personal ambition and behavior, and were overthrown by their disappointed colleagues or by other forces. Those who rose to power and ruled by the sword were destined sooner or later to perish by the sword when the means of violence at their disposal were no longer equal to those of their rivals. The officers, nevertheless, were unwilling to learn their lesson from the ugly procession of broken idols, and as one group of military upstarts after another tried to play its role as a so-called trustee for the people, the bewildered Arab people watched, often with indifference, hoping that the dangerous game would eventually end because the cost was too high, but the game never ended.

The very first leader of a coup in the emerging independent Arab countries was General Bakr Sidqi of Iraq who inaugurated his regime on October 29, 1936 by murdering the founder of the Iraqi army in cold blood. Less than ten months later Bakr Sidqi and his air force commander, Muhammad Ali Jawad, were murdered in Mosul on August 11, 1937 in a plot organized by their military rivals, while their civilian accomplice, Prime Minister Hikmet Sulaiman, was forced to resign. The four Iraqi colonels, known as the Golden Square, who forced the change of cabinets in their successive coups d'état and dragged Iraq into war with Britain after the seventh coup of April 1, 1941 were hunted down by the Iraqi government, tried, sentenced to death and executed. Their civilian partner, Rashid Ali al-Gailani, fled to Germany and after the end of the war was given asylum in Saudi Arabia. After the fall of the monarchy in July 1958 he returned to Baghdad, plotted against the dictator Abdul Karim Kassem and received a death sentence in January 1959, but the sentence was not executed. After the Iraqi coup of July 14, 1958 in which the royal family was massacred in cold blood, the leader General Kassem witnessed the execution of several officers who had cooperated with him in the coup but later attempted to overthrow him. Kassem survived an attempt on his life in the streets of Baghdad on October 7, 1959, and lived constantly in fear of being assassinated until he was ignominiously shot and exhibited on television on February 9, 1963 following the coup that sealed his fate on the preceding day. His former partner, General Aref, plotted against him soon after the coup of July 1958 and was jailed for three years. Aref seized power after Kassem's fall, but several conspiracies were organized against him by Baathist, Communist, and Nasserist elements. He was killed on April 13, 1966 in a helicopter crash between Qurna and Basra in southern Iraq and some reports speculated that the crash was the work of his enemies. The authors of the coup against the second Aref on July 17, 1968 were Colonels Abdul Razzaq Nayef and Ibrahim Daoud who became prime minister and defense minister, respectively, after their successful action. They held office for only two weeks in partnership with the Baath party and were dismissed and exiled by the Baath president Hasan al-Bakr. In early March 1970 Nayef was sentenced to death in absentia by a special court in Baghdad that convicted him of attempting to overthrow the Baath regime in December 1969.

In Syria the leader of the first coup of March 30, 1949, Colonel Husni al-Zaim was shot and killed along with his prime minister Dr. Barazi on August 14, 1949 in a suburb of Damascus by officers who had cooperated with him in the coup against the legitimate government four months and a half earlier. They criticized his misdeeds and claimed that they "saved the nation from the tyrant." The leader of the coup that overthrew Colonel Zaim was General Hinnawi and he was overthrown and arrested on December 19, 1949 by Colonel Shishakli who had cooperated with the leaders of the two previous coups. Hinnawi was released and was allowed to live in the capital of Lebanon but he was not destined to live long. He was assassinated near a street car stop in Beirut on October 31, 1950 by a young man of the Barazi family who thereby avenged the assassination of the former prime minister, Dr. Muhsin Barazi. Shishakli had a relatively long indirect and then direct rule. His regime ended in the coup of February 25, 1954 and those who had previously supported him now spoke of his "sinister rule" and complained that he "kept the officers at the mercy of spies." He was given asylum in Saudi Arabia and later lived in France after which he moved to Ceres in Brazil where he bought a farm. He was pursued and watched in Brazil by a Druze of the Abu-Ghazali family who wanted to avenge the death of many Druzes, including members of his own family, in the campaign that Shishakli had led against an insurrection in the Druze region in January 1954. The Druze young man shot and killed Shishakli in Ceres, Brazil, on September 27, 1964 more than ten years after his fall and after the anti-Druze campaign.

For nine years after the fall of Shishakli and until the Baath military strongmen took over in 1963, the Syrian officers who ruled by the sword did not perish by the sword. They received their punishment in other ways and their careers ended in frustration, disappointment and exile. The officers who were responsible for the unity of Syria and Egypt in the coup of mid-January 1958 were for the most part dispersed and humiliated and others were dismissed and watched after the merger, while the Baath civilian leaders who had supported unity were discredited and insulted and some of them, like Michel Aflaq, chose to live outside Syria. One of the chief architects of the United Arab Republic, Colonel Sarraj, was obliged to resign from his high post in Cairo in the summer of 1961 because he felt he had no power. After the fall of the UAR in the Syrian coup of September 28, 1961 he was kept in jail in Damascus and later escaped to Egypt where he was given a salary, like other pro-Nasserist Syrians who were not allowed to return to their country. Another architect of the

UAR who had also cooperated with all the military authors of coups and turned against them was Akram Hourani. He was often forced into exile in order not to be arrested, and his frustration as vice-president of the UAR led to his resignation at the end of 1959. He was later arrested and insulted by his former Baathist allies after 1963. One of the authors of the coup against the UAR, Colonel Nahlawi, was twice sent to exile after his two other coups against the civilian Qudsi regime. On April 2, 1962 his own military colleagues decided that he and five other officers who made the coup of March 28, 1962 should leave the country. He was again sent back to Europe after his attempt of January 13, 1963.

The leader of the coup of March 8, 1963, Colonel Ziad Hariri, ended the semi-constitutional Qudsi regime and was supported by Baathists and Nasserists. He enjoyed power for four months while the Baath needed him against their various opponents, but his power as minister of defense and chief of staff ended when the Baath in their search for exclusive power, succeeded in dismissing the officers who supported him and sent him to exile on July 8, 1963. Hariri was treated with relative kindness because he did not try to use force, but when the Nasserists led by Colonel Jassem Alwan attempted a coup against the Baath on July 18, the Baath strongman General Hafez acted differently. Besides those who were killed in the coup, twenty-seven participants were later tried and shot by the firing squad. Colonel Alwan and other officers were arrested later and remained in jail until they were allowed to leave for Egypt where they were given financial support by the Egyptian government. The Baath strongman, General Hafez, was challenged by his more radical colleagues and in the violent coup of February 23, 1966 he was wounded and later jailed, and two of his children received wounds. The radical Baathist victors under General Jedid attacked Hafez as well as the civilian party leaders Aflaq and Bitar, and heaped insults on them and accused them of reaction, treason and cooperation with imperialism. Hafez was later released and went with his civilian colleagues to live in Iraq after the restoration of Baathist rule in July 1968. One of the younger leaders of the bloody coup against Hafez was the Druze Captain Selim Hatoum. He was disappointed with his position and with the entire Alawi power structure after the success of the coup. He therefore tried to mount his own coup against General Jedid on September 8, 1966 but he failed and went to live and intrigue in Jordan. He returned to Syria after the June war with Israel and offered his services to his country, but the radical Baath regime gave him no chance. He was arrested and executed as a traitor.

The leader of the attempt against King Hussein of Jordan in the Zarqa incident of April 13, 1957 and the several other organizers of conspiracies were all allowed to leave the country or were kept in jail for a few years and were later pardoned by the king. It was reported at the time of the Zarqa attempt that General Ali Abu Nawar, according to an Arab tradition, asked King Hussein's protection by holding the edge of his coat when the furious loyal soldiers were seeking Abu Nawar's death, and the king protected him and allowed him to leave for Syria. The disloyal general later went to live in Egypt in Nasser's service until September 1964 when he was pardoned and was permitted to return to Jordan. In the Sudan, the two generals Shannan and Abdallah were arrested after their second coup of May 22, 1959 against the Abboud regime and were tried and sentenced to death, but the sentence was commuted to life in jail. The junior officers and cadets who made another attempt against the military rule of General Abboud on November 9, 1959 were not as lucky and five of them were sentenced to death and hanged on December 2, 1959. General Abboud himself was treated gently by the popular forces that revolted against the military regime in October 1964 probably because he and his generals accepted to end military rule and chose not to maintain themselves in power by the use of extreme violence against the wishes of the people.

In Yemen violence was met with violence and those who

assassinated Imam Yahya on February 17, 1948 and attempted to overthrow Imam Ahmad in April 1955 and March 1961 were tried and executed. The coup of September 26, 1962 led by General Sallal was met with royalist resistance and led to civil war. Sallal himself was eventually overthrown in a peaceful coup on November 5, 1967 by his own officers and former civilian aides after the withdrawal of Egyptian support. The coup was made while Sallal was out of the country in order to avoid bloodshed, and Sallal himself has gone into oblivion since he was given political asylum in Iraq.

The violent reaction of the Lebanese government against the attempt of Antun Saadeh, leader of the paramilitary forces of the Syrian Social National Party in early July 1949, has remained unique. No revolutionary leader in Lebanon has been summarily tried and executed within less than two days after his arrest as in Saadeh's case. The authors of the abortive coup of the SSNP at the end of December 1961 were given a long trial and their death sentence was commuted to life in jail, while the rebel leaders of the 1958 insurrection have retained their status and prestige as political leaders since the end of the crisis. Lebanon has witnessed no serious attempts by officers to rule by the sword, with the exception of the SSNP junior officers' badly conceived plan of December 1961 which was doomed to failure. The people of Lebanon and their rulers have discouraged and prevented the emergency of a military dictatorship, and the military leaders themselves have had evidently no desire to face the kind of hostile popular reaction that could have been produced by any miscalculation on their part.

The leaders of the Egyptian revolution of July 1952 were almost all forced to leave the political scene but they were allowed to live under strict supervision. They were not replaced by successive teams of officers who, as in Syria and Iraq, rose and fell in the game of the struggle for power. The reason was that one leader, Gamal Abdul Nasser, was able to maintain an overall dominance over his colleagues and with the support of those who remained by his side he dismissed those who had outlived their usefulness or refused to cooperate, and he promoted from the ranks those whom he chose as important aides. From the beginning he made it clear, when he arrested Rashad Muhanna and other officers in January 1953, that the army was not to involve itself in politics. General Naguib fell virtually at the end of March 1954 after a long quarrel but remained as a figurehead until he was deposed in November and was kept for many years under house arrest. Khalid Muhieddin, the Salem brothers, Baghdadi and Kemal Hussein, and after the June war of 1967 Abdul-Hakim Amer, Zakariya Muhieddin and Ali Sabri were among the important members of the original ruling group who lost their position and power. Nasser, however, was not always unchallenged, nor was he always safe and secure. His ability to remain in power was not necessarily a proof of his successful rule and in retrospect it would seem that it would have been better for Egypt and for the Arab world if he had not retained power for such a long time.[10] Nasser was challenged by Khalid Muhieddin and his cavalry and was obliged to return Naguib to his functions in February 1954. The Muslim Brethren tried to assassinate Nasser on October 26, 1954, and in July 1965 they organized a large conspiracy against him and his regime. His close friend of thirty years, Field Marshal Abdul Hakim Amer, who was also his designated successor as well as his first vice president and defense minister, conspired to overthrow him on August 27, 1967 and ended by committing suicide on September 14, 1967. The Syrian officers humiliated Nasser when they led a successful coup against his rule and forced the separation of their country from the UAR in September 1961. Dissenting Egyptian officers organized several conspiracies against Nasser after the secession of Syria and later as a result of deep involvement in the Yemen war. After the June war and the death of Amer, two plots were made by the officers to kill Nasser at the beginning of May and at the end of June 1968. Students demonstrated and rioted as they never had done before in February and November 1968 and asked for a change in the government system which was not granted.

Nasser's regime has succeeded in discovering the plots on time and in preventing the riots from becoming widespread popular revolutions. While he incited the people of the other Arab countries to revolt and murder their rulers for disagreeing with his policies, he dealt with his own opponents at home with tact and watched them closely but did not dispose of them.

B. Where Is The Dignity?
Democracy, the Socialist Revolution and Palestine

The military rulers tried to justify their seizure of power by directing their attacks against the corruption, instability, military weakness and arbitrary rule under the former legitimate regimes. The Palestine problem always provided them with arguments about the responsibility of the old regimes for defeat in 1948 and the need for change. After the success of their coups, the military promised to establish a "sound" democratic system, to strengthen the military establishment, encourage economic development, increase efficiency in the administration, defend national and individual dignity, realize social justice, achieve Arab unity and restore Arab rights in Palestine. The promises so far have not been fulfilled and, judged by their results not by their goals, and by what they became not by what they started with, the Arab radical military regimes and their socialist revolution should be generally viewed as a failure.

The results of military rule in the Arab countries over the last twenty years can be summarized in the following: first, the replacement of liberal constitutional democratic life by military dictatorships or by pseudo-democratic regimes based on one-party rule where freedoms are abolished and the police state has taken the place of the law-respecting state; second, economic stagnation, food shortages and curtailment of development projects following the nationalization of private enterprise, the attack on capitalism and private initiative, and the subjection of the economy to opportunistic political considerations; third, inefficiency, corruption and arrogance in the administration have remained on the same former level and were aggravated by the purging of hundreds of officials because they served under the old regime, the appointment of inefficient and inexperienced civilians and military from the poorer lower middle class in their place and in the newly nationalized services and projects, and the enormous expansion of the bureaucracy; fourth, weakness and ineffectiveness of the armed forces — in spite of the tremendous increase of modern weapons and equipment — due to the constant purges of military personnel as a result of recurring coups and conspiracies, the loss of discipline and competent training and organization, the general involvement of the military in politics and their inability to mobilize the human and natural resources in their country; fifth, collapse of the attempts to achieve Arab unity even among military regimes of the same ideological trend because of their mutual suspicions and fears and the instability that made the conclusion of binding agreements impossible, in addition to doctrinal differences and Arab division between so-called "liberated" revolutionary states and "reactionary" or conservative ones; sixth, the degradation rather than the restoration of national and individual dignity, and the increase of social injustice. The reason was the inability of the military regimes to provide for the defense and security of their country, and their unwillingness to guarantee the security of the individual's life, property and civil rights. The result was defeat and humiliation on the one hand, loss of personal freedom on the other, and division of the people into categories and classes with unequal rights and privileges as a result of the class struggle brought about by the socialist revolution. Another result was the exodus of thousands of intellectuals, competent economists, scientists and professional people who preferred to live in freedom and dignity outside their country.

In reviewing these results one has to distinguish between the individual dictatorial military regimes of the pre-doctrinal phase, and the totalitarian military regimes of the doctrinal phase. The former, such as those of Iraq under the colonels until 1941 and of Syria under Zaim and Shishakli were not under the influence of radical doctrines and were not committed to the destruction of the political and social order and to leading a socialist revolution. They attacked certain political leaders and certain parties but they did not condemn the entire democratic parliamentary system and the entire ruling class. They did not classify the people of the country into patriots and traitors or into progressives and reactionaries and did not grant or deny them civil rights on the basis of that classification. They tried to improve the economic and administrative systems but they did not abolish capitalism, confiscate property and nationalize private enterprise, and they did not initiate a class struggle in which the most ignorant and least qualified became the rulers. In the second phase after 1955 the military rulers set out to make a revolution. The "free officers" in Egypt set the example and the officers of the other Arab countries followed. The revolution had to be political and social at the same time because the socio-economic foundations of the power of the former ruling elite had to be destroyed in order to secure uncontested power for the new military ruling class and its allies. The revolution was given a national and a humanitarian justification, for it claimed that it sought to satisfy the aspirations of the masses and to give the country strength and a respectable position among the nations. The defense of Arab rights in Palestine was naturally included among the pretexts and goals of the revolution. The first and foremost preoccupation of the military, however, was to retain power but this, they claimed, was only in order to assure the protection and the continuance of the revolution. This is why their apologists have wondered who would exercise power if the officers were willing to surrender it, and if it would have been safe for them to abandon power. In the charters and provisional constitutions of the military regimes after 1962, one of the main functions of the national army came to be the protection of the revolution.

Conclusion: Results of Arab Revolution and Military Rule / 403

The military rulers and their civilian doctrinal supporters made a blunt attack on the parliamentary system or what they called "the reactionary democracy" and the entire liberal tradition under the false assumption that parliamentary democracy with its parties, factions and politicians had a divisive effect, represented a monopoly of power by a certain class and was responsible for Arab weakness. Writers and scholars echoed the claims of the military and added other false assumptions and errors. They viewed the recurrence of coups as a proof of weakness of representative government and of its abuse by unscrupulous leaders. They also thought that the shift that the military rulers made was not from democracy to dictatorship, but from one form of non-democratic rule to another.[11] The apologists evidently failed to realize that under the old parliamentary regime there was a recognized political opposition and freedom to criticize the government, and that the masses in whose name the revolution was later made exercised their right of voting more freely than under the regimented system of one-party rule. The parliamentary system, moreover, was becoming more and more representative of all social classes on the basis of achievement and leadership. When the military resorted to violence in support of certain doctrinal parties it was not because the opposition parties were suppressed by the former government or because democratic action was ineffective. It was because the doctrinal parties at the time had nothing worthwhile to offer, and their leaders had no popular appeal. The former government and the parliamentary system should not therefore be held responsible for their failure in the elections. It was the impatience of the frustrated leaders and their inability to reach power by due democratic process that explains their appeal to the military for support and the resort to violence. Moreover, the recurrence of military coups should be viewed as a cause of weakness of democratic liberal regimes rather than as a result or a proof of their weakness, for it was the constant military interventions and pressures that discredited and weakened the democratic system and made the success of the coups possible.

The radical military rulers of the Arab countries either exercised direct military rule or preferred to adopt a new kind of democracy — the so-called people's democracy — instead of strengthening the social and economic foundation of the old genuine liberal democracy. Their totalitarian rule was an imitation of the Fascist and Communist systems. It adopted the symbols and techniques of democratic government, spoke of freedom and of the people's will and rights, but it had no respect for such institutions of genuine democracy as rational discussion and free expression and consent. It controlled all aspects of life and viewed the way of the ruling clique and its one party organization as the only right way.[12] The military rulers drew support from the one party organization — such as the Socialist Union in Egypt and the Baath party in Syria and Iraq — but they virtually dominated the organization and determined who should be its delegates in the various ruling levels and assemblies. Freedom existed in theory but there were no free people. The Baath party believed, as its theorist Michel Aflaq arrogantly declared, that "destiny which entrusted the Baath with the task of carrying the message of Arab resurrection has given us the right to command with strength and with cruelty, for the Baath is the vanguard and the masses have to march behind."[13] The tyranny of the group over the individual was thus justified and the nation's will was to be determined by a small unrepresentative clique of leaders imposed by force. According to Jalal al-Sayyid, one of the Baath founding fathers who became disenchanted with the party, the Baath followed the principle that freedom could be granted only to its own party members.[14] The same leader, who was at one time one of the very few Baathist members of Parliament in Syria in the 1950's, came out in favor of genuine liberal democracy when the Baath turned to totalitarian rule under the control of its military wing. He declared that despite its many drawbacks and problems, "democracy always remains the best system and to it belongs the decisive word in the disagreements between citizens and in their various interpretations; it is preferable to the rule of one man or of an oligarchy."[15]

The socialist revolution was introduced by the military radicals with the slogans of social justice and equal opportunity and was represented as a means of awakening the masses and speeding economic development, but it was intended primarily to destroy the political opponents of the military and their radical supporters. Although the opposition to military rule was deprived of its press, its parties and its freedoms, the military remained horrified by the spectre of that opposition. Socialism was one effective way for its decisive liquidation. Despite its possible benefits, the socialist system was introduced at a very inopportune time and was implemented in a very unwise vindictive manner. It was perhaps the most serious error that the leaders of the Arab revolution made because it created divisions and hatreds within each country and between Arab countries at a time when the military and their supporters claimed to be preparing for Arab unity and for the Israeli challenge. But what the military claimed must have been different from what they effectively wanted and eventually did. Palestine and Arab national goals were not first priorities in their plans since they chose to divide the Arabs and to waste their energies on frivolous disputes at a time when their urgent need was for cooperation, unity, concentration on the serious problems of military training and organization and on a rational diplomacy.

One of the first priorities of the radical Arab military regimes was to spread socialism and revolution in the Arab world. Egypt led the way in the socialist laws of July 1961 and the charter of May 1962. The slogans of class struggle were introduced and the citizens were divided into traitors and reactionaires on the one hand, and patriots and progressives on the other on the basis of their wealth. For the first time in Arab history democracy was to be based on "the alliance of the working forces of the people" that consisted of farmers, laborers, revolutionary intellectuals and soldiers. For the first time the rulers confiscated the property of their subjects and satisfied their lust for vengeance against the former ruling classes and the prosperous citizens under the pretext of restoring to the Arab nation its dignity and giving the Arabs more strength. This was done in Arab countries and in a primarily Muslim society that knew of no formal social stratification or barriers and where the son of a peasant or of a laborer or anyone could improve constantly his social status within a short time on the basis of his improved intellectual, financial or professional position. The socialist system, while still in the experimental stage, became in the proclamations of Nasser and his spokesmen the basis for Arab unity, the subject of an Arab nationalist crusade, and the criterion for determining if an Arab country was "liberated" or reactionary, or if it was really nationalistic or a mere ally of imperialism and Zionism. The Egyptian officers who imposed socialism did not want to admit that it was an Arab variety of Marxism and worked hard to prove its relation with the message of Islam and thereby inflicted more indignities on an entire class of religious teachers who had to preach something they did not believe.

The Syrian Baath regime imposed the socialist system in several decrees between 1963 and 1965 although it promised after every step that it would be the last one. Socialism of Marxian type was thus established under the influence of the most radical Baath elements. One of the false premises by which the Baath justified its action was that "the bourgeois middle class was no longer capable of playing a positive role in the economic field and its opposition made it the ally of imperialism."[16] The resourceful middle class that made what is equivalent to a peaceful revolution in the Syrian economy between the two wars and after was thus condemned by a Baath unfounded sweeping statement, and more indignities in addition to material ruin were inflicted on entire classes of businessmen and shopkeepers. According to a well-known former Baath leader, the socialism mentioned in the Baath party constitution was not Marxian socialism but a kind of

Conclusion: Results of Arab Revolution and Military Rule / 407

state capitalism, because Marxian socialism is really Communism.[17] The same leader has maintained that socialism was intended to be implemented gradually in the unified Arab state when the circumstances could permit.

In Iraq as in Syria the rulers knew that the socialist transformation would be opposed and they consequently gave false promises about their intention not to impose socialism. When they did impose it they tried to explain, as Arab radicals have done in other countries, that socialism "springs from our Islamic traditions," and they gave it various names such as "constructive," "sound," "just" and "well-guided" socialism.[18] The economic future of these countries was thus arbitrarily decided, as it had never been before, on the basis of political expediency, and Arabism was sacrificed to socialism.

The most tragic and destructive aspects of radical military rule and of the socialist revolution that it imposed and promoted were reflected in the defeat of the socialist Arab states in the six day war of June 1967. They can be summarized as follows: first, the socialist regimes destroyed the military potential and weakened the preparedness of their countries by placing the security and interest of their regimes, of their revolution, and even of their particular factions and sects above the security and interest of their country. Commenting on sectarian influences within the Baath party, a former Baath leader has told us that the party pensioned off hundreds of Sunni Muslim officers from the Syrian urban centers after 1963 and that some units in the Syrian air force, marine, and mechanized forces were left without their main officers. On the other hand, new officers were admitted from the ranks of young government officials and teachers with no professional military experience and they were even promoted because they belonged to the Baath party and to certain religious sects.[19] The Baath regime in Syria, it was said, concentrated more forces around Damascus than on the war front because it feared a coup d'état and the surrender of the fortified Syrian positions on the Golan Heights by the Baath regime has remained a mystery. The Iraqi units that came to

Jordan during the June war were not issued ammunition until they reached the Jordanian border because the rulers were suspicious of their commanders, and the Iraqis were consequently unable to defend themselves against Israeli air raids. The Jordanian army, on the other hand, with every disadvantage of number, equipment, terrain and armament acquitted itself best during the June war and, as it has been observed, the simple old-fashioned tribal and monarchical loyalty was more effective in maintaining morale than the revolutionary socialism of Egypt and Syria.[20] After the June war, certain military observers have disclosed that there had been virtually no improvement in the capability of Arab officers and in Arab attempts to create an officer corps since 1949, and that there has even been some regression as Russian training has been substituted for the once dominant British influence.[21] A good picture of the indiscipline, time wasting, and adventurism that ruined the Syrian army under the Baath regime can be gained from reading the experiences of the Baath former national secretary-general, Munif al-Razzaz, and the memoirs of General Abdul Karim Zahreddin.[22]

A second destructive aspect of the socialist regime was the destruction of the material potential of the people by nationalizations, confiscations, shortages, and debts. It became a problem for certain people to fight under a regime that they hated because it deprived them of their property.[23] Third, the socialist regimes destroyed the spiritual resources of the Arabs and their traditional moral values and created a new Arab school based on lies, blackmail, suspicion and treachery. The new regimes attacked their opponents in the most ruthless terms calling them agents, hirelings, reactionaries and traitors although they were recognized nationalist leaders and rendered great national services before the military regimes ruled, but they were not revolutionary socialists. The people were demoralized and could no longer take the rulers seriously when one day, for example, they would send President Qudsi to jail as a traitor and two weeks later they would ask him to resume his duties as a noble patriotic president, or when Abdul Karim

Kassem would be called one day the "sole leader" and after his fall "The tyrannical beast and dirty despot." The people watched with dismay how the Baath rulers treacherously dismissed their colleagues who brought them to power while they were on a mission outside the country, and how the officers shifted loyalty and support from one ambitious strongman to another. They also saw how the ruling Baath faction poured insults and accusations on its former leaders Aflaq and Bitar and how the once powerful ally of the Baath, Akram Hourani, was jailed by a Baath government and accused of having used the officers to threaten parliament after 1954 and of having utilized socialism as a weapon to fight his political opponents.[24]

The fourth destructive aspect of the socialist regimes was their suppression of freedoms of all kinds for which the people and their recognized leaders had struggled so long under colonial rulers. The result was the arbitrary rule of one party or faction that accepted no criticism of its policy. Many of the serious errors and miscalculations under the socialist regimes could have been avoided if only there were genuinely representative bodies that had the power to advise and criticize. Included in this arbitrary power and the lack of freedom to correct it was the narrow partisanship of the ruling military radicals that led them to fill the administration with unqualified officials and to lose at the same time a great number of experts in various fields who preferred to leave their countries rather than live under a regime of repression, suspicion, and discrimination.

The Arab intellectuals under military rule have remained silent and uncreative except during the short spells of freedom between two military regimes. The Baath party once criticized the dictatorship of Colonel Zaim in 1949 but it took the Baath leader, Michel Aflaq, only a few days in jail, during which his hair was shaved and he was subjected to certain indignities, to recant in a formal letter to Zaim and to declare that he and his party were all wrong in their criticisms. Not one writer has had the courage of Milovan Djilas, the former Yugoslav Communist leader, for example, who held key positions in government and party and later was imprisoned from 1956-61 and 1962-66 because he declared in his writings that Communism as a system had degenerated into a bureaucratic tyranny. Not one has stood up, as Alexander Solzhenitsyn has done in the Soviet Union, to criticize and defy the ruling regime. Some have written continuously and with courage from their new home in Lebanon in spite of the atomosphere of fear that threatened at one time the critics of the radical military rulers and that witnessed the assassination of Kamil Mrowé, the liberal editor of al-Hayat in Beirut in May 1966. After the June war, the same Syrian writers living in Beirut wrote books and articles showing the relation between the socialist military regimes and Arab defeat.[25] Others who also lived in Beirut and wrote on the meaning of defeat chose to ignore completely the impact of arbitrary military rule and the divisive and weakening effects of the imposed socialist system, and emphasized only the Arab need for scientific and technological progress.[26]

Arab writers and intellectual leaders have mostly chosen not to approach the problem of military rule and socialist revolution and its impact on the weakness and the defeat of the Arab states for several reasons. First, they were afraid of being viewed as reactionaries or counter-revolutionaries at a time when military propaganda had represented the liberal moderate democrats who did not believe in socialism and radical military rule as traitors and reactionaires and when radicalism and revolution and everything critical of the status quo had their measure of popularity and prestige and their aspect of heroism. Second, they preferred to remain on good terms with the military regimes that ruled the majority of the fourteen Arab League states — in Iraq, Syria, Yemen and South Yemen in Asia, and Egypt, Sudan, Libya and Algeria in Africa — at the end of 1969. Third, the confusion between the new Palestinian revolution and its guerilla activities on the one hand and the Arab socialist revolution under military rule, on the other, and the fear of weakening the Palestinian Arab cause by criticizing the radical military regimes. This is why young Arab intellectuals living beyond the borders of the totalitarian Arab countries have repeated in their conferences the same slogans about the reactionary and counter-revolutionary forces and the confrontation of "the revolutionary forces of the Arab people with the combined forces of imperialism and Zionism." They have also emphasized the "imperative need for the revolutionary transformation of Arab society" in order "to translate Arab potential into reality."[27] Yet while they spoke about the need for transforming Arab society they failed to mention the negative effects of the class struggle on that same society and they did not attribute to the military regimes and their socialist revolution any share of responsibility in the defeat in 1967 in spite of the flagrant proofs of their ineptitude and their inability to defend their countries.

In contrast to what happened after the Palestine war of 1948, no belligerent Arab governments were attacked by intellectuals or popular forces after the 1967 defeat and none of them was overthrown. On the contrary two democratic regimes that were least involved in the war — Sudan and Libya in May and September 1969 respectively — were overthrown by military coups, and two military regimes in Iraq and South Yemen in July 1968 and June 1969 respectively — became more radical. The military regimes that were defeated in the June war have possibly drawn Arab sympathy because of the continued hostilities with Israel. The Arabs have possibly thought that for the sake of Palestine and the defense of the Arab countries along Israel's borders, the military rulers should not be weakened by criticism and riots, although there were some riots in February and November 1968 in Egypt and others in Iraq. The main reason, however, for the survival of the defeated regimes is that they are mainly military regimes and they are ready to supress any movement — as they have already done — that threatens their power. Moreover, they are supported by radical elements who played an important role in the riots against civilian rulers after 1948 but who are now contented with the rule of their radical military allies. These radicals, furthermore, are more interested in the success of socialism than the Palestine cause which they use as a pretext for spreading the socialist revolution. Some radicals have been even preaching a more complete social revolution since the war of June 1967 on the basis that socialism does not mean nationalization and planning only, but also a rebirth of the individual.[28]

VI. Back To The Barracks

The military rulers have been attracted and corrupted by political power and their officers have engaged in politics to the detriment of their professional military duties. The socialist revolution and the fiction of trusteeship for the masses have enabled the military and their radical supporters to retain power. But in the meantime, the countries that have been under their rule have suffered and they have been insensitive to their suffering. They were expected to defend Arab dignity, to enhance the Arab self image and to satisfy the Arab need for outside admiration. Instead, they have disgracefully led the Arabs to defeat, humiliation and shame by their ineptitude and by the mere fact of their deep involvement in radical politics and all its consequences. The leader of the socialist revolution who cruelly attacked the monarchs of such oil-producing countries as Saudi Arabia ended by living partly on the charity of these countries. In their fighting and in their diplomacy after 1967, the military regimes have been guided by one consideration, that of retaining power in their respective countries. The military defense pacts which they concluded since 1950 have been worthless militarily and have served only as political instruments to strengthen their regimes. After fifteen years of military preparation and training they have found out, among other things, that they had no pilots for all their planes, and Israel continued to expose the failure of these regimes by carrying the war into the heart of their homeland. Revolts and insurrections against military rule have been continuous and the latest were the attempts of mid-January 1970 against the Baath military rulers in Iraq, and the insurrection in the Sudan at the end of March 1970. Both ended in scores of executions and ruthless repression. The foreign policy of the military rulers and their radical allies has resulted in their dependence on one power, the Soviet Union, which is least interested in the solution of the problem of Palestine but whose primary interest lies in destroying the remnants of Western interests, perpetuating the turmoil and the "controlled chaos" in the Middle East, encouraging the establishment of increasingly radical Arab regimes and promoting their hostility to the West and the United States in particular. Under these various conditions and as a result of the failure of the military regimes, the only logical solution is to return the Arab countries to the rule of the legitimate representatives of the people under a liberal democratic system with free elections, and to return the military to their barracks and bring to an end the artificial class struggle imposed by the military rulers and their socialist system for their own advantage.

The return to liberal democracy would not mean the end of reform, modernization, and change but it would only mean the end of arbitrary and imposed change that created division, hatred, and inefficiency. It is only fair to remember that the Arab countries had already witnessed one of the most impressive peaceful revolutions in the interwar and post war periods before the intervention of the military in the early 1950's and without the help of military rule. The change was healthy and beneficial and would have continued its accelerated course without the tensions and the negative revengeful spirit that characterized it under the military. Among the aspects of change before the era of military coups were the following: the cultural revolution with its schools, universities, the superior standards of its students and teachers and cultural output; the economic and social revolution with its expanded and mechanized agriculture, its development projects, progress in industrialization, building activity, liberal labor codes, expanding and prospering banking and foreign trade, rising standards of living, and its emancipation of women, promotion of the poorer people from the urban and rural areas to participation in the various ranks of the military and civil service and to membership in parliament, and the emergence of a larger middle class whose status was based on financial, professional and intellectual achievement and which was replacing the landed aristocracy in social and political influence; the secular revolution with its notion of the nation-state as distinct from the Muslim state, its idea of citizenship and equal civil rights for the members of all communities, the weakening of the power of the clergy and the cooperation of all religious groups in the national endeavor; and last but not least, the national revolution that brought independence and freedom to the Arab countries after a long struggle that was accompanied by unity, sacrifice, and diplomatic skill and resulted in the establishment of constitutional liberal democratic governments based on respect for the rule of law and for the civil rights of individuals and groups.

The military rulers and their apologists have emphasized only the shortcomings of the liberal democratic regimes, but under their own military rule the Arab countries have witnessed more instability, more inefficiency, more demagogy, more lust and struggle for power, more humiliation and defeat, and less freedom, less equality and less prosperity than under the regimes that they have replaced. The reforms they were able to impose were the negative and easy ones that required the use of military force for the confiscation of property and the uprooting of the ruling elite. They have not been able to play the role of innovators, saviors, regenerators and educators as certain optimists expected. They could not evolve a political system that would allow popular participation. They followed the Communist regimes in their opposition to democratic reform movements and change because their interest could be best served by revolutionary reform under a military totalitarian regime. They even condoned the policies of their Communist friends when Czechoslovakia was invaded in August 1968 and force was used against the freedom of an entire people at a time when their own revolutionary regimes were advocating freedom and liberation for the Arabs including those of Palestine. They borrowed the Communist slogans on imperialism and neo-colonialism at a time when almost all the Arab countries had become independent. Their policy of close friendship with the Soviet Union and hostility to the West worked for the benefit of the Soviet Union itself and Israel more than for that of the Arabs. The Soviet Union and Israel have both favored the establishment of more extreme Arab governments and more Arab dependence on the Communist Bloc but for different reasons. The Russians wanted the Arabs to be completely dependent on them and exploited every Arab crisis with Israel to increase that dependence and to inflame Arab feelings against the West in the hope of wiping out completely Western, and particularly American interests in the Arab countries. Israel, on the other hand, wanted to portray the Arabs as enemies of the West and dangerous puppets of the Soviet Union, and to assume the role of defender of Western interests in order to have the exclusive support of the United States and other Western countries. The close friendship of the Arab revolutionaries with the Soviet Union brought them more weapons and more Russian expressions of support in diplomatic circles, but it did not give the Arabs more strength, and it neither helped them win a victory nor did it help in erasing the consequences of defeat.

Military rulers in the Arab states have so far disproved the assertions of those who saw in them a vanguard rather than a Praetorian guard, and who thought they were the only force for stability and reform in the Arab world. Military rulers have also proved to be a disappointment for those great powers, such as the United States, who thought that by promoting and backing them they could insure a greater measure of stability and cooperation that would help preserve and protect their interests.

Military dictatorship can no longer be defended by the argument that uses the autocratic past of the Arab countries to justify the present military autocracy, nor can it be supported by the reasoning that accepts the accession of the military to political power because the acquisition of political power by the military was not alien to Islamic tradition.[29] On the other hand, it cannot be said that military rule has been creating the socio-economic basis conducive to democracy[30] because the radical Arab military regimes have created only those economic and social conditions that were likely to perpetuate their rule with the support of one single party organization which they dominated and artificially created in certain cases. Moreover, military dictatorships have usually tended to distort the citizen's mentality and scale of values and to corrupt his judgment through propaganda and indoctrination in order to make the return to sound liberal democratic government more difficult and to maintain their own totalitarian rule. The training and experience in democratic government could not therefore be achieved under military rule because it is only in an atmosphere of freedom and free debate that this experience could be obtained and not in an atmosphere of indoctrination where all opposition was suppressed and where liberal democratic institutions have been under constant attack in order to undermine and destroy the people's faith in democracy. Military dictatorship in the Arab countries as a result has not been and will not be simply a period of transition to, and preparation for democracy, as it was in Kemalist Turkey, because the military rulers have opted for the totalitarian or false type of democracy and for the Marxian type of socialism that require the continued military presence because they can be maintained only by force. If, as it has been said, the final touchstone of achievement for an army regime is its success in making its continued existence unnecessary [31] the Arab military regimes then have not achieved much.

The notion that representative democracy is the product of a certain cultural tradition and climate, and that it requires a special type of character and therefore cannot succeed when transplanted to "the alien soil of the East which bred the thorns of despotism"[32] — this notion has been exaggerated and utilized to justify military dictatorships in Arab and non-Arab countries of the Middle East. It ignores the entire process of westernization and change in the last hundred years in Arab lands and the wholesale acquisition of various Western institutions and the disintegration of most traditionalist legal, educational, religious and social institutions. This notion would then favor the existence of a lop-sided Arab society that lives in the modern age in most aspects but goes back to the past and its depotism in its system of government. Representative democracy, moreover, need not mean the complete adoption of the Western parliamentary or presidential system because various countries can adapt democratic institutions, as Lebanon did, to their particular condition provided the essential elements of democratic life are preserved such as free elections, a constitution containing a bill of rights made by the people's representatives, and a constructive opposition that can criticize the ruling group and take its place by due democratic process.

It is difficult to prescribe the ways and means for putting an end to military coups and interventions and for removing the causes and pretexts that have hitherto led to them. Tensions, internal and external, personal ambitions, and imported ideologies that have produced the coups or encouraged them cannot be entirely removed, and no nation, particularly a developing one, can be entirely free of them. The military, however, can be prevented from exploiting the problems and tensions if they realize that their intervention would be met with resistance and revolt instead of indifference or faint protests on the part of the people and their political leaders. Yet, such hostile reaction to military coups would occur only if the people could appreciate the value of democratic life and institutions and the freedom that goes with them, and if their political leaders and rulers were able to promote and retain the people's respect and loyalty by responding to their economic and social needs and by learning how to live with the problems and rivalries without seeking the support of the army leaders.

In the present state of Arab hostilities with Israel it might seem strange to call for the return of the military to their barracks and for the disestablishment of the military regimes. Yet, the record of these regimes in two wars — in 1956 and 1967 — and particularly in the last one, and their diplomacy before and after the two wars have proved that they were incapable not only of waging war but also of waging peace. The military have moreover presided over regimes in which the state dangerously controlled everything but did not have stable political institutions,[33] and in which the economic and human resources could not be fully mobilized because the Marxian type of socialism introduced by these regimes and the recurring conspiracies, purges and struggles for power have created division, suspicion and hatred, provoked an exodus of active and much needed elements of the population, and weakened the nation's morale, defense forces, and economy. Those who at one time praised military rule as the possible remedy for the developing Arab states and saw in it the only force for stability and reform have mostly done so in the late 1950's and early 1960's before the recent debacle of 1967 and before the unfolding of the results of radical military rule and its imposed socialist system. At the present time it would seem that for the sake of the Arabs — including those of Palestine — and their dignity and future, it would be preferable to call for the return of the military rulers and officers to their barracks to concentrate on their professional duties and to leave the affairs of state to those who can reach decisions in the nation's interest after full consultation with representative bodies in a free exchange of ideas and not by arbitrary force for the benefit of a certain faction or doctrine. It is, moreover good to remind those who have struggled for freedom and repeated with ecstasy the slogans on liberation in the various Arab countries that the struggle for Palestine would defeat its purpose and would contradict Arab ideals and aspirations if it should become a pretext and a justification for maintaining a system of revolutionary military rule that deprives the Arabs of their freedoms and of all forms of private association and initiative and reduces the Arab individual to a mere statistical unit in a totalitarian state.

VII. After The End of Military Rule

One might wonder what would happen to the Arab states if their military regimes should fall and whether the expected democratic rule would be better than the rule of the military. Past experience has shown that the anarchy or the rule of the well-organized Communists and other extremists, which certain pessimists thought would follow the fall of the military dictators, did not take place. On the contrary, twice in Syria — in 1954 after the fall of Shishakli and in 1961 after the end of the Nasserist regime and the unity with Egypt — and once in the Sudan in 1964 after the fall of General Abboud, the people rallied around their old leaders and were overjoyed by the return of freedom. In the freely conducted elections they returned a moderate well balanced parliament. The Baath socialists of Aflaq and Bitar were so discredited that they were unable to obtain one single seat for their leaders in the Syrian elected Chamber of December 1961. The radical doctrinal parties have generally failed in every Arab country to have a popular following but it was the combination of Nasserist influence and intervention since 1955 and the pressures of the radical young officers that weakened the democratic governments and ended by overthrowing them by military force. This is why drastic changes should be made in the entire system of recruitment of officers and in the military organization in order to prevent the politicization of the army and assure the functioning of democratic rule, while the parties and particularly the radical militant ones should be carefully watched in order to prevent them from infiltrating and indoctrinating the officers and the cadets. But even in their relative weakness and while they were still experimenting with parliamentary rule, the democratic regimes have given the Arab countries more security, stability and prosperity than under the socialist military regimes. Similarly the democracies that could follow the fall of the present military rulers should be expected to do the same especially if an end is made to military intervention and pressure. The Arab individual would then be able to regain his dignity and enjoy freedom and the rule of law after the passing of the police state, and the safety of his person and property would be guaranteed. The uprooting and dispersion of the old ruling elite by the present military regimes should not mean that there would be a lack or a shortage of civilian leaders under a new democratic government, for the Arab countries, as most other countries, have always been able to produce new leaders among the rising generations and these, even the younger ones, have not all accepted the indoctrination of the radical one-party organizations and have not been all reduced to the status of obedient servants of the military rulers. Many of them have practiced what the old Arab proverb said about kissing the hand that you cannot bite and praying to God that it might be broken. Among those who joined the Baath party in Syria and Iraq because it was the ruling party, many would leave it as soon as the military who brought it to power are swept away.

With the fall of radical military rule it should not be feared that the Arab states would be weakened militarily under a democratic government and that they would be less capable of facing the Israeli challenge. In the past, with very modest forces at their disposal in the early period of their independence, the emerging Arab states fought in 1948 and did not have to endure the losses and the humiliation that they have endured under the present military regimes that had larger and better equipped armies. Under a new democratic rule and with the end of their conspiracies, political involvement and successive purges, the officers would be more secure, their promotions would be based on merit and not on political considerations, and they would be more dedicated to their profession, to their troops and to their state and its government. The political leaders, with more maturity and diplomatic skill and with no other interest to serve in their dealings with the great powers except that of their nation, would not commit the errors that the military rulers and their radical supporters made. They would be able to have more international support when their friendly relations are no longer restricted to one major power. In the world community the Arabs would also claim more respect under democratic regimes because the scandalous treason trials and the use of the firing squad, the arbitrary confiscations and nationalizations of the property of foreigners and natives, the recurring conspiracies, struggles and coups, and the angry speeches and attacks on sister Arab states and foreign powers alike would no longer be the object of derisive international comment.

The end of military rule would not mean the end of concern for social justice and of government regulatory power over the economy. Nor would it mean the weakening of Arab national feeling and of the aspirations for Arab unity, but it could mean the end of the socialist revolution and of radical Arab nationalism. It would be for the freely elected representatives of the people in the parliaments of the various Arab states to decide whether the socialist laws and the agrarian reform laws should be maintained, and the chances are that most of them would, as the experience of Syria after the end of unity with Egypt has proved. In the freely elected Syrian Parliament of December 1961 and early 1962 the agrarian laws were only slightly modified and those provisions of the socialist laws of July 1961 that awarded the laborer various benefits were maintained, but the nationalization of various business corporations that threatened to kill private initiative and damage the economy and give the state more responsibility than it could take were abolished. The Syrian radicals, however, were not as interested in the welfare of the laborer and peasant as they were in fighting and discrediting the democratic separatist regime, and with Nasser's help they led a violent campaign against it until they succeeded in wrecking it through a military coup. The democratic governments and even the traditionalist ones such as Saudi Arabia were not against social justice, and in the past they had always operated in fields where private enterprise was not capable of operating with the necessary efficiency, but they were against the Marxian socialism that the radical military regimes adopted and that was meant to discredit and destroy the entire bourgeois middle class and the ruling elite. The socialism that the liberal democrats fought and would probably not tolerate was the socialism that made the dictatorship of the military radicals possible, eliminated the role of private capital and enterprise, and created disunity and class struggle among the people.

In the 1960's several leaders of socialist regimes have fallen, while other personalities related to socialist parties have spoken out against the Marxian dogmatic type of socialism. Among the Afro-Asian idols who were broken by the indignant opposition of their colleagues and subjects was Sukarno of Indonesia, advocate of "guided democracy" and frivolous autocrat who was compromised in a Communist attempt to seize power in September 1965 and has been under palace arrest since March 1968. On February 24, 1966 the notorious Nkrumah of Ghana, the "Redeemer", and the champion of "scientific socialism" fell after nine years of dictatorship and extravagance during which he built up a colossal personal fortune. In July 1969 the co-founder of the Baath party, Salah Bitar, spoke out in Beirut against the demagogy and terror under the Arab socialist regimes and against the rigid dogmatism and the world of intruding foreign doctrines and ideologies and said that the Arab defeat in June 1967 was a just punishment for the Arab mistakes in thought and action.[34] In September 1969 Stalin's daughter confessed on American soil that "people who want to change democracy for socialism are blind," and that "life in Russia is a nightmare which has to end sometime."[35] The National Bank of Mexico declared in the summer of 1969 that "to a great extent the future of Mexico will depend on private enterprise." The government, it added, will continue to operate in those fields where private enterprise cannot, especially in fields of social importance. "This joint effort of government and private investment," the declaration concluded, "have benefited the economy and will continue to bring social justice to all."[36] This declaration was made in a country that has passed through one of the longest social revolutions in history after 1910 and which has achieved much in the field of economic and social reform.

As for the ideas of Arab nationalism and Arab unity, they were produced and promoted by the Arab liberal middle class intelligentsia in the last years of the Ottoman Empire and were adopted by Arab officers in the Ottoman army. They were introduced neither by the Baath party in Syria nor by the "free officers" in Egypt. The Arab nationalist leaders who led the struggle for independence between the two wars associated nationalism with freedom and democracy and were careful to establish liberal democratic regimes when their countries obtained independence. The doctrinal parties, such as the Baath, turned Arab nationalism into a chauvinistic dogma, associated it with socialism, and used it as an instrument of opposition against the ruling democratic regimes in order to reach power. They preached pan-Arab unity but did little to achieve it except if their party could draw prestige and power from it, and they opposed the various efforts to form a Fertile Crescent or a Greater Syria unity on the basis that these were imperialistic schemes. In the name of the Baath and of Arab unity, the army officers wrested power from the liberal nationalists and then set out in Syria and Iraq to implement a socialism of the Marxian type after 1963 in imitation of Nasser's Egypt. The socialist revolution for them became a necessity for fighting the old ruling classes and other opponents and for retaining power. Freedom was sacrificed and the role of the people was abolished under the pretext of protecting the revolution. In the hands of the Baath and other Arab radical groups, national endeavor was superseded by the effort to spread socialism and undermine those Arab regimes and leaders who refused it at a time when the Arabs thought they should be strong and united to restore Arab rights in Palestine. In Egypt the emergence of Nasser as an Arab national leader after 1955 was followed by a catastrophic series of interventions in other Arab countries that gave such Arab radicals as the Baathists the opportunity and the courage to attack the ruling regimes and eventually take their place. Belief in socialism and the acceptance of the official socio-economic system of the radical military regimes became the criterion for the recognition of a truly progressive Arab nationalist person or state. Governments and rulers who did not adopt the socialist system were classified as reactionaries and traitors. This is how Arab nationalism ended under military rule, and this is why socialism linked to nationalism succeeded in dividing and weakening the Arabs and in transforming the free democratic countries into totalitarian police states. No wonder that after the June War of 1967 certain Arab scholars who noted the division and weakness of the Arabs became disenchanted with Arab nationalism altogether and spoke of the "loss of faith" as a cause of Arab defeat,[37] and of the need for moral regeneration to fortify the Arabs' political and military strength. "I firmly believe," said one of them, "that Arab nationalism as a creed has been tried for a generation or two against Zionism and was found wanting. It has failed to maintain an Arab moral strength to any high degree that Islam did."[38]

Arab nationalism was not found wanting when it was liberal and when the Arabs struggled under its banner and wrested their independence from two great world powers, France and Britain, and laid the foundation of their economic independence and prosperity and of their cultural revival. Arab nationalism, however, could no longer inspire the Arabs when it was corrupted by the radical military upstarts and their selfish ideological mentors and became, through its association with Marxian socialism, an instrument of class warfare within the Arab countries and of division and suspicion between the Arab states. The Arabs were indeed demoralized and paralyzed and could no longer exert serious effort when they lost their freedom and dignity, when their leaders were discredited, insulted and forced into exile, when entire classes, including the most illiterate and nationally indifferent, replaced others in the military and civil service, and when suspicion and fear dominated the relation between Arab individuals and states. This is why the totalitarian military regimes and their imported ideologies should be replaced, as a preliminary step to any military effort, by liberal democratic regimes inspired by a liberal uncorrupted nationalism that could restore to the Arabs their freedom, dignity and faith, and re-establish between them the confidence and respect without which no cooperation and unity and no military strength could be achieved.

CHAPTER VI
NOTES

1. M. Khadduri, *Independent Iraq*, 84.
2. Muhammad Naguib, *Egypt's Destiny*, 17.
3. *al-Hayat* (Beirut), September 14, 1969 quoting a declaration by one of the Libyan leaders in the coup to *La Stampa* of Turino.
4. Article in *Time*, January 8, 1965 entitled "The Money Watchers."
5. One can always read with interest the general book of Edward Luttwak, *Coup d'état*: A Practical Handbook (Greenwich, Conn.: Fawcett Publications, 1969) especially chapters 3-5 on the strategy, the planning and the execution of the coup d'état.
6. See the first section of this chapter.
7. Anouar Abdel Malek quoted in Ayad al-Qazzaz, "Political Order, Stability and Officers: A Comparative Study of Iraq, Syria and Egypt from Independence till June 1967," *Middle East Forum*, XLV, 2 (1969), 33 n. 2.
8. See J. C. Hurewitz, *Middle East Politics: The Military Dimension* (New York: Praeger, 1969), 158 ff.
9. See an explanation of the differences between Egypt, and Syria and Iraq in Qazzaz, *loc. cit.*, 37 ff.
10. For an explanation of Nasser's ability to retain power, see supra the last pages of ch. 2 on Egypt and the last part of section 4 in this chapter.
11. See for the first assumption Vatikiotis, *The Egyptian Army in Politics*, 248; Sharabi, *Governments and Politics of the Middle East in the 20th Century*, 278, 281, for the second assumption.
12. For more on this method of government see, William Ebenstein, *Totalitarianism, New Perspectives* (New York: Holt, Rinehart and Winston, 1962).
13. Quoted by Adib Nassour in *al-Naksah wal-Khata'* (The Setback and the Error), (Beirut, 1968), 45.
14. See Jalal al-Sayyid's open letter of June 1964 to the president of the Syrian presidential council, General Amin Hafez, criticizing the Baath regime in *Opinions and Studies on Economic and Social Problems* (in Arabic), (Beirut, 1964) 44.
15. *Ibid.*

16. Resolutions of the Sixth national Baath Congress in Damascus, October 1963.
17. See Jalal al-Sayyid, *loc. cit.*, 40-41.
18. The Arabic terms used were *al-Ishtirakiyah al-Banna'ah, al-Salimah, al-Adilah, al-Rashidah.*
19. See Muta' al-Safadi, *Hizb al-Baath* (Beirut: Dar al-Adab, 1964), 339.
20. See Bernard Lewis in *Foreign Affairs* (January, 1968), 334.
21. See Hanson W. Baldwin in *Sunday N. Y. Times* March 16, 1969.
22. M. Razzaz, *al-Tajribah al-Murrah;* A. K. Zahreddin's *Memoirs;* see also Nassour, 111 ff.
23. For this and other destructive aspects of socialist regimes see the book written by Salaheddin Munajjed after the debacle of June 1967 entitled *A'midat al-Nakbah* (The Pillars of the Disaster) 2nd ed. (Beirut: Dar al-Kitab al Jadid; Feb. 1968). 56 ff.
24. Official Baath spokesman's declarations against Hourani when the latter was jailed on October 20, 1965 under the Zuayyen cabinet in *al-Hayat* October 22, 1965.
25. We have referred already to the books of Salaheddine Munajjed and Adib Nassour and the articles of Jubran Shamiyeh.
26. See for example Constantine Zurayk's, *Ma'na al-Nakbah Mujaddadan* (Beirut, 1967) that contains in the appendix a section from his book published in 1964 on the Arabs in the battle of civilization and mentions certain conditions by which the Arab revolutionary mentality could reach its goals but does not spell out any specific examples or results of the Arab socialist revolution.
27. See for example the statement at the close of the second annual convention of the Association of Arab-American University Graduates in Detroit, Dec. 5-6, 1969 in the *Newsletter of the AAUG* (Chicago, March 1970), 5-6.
28. See for example Nadim al-Bitar, *Min al-Naksah Ila al-Thawrah* (From the Setback to the Revolution), (Beirut, 1968), and review by John Mikhail in *MEJ* (Autumn, 1969), 539.
29. See Vatikiotis, *op. cit.*, 259.
30. See the opinion of Morroe Berger in his *Military Elite and Social Change in Egypt Since Napoleon* (Princeton, 1960), 28 ff.
31. See M. Halpern, *The Politics of Social Change,* 275.

32. See Charles Issawi, "Economic and Social Foundations of Democracy," in *The Middle East in Transition,* ed. W. Laqueur (Praeger, 1958), 33-51; Marguerite J. Fisher "New Concepts of Democracy in Southern Asia," in *The Western Political Quarterly* (Dec., 1962), 625-640.

33. See Albert Hourani, "Near Eastern Nationalism Yesterday and Today," *Foreign Affairs,* (October, 1963), 135.

34. Bitar's interview with the weekly *al-Hawadith* as reported in *al-Hayat,* July 13, 1969 by Zuhair al-Shulaq.

35. Declarations of Alliluyeva Stalin in a Meet the Press program as reported in the *Los Angeles Times,* September 22, 1969.

36. The declaration by the Banco Nacional de Mexico was made to *el-Universal* and quoted in *The News* (Mexico City), August 21, 1969.

37. See Salaheddine Munajjed's chapter I "Fuqdan al-Iman," (The Loss of Faith) in his *A'midat al Nakbah,* 9 ff.

38. See A. L. Tibawi, "Towards Understanding and Overcoming the Catastrophe," *Middle East Forum,* vol. 44, 3 (1968), 43.

APPENDIX

Chronology of Coups d'Etat and Revolutions

I. Egypt

1. July 23, 1952 (The Egyptian Revolution): Coup d'état by the Free Officers against King Farouk's regime followed on July 26 by the king's abdication and exile.

2. February 25, 1954 First coup against President Muhammad Naguib by Nasser and other members of the Revolution Command Council; Nasser became prime minister and head of RCC.

3. February 26, 1954 Counter-coup by Major Khalid Muhieddin, member of RCC, and his cavalry units forced Nasser to accept return of Naguib.

4. March 29, 1954 Second coup against Naguib by Nasser and other RCC members left Naguib powerless until he was deposed on November 14; decision to continue the transitional military rule until 1956, and defeat of Naguib's plan to restore democratic government.

5. August 25-27, 1967 Coup d'état planned by Marshal Abdul-Hakim Amer, former vice-president and deputy commander in chief, was foiled; Amer's suicide on September 14.

II. The Sudan

1. November 17, 1958 Coup d'état led by Lt. Gen. Ibrahim Abboud against Abdallah Khalil's cabinet; military rule began under Supreme Council of the Armed Forces.

2. March 2-4, 1959 Coup d'état in two stages with incomplete success by Generals Abdul Rahim Shannan and Muhieddin Abdallah against the Supreme Council of the Armed Forces.

3. May 22, 1959 Abortive coup by Generals Shannan and Abdallah against Supreme Council ended in their arrest, trial and death sentence commuted to life in jail.

4. November 9, 1959 Abortive coup by junior officers and cadets of the Infantry Training School at Omdurman; five of the leaders were sentenced to death and hanged on December 2, 1959.

5. October 22 – November 15, 1964 Popular revolution against military rule – the only successful people's revolution to end a military regime in the Arab world – forced dissolution of cabinet and Supreme Council of Armed Forces October 26, nomination of a civilian cabinet October 30, and resignation of General Abboud, November 15.

6. December 28, 1966 Abortive leftist coup by junior officers under Lt. Khalid Hussein Uthman during Sadeq al-Mahdi cabinet.
7. May 25, 1969 Leftist coup d'état by Col. Jaafar Numairi overthrew the Muhammad Mahjub cabinet and the civilian parliamentary regime.

III. Yemen

1. February 17, 1948 Coup against Imam Yahya by dissident civilian and military elements; Imam was assassinated, new Imam al-Wazir proclaimed, but Imam Ahmad ended the movement on March 13 and the new Imam and other leaders were executed.
2. April 2, 1955 Abortive coup against Imam Ahmad in Taiz led by Col. Thalaya; April 5 coup collapsed and leaders were executed.
3. March 26, 1961 Abortive coup against Imam Ahmad in Hodeida; Imam was wounded; leaders of coup were executed.
4. September 26, 1962 (The Yemeni revolution): Coup against new Imam Muhammad al-Badr and the Imamic regime under coup leader, Brig. Gen. Abdallah Sallal, led to civil war.
5. November 5, 1967 Coup against Sallal by military elements with civilian and foreign approval after end of Egyptian presence in Yemen.
6. March 22, 1968 Abortive attempt by extremist popular resistance in Hodeida against Gen. Hasan al-Amri cabinet.
7. August 27-8, 1968 Abortive leftist attempt with sectarian Shafii motivation under Col. Abdul-Wahab al-Raqib against al-Amri cabinet.

IV. Libya

1. September 1, 1969 Military coup d'état by junior officers calling themselves "The Free Unionists" overthrew the monarchy and proclaimed the Libyan Arab Republic.

December 12, 1969 Libyan Revolution Command Council disclosed that a plot to overthrow the new regime was discovered and the cabinet ministers, Colonels Adam Hawaz and Musa Ahmad, were arrested for participation in the plot.

SELECT BIBLIOGRAPHY
Documentary Records and Official Publications

Arab Political Documents. Eds. W. Khalidi and Y. Ibish. Beirut. Annual since 1963.

Basic Documents of the Arab Unifications. New York, Arab Information Center, 1958.

"Congressional Joint Resolution to Promote Peace and Stability in the Middle East" (Eisenhower Doctrine), *Department of State Bulletin,* vol. 36 (1957).

Dasatir al-Bilad al-Arabiyah (Constitutions of the Arab Countries). Cairo, League of Arab States, 1955.

Hanna, Sami A. and Gardner, George H. *Arab Socialism, A Documentary Survey.* Leiden, 1969.

Haqiqat al-Thawrah wa Ahdafuha (The Truth About the Revolution and its Goals). 2 vols. Dept. of Public Relations and Guidance of the Syrian Arab Army, Damascus 1961 (on the Syrian revolt of September 1961 and secession from UAR).

Hurewitz, J.C., ed. *Diplomacy in the Near and Middle East,* vol. II, Princeton, 1956.

Khalil, Muhammad, ed. *The Arab States and the Arab League: A Documentary Record.* 2 vols. Beirut, 1962.

"Land Reform Legislation of Syria, Egypt and Iran," *ME Journal,* VII, Winter, 1953.

Laqueur, W. Z. ed. *The Israeli-Arab Reader, A Documentary History of The Middle East Conflict.* New York, 1968.

Mahadir Jalsat Mubahathat al-Wahdah (Minutes of the Sessions on Unity Discussions) Cairo, 1963.

al-Marayati, Abid, ed. *Middle Eastern Constitutions and Electoral Laws.* New York, 1968.

Munajjed, Salaheddine, ed. *Suriyah Bayn al-Wahdah wa'l-Infisal* (Documents on the Unity and Secession of Syria). Beirut, 1962.

Nusous wa Watha'eq al-Shakwa al-Suriyah (Texts and Documents of the Syrian Complaint: presented to the special session of the Arab League Council at Shtura on August 22-30, 1962 against Nasserist intervention in Syria). Damascus, Ministry of Foreign Affairs, 1962.

Shamiyeh, Jubran ed. *Sijill al-Ara' wal-Waqa'i' al-Siyasiyah fil-Bilad al-Arabiyah* (Record of Political Opinion and Events in the Arab World.

Beirut Monthly (Arabic text since 1966, English issue since January 1969).

A Select Chronology and Background Documents Relating to the Middle East. USGPO, Washington D.C. 1969 (covers the period April 1946 to April 1969).

United States Policy in the Near East Crisis (Documents and Policy Statements May-July 1967). Washington D.C. Dept. of State. 1967.

"The Libyan Revolution in the Words of its Leaders", *Middle East Journal,* Spring 1970.

Lauterpacht, E. ed. *The Suez Canal Settlement: A Selection of Documents.* New York, Praeger, 1960.

——. *The United Nations Emergency Force: Basic Documents.* London, Stevens & Sons, 1960.

Muhakamat al-Thawrah (Trials Under the Revolution), containing the minutes of the sessions of the Tribunal of the Revolution. vol. IV Trial of Karim Tabet. Ed. Kemal Kirah, Cairo, 1954.

Mahkamat al-Shaab (The People's Court). 5 vols, containing the minutes of the court in the trial of the Muslim Brethren in November 1954, after the attempt against Nasser. Cairo, 1954.

Qala al-Ra'is (The President Said). Being selections from Nasser's speeches. Cairo, Dar al-Hilal, 1957.

Proceedings of the National Congress of Popular Forces May-July 1962. Cairo, Information Dept., 1962.

The Revolution After Five Years. Cairo, Information Dept., 1957.

United Arab Republic, al-Jaridah al-Rasmiyah (The Official Journal). Cairo, 1958-65.

——. *The Year Book.* Cairo, Information Dept.

——. *al-Mithaq* (The Charter). Cairo, Information Dept., 1962.

——. *al-Dustur* (The Constitution). Cairo, Information Dept., 1964.

——. *al-Qawanin al-Ishtirakiyah* (The Socialist Laws). Cairo, Information Dept., 1962.

——. *Projects of the Five-Year Plan for Economic and Social Development 1960-65.* Cairo, National Planning Committee, 1960. (In Arabic).

——. *Report on Education in the UAR 1960-61.* Cairo, Center for Educational Documents and Studies, 1961. (In Arabic)

——. *The High Dam.* By the General Committee for the Construction of the High Dam. Cairo, Ministry of the High Dam, 1963. (In Arabic).

Pocket Statistical Yearbook. Cairo, Statistics and Census Aministration. Annual.

United States Senate, Committee on Foreign Relations. 90th Congress, First Session. *Arms Sales to Near East and South Asian Countries, March-June 1967.* (Contains hearings before the Subcommittee on Near Eastern and South Asian Affairs).

General Works

Atassi, Adnan. *al-Dimuqratiyah al-Taqaddumiyah wal Ishtirakiyah al-Thawriyah* (Progressive Democracy and Revolutionary Socialism). Beirut, 1965.

Be'eri, Eliezer. *Army Officers in Arab Politics and Society.* Translation from Hebrew by Dov Ben-Abba. New York, 1970.

Berger, Morroe. "Les régimes militares du Moyen Orient." *Orient* No. 4 (1960, 3); *The Arab World Today.* Garden City, N.Y. 1962.

Binder, Leonard. *The Ideological Revolution in the Middle East.* New York, 1964.

Bitar, Nadim. *al-Idiyologiyah al-Inqilabiyah* (Revolutionary Ideology). Beirut, 1964.

Dumont, Jean. ed. *Les Coups d'état.* Paris, 1963.

Finer, S.E. *The Man on Horseback: The Role of the Military in Politics.* New York, 1962.

Fisher, Sydney N. ed. *The Military in the Middle East, Problems in Society and Government.* Columbus (Ohio), 1967.

Goodspeed, Donald J. *The Conspirators: A Study of the Coup d'état.* New York, 1962.

Haliq, Umar. *Dawr al-Marxiyah fil Ishtirakiyah al-Arabiyah* (The Role of Marxism in Arab Socialism). Beirut, 1965; *al-Ishtirakiyun al-Arab wal Shuyu'iyah al-Duwaliyah* (Arab Socialists and International Communism). Beirut, 1966.

Halpern, Manfred. *The Politics of Social Change in the Middle East and North Africa.* Princeton, 1963; "The Character and Scope of the Social Revolution in the Middle East," in William R. Polk ed., *The Developmental Revolution,* Washington D.C., 1963.

Hamon, Leo ed, *Le rôle extra-militaire de l'armée dams le Tiers Monde* Paris, 1966

Howard, Michael ed. *Soldiers and Governments.* Bloomington, Ind. 1961.

Hurewitz, J.C. *Middle East Politics: The Military Dimension.* New York, 1969; *Soviet-American Rivalry in the Middle East.* New York, 1969.

Janowitz, Morris. *The Military in the Political Development of the New Nations.* Chicago, 1964.

Johnson, John J. ed. *The Role of the Military in Underdeveloped Countries.* Princeton, 1962.

Kerr, Malcolm. "Arab Radical Notions of Democracy," *St. Anthony's Papers, M.E. Affairs* No. 3 Albert Hourani ed. Carbondale, Ill., 1963?; *The Arab Cold War 1958-1967.* 2nd ed. London, 1967.

Kirk, George E. *Contemporary Arab Politics.* New York, 1961.

Khadduri, Majid. "The Army Officer: His Role in Middle Eastern Politics," in *Social Forces in the Middle East,* ed. S.N. Fisher. Ithaca, 1955; *Political Trends in the Arab World: The Role of Ideas and Ideals in Politics.* Baltimore, 1970.

Lewis, Bernard. "The Middle East Reactions to Soviet Pressure," *M.E. Journal,* Spring 1956.

Lenczowski, George. "Radical Regimes in Egypt, Syria and Iraq: Some Comparative Observations on Ideologies and Practices," *Journal of Politics,* Gainesville, Flda., February, 1966.

Luttwak, Edward. *Coup d'état: A Practical Handbook.* Greenwich, Conn. 1969.

Munajjed, Salaheddin. *al-Tadlil al-Ishtiraki* (Socialist Deception). 2nd ed. Beirut, 1966; *Balshafat al-Islam* (The Bolshevization of Islam by Arab Marxists and Socialists).Beirut, 1966.

Nashashibi, Nasir. *Madha Jara fil Sharq al-Awsat* (What Happened in the Middle East). Beirut, 1961.

Polk, William R. *The United States and the Arab World.* Cambridge, Mass. 1965.

Rondot, Pierre. *The Changing Patterns of the Middle East.* New York 1961.

Sayegh, Fayez. *The Dynamics of Neutralism in the Arab World.* San Francisco, 1964.

Sebai, Mustafa. *Ishtirakiyat al-Islam* (Socialism in Islam). 2nd ed. Damascus, 1960.

Shaibani, Ahmad. *al-Akhlaqiyah al-Thawriyah wal Akhlaqiyah al-Arabiyah* (Revolutionary Ethics and Arab Ethics). Beirut, 1966.

Shamiyeh, Jibran. *Qadayana al-Arabiyah* (Our Arab Problems). Beirut, 1965.

Ya 'Uqala' al-'Arab Ittahidu (O Thoughtful Arabs, Unite) 3 vols. Beirut, 1965?

Sharabi, Hisham B. *Nationalism and Revolution in the Arab World.* Princeton, 1966.

Tully, Andrew. *CIA: The Inside Story.* New York, 1962.

Vernier, Bernard. *Armée et politique au Moyen Orient.* Paris, 1966.

Zartman, I. William. *Government and Politics in Northern Africa.* New York, 1963.

Chapters I and II

Abdel-Malek, Anouar. *Egypt: Military Society* (translated from the French). New York, 1968.

Abdel-Nasser, Gamal. *Egypt's Liberation, The philosophy of the Revolution.* Washington D.C., 1955.

Abul-Fath, Ahmad. *L'Affaire Nasser.* Paris, 1962. (also in Arabic, *Gamal Abdul Nasser* n.p. n.d. 1961?).

Ata, Muhammad. *Misr Bayn Thawratain.* Cairo, 1956.

Badeau, John S. "A Role in Search of a Hero: A Study of the Egyptian Revolution," *Middle East Journal,* Autumn 1955; "USA and UAR: Crisis in Confidence." *Foreign Affairs,* January, 1965.

Baha'uddin, Ahmad. *Farouk Malikan* (Farouk as King). Cairo, 1953.

Bar-Zohar, Michel. *Suez Ultra Secret.* Paris, 1964.

Barawi, Rashed. *The Military Coup in Egypt.* Cairo, 1952.

Berger, Morroe. *Bureaucracy and Society in Modern Egypt.* Princeton, 1957; *Military Elite and Social Change, Egypt since Napoleon.* Princeton, 1960.

Berque, Jacques. *L'Egypte: Impérialisme et Révolution.* Paris, 1970.

Bertier, Francis. "L'idéologie sociale de la révolution égyptienne." *Orient* no. 6, 1958.

Blomfield, L.M. *Egypt, Israel and the Gulf of Aqaba in International Law.* Toronto, 1957.

Chejne, Anwar. "Egyptian Attitudes Towards Pan-Arabism." *M.E. Journal,* Summer 1957.

Churchill, Randolph S. and Winston S. *The Six Day War.* Boston, 1967.

Colombe, Marcel. *L'évolution de l'Egypte 1924-1950.* Paris, 1951; "remarques sur la crise germano-arabe." *Orient* 32/33, 1964-1965.

Crecelius, Daniel. "al-Azhar in the Revolution," *M.E. Journal,* Winter 1966.

Cremeans, Charles. *The Arabs and the World: Nasser's National Arab Policy.* New York, 1963.

Dawn, C. Ernest. "The Egyptian Remilitarization of Sinai, May 1967," *Journal of Contemporary History,* July 1968.

Eden, Anthony. *Memoirs, Full Circle.* London, 1960.

Froelich, Jean-Claude. "L'Egypte et les peuples noirs," *Orient* 32/33, 1964-1965.

Garzouzi, Eva. *Old Ills and New Remedies in Egypt.* Cairo, 1958.

Glubb, John Bagot. *The Middle East Crisis, A Personal Interpretation.* London, 1967.

Haikal, Muhammad Hassanein. *Ma Lladhi Jara fi Suriyah* (What Happened in Syria), Cairo, 1962.

Haikal, Muhammad Hussein. *Mudhakkirat fil Siyasah al-Misriyah* (Memoirs on Egyptian Politics). 2 vols. Cairo, 1953.

Harris, Christina Phelps. *Nationalism and Revolution in Egypt: The Role of the Muslim Brotherhood.* Stanford, 1965.

Hanna, Sami A. and Gardner, George H. "Islamic Socialism," *Muslim World* vol. 56, 2 (1966).

Hopkins, Harry. *Egypt the Crucible.* London, 1969.

Hourani, Albert. "The Anglo-Egyptian Agreement: Some Causes and Implications," *M.E. Journal,* Summer 1955; "A Moment of Change: The Crisis of 1956," in *Vision of History,* Beirut, 1961.

Howard, Harry N. "The United States and the Middle East Crisis," *Current History,* December 1967; "The United Arab Republic," *Current History,* January, 1970.

Hussein, M. *La lutte des classes en Egypte de 1945 a 1968.* Paris, 1969.

al-Ishtirakiyah fil Tajarib al-Arabiyah (Socialism in Arab Experience), by "a group of thinkers." Beirut: Dar-al-Kitab al-Jadid, 1965.

Issawi, Charles. *Egypt in Revolution: An Economic Analysis.* London, 1963; "The United Arab Republic," *Current History,* February 1959.

Kadi, Leila S. *Arab Summit Conferences and the Palestine Question 1936-50, 1964-66.* Beirut, 1966.

Kanovsky, E. "The Aftermath of the Six Day War," *M.E. Journal,* Spring 1968.

Kenney, L. "The Aftermath of Defeat in Egypt." *International Journal* XXIII,1 (1967-68).

Kerr, Malcolm H. *Egypt Under Nasser.* New York, 1963; *The Middle East Conflict,* New York, 1968; "The Emergence of a Socialist Ideology in Egypt," *M.E. Journal* XVI (1962).

Khalid, Khalid Muhammad. *Min Huna Nabda'* (From Here We Start), Cairo, 1950. English translation by Ismail R. Faruqi. Washington D.C., 1953.

Khammash, Magdi. *Development and Planning in Egypt.* New York, 1968.

Lacouture, Jean and Simonne. *Egypt in Transition.* New York, 1958.

Laqueur, Walter Z. *The Road to Jerusalem: The Origins of the Arab-Israeli Conflict 1967.* New York, 1968.

Leiden, Carl. "Egypt: The Drift to the Left," *Middle Eastern Affairs,* December 1962 and January, 1963.

Lenczowski, George. "The Objects and Methods of Nasserism," *Journal of International Affairs* XIX, 1 (1965); "Arab Bloc Realignments," *Current History,* December, 1967.

Lewis, Bernard. "The Arab-Israeli War: The Consequences of Defeat." *Foreign Affairs,* January, 1968.

Little, Tom. *Modern Egypt.* New York, 1967; *High Dam at Aswan.* New York, 1965.

Mansfield, Peter. *Nasser's Egypt.* Baltimore, Penguin Books, 1965.

Mansur, George Yaqub ed. *al-Mu'jizah al-Ishtirakiyah* (The Socialist Miracle). Beirut, 1965. The title is sarcastic and the articles by Egyptian writers are very critical of the socialist administration.

Marlowe, John. *Arab Nationalism and British Imperialism.* New York, 1961.

McBride, Barrie St. Clair. *Farouk of Egypt, a Biography.* London, 1967.

McLeave, Hugh. *The Last Pharaoh: Farouk of Egypt.* New York, 1970.

Mead, Donald C. *Growth and Structural Change in the Egyptian Economy.* Homewood, Ill. 1967.

Mehdi, Mohammed. "The Cairo Declaration" (On the Federation Charter of April 17, 1963), *M.E. Forum,* Summer, 1963.

Monroe, Elizabeth. *Britain's Moment in the Middle East 1914-1956.* London, 1963.

Moussa, Tewfik. *al-Ishtirakiyah al-Misriyah wal Qadiyah al-Falastiniyah* (Egyptian Socialism and the Palestine Question) n.p. 1966?

Murad, Basim. *Abdul Nasser Bada' fi Dimashq wa Intaha fi Shtura* (Abdul Nasser Began in Damascus and Ended in Shtura). Damascus, 1962.

Muttali' (Pseud.) *al-Sarraj wa Mu'amarat al-Nasiriyah* (Sarraj and the Conspiracies of Nasserism). n.p. 1962?

Naguib, Mohammed. *Egypt's Destiny.* Garden City, N.Y. 1955.

Najjar, Fauzi M. "Islam and Socialism in the United Arab Republic," *Journal of Contemporary History,* July, 1968

"Nasserism," *Middle East Forum* (collection of articles), April, 1959.

Nutting, Anthony. *The Arabs.* New York, 1964; *No End of a Lesson, the Story of Suez,* New York, 1967.

O'Ballance, Edgar. *The Sinai Campaign of 1956.* New York, 1960.

O'Brien, Patrick. *The Revolution in Egypt's Economic System from Private Enterprise to Socialism 1952-1965.* London, 1966.

Palmer, Monte. "The United Arab Republic: An Assessment of Its Failure," *ME Journal,* Winter, 1966.

Parker, J.S.F. "The United Arab Republic," *International Affairs,* January 1962.

Peretz, Don. "Democracy and the Revolution in Egypt," *M.E. Journal* XIII (1959).

Rafi'i, Abdul Rahman. *Muqaddimat Thawrat 23 Yulio* (Preliminaries of the Revolution of 23 July). Cairo, 1953.

Robertson, Terence. *Crisis, The Inside Story of the Suez Conspiracy.* London, 1965.

Rostow, E. "The Middle East Crisis and Beyond," *Department of State Bulletin,* January 8, 1968.

Rouleau, Eric et al. *Israel et les Arabes: le 3 eme combat.* Paris, 1967.

Saab, Gabriel S. *The Egyptian Agrarian Reform 1952-1962.* New York. 1967.

Sadat, Anwar. *Revolt on The Nile.* London, 1957; *Qissat al-Thawrah Kamilah* (complete Story of the Revolution) Cairo, 1956.

St. John, Robert. *The Boss, The Story of Gamal Abdel-Nasser.* New York, 1960.

Said, Amin. *al-Thawrah* (The Revolution), Cairo, 1959; *al-Jumhuriyah al-Arabiyah al-Muttahidah* (The United Arab Republic), 2 vols. Cairo, 1959-60.

Sayegh, Anis. *al-Fikrah al-Arabiyah fi Misr* (The Idea of Arab Nationalism in Egypt). Beirut, 1959.

Sayegh, Fayez A. *Arab Unity, Hope and Fulfillment.* New York, 1958; "The Theoretical Structure of Nasser's Arab Socialism." *St. Antony's Papers,* ME Affairs no. 4 ed. Albert Hourani, London 1965.

Seale, Patrick. "The UAR and the Iraqi Challenge," *The World Today,* XVI (1960); "The Breakup of the United Arab Republic," *The World Today,* November, 1961; *The Struggle for Syria,* London, 1965.

Sedar, I. and Greenberg H. *Behind the Egyptian Sphinx.* Philadelphia, 1960.

Serafy, Salah. "Economic Development by Revolution: The Case of the UAR," *M.E. Journal* summer, 1963.

Sharabi, H. B. "The Egyptian Revolution," *Current History,* April 1962.

Shumais, Abdul Munem. *al-Zaim al-Tha'ir* (The Revolutionary Leader), Cairo, 1954; *Ishtirakiyatuna al-Arabiyah* (Our Arab Socialism), Cairo, 1961.

Shwadran, Benjamin. "Soviet Posture in the Middle East," *Current History,* December 1967.

Stevens, Georgiana. *Egypt, Yesterday and Today.* New York, 1963.

Stewart, Desmond. *Young Egypt.* London, 1958.

Surur, Taha Abdul Baqi. *Gamal Abdul Nasser.* Cairo, 1958.

Tamawi, Sulaiman. *Thawrat 23 Yulio Bayn Thawrat al-Alam* (The Revolution of 23 July Among World Revolutions). Cairo, 1966?

Tayib, Abbas Muhammad. *Batal al-Thawrah al-Qa'id Muhammad Naguib* (The Hero of the Revolution General Muhammad Naguib). Cairo, 1963.

Tomiche, Nada. *L'Egypte Moderne.* Paris, 1966.

Vatikiotis, P.J. *The Egyptian Army in Politics.* Bloomington, 1961; *Modern History of Egypt,* New York 1969; ed. *Egypt Since the Revolution,* New York, 1968; "Islam and the Foreign Policy of Egypt," in J. Harris Proctor ed. *Islam and International Relations,* New York 1965; "Egypt 1966: The Assessment of a Revolution," *The World Today,* June 1966.

Vernier, Bernard. "L'évolution du régime militaire en Egypte," *Revue Française de Science Politique,* September, 1963.

Vigneau, Jean. "The Ideology of the Egyptian Revolution," in W. Z. Laqueur, ed. *The Middle East in Transition,* New York, 1956.

Warriner, Doreen. "Land Reform in Egypt and its Repercussions," *International Affairs,* January, 1953.

Wheelock, Keith. *Nasser's New Egypt.* New York, 1960.

Wilber, Donald N. Ed. *United Arab Republic — Egypt, Its People, Its Society, Its Culture.* New York, 1969.

Wynn, Wilton. *Nasser of Egypt, the Search for Dignity.* Cambridge, Mass. 1959.

Yost, Charles W. "The Arab Israeli War: How it Began." *Foreign Affairs,* January 1968.

Ziadeh, Farhat J. *Lawyers, the Rule of Law and Liberalism in Modern Egypt.* Stanford, 1968.

Chapter III

Collins, Robert O. and Tignor, Robert L. *Egypt and the Sudan.* Englewood Cliffs, 1967.

Daniel, Aristide. "Une république africaine indépendante: Le Soudan," *Orient,* no. 3, July 1957.

Directory of the Republic of the Sudan. London, 1959.

Fauzi, Saad el-Din. *The Labor Movement in the Sudan 1945-1955.* New York, 1957.

Gosnell, Harold F. "The 1958 Elections in the Sudan," *ME Journal,* Autumn, 1958.

Henderson, K.D.D. *Sudan Republic.* London, 1965.

Hill, Richard L. *Biographical Directory of the Anglo-Egyptian Sudan.* rev. ed. Oxford, 1966.

Holt, P.M. *A Modern History of the Sudan.* New York, 1961; "Sudanese Nationalism and Self Determination," *ME Journal,* Spring and Summer, 1956.

Kilner, Peter. "Military Government in Sudan: The Past Three Years," *The World Today,* June 1962.

Mac Michael, Sir Harold A. *The Sudan.* London, 1954.

Nyquist, Thomas E. "The Sudan: Prelude to Elections," *ME Journal,* Summer 1965.

Oduho, Joseph and Deng, William. *The Problem of the Southern Sudan.* London, 1963.

Ribaud, André. "Où en est le Soudan," *Orient* no. 12 (1959, 4).

Shibeika, Mekki. *The Independent Sudan.* New York, 1960.

Sudanese Government. *Ten Year Plan of Economic and Social Development 1961-1971.* Khartoum, 1962.

Chapter IV

Attar, Muhammad Said. *al-Takhalluf al-Iqtisadi wal Ijtima'i fil Yemen* (Economic and Social Underdevelopment in Yemen). Beirut, 1965.

Bethman, Eric W. *Yemen on the Threshold.* Washington D.C., 1960.

Brown, William R. "The Yemeni Dilemma," *ME Journal,* Autumn 1963.

Colombe, Marcel. "Coup d'état au Yemen," *Orient* no. 23 (1962, 3).

Helfritz, H. *The Yemen: A Secret Journey.* London, 1958.

Heyworth-Dunne, J. *al-Yemen: A General Social, Political and Economic Survey.* Cairo, 1952; "Témoiguage sur le Yemen," *Orient,* no. 31 (1964, 3).

Ingrams, Harold. *The Yemen: Imams, Rulers, Revolutions.* London, 1963.

Khadduri, Majid. "Coup and Counter-Coup in the Yemen 1948," *International Affairs,* January 1952.

Kilner, P. "South Arabian Independence," *The World Today,* August 1967.

Macro, Eric. *Yemen and the Western World 1571-1964.* New York, 1968.

Pawelke, Gunther. *Yemen The Forbidden Land.* Dusseldorf, 1959.

Saqqaf, Ahmad Muhammad Zein. *Ana 'Aaed min al-Yemen* (Returning from Yemen), 3rd ed., Beirut, 1962?

Schmidt, Dana Adams. *Yemen: The Unknown War.* New York, 1968.

Shahhari, Muhammad Ali. *Tariq al-Thawrah al-Yemeniyah.* Cairo, 1966 (English Version: The Road of the Yemeni Revolution, Washington D.C.: Joint Publications Research Service, 1967).

Shami, Ahmad Muhammad. *Imam al-Yemen Ahmad Hamiduddin.* Beirut, 1965.

Shamiyeh, Jubran. *Ya Uqala' al-Arab Ittahidu.* vol. 3, Beirut, 1965?

Sharaf al-Din, Ahmad Hussein. *al-Yemen Ibr al-Tarikh* (Yemen in History). Cairo, 1964.

Sommerville-Large, Peter. *Tribes and Tribulations, A Journey in Republican Yemen.* London, 1967.

Surieu, Robert. "Problemes Yéménites," *Orient* no. 7 (1958, 3).

Wenner, Manfred W. *Modern Yemen 1918-1966.* Baltimore, 1967.

Chapter V

Barbour, Nevill ed. *A Survey of Northwest Africa.* 2nd ed. London, 1962.

Brown, L. Carl ed. *State and Society in Independent North Africa.* Washington D.C., 1966.

442 / Select Bibliography

Cecil, Charles O. "The Determinants of Libyan Foreign Policy," *ME Journal,* Winter, 1965.

"The Constitution of the United Kingdom of Libya: Background and Summary," *ME Journal,* Winter, 1952.

Dearden, Ann. "Independence for Libya: The Political Problems," *ME Journal,* October, 1950.

Epton, Nina. *Oasis Kingdom: The Libyan Story.* London, 1952.

F.S. "Libya: Seven Years of Independence, *The World Today,* February 1959.

IBRD. *The Economic Development of Libya.* Baltimore, 1960.

Khadduri, Majid. *Modern Libya: A Study in Political Development.* Baltimore, 1963.

Khalidi, Ismail Raghib. *Constitutional Development in Libya.* Beirut, 1956.

Kiker, Douglas. "Libya," *The Atlantic,* June 1970.

Kubbah, Abdul Amir Qasim. *al-Mamlakah al-Libiyah* (The Libyan Kingdom). Beirut, 1963.

Legg, H. J. *Economic and Commercial Conditions in Libya.* London, 1952.

Lewis, William H. and Gordon, Robert. "Libya After Two Years of Independence," *ME Journal,* Winter 1954.

Lewis, William H. "Libya, The End of Monarchy," *Current History,* January 1970.

Lindberg, John. *A General Economic Appraisal of Libya.* New York, 1952.

Mallakh, Ragaei. "The Economics of Rapid Growth: Libya," *ME Journal,* Summer 1969.

Rivlin, Benjamin. "Unity and Nationalism in Libya," *ME Journal,* April 1949.

Thomas, Frederick C. "The Libyan Oil Worker," *ME Journal,* Summer 1961.

Villard, Henry Sarrano. *Libya, The New Arab Kingdom of North Africa.* Ithaca, 1956.

Ziadeh, Nicola A. *Sanusiyah: A Study of a Revivalist Movement in Islam.* Leiden, 1958.

Chapter VI

Azem, Sadeq Jalal. *al-Naqd al-Dhati Ba'd al-Hazimah* (Self Criticism after the Defeat). Beirut, 1969.

Be'eri, Eliezer. "A note on coups d'état in the Middle East." *Journal of Contemporary History,* vol. 5 no. 2 (1970).

Bitar, Nadim. *Min al-Naksah ila al-Thawrah* (From the Setback to the Revolution). Beirut, 1968.

Ebenstein, William. *Totalitarianism, New Perspectives.* New York, 1962.

Hourani, Albert. "Near Eastern Nationalism Yesterday and Today," *Foreign Affairs,* October 1963.

Issawi, Charles. "Economic and Social Foundations of Democracy," in *The Middle East in Transition* ed. W. Z. Laqueur, New York, 1958.

Kimche, David and Bawly, Don. *The Sandstorm, The Arab-Israeli War of June 1967: Prelude and Aftermath.* London, 1968.

Khouri, Fred J. *The Arab-Israeli Dilemma.* Syracuse, N.Y., 1968.

Luttwak, Edward. *Coup d'état: A Practical Handbook.* Greenwich, Conn., 1969.

Laqueur, Walter Z. *The Struggle for the Middle East: The Soviet Union and the Middle East 1958-68.* New York, 1969.

Munajjed, Salaheddin. *A'midat al-Nakbah* (The Pillars of the Disaster). 2nd ed. Beirut, 1968.

Nassour, Adib. *al-Naksah wal Khata'* (The Setback and the Error: the intellectual and ideological errors that led to the catastrophe). Beirut, 1968?

Qazzaz, Ayad. "Political Order, Stability and Officers: A Comparative Study of Iraq, Syria and Egypt from Independence till June 1967," *ME Forum,* vol. 45 no. 2 (1969).

Razzaz, Munif. *al-Tajribah al-Murrah* (The Bitter Experiment). Beirut, 1967.

Safadi, Muta'. *Hizb al-Baath: Ma'sat al-Mawlid, Ma'sat al-Nihayah* (The Baath Party: Tragedy of the Beginning, Tragedy of the End). Beirut, 1964.

Safran, Nadav. *From War to War: The Arab-Israeli Confrontation 1948-67.* New York, 1967.

Sharabi, Hisham. *Palestine and Israel, The Lethal Dilemma.* New York, 1969.

Sayyid, Jalal. "Open Letter to the President of the Syrian Presidential Council, General Amin Hafez" in *Opinions and Studies on Economic and Social Problems* (in Arabic), Beirut, 1964.

Tibawi, A. L. "Towards Understanding and Overcoming the Catastrophe," *ME Forum,* vol. 44 no. 3 (1968).

Zurayk, Constantine. *Ma'na al-Nakbah Mujaddadan* (The Meaning of the Disaster, A New Statement). Beirut, 1967.

Other Publications

al-Ahram, Akhbar al-Yawm, al-Gumhouriyah, Rose al-Yusif, al-Misri, al-Musawwar, Egyptian Gazette, The Scribe, The Arab Observer, Minbar al-Islam, Majallat al-Azhar (Cairo), al-Nasr, al-Bina', al-Baath, al-Thawrah, al-Sarkhah. al-Ayyam (Damascus), al-Nahar, al-Anwar, al-Hayat, Daily Star, al-Safa, al-Zaman, al-Anba', al-Jaridah, L'Orient, al-Sayyad, Mideast Mirror (Beirut), al-Ra'ed, Tripoli Mirror (Tripoli-Libya), Libyan Times (Benghazi), al-Sahafah, al-'Alam (Khartoum), Oriente Moderno (Rome), The Times, Daily Express, The Observer, The Guardian, The Daily Mail, The Economist, Mizan Newsletter, New Africa, The Middle East and North Africa (London), Cahiers de l'Orient Contemporain, Le Figaro, Le Monde, The International Herald Tribune (Paris), The New York Times, Arab News and Views, al-Bayan, Action, The Heritage, Time, Newsweek (New York), The Christian Science Monitor, The Atlantic (Boston), Mid East (Washington D.C.), The Los Angeles Times.

INDEX

Abaza, Fikri 97
Abbas, Prince of Yemen 227, 235
Abbasiya 21
Abboud, Gen. Ibrahim 183 ff., 190 ff., 200, 212, 215, 352, 371, 377, 397
Abdallah, King of Jordan 5
Abdallah, Prince of Yemen 224, 231 ff.
Abdallah, Capt. Farouk 211
Abdallah, Brig. Muhieddin 186 ff., 209, 397
Abdin Palace 38
Abdul-Hadi, Ibrahim 32 ff.
Abdul-Karim, Col. Ahmad 100
Abdul-Latif, Mahmud 42
Abdul-Mun'em, Prince 27, 31
Abdul-Nasser, Gamal (see Nasser)
Abdul Quddus, Ihsan 9
Abdul-Rahman, Ali 183, 203
Abdul Rauf, Abdul Mun'em 12, 41
Abdul-Razzaq, Col. Aref 361, 375
Abdul-Wahab, Gen. Ahmad 186 ff.
Abu-Assaf, Col. Amin 367
Abu-Isa, Farouk 212, 216
Abu-Nawar, Gen. Ali 397
Abu-Ramada 182
Abu-Shweirib, Saadeddin 325, 330
Abu-Taleb, Abdul Rahman 254
Abul Fateh, Ahmad 13, 17, 19, 28
Abul Nour, Abdul Muhsen 165
Accra Conference 206
al-Adem 319, 328, 335 ff.
Aden 138, 222, 224 ff., 236, 256, 260, 278, 283 ff., 292 ff.
Adventist Hospital (Libya) 340
Afifi, Jamal 126
Aflaq, Michel 390, 395 ff., 404, 409
Africa 106, 108 ff.
Afro-Asian world 147
Agrarian reform 28, 31, 54, 58, 64, 144, 384 ff., 421
Ahali group 358
Ahmad, Imam of Yemen 146, 223 ff., 229 ff.

Ahmad Fuad, Crown Prince of Egypt 11, 24 ff., 32
Ahmad, Col. Musa 330, 343 ff.
al-Ahram 67, 91 ff., 102, 104, 127, 154, 159, 197, 279, 345
al-Akhbar (Cairo) 104, 137
Alafi, Lt. Muhammad 239 ff.
Alawi officers 386
Aleppo 374
Alexandria 14, 17, 23, 28, 81, 93, 101, 127 ff., 130 ff., 138
Algeria 81, 91, 132, 257, 318, Algiers 94
Ali ibn Ahmad Ibrahim 254
Alwan, Col. Jassem 396
Amer, Abdul Hakim 12, 19, 22, 39, 42, 51, 64, 67, 80, 104, 118, 123 ff., 252, 260 ff., 282, 355, 399
Amer, Gen. Hussein Sirri 16 ff., 20
American University of Beirut 175
American (see United States)
Amin, Abdul Mun'em 12, 41
al-Amin, Maqbul 187
Amman 156
al-Amri, Abdallah 226
al-Amri, Col. Hasan 227, 267 ff., 290 ff., 295 ff., 389
Anglo-Egyptian treaty (1936) 176 ff.
Ansar 176 ff., 191, 210
Anya Nya 214
Aqaba, Gulf of 86, 99, 114 ff.
Arab countries 1, 12, 67, 87, 98, 106, 109, 136, 140, 154, 223, 328, 365, 413 ff.; Arab world 58, 81, 104, 116, 132 ff., 140, 147, 152, 155, 260, 277, 281, 315
Arab Higher Defense Council 111
Arab League 5, 100, 112, 222, 227, 229, 271
Arab Legion 356
Arab nationalism, Arabism 83 ff., 143, 153, 386 ff., 423 ff.
Arab Nationalists' Movement 325, 331, 347
Arab Revolution 91, 111, 132, 143, 260 ff., 347

Arab Socialist Union 45, 48 ff., 61, 63, 127, 129 ff., 137, 153, 159 ff., 404
Arab unity 83, 90, 95, 143, 332, 359, 386 ff., 401, 421, 423
Arabi Pasha 3, Arabi revolt 20
Arabia, Arabian Peninsula 2, 117, 133, 138, 260 ff., 265, 274, 281
Arabic, Arabization 341 ff.
Arabs 84 ff., 87 ff., 95 ff., 106, 109, 114, 117, 132, 135 ff., 141, 145 ff., 161
Arafat, Yasser 134, 157
Aref, Col. Abdul Rahman 375 ff.
Aref, Col. Abdul Salam 365, 376 ff., 386, 394
Arish 22
Arms deal 56, 84 ff., 97, 103, 144, defective arms 7, 15
Asad, Gen. Hafez 133 ff., 163
Ashiqqa party 175 ff.
Asir 221
Askari, Jaafar Pasha 378
Asnag, Abdallah 238
Astal 125
Aswan Dam 66, 85, 104, 145, 182, 189
Ataturk, Mustafa Kemal 150 ff.
Atassi, Col. Faisal 367
Atassi Nureddin 111, 163
Awadallah, Babakr (Abu Bakr) 209 ff., 214, 216
Al-Ayni, Muhsim 242, 250 ff., 263, 273, 286 ff.
al-Azhar 63, 108
Azhari, Ismail 175, 178 ff., 192, 204 ff., 210, 213

Baath, party 89, 133, 321, 331, 366, 370 ff., 385, 404 ff., 423; Baathists 92, 94, 102, 366, 374 ff., 419; regime 106, 114, 277, 390 ff., 406 ff.
Babakri, Sheikh Ali 283
Badawi, Abdul Hamid 4
Badeau, John 265
al-Badr, Imam Muhammad 106, 220 ff., 226, 231, 233, 235 ff., 244 ff., 263 ff., 273, 278, 292, 356, 362
Badran, Shamseddin 117, 122 ff., 125

Baghdad 133, 242, 285, 374 ff.
Baghdad Pact 56, 83 ff., 95, 98, 103, 109, 139, 147, 353, 360 ff., 386 ff.
Baghdadi, Abdul Latif 12 ff., 33, 80, 162, 399
Bahauddin, Ahmad 141
Baidani, Abdul Rahman 236 ff., 242 ff., 246, 250 ff., 266 ff.
Bakii tribes 227, 235, 239
Bakkush, Abdul Hamid 324
al-Bakr, Ahmad Hasan 391, 394
Banco di Roma 340
Bandung Conference 56, 84
Banna, Hasan 6
Baquri, Sheikh Hasan 52
Barazi, Dr. Muhsin 394 ff.
Barcays Bank 340
al-Barduni, Abdallah 230
Bashair Palace (San'a) 248
Bashir, Gen. Hasan 186, 188, 197
Bazzaz, Abdul Rahman 381
Beida (Libya) 324
Beihan 259, 271
Beirut 113, 120, 156, 229, 288, 373, 410
Belgium, Belgian 57, 106, 144
Benghazi 309 ff., 314, 327, 340
Beni Merr 14
Bitar, Salaheddin 389, 396, 409, 422
Black Saturday 11, 131, 370
Bolshevization of Islam 62 ff.
Bonn 237
Bourguiba, Habib 95, 141, 278
Brezhnev, Leonid 137
Britain, British 4 ff., 10, 16, 20, 23, 56, 82, 86 ff., 98, 109, 119, 132, 138, 140, 174 ff., 221, 225, 231, 256, 259 ff., 283 ff., 309 ff., 318 ff., 328, 334, 346, 360
Bunche, Ralph 275
Bunker, Ellsworth 276
Bureaucracy 64
Burlos, Lake 120
Bursa 325
Buwaysir, Saleh 326

Caffery, James 25
Cairo 40, 94, 100, 106, 108, 110 ff., 127, 135, 154, 156 ff., 214, 232, 246 ff., 281, 285 ff., 319, 333, 353; burning of 11, Conference 93, 107, University 14, 21, 28, 36
Canal zone (see Suez Canal zone)
Capitalism 27, 57, 144 ff., 148 state 56 ff.
Capitulations 3
Casablanca summit conference 93, 205, 271, 279
Central Intelligence Agency (CIA) 20
Ceres (Brazil) 395
Chamoun, Camille 257
Charter (Egypt) see National Charter
Chehab, Gen. Fuad 362
Chelebi, Ra'fat 31
China, Communist 86, 107, 231, 237, 245, 341
Class struggle 54, 67, 150, 153, 385, 402, classless society 57
Cold war 96, Arab 96, 143
Collective leadership (Egypt) 48
Combined rural centers 55
Commandos 133 ff.
Communism, Communists 5, 31, 50, 56, 61 ff., 89, 104, 140, 148, 370, 414 ff., 422, Communist bloc 85, 137, 145, in Sudan 180, 192, 197 ff., 202 ff., 207 ff., 238, in Libya 314, 320
Condominium (Sudan) 174 ff.
Congo 106 ff., 277
Constitutions, Constitutional rule in Egypt 29, 30, 34, 44 ff., 46, 48, 142, in Sudan 179, in Yemen 251 ff., 267 ff., in Libya 309, general 380 ff.
Cooperatives 54 ff.
Copts, Coptic 53
Coups d'etat, General remarks 352 ff., motives of 357 ff., patterns of 369 ff., in Egypt 11, 21 ff., 36 ff., 40 ff., in Syria 60, 90, in Sudan 183 ff., in Yemen 221 ff., in Libya 308 ff.
Crusaders 150
Cuba 102, 107
Cyrenaica 308 ff., 318, 327, 330, defense force 322, 327
Czech arms deal (see arms deal)

Da'an, treaty of 221
Dabbi, Col. Abdallah 247, 249, 287
Daifallah, Gen. Hamad al Nil 213
Damanhuri, Muhammad 31
Damascus 100, 102, 111, 113, 115, 373 ff., 407
Damietta 82
Daoud, Gen. Ibrahim 391, 394
Dayan, Moshe 116
Democracy 27, 35, 38, 44 ff., 127, 400 ff., 413 ff., "sound" 380, 400, totalitarian 47 ff., 383, 404 ff., 415
Derna 314
Dictatorship, Egypt 28, 30, 41 ff., 54, general military 400, 402, 416 ff.
Djilas, Milovan 410
Dogheishy, Hamid 126
Druze 367, 395
Dulles, John Foster 85 ff.

Economy 57, 64, 312 ff., 338, 401
Eden, Anthony 87, 115
Education 51, 312, 314 ff.
Egypt, Revolution and Socialism in, ch. 1, 1 ff., Nasserism ch. 2, 78 ff.; 174 ff., 182, 199, 237, 245, 256 ff., 268 ff., 308 ff., 328, 353 ff., 360 ff., 389 ff.
Egyptian, old regime 1 ff., character 2, army 10, 15, 142, 152, Egyptians 53, 88, 121, 147, 154, 161, 230 ff., 257 ff., 282, 284 ff., 312 ff., 318, 340 ff.
Egypt's Destiny 15
Eisenhower, President 86, 98, Doctrine 98
Equatoria province 179
Erhard, Chancellor 110
Erkwit 268, 278
Eshkol, Levi 115
Esso Standard Libya 314
Ethiopia 205
Europe, European Communities 3, Western 328

Faisal, King of Saudi Arabia 93, 95, 133, 147, 271, 274 ff., 279 ff., 284, 289 ff., 347
Faluja 14

Farid, Gen. Hussein 21
Farida, Queen of Egypt 6 ff.
Farouk, King 2, 5 ff., 11, 16, 20, 23 ff., 30, 142, 175, 355, 360
Fateh organization 134, 157
Fawzi, Mahmud 164
Fawzi, Gen. Muhammad 114, 123, 159
February 4 incident (1942) 6, 10, 14
Fedayeen 86, 99
Federation Charter (April 1963) 92
Fekini, Muhieddin 319
Fertile Crescent 2, 369, unity 5, 83, 423
Feudalism 27, 54, 64
Fezzan 309
Figaro 330
Foreign trade (Egypt) 59, business (Libya) 316
France, French 86, 98 ff., 328, 334, 337, 346, property 56
Freedom 52, 59, 95, 129, 150, 400 ff., 409, 418 ff.
Free officers, Egypt 11 ff., 21 ff., 51, 120, 363, 365, 370, 373, 402, Sudan 197, Yemen 238, 247
Free unionist officers (Libya) 325, 331
Free Yemenis 223 ff., 231 ff., 238, 245, 255 ff.
Front for the Liberation of Occupied South Yemen (Flosy) 283, 293

Gadaref 188
Gailani, Rashid Ali 359, 381, 393 ff.
Gaza, Gaza Strip 84, 86, 96, 99 ff., 150
Germany, Germans, West 66, 109 ff., 112, 121, East 110 ff., 212, 309
Gezira Palace 36, 154
Giza 125
Golan Heights 408
Golden Square 393
Gordon, General 186, Gordon College 175
Graduates General Congress 175
Greeks 60
Gromyko, Andrei 116, 135
Guerrillas (Palestinian) 156
Gum'a, Sharawi 129, 159

Hadeto 13
Hafez, Gen. Amin 364, 374, 396 ff.
Hafez, Sulaiman 28
Haidar Pasha, Gen. Muhammad 16 ff.
Haikal, Muhammad Hassanein 91, 102, 120 127, 140 ff., 154, 159
Hajja 227, 235, 242, 248 ff., 254
Hamdun, Capt. Mustafa 367
Hamiduddin dynasty 224
Hammarskjold, Dag 99
Harad Conference 271, 279
Hariri, Col. Ziad 365, 371, 373 ff., 396
al-Hasan, Prince of Yemen 224, 227, 235, 237 ff., 247, 250
Hasan ibn Ibrahim 253
Hasan, Muhammad 24
Hashemites 147, 360
Hashid tribes 227, 235, 239
Hassanein, Magdi 46, 51
Hatem, Abdul Qader 58
Hatum, Capt. Selim 397
Hawaz, Col. Adam 330, 332, 343 ff.
al-Hayat (Beirut) 200, 410
Haziz 226
Heath, Lord Privy Seal 264
Heliopolis 21
Helou, Charles 282
Helwan, steel factory 66, demonstration 127
High Dam (see Aswan Dam)
Higher Council of Letters, Arts and Sciences 52
Higher Socialist Institute 63
Hilali Pasha cabinets 17, 23
Hindwan, Muhsin 239
Hinnawi, Mustafa 135
Hinnawi, Brig. Sami 360, 362, 372, 395
Hodeiby, Hasan 40
Hodeida 227, 231 ff., 239 ff., 257, 286, 290 ff.
Homs 367
Hourani, Akram 100, 366 ff., 371, 396, 409
Hreidi, Jalal 125
Humphrey, Hubert 108
Hussein, King of Jordan 93 ff., 111, 113, 116, 132, 138, 146, 156 ff., 241, 246, 263 ff., 397

al-Hussein, Prince of Yemen 226
Hussein, Ahmad 11
Hussein, Kemal al-Din 12, 40, 80, 162, 399
Hussein, Taha 4 ff.
Husseini, Haj Amin 363

Ibn al-Ahmar 239
Ibn Saud, King Abdul Aziz 229
Ibrahim, Prince of Yemen 224, 226 ff.
Ibrahim, Hasan 12, 33, 41
Ideology, Ideological 57, 359 ff.
Idris, King (see al-Sanusi)
Imamate of Yemen 91, 146, 220 ff., 229 ff., 240 ff., 245, 255, 273, 289, Imamic regime 353
Imams 225, 368
Imperialism 16, 27, 60, 88, 109, 111, 145, 347, 359
Independence 3, 359 ff.
India 109
Indian Ocean 138
Institute of Socialist Youth 63
Interventionism (Nasserist) 91, 106, 108
Iran 83
Iraq 64, 83 ff., 90 ff., 120, 132, 147, 225, 257, 353 ff., 357 ff., 372 ff., 408, 411
Iraq Petroleum Co. pipeline 87
Irwa, Gen. Ahmad 196
Iryani, Sheikh Abdul Rahman 227, 268 ff., 286 ff.
Iryani, Col. Muhammad 286
Islam, Islamic (see Muslim)
Islamic Charter party (Sudan) 204
Ismail, Khedive 151
Ismail, Prince of Yemen 232
Israel, Israeli 7, 80, 84, 86 ff., 93 ff., 96 ff., 100 ff., 105 ff., 108 ff., 113 ff., 118 ff., 128, 134 ff., 137, 140 ff., 147, 155, 214, 277 ff., 296, 332, 334, 363, 411, 415, 418
Italy, Italian 308 ff., 322, 326, 339

Jabr, Saleh 353
Jamali, Hafez 150, 204
Jamil, Col. Jamal 225 ff.
Jayfi, Brig. Hammud 227, 268 ff., 296

Jedid, Gen. Salah 364, 374, 396 ff.
Jerusalem 150
Jews, Jewish 56, 60, 339
Jidda, agreement 93, 271, 279 ff., 284, pact 237
Jizan 249, 276, 280
Johnson, Lyndon 107
Jordan 64, 90 ff., 101, 106, 111 ff., 133, 140, 143, 156, 246, 257, 275, 278, 355 ff., 366, 408, river waters 93, 100 ff.
Junta (see Revolution Command Council)

Karami cabinet 353
Kassem, Brig. Abdul Karim 90 ff., 103, 353, 362, 371, 376 ff., 394, 409
Keladi, Sheikh Ali 283
Kennedy, John F. Administration 105, 263, 265 ff., 275
Kerdasa 82
Ketaf (Yemen) 276
Khalid, Khalid Muhammad 9
Khalifa, Sirr al-Khatem 198, 200 ff.
Khalil, Abdallah 177, 181, 185
Khamr 270
Khartoum 175, 183 ff., 187, 333, 337, summit conference and agreement 124, 132, 284, 297, 320, University of 189, 193 ff., 201, 211
Khashaba, Ali 182
Khashm al-Girba 203
Khatmiyya Brotherhood 175 ff., 185
Khatri, Col. 285
Khawad, Gen. Muhammad 200, 213
Khawli, Hasan Sabri 134
Khawli, Lutfi 63
Khouri, Beshara 352, 368
Khruschev, Nikita 63, 84, 97, 104
Kibsi, Hussein 226
Kitchener, Gen. Herbert 186
Kosygin, Alexei 94, 117, 137, 158, 281, 290
Ku'bar, Abdul Mejid 316
Kuwait 66, 133, 140, 272, 313

Labib, Ismail 126
Lampson, Sir Miles 6

Lebanon 64, 90, 101, 120, 133 ff., 143, 257, 277, 281 ff., 352 ff., 355 ff., 361 ff., 366, 378, 398, 410, 417

Liberation, Province 46, 51, 55, 104, of Palestine 97, Rally 36, 40, 44, Liberated Arab states 91, 95

Libya 133, 364, 378 ff., 411, officers' coup and new republic, ch. 5, 308 ff.

al-Liqya, Abdallah 239

Lumumba, Patrice 106

Maarib 257, 259

Mabahith 79

Maghribi, Mahmud 325, 330, 338, 341, 343

Mahdi, Sayyid Abdul Rahman 176 ff., 184

Mahdi, Sayyid al-Hadi 192, 206, 210

Mahdi, Sayyid Sadeq 192, 206 ff., 210, 213

Mahdi, Sayyid Saddiq 185, 191

Mahdists 175, 192, 337

Maher, Ali 23 ff., 27 ff.

Mahjub, Abdul Khaleq 212

Mahjub, Muhammad Ahmad 192, 204 ff., 210 ff., 284

Mahmud, Muhammad Sidqi 113, 126

Mahmud, Gen. Nureddin 353

Majali, Hazza 353, 362

Makawi, Abdul Qawi 283

Makki, Hasan 289

Mamelukes 52, 151

Managil Canal 190

Mansoura 130 ff.

al-Maqbul, al-Taher 197

Maronite Patriarch 282

Marsa al-Brega 314

Marxism, Marxist 54, 57, 61 ff., 144, 152

Mboro, Clement 201, 214

Mediterranean 118, 138

Mer'i, Mustafa 8

Mexico 422 ff.

Middle East 2, 83, 87, 98, 136 ff., 417

Military Academy (Egypt) 13 ff., 21

Military dictatorship (see dictatorship, military rule).

Military regimes, rule 354 ff., 402 ff., 410, 412 ff., 418, 424, characteristics of 379 ff., results of 393 ff., end of 417 ff.

Mirghani, Sayyid Ali 175, 181

Misr, Bank complex, Organization 57

al-Misri 9, 13, 28

al-Misri, Gen. Aziz 18

Mocha 231

Montreux conference 3

Morocco 140

Moscow 117, 124, 130, 138, 285, 295

Mosul, 374 ff., 393, coup 103

Mrow'e, Kamil 410

Muhammad, Prophet 62

Muhammad Ali 1, 4, 148, 151, 261 dynasty 32, 360

Muhammad ibn al-Hussein 273, 288 ff., 292, 295

Muhanna, Col. Rashad 16, 27, 31, 389, 399

Muhieddin, Khalid 12 ff., 21, 37, 41, 104, 399

Muhieddin, Zakaria 12, 23, 50, 65, 125, 128, 158 ff., 399

al-Muhsin, Prince of Yemen 226

Munassar, Qasim 295

Muntasir, Mahmud 319

Muntazah Palace 24

Muqdami, Hussein 240

al-Musawar 141

Muslim, Islam, Islamic 53, 57, 151, 337, 342, Islamic centers 108, Islam and Socialism 62 ff., 406, Muslim pact 94 ff., 147, Muslim solidarity 93 ff., 280 ff.

Muslim Brotherhood, in Egypt 5, 13, 29, 36, 40, 42, 82, 131, 225, 281, 399, 416, 424, in Sudan 194, 203, 207

Naguib, Gen. Ali 21

Naguib, Gen. Muhammad 6 ff., 12, 15 ff., 18 ff., 25, 28 ff., 32 ff., 42, 142, 146, 177, 355, 358, 371, 382, 399

Nahas, Mustafa 5, 9 ff., 28 ff., 82

Nahlawi, Col. Abdul Karim 367, 379, 396

Najran 221, 259, 280

Nariman, Queen 7

al-Nasr (Damascus) 79

Nasr, car factory 67, Organization 57

Nasr, Salah 124
Nasser, Nasserists 11 ff., 20 ff., 28, 31 ff., 43 ff., 49 ff., 58 ff., 61 ff., 79 ff., 88 ff., 100 ff., 104 ff., 114 ff., 122 ff., 127 ff., 136, 139, 143 ff., 146 ff., 153 ff., (death), 157 ff., (succession), 183, 190, 201, 237 ff., 246, 257 ff., 276 ff., 284 ff., 318 ff., 333, 355, 362 ff., 387, 392, 399, 424, Nasser cult 80 ff., 155
Nasserism 140, 143, 145, 149, 151, 155, 162, 311, 359 ff., methods and results ch. 2, 78 ff., and six day war 113 ff.
National assembly (Egypt) 45 ff., 48, 58, 60, 67, 127, 130
National Charter (Egypt) 47, 59, 61, 91, 144, 260, 385
National congress of popular forces 47
National congress party (Libya) 309, 317
National guard (Egypt) 40
National liberation front (South Yemen) 283 ff., 292 ff., 390
National Union (Egypt) 45 ff., 60
National Unionist party (Sudan) 178 ff., 203
Nationalization 56 ff., 66, 85, 144, 151, 401, 408
Nayef, Col. Abdul Razzaq 394
Near East 151
Negev 93
Neutralism, neutralist 56, 84 ff., 97, 103, 109, 385
New York 238, 240, 247, 250, 342
New York Times 200, 264
Nile, Valley 125, 368, water agreement 189
Nkrumah, Kwame 422
Nolte, Richard 116
Non-alignment 136, 142 ff., non-aligned conference 107
North Atlantic Treaty Organization (NATO) 139
Nufuri, Col. Amin 100
Numairi, Col. Jaafar 209 ff., 214 ff., 333, 337, 344, 391
Nu'man, Ahmad Muhammad 227, 232, 267 ff., 286 ff.
Nuqrashi, Mahmud Fahmi 6
Nutting, Anthony 87

Officers, Egypt 16 ff., 20, 79, 143, Syria 15, Sudan 195, 209, 215, Libya 308 ff., 321 ff., role in coups 352 ff., 357 ff., general 420 ff.
Oil, interests, resources 120, 261, 308 ff., 311 ff., 323, 338, embargo 132
Okasha, Sarwat 12, 17
Omdurman 183, 189, 192, 211, 213
Ottoman Empire, Ottomans 1, 52, 261, 423

Pakistan 83, 109
Palestine 5, 95, 106, 116, 143, 150, 278, 318, 323, 332, 336 ff., 346, 363, 368, 418, War of 1948, 6, 9, 13, 16, 22, 96, 363, Nasserism, great powers and Palestine 96 ff., resistance movement 134, 333, 410, Palestinians 97, 100, 119, Palestine Liberation Organization 95, 101 ff., 108, 111, 118, 133, 156, 164
Parliamentary rule, Egypt 5 ff., Sudan 180, 184, 200 ff., Libya 316 ff., General 358, 380, 402 ff., 417
Parties, Egypt 9, 29, 31, Sudan 181 ff., 184, 197
Peasants 3, 28, 47 ff., 64
People's party (Syria) 366 ff.
People's democratic party (Sudan) 181, 202 ff.
People's republic of South Yemen 293
Persian Gulf 136, 138
Philosophy of the Revolution 20, 27
Podgorny, Nikolai 137
Police, secret 79 ff., 339, state 400, 420
Popular front for the liberation of Palestine (PFLP) 347
Port Said 65, 86 ff., 107, 120, 138
Portsmouth, treaty 353
Pravda 63, 135
Press, Egypt 30, 41, 52 ff., 67, 127, 129, 137, 280, Arab 281, Libya 340, general 383 ff., nationalization of 53, 57
Primakof, E. 63
Progressive, Arab states 91, 94, movements 143 ff.
Propaganda, Egypt 80, 88 ff.
Ptolemies 148
Pulli, Antonio 24

Qadhafi, Col. Mu'ammar 330 ff., 343 ff., 371
Qadhafi, Wanis 320, 323
Qasr al-Ayni hospital 67
Qena 134
Qubba Palace 100, 128, 154
Qudsi, Nazem 91, 246, 353, 408

Rabat, summit conference 333
Radicalism, radicals 163, 359, 363 ff., 369, 402, radical republics, regimes 308, 405 ff., 411, 418, 424
Radwan, Abbas 125
Rahumi, Lt. Col. Ahmad 286
Raquib, Lt. Col. Abdul Wahab 296
Ras al-Tin Palace 24
Razzaz, Munif 408
Reaction, Reactionaries 60 ff., 66, 131 ff., 145, 359, reactionary states, rulers 94 ff., 101, 111, 115, 280 ff., 332, 335, 387, 401
Red Sea 138
Reform, general 384 ff., Social 9, 27, 54, 152, 358
Regency council (Egypt) 27, 31
Religion, and socialism 61 ff., religious discrimination 53
Republics, establishment of 380 ff.
Revolutions, Egypt 4, 20 ff., 26, 54, 59 ff., 144, Sudan 194 ff., Yemen 244 ff., revolutionary change 35, 144, Sudan 215, Yemen 253, revolutionary states, regimes 94, 111, 337, 387, 401
Revolutions and military rule, general remarks 352 ff., motives 357 ff., characteristics 379 ff., results 393 ff.
Revolution Command Council (RCC), Egypt 27 ff., 30 ff., 45, 79, 146, 392, Yemen 250 ff., 267, Libya 326 ff., 332 ff., 343 ff.
Rhodesia 109
Riad, Mahmud 112
al-Rida, Muhammad 317
al-Rida, Hasan 317, 326 ff.
Rikhye, Gen. Indar 114
Riyad 229, 259, 282 ff.
Rogers, William 156
Rome 238

Rose al-Yusif 9, 20, 102
Ru'aini, Muhammad 240
Rumania 137
Russia, Russians 97 ff., 102, 104, 116 ff., 121, 124, 136 ff, 139, 158, 231, 237, 255, 291, 408

Saada 276
Saadawi, Bashir 310
Saadeddin, Ibrahim 63
Saadeh, Antun 398
Sabri, Ali 48 ff., 125, 128 ff., 158 ff., Sabri brothers 12
Sadat, Anwar 12 ff., 19, 22, 33, 35 ff., 41 ff., 47, 157 ff., 237, 282, 337
Sadeq, Gen. Fuad 18
Saddiq, Col. sYusif 12 ff., 22, 41
al-Safa (Beirut) 103
al-Sahafa (Khartoum) 208
Sa'id, Ahmad 129
al-Sa'id, Nuri Pasha 5, 83, 90
Saiqa guerrillas 163
Saladin 81, 84, 150
Salem, Gamal 12, 22, 24 ff., 42
Salem, Salah 12, 22, 35 ff., 39, Salem brothers 399
Salih Pasha, Abdul Mejid 14
Sallal, Brig. Abdallah 227, 233, 240, 242, 244 ff., 266 ff., 284 ff., 389, 398
Sammu' 94, 106, 111
San'a 221, 223, 225 ff., 244 ff., 260, 275 ff., 285 ff., 289 ff.
Sanhonri, Abdul Razzaq 26, 39, 41
al-Sanusi, Muhammad Ali 309
al-Sanusi, King Muhammad Idris 309 ff., 318 ff.
al-Sanusi, Gen. Hamdeddin 327
Sanusi, brotherhood, kingdom, tribesmen 308 ff., 327, 390
Sarraj, Abdul Hamid 104, 362, 395
Saud, King 39, 41, 241, 246, 263 ff., 275, 282, 362
Saudi Arabia 64, 83, 91, 93 ff., 112, 117, 133, 147, 221, 235, 237, 248 ff., 256 ff., 274 ff., 278 ff., 313, 347, 362, 373
Sawi, Sawi Ahmad 40

Sawt al-Yemen 223, 225
al-Sayyid, Jalal 404
Sayyids 222 ff., 250, 253
Second World War 5, 309, 322
Security Council 134, 156, 182
Serageddin, Fuad 13, 32 ff.
Shaabi, Qahtan 283, 293 ff., 390
Shafi'i, Hussein 12, 22, 41 ff., 125, 128, 157, 286
Shafi'ite Muslims 223 ff., 228, 239, 247, 287
al-Shalhi, Busiri 316
al-Shalhi, Ibrahim 312; Shalhi family 324
al-Shami, Muhammad Abdallah 254
Shannan, Brig. Abdul Rahman 186, 204, 397
Shanshal, Muhammad Saddiq 120
Sharaf, Sami 159
Shawaf, Col. Abdul Wahab 361, 375, 378
Shawqi, Col. Ahmad 12, 22
Shelepin 110
Shepilov 86
al-Shibli, Amin 212
Shirine, Ismail 17
Shishakli, Col. Adib 354, 360, 362, 366, 375, 380 ff., 395
Shita, Selim 321
Shtura conference 261
Shukri, Ahmad 272
Shuqair, Labib 161
Shuqairi, Ahmad 95, 102, 111 ff., 133
Sidqi, Gen. Bakr 354, 357, 377 ff., 393
Sidqi-Bevin, negotiations 176
Sinai 86 ff., 99, 112, 114, 119, 150, 278
Sirri, Hussein, cabinet 17
Sirt 330
Sirwah 259
Six day war 118 ff., 313, 320, 397, 399, 407 ff.
Smith, Hedrick 200
Social justice 9, 27, 54, 152, 358
Socialism, Egypt 54 ff., 58, 61 ff., 98, 144 ff., 151, 241, 384, Arab countries 140, 143, 265 ff., 278, 282, 308, 337 ff., 364, 418 ff., socialist revolution 90 ff., 98, 152, 274, 405 ff., 421
Socialist Union (see Arab Socialist Union)
Solod, Daniel 97

Solzhenitsyn, Alexander 410
South Arabian federation 231, 238, 256, 25. 283 ff., 292 ff.
Southern Sudan 126 ff., 181 ff., 193, 214
Southern Yemen 267, 391, 411
Sovereignty Council (Sudan) 204
Soviet Union 50 ff., 66, 84 ff., 97 ff., 104 ff., 110 ff., 116 ff., 122, 124, 126, 135 ff., 138 ff., 142, 144, 152 ff., 158 ff., 237, 262, 277, 280, 290 ff., 328, 346, 363, 413, 415
Srur, Taha Abdul Baqi 81
Staff College (Egypt) 13 ff.
Stookey, Robert 263
Sudan 1, 9, 19, 36 ff., 82, 141, ch. 3, 174 ff., 284, 344, 354, 361, 389, 411, 419
Sudan African National Union (SANU) 193
Suez Canal, Zone 4, 10, 20, 23, 82, 360, Company 56, 85 ff., 144 ff., Suez Canal 87, 119, 133 ff., 138 ff., 151, 313
Suez War 56, 86 ff., 98 ff., 122, 363
Sukarno, Ahmad 422
Sulaiman, Ahmad 199
Sulaiman, Muhammad Sidqi 50, 113
Summit conferences, spirit 93, 100 ff., 112
Supreme council of the armed forces (Sudan) 183 ff., 195 ff.
Supreme court (Sudan) 207
Sweidani, Col. Ahmad 113
Syria 2, 46, 58, 83, 87, 90 ff., 94, 100 ff., 112 ff., 115, 120, 132, 136 ff., 143, 257, 262, 281, 291, 353 ff., 357 ff., 372 ff., 388 ff., 406 ff., 419 Greater Syria 5, 423
Syrian Social National Party 378, 398
Syro-Lebanese 60

Tabet, Karim 7 ff.
Tabi'i, Muhammad 137
Taif, treaty of 221
Taiz 225 ff., 231, 234 ff., 239, 243, 263, 273, 281, 286
Takriti, Hardan 163
al-Tali'a 63
Tell, Wasfi 163
Tewfik, Saad 21
Thalaya, Col. Ahmad 232 ff.

al-Thawrah 340
Tiran, Straits of 86, 99, 114
Tito, President 98
Tobruk 311, 314, 319, 328, 335
Transitional period (Egypt) 29 ff.
Trevelyan, Sir Humphrey 293
Tribunal of the Revolution (Egypt) 8, 32 ff.
Tripoli, Tripolitania 309, 319 ff., 326, 333
Tunisia 133
Turkey, Turks 83, 150 ff., 221, 326, Kemalist Turkey 416

Ulama, and socialism 63
Ulbricht, Walter 110
Umma party (Sudan) 176, 178, 202 ff., 207 ff.
Unified Arab command 101 ff., 111 ff., 118
United Arab Republic (Egypt and Syria) 46, 88, 90, 103, 105 ff., 237, 241, 260 ff., 280 ff., 354, 395 ff.
United Arab States 237, 241
United Democratic party (Sudan) 206
United National Front (Sudan) 196 ff.
United Nations 86, 176, 264, 276, 282, Emergency Force 99, 101, 112, 114, General Assembly 137, 309
United States, American, 20, 38, 55, 65 ff., 85 ff., 97 ff., 103, 105, 107, 111 ff., 117 ff., 122, 132, 136 ff., 140, 147, 181, 185 ff., 214, 231 ff., 263 ff., 275 ff., 311 ff., 320 ff., 328, 334 ff., 337, 373, 415
Universities 128, 131, 312
Uqba ibn Nafi airfield 336
U Thant 114, 116, 282
Uthman, Lt. Khalid Hussein 208
Uthman, Muhammad Ali 286
Uways, Daoud 79

Van Horn, Gen. Carl 276
Vietnam 107, 136, 141, 212, 277
Vinogradov, Sergei 140
Voice of the Arabs radio 129, 241 ff.

Wadi Halfa 189
Wafd party 5, 9 ff., 13, 16, 28 ff., 175, 383
Waqfs 52
Wartalani, al-Fadil 225 ff.
Washington 120
Wau 190
al-Wazir, Sayyid Abdallah 223 ff.
al-Wazir, Sayyid Ali 223, 226
al-Wazir, Sayyid Ibrahim Ali 269, 273
Western powers, West 83 ff., 97 ff., 106, 108 ff., 117, 119, 136, 139 ff., 145, 314, 318 ff., 328, 334, 346, 386 ff., 413, 415, Western pacts 84
Western Desert 120
Wheeler airfield 311, 319, 335 ff.
Working forces of the people 48 ff., oil workers (Libya) 315

Yahya, Imam 221 ff., 226 ff., 242, 356, 378, 398
Yemen 51, 67, 90 ff., 138, 362, 365, 378, 398, civil war in, 79 ff., 91, 93, 106, 115, 120, 133, ch. 4, 220 ff., 355 ff.
Yemen First front 271, 273
Young Egypt party 5
Yugoslavia 56, 98

Zaghlul, Saad 5
Zahreddin, Gen. Abdul Karim 408
Za'im, Col. Husni 354, 357, 360, 362, 368, 394, 409
al-Zaman (Beirut) 111
Zarqa incident 397
Zaydis 220, 222, 228, 237, 247, 287
Zionism, Zionist 111, 113, 131, 145, 348, 406, 424
Zu'aiter, Akram 112
Zubayri, Qadi Muhammad Mahmud 223, 226 ff., 232, 242, 250, 268 ff.